VOLUME 1 • LESSONS 1–6   SIXTH EDITION

VISTAS

INTRODUCCIÓN A LA LENGUA ESPAÑOLA

José A. Blanco

Philip Redwine Donley, late
Austin Community College

VISTA®
HIGHER LEARNING

Boston, Massachusetts

On the cover:
Machu Picchu, Peru

Creative Director: José A. Blanco
Publisher: Sharla Zwirek
Editorial Development: Judith Bach, Camilo Cerpa, María Victoria Echeverri, Jo Hanna Kurth
Project Management: Tiffany Kayes, Faith Ryan
Rights Management: Annie Pickert Fuller, Ashley Poreda
Technology Production: David Duque, Jamie Kostecki, Paola Ríos Schaaf
Design: Radoslav Mateev, Gabriel Noreña, Andrés Vanegas
Production: Oscar Díez, Sebastián Díez, Alejandro Rojas

Student Text (Casebound) ISBN: 978-1-54330-129-8
Instructor's Annotated Edition ISBN: 978-1-54330-131-1

Library of Congress Control Number: 2018934157

5 6 7 8 9 TC 24 23 22 21

Printed in Canada.

Introduction

To Vista Higher Learning's great pride, **Vistas** became the best-selling new introductory college Spanish program in more than a decade in its first edition, and its success has only grown over time. It is now our pleasure to welcome you to **Vistas, Sixth Edition**, your gateway to the Spanish language and to the vibrant cultures of the Spanish-speaking world.

A direct result of extensive reviews and ongoing input from students and instructors, **Vistas 6/e** includes both the highly successful, ground-breaking features of the original program, plus exciting new elements designed to keep **Vistas** the most student-friendly program available.

Original, hallmark features

- A unique, easy-to-navigate design built around color-coded sections that appear either completely on one page or on spreads of two facing pages
- Integration of an appealing video, up-front in each lesson of the student text
- Practical, high-frequency vocabulary in meaningful contexts
- Clear, comprehensive grammar explanations with high-impact graphics and other special features that make structures easier to learn and use
- Ample guided practice to make you comfortable with the vocabulary and grammar you are learning and to give you a solid foundation for communication
- An emphasis on communicative interactions with a classmate, small groups, the full class, and your instructor
- A process approach to the development of reading, writing, and listening skills
- Coverage of the entire Spanish-speaking world and integration of everyday culture
- Unprecedented learning support through on-the-spot student sidebars and on-page correlations to the print and technology components for each lesson section
- A complete set of print and technology components to help you learn Spanish

NEW! to the Sixth Edition

- Pronunciation tutorials with speech recognition
- 7 new **En pantalla** videos
- 5 new **Cultura** readings
- 3 new literary readings in **Lectura**
- New **Panorama cultural** videos
- Video Virtual Chats
- Redesigned textbook icons, including easy-to-identify chat activities
- New music feature **Con ritmo hispano**

Vistas 6/e has eighteen lessons, each of which is organized exactly the same way. To familiarize yourself with the organization of the text, as well as its original and new features, take the **at-a-glance** tour.

table of contents

	contextos	fotonovela

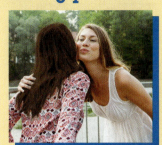

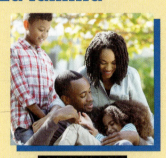
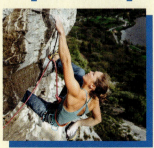

cultura	estructura	adelante

contextos	fotonovela

contexts	fotonovela

Lección 9
Las fiestas

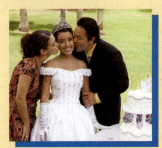

Volume 2

Lección 10
En el consultorio

Volume 2

Lección 11
La tecnología

Volume 2

Lección 12
La vivienda

Volumes 2 & 3

cultura	estructura	adelante

	contextos	fotonovela

Lección 13
La naturaleza

Volume 3

Lección 14
En la ciudad

Volume 3

Lección 15
El bienestar

Volume 3

Lección 16
El mundo del trabajo

Volume 3

cultura	estructura	adelante

	contextos	fotonovela

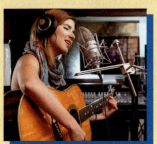

Consulta (*Reference*)   Volumes 1–3

cultura	estructura	adelante

Icons

Familiarize yourself with these icons that appear throughout **Vistas**.

Presentational content for this section available online

Textbook activity available online

Partner Chat or Video Virtual Chat activity available online

Pair activity

Group activity

Activity with handout

Listening activity/section

Video available for this paragraph of **Panorama**

More activities

| vhlcentral | LM p. 0 | WB pp. 00–00 | Online activities |

The **More activities** box indicates additional print and online activities.

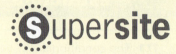

Supersite

Each section of your textbook comes with activities on the **Vistas** Supersite, many of which are auto-graded for immediate feedback. Plus, the Supersite is iPad®-friendly*, so it can be accessed on the go! Visit **vhlcentral.com** to explore this wealth of exciting resources.

CONTEXTOS
- Vocabulary hotspots with audio
- Textbook activities and additional activities for extra practice
- Audio activities
- Chat activities for conversational skill-building and oral practice

FOTONOVELA
- Streaming video of **Fotonovela**, with instructor-managed options for subtitles and transcripts in Spanish and English
- Pronunciation tutorials with speech recognition
- Textbook activities and additional activities for extra practice
- Audio files for **Pronunciación**
- Record-compare practice

CULTURA
- **Con ritmo hispano** information and activities
- **Conexión Internet** activity
- Textbook activities and additional activities for extra practice
- Additional reading

ESTRUCTURA
- Interactive grammar tutorials
- Textbook activities and additional activities for extra practice
- Chat activities for conversational skill-building and oral practice
- Diagnostics in **Recapitulación** section

ADELANTE
- Audio-sync reading in **Lectura**
- Additional reading
- Writing activity in **Escritura** with composition engine
- Audio files for listening activity in **Escuchar**
- Textbook activities and additional activities for extra practice
- Streaming **En pantalla** TV clips or short films, with instructor-managed options for subtitles and transcripts in Spanish and English
- Streaming video of **Flash cultura** series, with instructor-managed options for subtitles and transcripts in Spanish and English

PANORAMA
- Textbook activities and additional activities for extra practice
- **Conexión Internet** activity
- Streaming video of **Panorama cultural** series, with instructor-managed options for subtitles and transcripts in Spanish and English

VOCABULARIO
- Vocabulary list with audio
- Customizable study lists

Plus! Also found on the Supersite:
- All textbook and lab audio MP3 files
- Communication center for instructor notifications and feedback
- Live Chat tool for video chat, audio chat, and instant messaging without leaving your browser
- A single gradebook for all Supersite activities
- WebSAM online Workbook/Video Manual/Lab Manual

*Students must use a computer for audio recording and select presentations.

Lesson Openers
outline the content and features of each lesson.

Las vacaciones 5

Communicative Goals
You will learn how to:
• Discuss and plan a vacation
• Describe a hotel
• Talk about how you feel
• Talk about the seasons and the weather

contextos
pages 152–157
• Travel and vacation
• Months of the year
• Seasons and weather
• Ordinal numbers

fotonovela
pages 158–161
Felipe plays a practical joke on Miguel, and the friends take a trip to the coast. They check in to their hotel and go to the beach, where Miguel gets his revenge.

cultura
pages 162–163
• El Viejo San Juan
• Punta del Este

estructura
pages 164–179
• **Estar** with conditions and emotions
• The present progressive
• **Ser** and **estar**
• Direct object nouns and pronouns
• **Recapitulación**

adelante
pages 180–187
Lectura: A hotel brochure from Puerto Rico
Escritura: A travel brochure for a hotel
Escuchar: A weather report
En pantalla: A tourism ad
Flash cultura: A video about Machu Picchu
Panorama: Puerto Rico

A PRIMERA VISTA
• ¿La persona es viejo o joven?
• ¿Lleva una pelota o una mochila?
• ¿Pasea o ve una película? ¿Anda en patineta o va de excursión?
• ¿Es posible nadar en este lugar?

A primera vista activities jump-start the lessons, allowing you to use the Spanish you know to talk about the photos.

Communicative goals highlight the real-life tasks you will be able to carry out in Spanish by the end of each lesson.

Supersite

• Supersite resources are available for every section of the lesson at **vhlcentral.com**. Icons show you which textbook activities are also available online, and where additional practice activities are available. The description next to the Ⓢ icon indicates what additional resources are available for each section: videos, recordings, tutorials, and more!

• Textbook activity

Supersite features vary by access level.

Contextos
presents vocabulary in meaningful contexts.

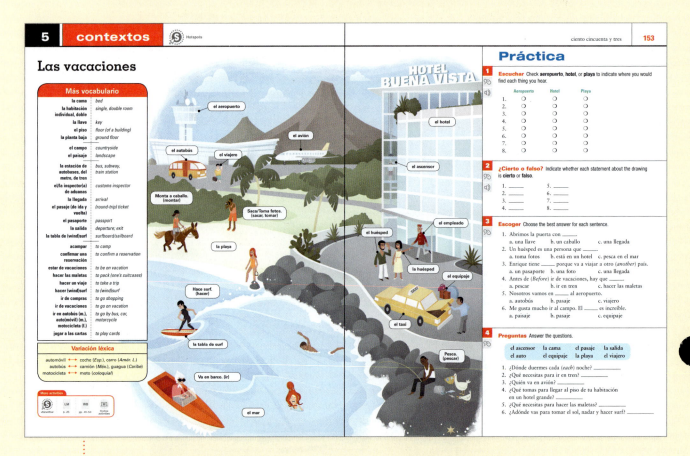

Más vocabulario boxes call out other important theme-related vocabulary in easy-to-reference Spanish-English lists.

Variación léxica presents alternate words and expressions used throughout the Spanish-speaking world.

Illustrations High-frequency vocabulary is introduced through expansive, full-color illustrations.

More activities The icons in the **More activities** boxes let you know exactly which print and technology components you can use to reinforce and expand on every section of every lesson.

Práctica This section always begins with two listening exercises and continues with activities that practice the new vocabulary in meaningful contexts.

Comunicación activities allow you to use the vocabulary creatively in interactions with a partner, a small group, or the entire class.

Supersite

- Audio support for vocabulary presentation
- Textbook activities
- Additional online-only practice activities
- Chat activities for conversational skill-building and oral practice
- Vocabulary activities in Activity Pack

Supersite features vary by access level.

Fotonovela
follows the adventures of a group of students living and traveling in Mexico.

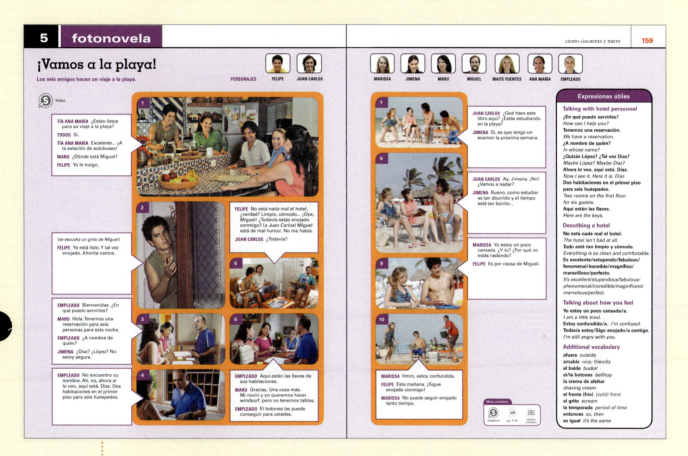

Personajes The photo-based conversations take place among a cast of recurring characters—a Mexican family with two college-age children, and their group of friends.

Icons signal activities by type (pair, group, audio, handout) and let you know which activities can be completed online.

Fotonovela Video The video episodes that correspond to this section are available for viewing online.

Expresiones útiles These expressions organize new, active structures by language function so you can focus on using them for real-life, practical purposes.

Conversations Taken from the **Fotonovela** Video, the conversations reinforce vocabulary from **Contextos**. They also preview structures from the upcoming **Estructura** section in context and in a comprehensible way.

Ⓢupersite

- Streaming video of the **Fotonovela** episode
- Textbook activities
- Additional online-only practice activities

Supersite features vary by access level.

Pronunciación & Ortografía
present the rules of Spanish pronunciation and spelling.

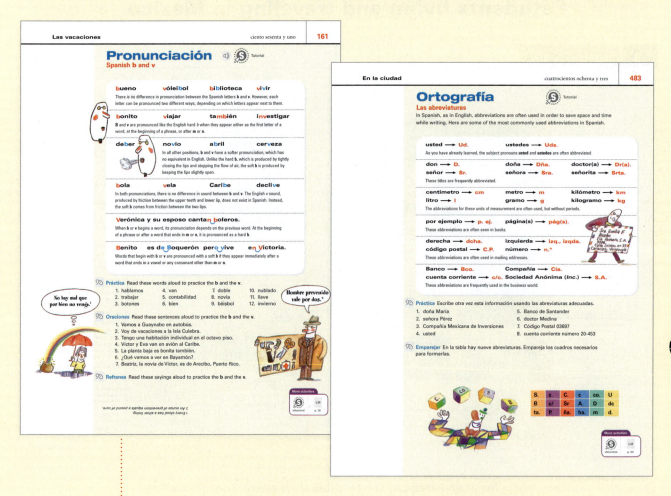

Pronunciación explains the sounds and pronunciation of Spanish in Lessons 1–9.

Ortografía focuses on topics related to Spanish spelling in Lessons 10–18.

Supersite

- Pronunciation tutorials with speech recognition
- Spelling tutorials
- Record-compare textbook activities

Supersite features vary by access level.

Cultura
exposes you to different aspects
of Hispanic culture tied to the lesson theme.

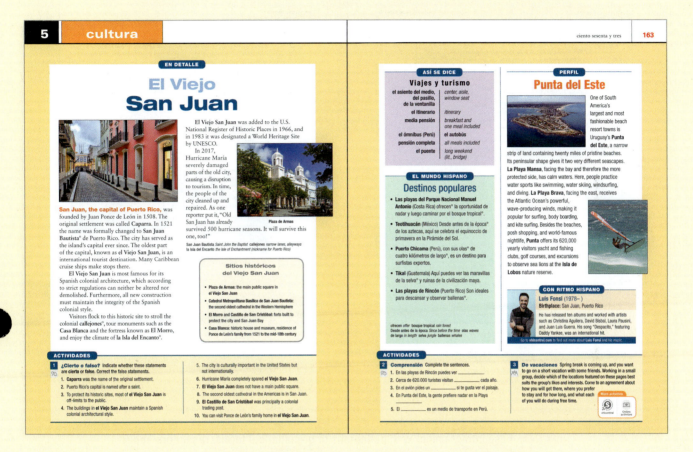

En detalle & Perfil Two articles on the lesson theme focus on a specific place, custom, person, group, or tradition in the Spanish-speaking world. In Spanish starting in Lesson 7, these features also provide reading practice.

Coverage While the **Panorama** section takes a regional approach to cultural coverage, **Cultura** is theme-driven, covering several Spanish-speaking regions in every lesson.

Así se dice & El mundo hispano Lexical and comparative features expand cultural coverage to people, traditions, customs, trends, and vocabulary throughout the Spanish-speaking world.

Con ritmo hispano This new feature profiles musicians of the Spanish-speaking world.

Supersite

- **Con ritmo hispano** information and activities
- Textbook activities
- Additional online-only practice activities

- **Conexión Internet** activity with questions and keywords related to lesson theme
- Additional cultural reading

Supersite features vary by access level.

Estructura
presents Spanish grammar in a graphic-intensive format.

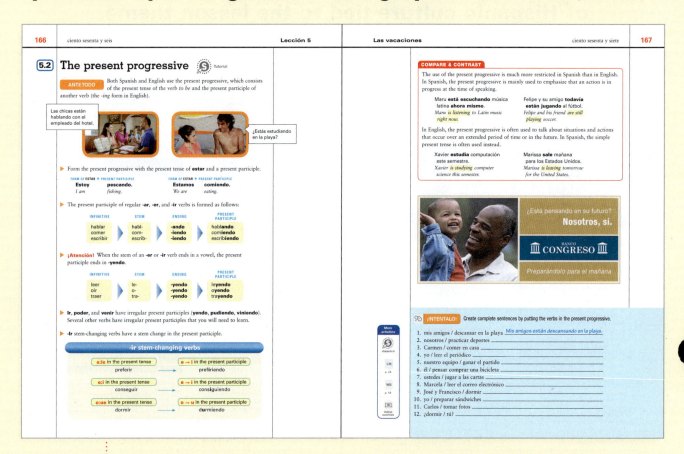

Ante todo Ease into grammar with definitions of grammatical terms, reminders about what you already know of English grammar, and Spanish grammar you have learned in earlier lessons.

Charts To help you learn, colorful, easy-to-use charts call out key grammatical structures and forms, as well as important related vocabulary.

Compare & Contrast This feature focuses on aspects of grammar that native speakers of English may find difficult, clarifying similarities and differences between Spanish and English.

Student sidebars provide you with on-the-spot linguistic, cultural, or language-learning information directly related to the materials in front of you.

Diagrams Clear and easy-to-grasp grammar explanations are reinforced by colorful diagrams that present sample words, phrases, and sentences.

¡Inténtalo! offers an easy first step into each grammar point.

Supersite

- Interactive, animated grammar tutorials with quick checks
- Textbook activities

Supersite features vary by access level.

Estructura
provides directed and communicative practice.

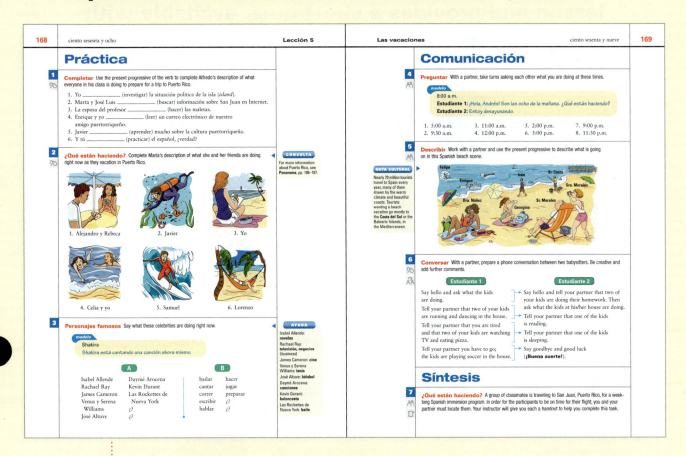

Práctica Guided, yet meaningful exercises weave current and previously learned vocabulary together with the current grammar point.

Activities with handouts In information gap activities, you and your partner each have only half of the information you need, so you must work together to accomplish the task at hand. Other activities with handouts include surveys.

Comunicación Opportunities for creative expression use the lesson's grammar and vocabulary.

Sidebars The **Notas culturales** expand coverage of the cultures of Spanish-speaking peoples and countries, while the other sidebars provide on-the-spot language support.

Síntesis activities integrate the current grammar point with previously learned points, providing built-in, consistent review.

Supersite

- Textbook activities
- Additional online-only practice activities
- Chat activities for conversational skill-building and oral practice
- Grammar activities in Activity Pack

Supersite features vary by access level.

Estructura
Recapitulación reviews the grammar of each lesson and provides a short quiz, available with auto-grading on the Supersite.

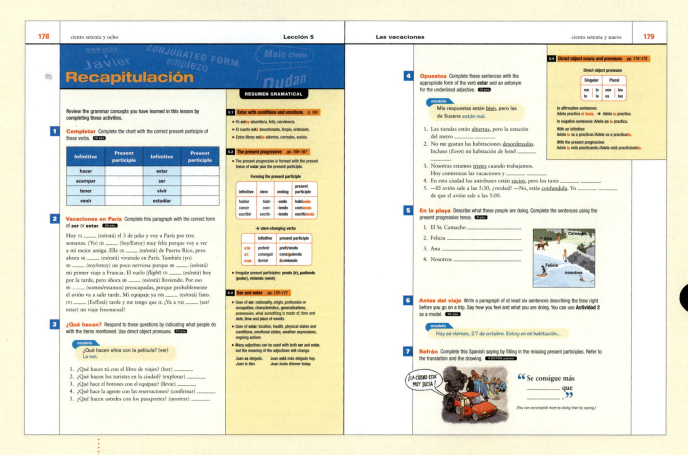

Resumen gramatical This review panel provides you with an easy-to-study summary of the basic concepts of the lesson's grammar, with page references to the full explanations.

Points Each activity is assigned a point value to help you track your progress. All **Recapitulación** sections add up to one hundred points, plus four additional points for successfully completing the bonus activity.

Activities A series of activities, moving from directed to open-ended, systematically test your mastery of the lesson's grammar. The section ends with a riddle or puzzle using the grammar from the lesson.

Supersite

- Textbook activity with diagnostics
- Additional online-only review activities
- Review activities in Activity Pack
- Vocabulary practice quiz with diagnostics

Supersite features vary by access level.

Adelante

Lectura develops reading skills in the context of the lesson theme.

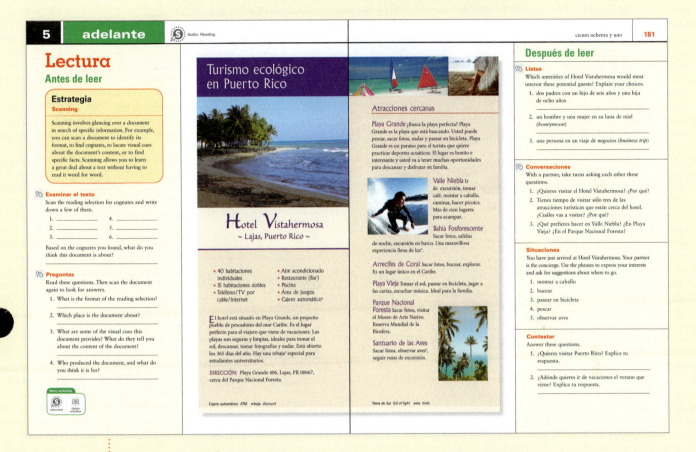

Antes de leer Valuable reading strategies and pre-reading activities strengthen your reading abilities in Spanish.

Readings Selections related to the lesson theme recycle vocabulary and grammar you have learned. The selections in Lessons 1–12 are cultural texts, while those in Lessons 13–18 are literary pieces.

Después de leer Activities include post-reading exercises that review and check your comprehension of the reading as well as expansion activities.

Supersite

- Audio-sync reading that highlights text as it is being read
- Textbook activities
- Additional reading

Supersite features vary by access level.

Adelante

Escritura develops writing skills while *Escuchar* practices listening skills in the context of the lesson theme.

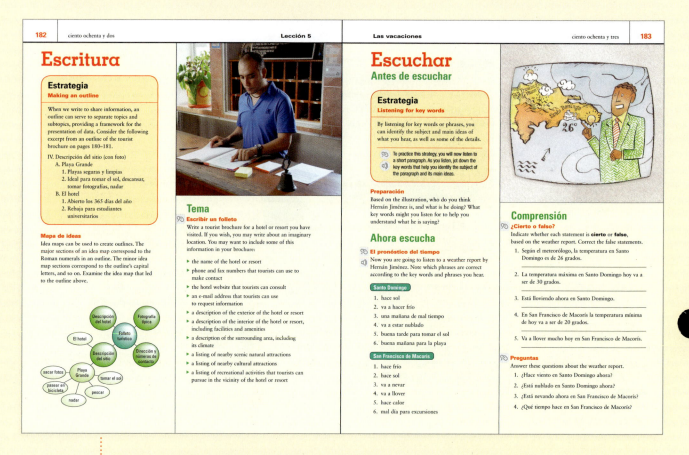

Estrategia Strategies help you prepare for the writing and listening tasks to come.

Escritura The **Tema** describes the writing topic and includes suggestions for approaching it.

Escuchar A recorded conversation or narration develops your listening skills in Spanish. **Preparación** prepares you for listening to the recorded passage.

Ahora escucha walks you through the passage, and **Comprensión** checks your listening comprehension.

Supersite

- Composition engine for writing activity in **Escritura**
- Audio for listening activity in **Escuchar**
- Textbook activities

Supersite features vary by access level.

Adelante

En pantalla and *Flash cultura* present additional video tied to the lesson theme.

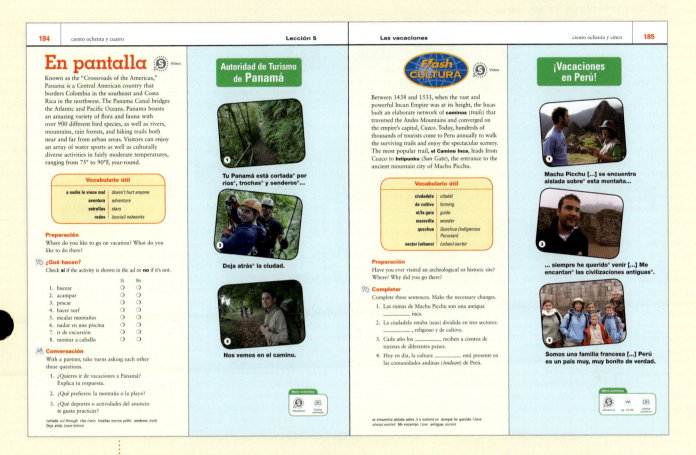

En pantalla TV clips, many **NEW!** to this edition, give you additional exposure to authentic language. The clips include commercials, documentaries, public service announcements, and short films that feature the language, vocabulary, and theme of the lesson.

Presentation Cultural notes, video stills with captions, and vocabulary support all prepare you to view the clips. Activities check your comprehension and expand on the ideas presented.

Flash cultura An icon lets you know that the enormously successful **Flash cultura** Video offers specially shot content tied to the lesson theme.

Activities Due to the overwhelming popularity of the **Flash cultura** Video, previewing support and comprehension activities are integrated into the student text.

Ⓢupersite

- Streaming video of **En pantalla** and **Flash cultura**
- Textbook activities
- Additional online-only practice activities

Supersite features vary by access level.

Panorama
presents the nations of the Spanish-speaking world.

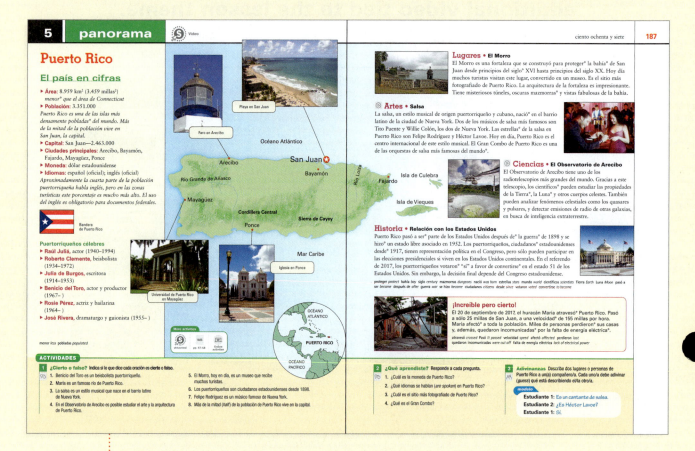

El país en cifras presents interesting key facts about the featured country.

Maps point out major cities, rivers, and geographical features and situate the country in the context of its immediate surroundings and the world.

Readings A series of brief paragraphs explores facets of the country's culture such as history, places, fine arts, literature, and aspects of everyday life.

¡Increíble pero cierto! highlights an intriguing fact about the country or its people.

Activities Three activities related to the lesson's vocabulary, grammar, and/or theme check your comprehension.

Panorama cultural Video This video provides an exciting visual companion for two of the **Panorama** paragraphs about the featured country.

Supersite

- Streaming video of the **Panorama cultural** program
- Textbook activities
- Additional online-only practice activities
- **Conexión Internet** activity with questions and keywords related to lesson theme

Supersite features vary by access level.

Vocabulario
summarizes all the active vocabulary of the lesson.

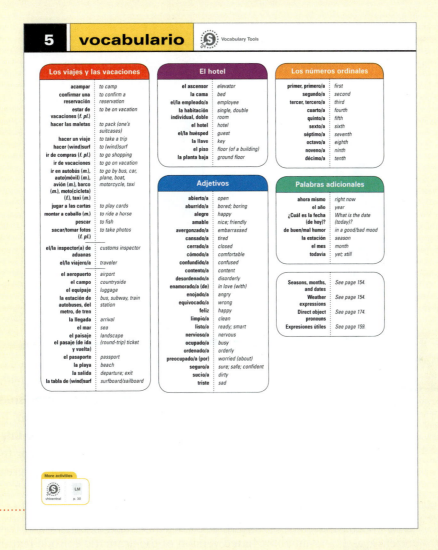

5 vocabulario — Vocabulary Tools

Los viajes y las vacaciones

acampar	to camp
confirmar una reservación	to confirm a reservation
estar de vacaciones (*f. pl.*)	to be on vacation
hacer las maletas	to pack (one's suitcases)
hacer un viaje	to take a trip
hacer (wind)surf	to (wind)surf
ir de compras (*f. pl.*)	to go shopping
ir de vacaciones	to go on vacation
ir en autobús (*m.*), auto(móvil) (*m.*), avión (*m.*), barco (*m.*), moto(cicleta) (*f.*), taxi (*m.*)	to go by bus, car, plane, boat, motorcycle, taxi
jugar a las cartas	to play cards
montar a caballo (*m.*)	to ride a horse
pescar	to fish
sacar/tomar fotos (*f. pl.*)	to take photos
el/la inspector(a) de aduanas	customs inspector
el/la viajero/a	traveler
el aeropuerto	airport
el campo	countryside
el equipaje	luggage
la estación de autobuses, del metro, de tren	bus, subway, train station
la llegada	arrival
el mar	sea
el paisaje	landscape
el pasaje (de ida y vuelta)	(round-trip) ticket
el pasaporte	passport
la playa	beach
la salida	departure; exit
la tabla de (wind)surf	surfboard/sailboard

El hotel

el ascensor	elevator
la cama	bed
el/la empleado/a	employee
la habitación individual, doble	single, double room
el hotel	hotel
el/la huésped	guest
la llave	key
el piso	floor (of a building)
la planta baja	ground floor

Adjetivos

abierto/a	open
aburrido/a	bored; boring
alegre	happy
amable	nice; friendly
avergonzado/a	embarrassed
cansado/a	tired
cerrado/a	closed
cómodo/a	comfortable
confundido/a	confused
contento/a	content
desordenado/a	disorderly
enamorado/a (de)	in love (with)
enojado/a	angry
equivocado/a	wrong
feliz	happy
limpio/a	clean
listo/a	ready; smart
nervioso/a	nervous
ocupado/a	busy
ordenado/a	orderly
preocupado/a (por)	worried (about)
seguro/a	sure; safe; confident
sucio/a	dirty
triste	sad

Los números ordinales

primer, primero/a	first
segundo/a	second
tercer, tercero/a	third
cuarto/a	fourth
quinto/a	fifth
sexto/a	sixth
séptimo/a	seventh
octavo/a	eighth
noveno/a	ninth
décimo/a	tenth

Palabras adicionales

ahora mismo	right now
el año	year
¿Cuál es la fecha (de hoy)?	What is the date (today)?
de buen/mal humor	in a good/bad mood
la estación	season
el mes	month
todavía	yet; still

Seasons, months, and dates	See page 154.
Weather expressions	See page 154.
Direct object pronouns	See page 174.
Expresiones útiles	See page 159.

More activities
vhlcentral — LM p. 30

Vocabulario The end-of-lesson page lists the active vocabulary from each lesson. This is the vocabulary that may appear on quizzes or tests.

Supersite

- Audio for all vocabulary items
- Customizable study lists
- Summative vocabulary activity with speech recognition
- Practice test with diagnostics
- Oral practice

Supersite features vary by access level.

Fotonovela Video Program

The cast

Here are the main characters you will meet in the **Fotonovela** Video:

From Mexico,
Jimena Díaz Velázquez

From Argentina,
Juan Carlos Rossi

From Mexico,
Felipe Díaz Velázquez

From the U.S.,
Marissa Wagner

From Mexico,
María Eugenia (Maru) Castaño Ricaurte

From Spain,
Miguel Ángel Lagasca Martínez

The **Vistas 6/e Fotonovela** Video is a dynamic and contemporary window into the Spanish language. The video centers around the Díaz family, whose household includes two college-aged children and a visiting student from the U.S. Over the course of an academic year, Jimena, Felipe, Marissa, and their friends explore **Mexico City** and other parts of Mexico as they make plans for their futures. Their adventures take them through some of the greatest natural and cultural treasures of the Spanish-speaking world, as well as the highs and lows of everyday life.

The **Fotonovela** section in each textbook lesson is actually an abbreviated version of the dramatic episode featured in the video. Therefore, each **Fotonovela** section can be done before you see the corresponding video episode, after it, or as a section that stands alone.

In each dramatic segment, the characters interact using the vocabulary and grammar you are studying. As the storyline unfolds, the episodes combine new vocabulary and grammar with previously taught language, exposing you to a variety of authentic accents along the way. At the end of each episode, the **Resumen** section highlights the grammar and vocabulary you are studying.

We hope you find the **Fotonovela** Video to be an engaging and useful tool for learning Spanish!

En pantalla Video Program

The **Vistas** Supersite features an authentic video clip for each lesson. Clip formats include commercials, documentaries, and even short films. These clips, many **NEW!** to the Sixth Edition, have been carefully chosen to be comprehensible for students learning Spanish, and are accompanied by activities and vocabulary lists to facilitate understanding. More importantly, though, these clips are a fun and motivating way to improve your Spanish!

Here are the countries represented in each lesson in **En pantalla**:

Lesson 1 U.S.	Lesson 7 Argentina	Lesson 13 Spain
Lesson 2 Chile	Lesson 8 Colombia	Lesson 14 Honduras
Lesson 3 Argentina	Lesson 9 Chile	Lesson 15 Mexico
Lesson 4 Spain	Lesson 10 Spain	Lesson 16 Spain
Lesson 5 Panama	Lesson 11 Spain	Lesson 17 Spain
Lesson 6 Spain	Lesson 12 Spain	Lesson 18 Chile

Flash cultura Video Program

In the dynamic **Flash cultura** Video, young people from all over the Spanish-speaking world share aspects of life in their countries with you. The similarities and differences among Spanish-speaking countries that come up through their adventures will challenge you to think about your own cultural practices and values. The segments provide valuable cultural insights as well as linguistic input; the episodes will introduce you to a variety of accents and vocabulary as they gradually move into Spanish.

Panorama cultural Video Program

The **Panorama cultural** Video provides visuals for two of the **Panorama** paragraphs about the featured country.

acknowledgments

On behalf of its authors and editors, Vista Higher Learning expresses its sincere appreciation to the many instructors and college professors across the U.S. and Canada who contributed their ideas and suggestions.

Vistas, Sixth Edition, is the direct result of extensive reviews and ongoing input from both students and instructors using the Fifth Edition. Accordingly, we gratefully acknowledge those who shared their suggestions, recommendations, and ideas as we prepared this Sixth Edition.

We express our sincere appreciation to the instructors who completed our online review.

Reviewers

Elizabeth Aguilar
University of Illinois at Chicago

Soraya Alamdari, PhD
Glendale Community College, CA

Pilar Alcalde, PhD
University of Memphis, TN

Tim Altanero, PhD
Austin Community College, TX

Felipe Amaro
University of Illinois at Chicago

Isabel Anievas-Gamallo
San Joaquin Delta College, CA

Rosalind Arthur
Clark Atlanta University, GA

Collin Ashmore
Washington College, MD

Inge R. Baird
Anderson University, IN

Tim Barnett
St. Mary's University, TX

Wanda Baumgartel
Somerset Community College, KY

Kevin Beard
Richland College, TX

Sarah Beeman
University of St. Thomas, MN

Janet Bell
Tarleton State University, TX

Martha Black de Frías
University of Alaska Anchorage

Tom Blodget
Butte College, CA

Jeanne A. Boettcher
Madison Area Technical College, WI

Stella M. Boghosian
Queens College, CUNY

Teresa L. Borden
Columbia College, CA

Sara Blossom Bostwick
Lansing Community College, MI

Teresa Buzo Salas
Georgia Southern University

Silvia Castellini-Patel
West Valley College, CA

Lisa Celona
Tunxis Community College, CT

Gabriela Cerghedean
Beloit College, WI

Dr. Silvia Choi
Georgia Gwinnett College

Sonia Ciccarelli
San Joaquin Delta College, CA

Carrie Y. Clay
Anderson University, IN

Scott Cooper
Anne Arundel Community College, MD

Fina Coronel
Fresno City College, CA

Miryam Criado, PhD
Hanover College, IN

José V. Cruz
Fayetteville Technical Community College, NC

Walberto Diaz
San Diego City College, CA

Dr. Karen Dollinger
University of Pikeville, KY

Danion L. Doman
Truman State University, MO

Mark A. Dowell
St. Charles Community College, MO

Scott Estes
North Idaho College

Kim Faber
Oberlin College, OH

Kelly Montijo Fink
Kirkwood Community College, IA

Catherine Fountain
Appalachian State University, NC

Lloyd J. Frias
Loyola University Maryland

Lucas Fricke
Bethany Lutheran College, MN

Dr. Vasant Gadre
Richland College, TX

Angélica Galván
Tennessee Tech University

Dr. Eduardo Garcia
Drake University, IA

Raquel Gaytán
Rice University, TX

Hasmik Gharaghazaryan
Richland College, TX

Michael Gismondi
University of Illinois at Chicago

Jill R. Gomez
Miami University Hamilton, OH

Lucila González Cirre
Cerro Coso Community College, CA

Ana González-Gómez
Northern Arizona University

Kate Grovergrys
Madison Area Technical College, WI

Cassandra Gulam
Washington State University Vancouver

Kenneth Habecker, MA
Columbia College, CA

Michael Harrison
San Diego Mesa College, CA

Richard A. Heath
Kirkwood Community College, IA

Valerie Hecht
College of Southern Nevada

Dawn Heston
University of Missouri

Matt Hoch
Northern Arizona University

Lourdes Huici Clever, MA
Community College of Aurora, CO

Rene Iraheta
West Hills College Lemoore, CA

Becky S. Jaimes
Austin Community College, TX

Stacy Jazán, PhD
Glendale Community College, CA

Aggie Johnson
Flagler College, FL

Stephanie H. Langston
Perimeter College at Georgia State University

Katie MacLean, PhD
Kalamazoo College, MI

María José Maguire
Flagler College, FL

Donna Marqués
MiraCosta College, CA

Dr. Cecilia Marrugo
Tarleton State University, TX

Dr. Mark McGraw
Ouachita Baptist University, AR

José Mendoza
Beaufort County Community College, NC

Dr. Joshua Mora
Wayland Baptist University, TX

Arturo Morales
LeTourneau University, TX

Anna Moreno
West Hills Community College, CA

Antonio Olivas
East Los Angeles College, CA

Ruth Ore' Giron
Pima Community College, AZ

Lucía Osa-Melero
Duquesne University, PA

Lulú De Panbehchi
Virginia Commonwealth University

George Pappas
Pace University, NY

Jeana Paul-Ureña
Stephen F. Austin State University, TX

Chachi Perez
Richland College, TX

Susana Pérez Castillejo
University of St. Thomas, MN

Mary Perley
Cairn University, PA

Zorayda H. Pina
Owens Community College, OH

Karry Putzy
Kirkwood Community College, IA

Micaela Ramos
University of San Diego, CA

Aida Ramos-Sellman
Goucher College, MD

Liz Rangel Arriola
Pima Community College, AZ

Dr. John W. Reed
Saint Mary's University of Minnesota

Timothy Reed
Ripon College, WI

Jesus Reyes
Hartnell College, CA

Steve Richman
Mercer County Community College, NJ

Vanessa Rocha
San Joaquin Delta College, CA

Monica Pilar Rodriguez
Lyon College, AR

Linda A. Roy
Tarrant County College - South Campus, TX

Marilin Sarria
Fairfield University, CT

Eduardo Santa Cruz, PhD
Hanover College, IN

Dora Schoenbrun-Fernandez
San Diego Mesa College, CA

Mariana R. Segovia
Palomar College, CA

Albert Shank
Scottsdale Community College, AZ

Angeles Solana
SUNY Cortland

Stacy Spears
Texarkana College, TX

Abbey Stell
Butte College, CA

Cristina Szterensus
Rock Valley College, IL

Karen Tharrington, PhD
Sandhills Community College, NC

Daniel G. Tight
University of St. Thomas, MN

Dr. Ivelisse Urbán
Tarleton State University, TX

Silvia Vazquez
MiraCosta College, CA

Alexandra Vinarov, PhD
LIM College, NY

F. Vivar
University of Memphis, TN

Dr. Lynn Vogel-Zuiderweg
East Los Angeles College, CA

Montana Walsh
Northern New Mexico College

Dr. Wesley J. Weaver III
SUNY Cortland

Sarah Willoughby
Everett Community College, WA

James R. Wilson
Madison Area Technical College, WI

Aurora Wold-Krogmann
Temple College, TX

Mikela Zhezha-Thaumanavar
Kalamazoo College, MI

Hola, ¿qué tal?

1

A PRIMERA VISTA
- Guess what the people on the photo are saying:
  a. Adiós. b. Hola. c. salsa
- Most likely they would also say:
  a. Gracias. b. fiesta c. Buenos días.
- The women are:
  a. amigas b. chicos c. señores

Hola, ¿qué tal?

Más vocabulario

Hola.	*Hi.*
Buenos días.	*Good morning.*
Buenas noches.	*Good evening; Good night.*
Hasta la vista.	*See you later.*
Hasta pronto.	*See you soon.*
¿Cómo se llama usted?	*What's your name? (form.)*
Le presento a…	*I would like to introduce you to (name). (form.)*
Te presento a…	*I would like to introduce you to (name). (fam.)*
el nombre	*name*
¿Cómo estás?	*How are you? (fam.)*
No muy bien.	*Not very well.*
¿Qué pasa?	*What's happening?; What's going on?*
por favor	*please*
De nada.	*You're welcome.*
No hay de qué.	*You're welcome.*
Lo siento.	*I'm sorry.*
Gracias.	*Thank you; Thanks.*
Muchas gracias.	*Thank you very much; Thanks a lot.*

Variación léxica

Items are presented for recognition purposes only.

Buenos días. ⟷ Buenas.
De nada. ⟷ A la orden.
Lo siento. ⟷ Perdón.
¿Qué tal? ⟷ ¿Qué hubo? (*Col.*)
Chau. ⟷ Ciao; Chao.

More activities

 vhlcentral | LM p. 1 | WB pp. 1–2 | Online activities

1
ELENA Patricia, le presento a Jorge Perales.
PATRICIA Encantada.
SEÑOR PERALES Igualmente. ¿De dónde es usted, señorita?
PATRICIA Soy de México. ¿Y usted?
SEÑOR PERALES De Puerto Rico.

3
SEÑOR VARGAS Buenas tardes, señora Wong. ¿Cómo está usted?
SEÑORA WONG Muy bien, gracias. ¿Y usted, señor Vargas?
SEÑOR VARGAS Bien, gracias.
SEÑORA WONG Hasta mañana, señor Vargas. Saludos a la señora Vargas.
SEÑOR VARGAS Adiós.

5
CARMEN Buenas tardes. Me llamo Carmen. ¿Cómo te llamas tú?
ANTONIO Buenas tardes. Me llamo Antonio. Mucho gusto.
CARMEN El gusto es mío. ¿De dónde eres?
ANTONIO Soy de los Estados Unidos, de California.

2
TOMÁS ¿Qué tal, Alberto?
ALBERTO Regular. ¿Y tú?
TOMÁS Bien. ¿Qué hay de nuevo?
ALBERTO Nada.

4
BERTA Hasta luego, Tere.
TERESA Chau, Berta. Nos vemos mañana.

AYUDA

In Spanish, people can be addressed either formally or informally. Dialogues 1 and 3 are formal exchanges and use **usted** (*you*) forms. Dialogues 2, 4, and 5 are informal and use the familiar **tú** (*you*) form or other informal expressions. You will learn more about this in **Estructura 1.3**.

Práctica

1 **Indicar** Check **sí** if you might use the expression you hear to greet someone or **no** if you would not.

	Sí	No		Sí	No
1.	○	○	5.	○	○
2.	○	○	6.	○	○
3.	○	○	7.	○	○
4.	○	○	8.	○	○

2 **Escuchar** Choose the correct response for each question or statement you hear.

1. a. Muy bien, gracias.   b. Me llamo Graciela.
2. a. Lo siento.   b. Mucho gusto.
3. a. Soy de Puerto Rico.   b. No muy bien.
4. a. No hay de qué.   b. Regular.
5. a. Mucho gusto.   b. Hasta pronto.
6. a. Nada.   b. Igualmente.
7. a. Me llamo Guillermo Montero.   b. Muy bien, gracias.
8. a. Buenas tardes. ¿Cómo estás?   b. El gusto es mío.

3 **Escoger** For each expression, write another word or phrase that expresses a similar idea.

> **modelo**
> ¿Cómo estás? ¿Qué tal?

1. De nada.
2. Encantado.
3. Adiós.
4. Mucho gusto.
5. Hasta la vista.

4 **Ordenar** Work with a partner to put this scrambled conversation in order. Then act it out.

—Soy de México. ¿Y tú?
—Muy bien, gracias. Soy Rosabel.
—Mucho gusto, Rosabel.
—Hola. Me llamo Carlos. ¿Cómo estás?
—Soy de Argentina.
—Igualmente. ¿De dónde eres, Carlos?

CARLOS _____

ROSABEL _____

CARLOS _____

ROSABEL _____

CARLOS _____

ROSABEL _____

5 Seleccionar Choose the best word or phrase to complete each mini-conversation.

1. —Nos vemos mañana.
   —_____
   a. Gracias.   b. ¡Chau!   c. ¿Y usted?
2. —¿Qué tal?
   —_____
   a. Lo siento.   b. Igualmente.   c. Regular.
3. —Mucho gusto, señora Ochoa.
   —_____
   a. Muy bien.   b. No hay de qué.   c. Encantada, señor Rubio.
4. ¿De dónde eres?
   —_____
   a. De California.   b. El gusto es mío.   c. De nada.
5. —_____
   —No muy bien.
   a. ¿Qué pasa?   b. Hasta la vista.   c. ¿Cómo está usted?

6 Completar Work with a partner to complete these dialogues.

modelo
Estudiante 1: ¿Cómo estás?
Estudiante 2: Muy bien, gracias.

1. **Estudiante 1:** _____
   Estudiante 2: Buenos días. ¿Qué tal?
2. **Estudiante 1:** _____
   Estudiante 2: Me llamo Carmen Sánchez.
3. **Estudiante 1:** _____
   Estudiante 2: De Canadá.
4. **Estudiante 1:** Te presento a Marisol.
   Estudiante 2: _____
5. **Estudiante 1:** Gracias.
   Estudiante 2: _____
6. **Estudiante 1:** _____
   Estudiante 2: Nada.

7 Cambiar Work with a partner and correct the second part of each conversation to make it logical.

modelo
Estudiante 1: ¿Qué tal?
Estudiante 2: ~~No hay de qué.~~ Bien. ¿Y tú?

1. **Estudiante 1:** Hasta mañana, señora Ramírez. Saludos al señor Ramírez.
   Estudiante 2: *Muy bien, gracias.*
2. **Estudiante 1:** ¿Qué hay de nuevo, Alberto?
   Estudiante 2: *Sí, me llamo Alberto. ¿Cómo te llamas tú?*
3. **Estudiante 1:** Gracias, Tomás.
   Estudiante 2: *Regular. ¿Y tú?*
4. **Estudiante 1:** Miguel, te presento a la señorita Perales.
   Estudiante 2: *No hay de qué, señorita.*
5. **Estudiante 1:** ¿De dónde eres, Antonio?
   Estudiante 2: *Muy bien, gracias. ¿Y tú?*
6. **Estudiante 1:** ¿Cómo se llama usted?
   Estudiante 2: *El gusto es mío.*

¡LENGUA VIVA!

The titles **señor**, **señora**, and **señorita** are abbreviated **Sr.**, **Sra.**, and **Srta.** Note that these abbreviations are capitalized, while the titles themselves are not.

There is no Spanish equivalent for the English title *Ms.;* women are addressed as **señora** or **señorita**.

Comunicación

8 **Diálogos** With a partner, complete and act out these conversations.

> ### Conversación 1
>
> —Hola. Me llamo Teresa. ¿Cómo te llamas tú?
>
> —_____
>
> —Soy de Puerto Rico. ¿Y tú?
>
> —_____

> ### Conversación 2
>
> —_____
>
> —Muy bien, gracias. ¿Y usted, señora López?
>
> —_____
>
> —Hasta luego, señora. Saludos al señor López.
>
> —_____

> ### Conversación 3
>
> —_____
>
> —Regular. ¿Y tú?
>
> —_____
>
> —Nada.

9 **Conversaciones** Write four short conversations based on what the people would say.

10 **Situaciones** In groups of three, write and act out these situations.

1. On your way out of class on the first day of school, you strike up a conversation with the two students who were sitting next to you. You find out each student's name and where he or she is from before you say goodbye and go to your next class.

2. At the next class you meet up with a friend and find out how he or she is doing. As you are talking, your friend Elena enters. Introduce her to your friend.

3. As you're leaving the bookstore, you meet your parents' friends Mrs. Sánchez and Mr. Rodríguez. You greet them and ask how each person is. As you say goodbye, you send greetings to Mrs. Rodríguez.

4. Make up and act out a real-life situation that you and your classmates can role-play with the language you've learned.

Bienvenida, Marissa

Marissa llega a México para pasar un año con la familia Díaz.

 Video

MARISSA ¿Usted es de Cuba?

SRA. DÍAZ Sí, de La Habana. Y Roberto es de Mérida. Tú eres de Wisconsin, ¿verdad?

MARISSA Sí, de Appleton, Wisconsin.

MARISSA ¿Quiénes son los dos chicos de las fotos? ¿Jimena y Felipe?

SRA. DÍAZ Sí. Ellos son estudiantes.

DON DIEGO ¿Cómo está usted hoy, señora Carolina?

SRA. DÍAZ Muy bien, gracias. ¿Y usted?

DON DIEGO Bien, gracias.

DON DIEGO Buenas tardes, señora. Señorita, bienvenida a la Ciudad de México.

MARISSA ¡Muchas gracias!

MARISSA ¿Cómo se llama usted?

DON DIEGO Yo soy Diego. Mucho gusto.

MARISSA El gusto es mío, don Diego.

SRA. DÍAZ Ahí hay dos maletas. Son de Marissa.

DON DIEGO Con permiso.

DON DIEGO

SR. DÍAZ

FELIPE

JIMENA

7

SR. DÍAZ ¿Qué hora es?

FELIPE Son las cuatro y veinticinco.

8

SRA. DÍAZ Marissa, te presento a Roberto, mi esposo.

SR. DÍAZ Bienvenida, Marissa.

MARISSA Gracias, señor Díaz.

9

JIMENA ¿Qué hay en esta cosa?

MARISSA Bueno, a ver, hay tres cuadernos, un mapa... ¡Y un diccionario!

JIMENA ¿Cómo se dice mediodía en inglés?

FELIPE "Noon".

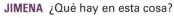

10

FELIPE Estás en México, ¿verdad?

MARISSA ¿Sí?

FELIPE Nosotros somos tu diccionario.

More activities

vhlcentral | VM pp. 1–2 | Online activities

Expresiones útiles

Identifying yourself and others

¿Cómo se llama usted?
What's your name?

Yo soy Diego, el portero. Mucho gusto.
I'm Diego, the doorman. Nice to meet you.

¿Cómo te llamas?
What's your name?

Me llamo Marissa.
My name is Marissa.

¿Quién es...? / ¿Quiénes son...?
Who is...? / Who are...?

Es mi esposo.
He's my husband.

Tú eres..., ¿verdad?/¿cierto?/¿no?
You are..., right?

Identifying objects

¿Qué hay en esta cosa?
What's in this thing?

Bueno, a ver, aquí hay tres cuadernos...
Well, let's see, here are three notebooks...

Oye/Oiga, ¿cómo se dice *suitcase* en español?
Hey, how do you say suitcase in Spanish?

Se dice *maleta*.
You say maleta.

Saying what time it is

¿Qué hora es?
What time is it?

Es la una. / Son las dos.
It's one o'clock. / It's two o'clock.

Son las cuatro y veinticinco.
It's four twenty-five.

Polite expressions

Con permiso.
*Pardon me; Excuse me.
(to request permission)*

Perdón.
Pardon me; Excuse me. (to get someone's attention or excuse yourself)

¡Bienvenido/a! *Welcome!*

¿Qué pasó?

1

¿Cierto o falso? Indicate if each statement is **cierto** or **falso**. Then correct the false statements.

	Cierto	Falso
1. La Sra. Díaz es de Caracas.	○	○
2. El Sr. Díaz es de Mérida.	○	○
3. Marissa es de Los Ángeles, California.	○	○
4. Jimena y Felipe son profesores.	○	○
5. Las dos maletas son de Jimena.	○	○
6. El Sr. Díaz pregunta "¿qué hora es?".	○	○
7. Hay un diccionario en la mochila (*backpack*) de Marissa.	○	○

2

Identificar Indicate which person says the equivalent of each statement.

1. Son las cuatro y veinticinco, papá.
2. Roberto es mi esposo.
3. Igualmente, don Diego.
4. ¿Qué hay de nuevo, doña Carolina?
5. Yo soy de Cuba.
6. ¿Qué hay en la mochila, Marissa?

MARISSA **FELIPE** **SRA. DÍAZ**

DON DIEGO **JIMENA** ◄

3

Completar Complete this new version of the conversation between Don Diego and Marissa.

DON DIEGO Hola, (1)_____.
MARISSA Hola, señor. ¿Cómo se (2)_____ usted?
DON DIEGO Yo me llamo Diego, ¿y (3)_____?
MARISSA Yo me llamo Marissa. (4)_____.
DON DIEGO (5)_____, señorita Marissa.
MARISSA Nos (6)_____, don Diego.
DON DIEGO Hasta (7)_____, señorita Marissa.

4

Conversar With a partner, prepare a conversation between two travelers at an airport.

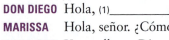 Estudiante 1   Estudiante 2

Estudiante 1	Estudiante 2
Say "good afternoon" to your partner and ask for his or her name.	→ Say hello and what your name is. Then ask what your partner's name is.
Say what your name is and that you are glad to meet your partner.	→ Say that the pleasure is yours.
Ask how your partner is.	→ Say that you're doing well, thank you.
Ask where your partner is from.	→ Say where you're from.
Say it's one o'clock and say goodbye.	→ Say goodbye.

Pronunciación
 Tutorial
The Spanish alphabet

The Spanish and English alphabets are almost identical, with a few exceptions. For example, the Spanish letter **ñ (eñe)** doesn't occur in the English alphabet. Furthermore, the letters **k (ka)** and **w (doble ve)** are used only in words of foreign origin. Examine the chart below to find other differences.

¡LENGUA VIVA!

Note that **ch** and **ll** are digraphs, or two letters that together produce one sound. Conventionally they have been considered part of the alphabet, but **ch** and **ll** do not have their own entries when placing words in alphabetical order, as in a glossary.

Letra	Nombre(s)	Ejemplos	Letra	Nombre(s)	Ejemplos
a	a	adiós	m	eme	mapa
b	be	bien, problema	n	ene	nacionalidad
c	ce	cosa, cero	ñ	eñe	mañana
ch	che	chico	o	o	once
d	de	diario, nada	p	pe	profesor
e	e	estudiante	q	cu	qué
f	efe	foto	r	ere	regular, señora
g	ge	gracias, Gerardo, regular	s	ese	señor
			t	te	tú
h	hache	hola	u	u	usted
i	i	igualmente	v	ve	vista, nuevo
j	jota	Javier	w	doble ve	*walkman*
k	ka, ca	kilómetro	x	equis	existir, México
l	ele	lápiz	y	i griega, ye	yo
ll	elle	llave	z	zeta, ceta	zona

El alfabeto Repeat the Spanish alphabet and example words after your instructor.

AYUDA

The letter combination **rr** produces a strong trilled sound that does not have an English equivalent. English speakers commonly make this sound when imitating the sound of a motor. This sound occurs with the **rr** between vowels and with the **r** at the beginning of a word: **puertorriqueño, terrible, Roberto**, etc. See **Lección 7**, p. 233 for more information.

Práctica Spell these words aloud in Spanish.

1. nada
2. maleta
3. quince
4. muy
5. hombre
6. por favor
7. San Fernando
8. Estados Unidos
9. Puerto Rico
10. España
11. Javier
12. Ecuador
13. Maite
14. gracias
15. Nueva York

Refranes Read these sayings aloud.

Ver es creer.[1]

En boca cerrada no entran moscas.[2]

1 Seeing is believing. 2 Silence is golden.

More activities

vhlcentral   LM   p. 2

Saludos y besos en los países hispanos

In Spanish-speaking countries, kissing on the cheek is a customary way to greet friends and family members. Even when people are introduced for the first time, it is common for them to kiss, particularly in non-business settings. Whereas North Americans maintain considerable personal space when greeting, Spaniards and Latin Americans tend to decrease their personal space and give one or two kisses (**besos**) on the cheek, sometimes accompanied by a handshake or a hug. In formal business settings, where associates do not know one another on a personal level, a simple handshake is appropriate.

Greeting someone with a **beso** varies according to gender and region. Men generally greet each other with a hug or warm handshake, with the exception of Argentina, where male friends and relatives lightly kiss on the cheek. Greetings between men and women, and between women, generally include kissing, but can differ depending on the country and context. In Spain, it is customary to give **dos besos**, starting with the right cheek first. In Latin American countries, including Mexico, Costa Rica, Colombia, and Chile, a greeting consists of a single "air kiss" on the right cheek. Peruvians also "air kiss," but

strangers will simply shake hands. In Colombia, female acquaintances tend to simply pat each other on the right forearm or shoulder.

Tendencias

País	Beso	País	Beso
Argentina	💋	España	💋💋
Bolivia	💋	México	💋
Chile	💋	Paraguay	💋💋
Colombia	💋	Puerto Rico	💋
El Salvador	💋	Venezuela	💋/💋💋

ACTIVIDADES

1 **¿Cierto o falso?** Indicate whether these statements are true (**cierto**) or false (**falso**). Correct the false statements.

1. In Spanish-speaking countries, people use less personal space when greeting than in the U.S.

2. Men never greet with a kiss in Spanish-speaking countries.

3. Shaking hands is not appropriate for a business setting in Latin America.

4. Spaniards greet with one kiss on the right cheek.

5. In Mexico, people greet with an "air kiss."

6. Gender can play a role in the type of greeting given.

7. If two women acquaintances meet in Colombia, they should exchange two kisses on the cheek.

8. In Peru, a man and a woman meeting for the first time would probably greet each other with an "air kiss."

EL MUNDO HISPANO

Parejas y amigos famosos

Here are some famous couples and friends from the Spanish-speaking world.

- **Penélope Cruz** (España) y **Javier Bardem** (España) Both Oscar-winning actors, the couple married in 2010. They starred together in *Vicky Cristina Barcelona* (2008) and *Loving Pablo* (2017).

- **Gael García Bernal** (México) y **Diego Luna** (México) These lifelong friends became famous when they starred in the 2001 Mexican film *Y tu mamá también*. They continue to work together on projects, such as the 2012 film *Casa de mi padre.*

- **Salma Hayek** (México) y **Penélope Cruz** (España) These two close friends developed their acting skills in their home countries before meeting in Hollywood.

PERFIL

La plaza principal

In the Spanish-speaking world, public space is treasured. Small city and town life revolves around the **plaza principal**. Often surrounded by cathedrals or municipal buildings like the **ayuntamiento** (*city hall*), the pedestrian **plaza** is designated as a central meeting place for family and friends. During warmer months, when outdoor cafés usually line the **plaza**, it is a popular spot to have a leisurely

La Plaza Mayor de Salamanca

cup of coffee, chat, and people watch. Many town festivals, or **ferias**, also take place in this space. One of the most famous

La Plaza de Armas, Lima, Perú

town squares is the **Plaza Mayor** in the university town of Salamanca, Spain. Students gather underneath its famous clock tower to meet up with friends or simply take a coffee break.

CON RITMO HISPANO

Lin-Manuel Miranda (1980–)
Birthplace: New York City, New York

He won two Tony Awards for his musical *Hamilton* (2016) and one for *In the Heights* (2008), his musical about the predominantly Latino New York neighborhood of Washington Heights.

Go to **vhlcentral.com** to find out more about **Lin-Manuel Miranda** and his music.

ACTIVIDADES

2 Comprensión Answer these questions.
1. What are two types of buildings found on the **plaza principal?**
2. What two types of events or activities are common at a **plaza principal?**
3. How would Diego Luna greet his friends?
4. Would Salma Hayek and Gael García Bernal greet each other with one kiss or two?

3 Saludos Role-play these greetings with a partner. Include a verbal greeting as well as a kiss or handshake, as appropriate.
1. friends in Mexico
2. business associates at a conference in Chile
3. friends meeting in Madrid's Plaza Mayor
4. Peruvians meeting for the first time
5. relatives in Argentina

More activities
 vhlcentral   Online activities

1.1 Nouns and articles Tutorial

Spanish nouns

ANTE TODO A noun is a word used to identify people, animals, places, things, or ideas. Unlike English, all Spanish nouns, even those that refer to non-living things, have gender; that is, they are considered either masculine or feminine. As in English, nouns in Spanish also have number, meaning that they are either singular or plural.

Nouns that refer to living things

Masculine nouns		Feminine nouns	
el hombre	*the man*	**la mujer**	*the woman*
ending in –o		**ending in –a**	
el chico	*the boy*	**la chica**	*the girl*
el pasajero	*the (male) passenger*	**la pasajera**	*the (female) passenger*
ending in –or		**ending in –ora**	
el conductor	*the (male) driver*	**la conductora**	*the (female) driver*
el profesor	*the (male) teacher*	**la profesora**	*the (female) teacher*
ending in –ista		**ending in –ista**	
el turista	*the (male) tourist*	**la turista**	*the (female) tourist*

▶ Generally, nouns that refer to males, like **el hombre**, are masculine, while nouns that refer to females, like **la mujer**, are feminine.

▶ Many nouns that refer to male beings end in **–o** or **–or**. Their corresponding feminine forms end in **–a** and **–ora**, respectively.

el conductor

la profesora

▶ The masculine and feminine forms of nouns that end in **–ista**, like **turista**, are the same, so gender is indicated by the article **el** (masculine) or **la** (feminine). Some other nouns have identical masculine and feminine forms.

el joven
the young man

la joven
the young woman

el estudiante
the (male) student

la estudiante
the (female) student

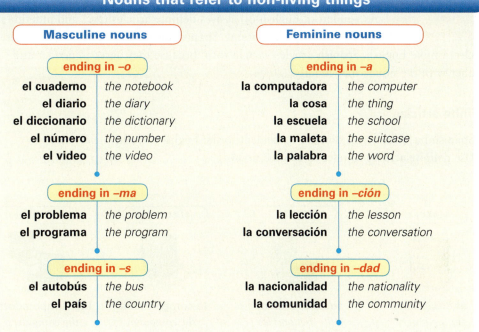

Nouns that refer to non-living things

Masculine nouns		Feminine nouns	
ending in –o		**ending in –a**	
el cuaderno	*the notebook*	la computadora	*the computer*
el diario	*the diary*	la cosa	*the thing*
el diccionario	*the dictionary*	la escuela	*the school*
el número	*the number*	la maleta	*the suitcase*
el video	*the video*	la palabra	*the word*
ending in –ma		**ending in –ción**	
el problema	*the problem*	la lección	*the lesson*
el programa	*the program*	la conversación	*the conversation*
ending in –s		**ending in –dad**	
el autobús	*the bus*	la nacionalidad	*the nationality*
el país	*the country*	la comunidad	*the community*

¡LENGUA VIVA!

The Spanish word for *video* can be pronounced with the stress on the **i** or the **e**. For that reason, you might see the word written with or without an accent: **video** or **vídeo**.

▶ As shown above, certain noun endings are strongly associated with a specific gender, so you can use them to determine if a noun is masculine or feminine.

▶ Because the gender of nouns that refer to non-living things cannot be determined by foolproof rules, you should memorize the gender of each noun you learn. It is helpful to learn each noun with its corresponding article, **el** for masculine and **la** for feminine.

▶ Another reason to memorize the gender of every noun is that there are common exceptions to the rules of gender. For example, **el mapa** (*map*) and **el día** (*day*) end in **–a**, but are masculine. **La mano** (*hand*) ends in **–o**, but is feminine.

Plural of nouns

▶ To form the plural, add **–s** to nouns that end in a vowel. For nouns that end in a consonant, add **–es**. For nouns that end in **z**, change the **z** to **c**, then add **–es**.

el chic**o** ⟶ los chic**os**   la nacionalida**d** ⟶ las nacionalida**des**

el diari**o** ⟶ los diari**os**   el paí**s** ⟶ los paí**ses**

el problem**a** ⟶ los problem**as**   el lápi**z** (*pencil*) ⟶ los lápi**ces**

CONSULTA

You will learn more about accent marks in **Lección 4, Pronunciación,** p. 123.

▶ In general, when a singular noun has an accent mark on the last syllable, the accent is dropped from the plural form.

la lecci**ón** ⟶ las lecci**ones**   el autob**ús** ⟶ los autob**uses**

▶ Use the masculine plural form to refer to a group that includes both males and females.

1 pasajer**o** + 2 pasajer**as** = 3 pasajer**os**   2 chic**os** + 2 chic**as** = 4 chic**os**

Spanish articles

ANTE TODO As you know, English often uses definite articles (*the*) and indefinite articles (*a*, *an*) before nouns. Spanish also has definite and indefinite articles. Unlike English, Spanish articles vary in form because they agree in gender and number with the nouns they modify.

Definite articles

▶ Spanish has four forms that are equivalent to the English definite article *the*. Use definite articles to refer to specific nouns.

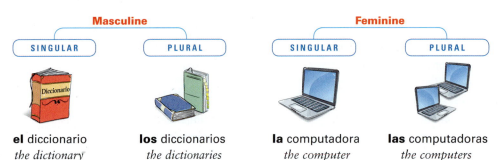

Masculine		Feminine	
SINGULAR	PLURAL	SINGULAR	PLURAL
el diccionario	**los** diccionarios	**la** computadora	**las** computadoras
the dictionary	*the dictionaries*	*the computer*	*the computers*

Indefinite articles

▶ Spanish has four forms that are equivalent to the English indefinite article, which according to context may mean *a*, *an*, or *some*. Use indefinite articles to refer to unspecified persons or things.

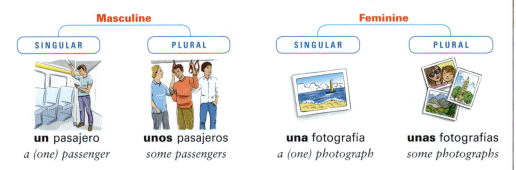

Masculine		Feminine	
SINGULAR	PLURAL	SINGULAR	PLURAL
un pasajero	**unos** pasajeros	**una** fotografía	**unas** fotografías
a (one) passenger	*some passengers*	*a (one) photograph*	*some photographs*

¡LENGUA VIVA!

Feminine singular nouns that begin with a stressed **a-** or **ha-** require the masculine articles **el** and **un**. This is done in order to avoid repetition of the **a** sound. The plural forms still use the feminine articles.
el agua *water*
las aguas *waters*
un hacha *ax*
unas hachas *axes*

¡LENGUA VIVA!

Since **la fotografía** is feminine, so is its shortened form, **la foto**, even though it ends in **–o**.

¡INTÉNTALO! Provide a definite article for each noun in the first column and an indefinite article for each noun in the second column.

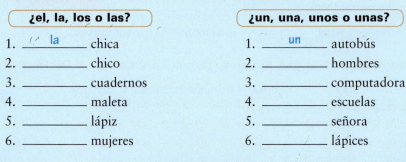

¿el, la, los o las?

1. _____la_____ chica
2. _____ chico
3. _____ cuadernos
4. _____ maleta
5. _____ lápiz
6. _____ mujeres

¿un, una, unos o unas?

1. _____un_____ autobús
2. _____ hombres
3. _____ computadora
4. _____ escuelas
5. _____ señora
6. _____ lápices

More activities

vhlcentral

LM p. 3

WB p. 3

Online activities

Práctica

1 **¿Singular o plural?** If the word is singular, make it plural. If it is plural, make it singular.

> **modelo**
>
> el hombre   los hombres
> unas señoritas   una señorita

1. el número
2. un diario
3. la estudiante
4. el conductor
5. el país
6. las cosas
7. unos turistas
8. las nacionalidades
9. unas computadoras
10. los problemas
11. los profesores
12. la señora

2 **Identificar** Provide the nouns with their corresponding definite and indefinite articles.

> **modelo**
>
> las computadoras, unas computadoras

1. _____

2. _____

3. _____

4. _____

5. _____

6. _____

7. _____

8. _____

Comunicación

3 **Charadas** In groups, play a game of charades. Individually, think of two nouns for each charade, for example, a boy using a computer (**un chico**; **una computadora**). The first person to guess correctly acts out the next charade.

1.2 # Numbers 0–30   Tutorial

Los números 0 a 30		
0 cero		
1 uno	**11** once	**21** veintiuno
2 dos	**12** doce	**22** veintidós
3 tres	**13** trece	**23** veintitrés
4 cuatro	**14** catorce	**24** veinticuatro
5 cinco	**15** quince	**25** veinticinco
6 seis	**16** dieciséis	**26** veintiséis
7 siete	**17** diecisiete	**27** veintisiete
8 ocho	**18** dieciocho	**28** veintiocho
9 nueve	**19** diecinueve	**29** veintinueve
10 diez	**20** veinte	**30** treinta

AYUDA

Though it is less common, the numbers 16 through 29 (except 20) can also be written as three words: **diez y seis, diez y siete…**

▶ The number **uno** (*one*) and numbers ending in **–uno**, such as **veintiuno**, have more than one form. Before masculine nouns, **uno** shortens to **un**. Before feminine nouns, **uno** changes to **una**.

un hombre ⟶ veinti**ún** hombres   **una** mujer ⟶ veinti**una** mujeres

▶ **¡Atención!** The forms **uno** and **veintiuno** are used when counting (**uno, dos, tres… veinte, veintiuno, veintidós…**). They are also used when the number *follows* a noun, even if the noun is feminine: **la lección uno**.

▶ To ask *how many people* or *things* there are, use **cuántos** before masculine nouns and **cuántas** before feminine nouns.

▶ The Spanish equivalent of both *there is* and *there are* is **hay**. Use **¿Hay…?** to ask *Is there…?* or *Are there…?* Use **no hay** to express *there is not* or *there are not*.

—**¿Cuántos** estudiantes **hay**?
How many students are there?

—**Hay** seis estudiantes en la foto.
There are six students in the photo.

—**¿Hay** chicos en la fotografía?
Are there guys in the picture?

—**Hay** tres chicas y **no hay** chicos.
There are three girls, and there are no guys.

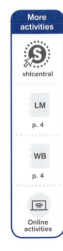

More activities

vhlcentral

LM
p. 4

WB
p. 4

Online activities

¡INTÉNTALO! Provide the Spanish words for these numbers.

1. **7** _siete_
2. **15** _____
3. **29** _____
4. **1** _____

5. **0** _____
6. **16** _____
7. **21** _____
8. **9** _____

9. **23** _____
10. **11** _____
11. **10** _____
12. **4** _____

13. **12** _____
14. **28** _____
15. **14** _____
16. **30** _____

Práctica

1

Contar Following the pattern, write out the missing numbers in Spanish.

1. 1, 3, 5, ..., 29
2. 2, 4, 6, ..., 30
3. 3, 6, 9, ..., 30
4. 30, 28, 26, ..., 0
5. 28, 24, 20, ..., 0
6. 30, 25, 20, ..., 0

2

Resolver Solve these math problems with a partner.

> **modelo**
>
> 5 + 3 =
>
> **Estudiante 1:** *cinco más tres son…*
> **Estudiante 2:** *ocho*

AYUDA		
+	→	**más**
−	→	**menos**
=	→	**son**

1. **2 + 15 =**
2. **5 + 7 =**
3. **20 − 1 =**
4. **18 + 12 =**
5. **3 + 22 =**

6. **6 − 3 =**
7. **11 + 12 =**
8. **8 + 5 =**
9. **7 − 2 =**
10. **23 − 14 =**

3

¿Cuántos hay? How many persons or things are there in these drawings?

> **modelo**
>
> Hay tres maletas.

1. _____   2. _____

3. _____   4. _____   5. _____

6. _____   7. _____   8. _____

Comunicación

4

En la clase With a partner, take turns asking and answering these questions about your classroom.

1. ¿Cuántos estudiantes hay?
2. ¿Cuántos profesores hay?
3. ¿Hay una computadora?
4. ¿Hay una maleta?
5. ¿Cuántos mapas hay?

6. ¿Cuántos lápices hay?
7. ¿Hay cuadernos?
8. ¿Cuántos diccionarios hay?
9. ¿Hay hombres?
10. ¿Cuántas mujeres hay?

5

Preguntas With a partner, take turns asking and answering questions about the drawing. Talk about:

1. how many children there are
2. how many women there are
3. if there are some photographs
4. if there is a boy
5. how many notebooks there are

6. if there is a bus
7. if there are tourists
8. how many pencils there are
9. if there is a man
10. how many computers there are

1.3 | Present tense of *ser* Tutorial

Subject pronouns

ANTE TODO In order to use verbs, you will need to learn about subject pronouns. A subject pronoun replaces the name or title of a person and acts as the subject of a verb.

Subject pronouns

SINGULAR		PLURAL	
yo	*I*	**nosotros**	*we* (masculine)
		nosotras	*we* (feminine)
tú	*you* (familiar)	**vosotros**	*you* (masc., fam.)
usted (Ud.)	*you* (formal)	**vosotras**	*you* (fem., fam.)
		ustedes (Uds.)	*you*
él	*he*	**ellos**	*they* (masc.)
ella	*she*	**ellas**	*they* (fem.)

¡LENGUA VIVA!

In Latin America, **ustedes** is used as the plural for both **tú** and **usted**. In Spain, however, **vosotros** and **vosotras** are used as the plural of **tú**, and **ustedes** is used only as the plural of **usted**.

•••

Usted and **ustedes** are abbreviated as **Ud**. and **Uds.**, or occasionally as **Vd.** and **Vds.**

▶ Spanish has two subject pronouns that mean *you* (singular). Use **tú** when addressing a friend, a family member, or a child you know well. Use **usted** to address a person with whom you have a formal or more distant relationship, such as a superior at work, a professor, or an older person.

Tú eres de Canadá, ¿verdad, David?
You are from Canada, right, David?

¿**Usted** es la profesora de español?
Are you the Spanish professor?

▶ The masculine plural forms **nosotros**, **vosotros**, and **ellos** refer to a group of males or to a group of males and females. The feminine plural forms **nosotras**, **vosotras**, and **ellas** can refer only to groups made up exclusively of females.

nosotros, vosotros, ellos

nosotros, vosotros, ellos

nosotras, vosotras, ellas

▶ There is no Spanish equivalent of the English subject pronoun *it*. Generally *it* is not expressed in Spanish.

Es un problema.
It's a problem.

Es una computadora.
It's a computer.

The present tense of ser

In **Contextos** and **Fotonovela**, you have already used several present-tense forms of **ser** (*to be*) to identify yourself and others, and to talk about where you and others are from. **Ser** is an irregular verb; its forms do not follow the regular patterns that most verbs follow. You need to memorize the forms, which appear in this chart.

The verb ser (*to be*)		
SINGULAR FORMS	yo **soy**	*I am*
	tú **eres**	*you are* (fam.)
	Ud./él/ella **es**	*you are* (form.); *he/she is*
PLURAL FORMS	nosotros/as **somos**	*we are*
	vosotros/as **sois**	*you are* (fam.)
	Uds./ellos/ellas **son**	*you are; they are*

Uses of *ser*

▶ Use **ser** to identify people and things.

—¿Quién **es** él?
Who is he?

—**Es** Felipe Díaz Velázquez.
He's Felipe Díaz Velázquez.

—¿Qué **es**?
What is it?

—**Es** un mapa de España.
It's a map of Spain.

Es Marissa.

Es una maleta.

▶ **Ser** also expresses possession, with the preposition **de**. There is no Spanish equivalent of the English construction [*noun*] + 's (*Maru's*). In its place, Spanish uses [*noun*] + **de** + [*owner*].

—¿**De** quién **es**?
Whose is it?

—**Es** el diario **de** Maru.
It's Maru's diary.

—¿**De** quién **son**?
Whose are they?

—**Son** los lápices **de** la chica.
They are the girl's pencils.

▶ When **de** is followed by the article **el**, the two combine to form the contraction **del**. **De** does *not* contract with **la**, **las**, or **los**.

—**Es** la computadora **del** conductor.
It's the driver's computer.

—**Son** las maletas **del** chico.
They are the boy's suitcases.

▶ **Ser** also uses the preposition **de** to express origin.

¿De dónde eres?

Yo soy de Wisconsin.

¿De dónde es usted?

Yo soy de Cuba.

—¿**De** dónde **es** Juan Carlos?
Where is Juan Carlos from?

—Es **de** Argentina.
He's from Argentina.

—¿**De** dónde **es** Maru?
Where is Maru from?

—**Es de** Costa Rica.
She's from Costa Rica.

▶ Use **ser** to express profession or occupation.

Don Francisco **es conductor**.
Don Francisco is a driver.

Yo **soy estudiante**.
I am a student.

▶ Unlike English, Spanish does not use the indefinite article (**un, una**) after **ser** when referring to professions, unless accompanied by an adjective or other description.

Marta **es** profesora.
Marta is a teacher.

Marta **es una** profesora excelente.
Marta is an excellent teacher.

Somos Perú

LATAMPerú

¡INTÉNTALO! Provide the correct subject pronouns and the present forms of **ser**.

1. Gabriel _él_ _es_
2. Óscar y Flora _____ _____
3. Juan y yo _____ _____
4. Adriana _____ _____

5. las turistas _____ _____
6. los conductores _____ _____
7. el chico _____ _____
8. los señores Ruiz _____ _____

Práctica

1

Pronombres What subject pronouns would you use to (a) talk *to* these people directly and (b) talk *about* them to others?

> **modelo**
> un joven　tú, él

1. una chica
2. el presidente de México
3. tres chicas y un chico
4. la señora Ochoa
5. un estudiante
6. dos profesoras

2

Identidad y origen With a partner, take turns asking and answering these questions about the people indicated: **¿Quién es?/¿Quiénes son?** and **¿De dónde es?/¿De dónde son?**

> **modelo**
> Selena Gomez (Estados Unidos)
> **Estudiante 1:** ¿Quién es?　　**Estudiante 1:** ¿De dónde es?
> **Estudiante 2:** Es Selena Gomez.　**Estudiante 2:** Es de los Estados Unidos.

1. Enrique Iglesias (España)
2. Gustavo Dudamel (Venezuela)
3. America Ferrera y Marc Anthony (Estados Unidos)
4. Carlos Santana y Salma Hayek (México)
5. Shakira (Colombia)
6. Sergio García y Penélope Cruz (España)
7. Ariana Grande y Michael Peña (Estados Unidos)
8. José Abreu (Cuba)

3

¿Qué es? Ask your partner what each object is and to whom it belongs.

> **modelo**
> **Estudiante 1:** ¿Qué es?　　**Estudiante 1:** ¿De quién es?
> **Estudiante 2:** Es un diccionario.　**Estudiante 2:** Es del profesor Núñez.

1.　　2.　　3.　　4.

Comunicación

4

Preguntas Ask your partner questions about the ad. Be imaginative in your responses.

¿Cuántas?	¿De dónde?	¿Qué?
¿Cuántos?	¿De quién?	¿Quién?

SOMOS ECOTURISTA, S.A.

Los autobuses oficiales de la Ruta Maya

- 25 autobuses en total
- 30 conductores del área
- pasajeros internacionales
- mapas de la región

¡Todos a bordo!

5

¿Quién es? In small groups, take turns pretending to be a famous person from a Spanish-speaking country. Use the list of professions to think of people from a variety of backgrounds. Your partners will ask you questions and try to guess who you are.

actor *actor*	cantante *singer*	escritor(a) *writer*
actriz *actress*	deportista *athlete*	músico/a *musician*

modelo

Estudiante 3: ¿Eres de Puerto Rico?
Estudiante 1: No. Soy de Colombia.
Estudiante 2: ¿Eres hombre?
Estudiante 1: Sí. Soy hombre.
Estudiante 3: ¿Eres escritor?
Estudiante 1: No. Soy actor.
Estudiante 2: ¿Eres John Leguizamo?
Estudiante 1: ¡Sí! ¡Sí!

1.4 **Telling time** Tutorial

ANTE TODO In both English and Spanish, the verb *to be* (**ser**) and numbers are used to tell time.

▶ To ask what time it is, use **¿Qué hora es?** When telling time, use **es + la** with **una** and **son + las** with all other hours.

Es la una.   Son las dos.   Son las seis.

▶ As in English, you express time in Spanish from the hour to the half hour by adding minutes.

Son las cuatro **y cinco**.   Son las once **y veinte**.

▶ You may use either **y cuarto** or **y quince** to express fifteen minutes or quarter past the hour. For thirty minutes or half past the hour, you may use either **y media** or **y treinta**.

Es la una **y cuarto**.   Son las nueve **y quince**.   Son las doce **y media**.   Son las siete **y treinta**.

▶ You express time from the half hour to the hour in Spanish by subtracting minutes or a portion of an hour from the next hour.

Es la una **menos cuarto**.   Son las tres **menos quince**.   Son las ocho **menos veinte**.   Son las tres **menos diez**.

▶ To ask at what time a particular event takes place, use the phrase **¿A qué hora (...)?** To state at what time something takes place, use the construction **a la(s)** + *time*.

¿A qué hora es la clase de biología?
(At) what time is biology class?

La clase es **a las dos**.
The class is at two o'clock.

¿A qué hora es la fiesta?
(At) what time is the party?

A las ocho.
At eight.

¡LENGUA VIVA!

Other useful expressions for telling time:
Son las doce (del día). It is twelve o'clock (p.m.).
Son las doce (de la noche). It is twelve o'clock (a.m.).

▶ Here are some useful words and phrases associated with telling time.

Son las ocho **en punto**.
It's 8 o'clock on the dot/sharp.

Son las nueve **de la mañana**.
It's 9 a.m./in the morning.

Es **el mediodía**.
It's noon.

Son las cuatro y cuarto **de la tarde**.
It's 4:15 p.m./in the afternoon.

Es **la medianoche**.
It's midnight.

Son las diez y media **de la noche**.
It's 10:30 p.m./at night.

¿Qué hora es?

Son las cuatro menos diez.

¿Qué hora es?

Son las cuatro y veinticinco.

¡INTÉNTALO! Practice telling time by completing these sentences.

1. (1:00 a.m.) Es la _____una_____ de la mañana.
2. (4:15 p.m.) Son las cuatro y _____ de la tarde.
3. (2:50 a.m.) Son las tres _____ diez de la mañana.
4. (8:30 p.m.) Son las ocho y _____ de la noche.
5. (9:15 a.m.) Son las nueve y quince de la _____.
6. (12:00 p.m.) Es el _____.
7. (6:00 a.m.) Son las seis de la _____.
8. (4:05 p.m.) Son las cuatro y cinco de la _____.
9. (12:00 a.m.) Es la _____.
10. (2:15 a.m.) Son las _____ y cuarto de la mañana.
11. (3:45 a.m.) Son las cuatro menos _____ de la mañana.
12. (1:25 p.m.) Es la una y _____ de la tarde.
13. (6:50 a.m.) Son las _____ menos diez de la mañana.
14. (10:40 p.m.) Son las once menos veinte de la _____.

More activities

vhlcentral

LM
p. 6

WB
pp. 7–8

Online activities

Práctica

1

Ordenar Put these times in order, from the earliest to the latest.

a. Son las dos de la tarde.

b. Son las once de la mañana.

c. Son las siete y media de la noche.

d. Son las seis menos cuarto de la tarde.

e. Son las ocho y veintidós de la mañana.

f. Son las dos menos diez de la tarde.

2

¿Qué hora es? Give the times shown.

modelo

Son las cuatro y cuarto/quince de la tarde.

1. _____ 2. _____ 3. _____ 4. _____

5. _____ 6. _____ 7. _____ 8. _____

3

¿A qué hora? Ask your partner at what time these events take place. Your partner will answer according to the cues provided.

modelo

la clase de matemáticas (2:30 p.m.)

Estudiante 1: *¿A qué hora es la clase de matemáticas?*

Estudiante 2: *Es a las dos y media de la tarde.*

1. el programa *Las cuatro amigas* (*11:30 a.m.*)
2. el drama *La casa de Bernarda Alba* (*7:00 p.m.*)
3. el programa *Las computadoras* (*8:30 a.m.*)
4. la clase de español (*10:30 a.m.*)
5. la clase de biología (*9:40 a.m.*)
6. la clase de historia (*10:50 a.m.*)
7. el partido (*game*) de béisbol (*5:15 p.m.*)
8. el partido de tenis (*12:45 p.m.*)
9. el partido de baloncesto (*basketball*) (*7:45 p.m.*)

NOTA CULTURAL

Many Spanish-speaking countries use both the 12-hour clock and the 24-hour clock (that is, military time). The 24-hour clock is commonly used in written form on signs and schedules. For example, 1 p.m. is **13h**, 2 p.m. is **14h** and so on. See the photo on p. 33 for a sample schedule.

NOTA CULTURAL

La casa de Bernarda Alba is a famous play by Spanish poet and playwright **Federico García Lorca** (1898–1936). Lorca was one of the most famous writers of the 20th century and a close friend of Spain's most talented artists, including the painter Salvador Dalí and the filmmaker Luis Buñuel.

Comunicación

4

En la televisión With a partner, take turns asking questions about these television listings.

> *modelo*
>
> **Estudiante 1:** ¿A qué hora es el documental *Las computadoras*?
> **Estudiante 2:** Es a las nueve en punto de la noche.

TV Hoy - Programación

11:00 am	Telenovela: *La casa de la familia Díaz*
12:00 pm	Película: *El cóndor* (drama)
2:00 pm	Telenovela: *Dos mujeres y dos hombres*
3:00 pm	Programa juvenil: *Fiesta*
3:30 pm	Telenovela: *¡Sí, sí, sí!*
4:00 pm	Telenovela: *El diario de la Sra. González*
5:00 pm	Telenovela: *Tres mujeres*
6:00 pm	Noticias
7:00 pm	Especial musical: *Música folklórica de México*
7:30 pm	La naturaleza: *Jardín secreto*
8:00 pm	Noticiero: *Veinticuatro horas*
9:00 pm	Documental: *Las computadoras*

5

Preguntas With a partner, answer these questions based on your own knowledge.

1. Son las tres de la tarde en Nueva York. ¿Qué hora es en Los Ángeles?

2. Son las ocho y media en Chicago. ¿Qué hora es en Miami?

3. Son las dos menos cinco en San Francisco. ¿Qué hora es en San Antonio?

4. ¿A qué hora es el programa *Saturday Night Live*?

Síntesis

6

Situación With a partner, play the roles of a journalism student interviewing a visiting literature professor (**profesor(a) de literatura**) from Venezuela. Be prepared to act out the conversation for your classmates.

Estudiante	**Profesor(a) de literatura**
Ask the professor his/her name.	→ Ask the student his/her name.
Ask the professor what time his/her literature class is.	→ Ask the student where he/she is from.
Ask how many students are in his/her class.	→ Ask to whom the notebook belongs.
Say thank you and goodbye.	→ Say thank you and you are pleased to meet him/her.

Recapitulación

SUBJECT
Javier
CONJUGATED FORM
empiezo
Main clause
Dudan

Review the grammar concepts you have learned in this lesson by completing these activities.

1 **Completar** Complete the charts according to the models. **28 pts.**

Masculino	Femenino
el chico	la chica
	la profesora
	la amiga
el señor	
	la pasajera
el estudiante	
	la turista
el joven	

Singular	Plural
una cosa	unas cosas
un libro	
	unas clases
una lección	
un conductor	
	unos países
	unos lápices
un problema	

2 **En la clase** Complete each conversation with the correct word. **22 pts.**

César   Beatriz

CÉSAR ¿(1) _____ (Cuántos/Cuántas) chicas hay en la (2) _____ (maleta/clase)?

BEATRIZ Hay (3) _____ (catorce/cuatro) [*14*] chicas.

CÉSAR Y, ¿(4) _____ (cuántos/cuántas) chicos hay?

BEATRIZ Hay (5) _____ (tres/trece) [*13*] chicos.

CÉSAR Entonces (*Then*), en total hay (6) _____ (veintiséis/veintisiete) (7) _____ (estudiantes/chicas) en la clase.

ARIANA ¿Tienes (*Do you have*) (8) _____ (un/una) diccionario?

Ariana   Daniel

DANIEL No, pero (*but*) aquí (9) _____ (es/hay) uno.

ARIANA ¿De quién (10) _____ (son/es)?

DANIEL (11) _____ (Son/Es) de Carlos.

RESUMEN GRAMATICAL

1.1 Nouns and articles *pp. 12–14*

Gender of nouns

Nouns that refer to living things

	Masculine		Feminine
-o	el chico	-a	la chica
-or	el profesor	-ora	la profesora
-ista	el turista	-ista	la turista

Nouns that refer to non-living things

	Masculine		Feminine
-o	el libro	-a	la cosa
-ma	el programa	-ción	la lección
-s	el autobús	-dad	la nacionalidad

Plural of nouns

▶ ending in vowel + *-s*   la chica → las chicas

▶ ending in consonant + *-es*   el señor → los señores

  (-z → -ces un lápiz → unos lápices)

▶ Definite articles: el, la, los, las

▶ Indefinite articles: un, una, unos, unas

1.2 Numbers 0–30 *p. 16*

0	cero	8	ocho	16	dieciséis
1	uno	9	nueve	17	diecisiete
2	dos	10	diez	18	dieciocho
3	tres	11	once	19	diecinueve
4	cuatro	12	doce	20	veinte
5	cinco	13	trece	21	veintiuno
6	seis	14	catorce	22	veintidós
7	siete	15	quince	30	treinta

1.3 Present tense of *ser* *pp. 19–21*

yo	soy	nosotros/as	somos
tú	eres	vosotros/as	sois
Ud./él/ella	es	Uds./ellos/ellas	son

3 **Presentaciones** Complete this conversation with the correct form of the verb **ser**. `12 pts.`

JUAN ¡Hola! Me llamo Juan. (1) _____ estudiante en la clase de español.

DANIELA ¡Hola! Mucho gusto. Yo (2) _____ Daniela y ella (3) _____ Mónica. ¿De dónde (4) _____ (tú), Juan?

JUAN De California. Y ustedes, ¿de dónde (5) _____ ?

MÓNICA Nosotras (6) _____ de Florida.

1.4	Telling time	pp. 24–25

Es la una.	It's 1:00.
Son las dos.	It's 2:00.
Son las tres y diez.	It's 3:10.
Es la una **y cuarto/ quince**.	It's 1:15.
Son las siete **y media/ treinta**.	It's 7:30.
Es la una **menos cuarto/quince**.	It's 12:45.
Son las once **menos veinte**.	It's 10:40.
Es **el mediodía**.	It's noon.
Es **la medianoche**.	It's midnight.

4 **¿Qué hora es?** Write out in words the following times, indicating whether it's morning, noon, afternoon, or night. `10 pts.`

1. It's 12:00 p.m.

_____

2. It's 7:05 a.m.

_____

3. It's 9:35 p.m.

_____

4. It's 5:15 p.m.

_____

5. It's 1:30 p.m.

_____

5 **¡Hola!** Write five sentences introducing yourself and talking about your classes. You may want to include your name, where you are from, who your Spanish teacher is, the time of your Spanish class, how many students are in the class, etc. `28 pts.`

_____
_____
_____
_____

6 **Canción** Choose the appropriate words to complete this children's song. `4 EXTRA points!`

cinco	cuántas	cuatro	media	quiénes

" _____ patas°
tiene un gato°?
Una, dos, tres y
_____ . "

patas *legs*   tiene un gato *does a cat have*

Lectura

Antes de leer

Estrategia
Recognizing cognates

As you learned earlier in this lesson, cognates are words that share similar meanings and spellings in two or more languages. When reading in Spanish, it's helpful to look for cognates and use them to guess the meaning of what you're reading. But watch out for false cognates. For example, **librería** means *bookstore*, not *library*, and **embarazada** means *pregnant*, not *embarrassed*. Look at this list of Spanish words, paying special attention to prefixes and suffixes. Can you guess the meaning of each word?

importante	oportunidad
farmacia	cultura
inteligente	activo
dentista	sociología
decisión	espectacular
televisión	restaurante
médico	policía

🔗 Examinar el texto
Glance quickly at the reading selection and guess what type of document it is. Explain your answer.

🔗 Cognados
Read the document and make a list of the cognates you find. Guess their English equivalents, then compare your answers with those of a partner.

More activities
vhlcentral   Online activities

Joaquín Salvador Lavado nació (*was born*) en Argentina en 1932 (mil novecientos treinta y dos). Su nombre profesional es **Quino**. Es muy popular en Latinoamérica, Europa y Canadá por sus tiras cómicas (*comic strips*). Mafalda es su serie más famosa. La protagonista, Mafalda, es una chica muy inteligente de seis años (*years*). La tira cómica ilustra las aventuras de ella y su grupo de amigos. Las anécdotas de Mafalda y los chicos también presentan temas (*themes*) importantes como la paz (*peace*) y los derechos humanos (*human rights*).

Después de leer

🔗 Preguntas
Answer these questions.

1. What is Joaquín Salvador Lavado's pen name?
2. What is Mafalda like?
3. Where is Mafalda in panel 1? What is she doing?
4. What happens to the sheep in panel 3? Why?
5. Why does Mafalda wake up?
6. What number corresponds to the sheep in panel 5?
7. In panel 6, what is Mafalda doing? How do you know?

Los animales

This comic strip uses a device called onomatopoeia: a word that represents the sound that it stands for. Did you know that many common instances of onomatopoeia are different from language to language? The noise a sheep makes is *baaaah* in English, but in Mafalda's language it is **béeeee**.

Do you think you can match these animals with their Spanish sounds? First, practice saying aloud each animal sound in group B. Then, match each animal with its sound in Spanish. If you need help remembering the sounds the alphabet makes in Spanish, see p. 9.

A

 1. ____ **gato**   2. ____ **perro**   3. ____ **vaca**   4. ____ **gallo**

 5. ____ **rana**   6. ____ **pato**   7. ____ **cerdo**

B

a. kikirikí   b. muuu   c. croac   d. guau

e. cuac cuac   f. miau   g. oinc

Escritura

Estrategia
Writing in Spanish

Why do we write? All writing has a purpose. For example, we may write an e-mail to share important information or compose an essay to persuade others to accept a point of view. Proficient writers are not born, however. Writing requires time, thought, effort, and a lot of practice. Here are some tips to help you write more effectively in Spanish.

DO

▶ Try to write your ideas in Spanish

▶ Use the grammar and vocabulary that you know

▶ Use your textbook for examples of style, format, and expression in Spanish

▶ Use your imagination and creativity

▶ Put yourself in your reader's place to determine if your writing is interesting

AVOID

▶ Translating your ideas from English to Spanish

▶ Simply repeating what is in the textbook or on a web page

▶ Using a dictionary until you have learned how to use foreign language dictionaries

Tema

Hacer una lista

Create a telephone/address list that includes important names, numbers, and websites that will be helpful to you in your study of Spanish. Make whatever entries you can in Spanish without using a dictionary. You might want to include this information:

▶ The names, phone numbers, and e-mail addresses of at least four other students

▶ Your professor's name, e-mail address, and office hours

▶ Three phone numbers and e-mail addresses of campus offices or locations related to your study of Spanish

▶ Five electronic resources for students of Spanish, such as chat rooms and sites dedicated to the study of Spanish as a second language

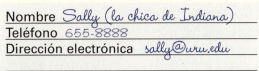

Nombre *Sally (la chica de Indiana)*
Teléfono 655-8888
Dirección electrónica *sally@uru.edu*

Nombre *Profesor José Ramón Casas*
Teléfono 655-8090
Dirección electrónica *jrcasas@uru.edu*
Horas de oficina 12 a 12:30

Nombre *Biblioteca* 655-7000
Dirección electrónica *library@uru.edu*

●Escuchar

Antes de escuchar

Estrategia
Listening for words you know

You can get the gist of a conversation by listening for words and phrases you already know.

To help you practice this strategy, listen to the following sentence and make a list of the words you have already learned.

Preparación

Based on the photograph, what do you think Dr. Cavazos and Srta. Martínez are talking about? How would you get the gist of their conversation, based on what you know about Spanish?

●Ahora escucha

Palabras y frases

Now you are going to hear Dr. Cavazos's conversation with Srta. Martínez. List the familiar words and phrases each person says.

Dr. Cavazos	Srta. Martínez
1. _____	9. _____
2. _____	10. _____
3. _____	11. _____
4. _____	12. _____
5. _____	13. _____
6. _____	14. _____
7. _____	15. _____
8. _____	16. _____

With a partner, use your lists of familiar words as a guide to come up with a summary of what happened in the conversation.

Comprensión

Identificar

Who would say the following things, Dr. Cavazos or Srta. Martínez?

1. Me llamo…
2. De nada.
3. Gracias. Muchas gracias.
4. Aquí tiene usted los documentos de viaje (*trip*), señor.
5. Usted tiene tres maletas, ¿no?
6. Tengo dos maletas.
7. Hola, señor.
8. ¿Viaja usted a Buenos Aires?

Contestar

1. Does this scene take place in the morning, afternoon, or evening? How do you know?
2. How many suitcases does Dr. Cavazos have?
3. Using the words you already know to determine the context, what might the following words and expressions mean?
   - boleto
   - pasaporte
   - un viaje de ida y vuelta
   - ¡Buen viaje!

En pantalla

Video

Latinos form the largest minority group in the United States. The Census Bureau projects that by the year 2060, the Latino population will grow to 30 percent. Viewership of the two major Spanish-language TV stations, **Univisión** and **Telemundo**, has skyrocketed, at times surpassing that of the four major English-language networks. With Latino purchasing power estimated at 1.5 trillion dollars a year, many companies have responded by adapting successful marketing campaigns to target a Spanish-speaking audience. Turn on a Spanish-language channel, and you'll see ads for the world's biggest consumer brands, from soft drinks to car makers; many of these advertisements are adaptations of their English-language counterparts.

Vocabulario útil

carne en salsa	*beef with sauce*
copa de helado	*cup of ice cream*
no tiene precio	*priceless*
plato principal	*main course*
un domingo en familia	*Sunday with the family*

Preparación

Have you seen any Spanish versions of English-language commercials? If so, which ones? How are they different from the originals? Have you seen any bilingual ads? If so, when did they air and what did they advertise?

Emparejar

Match each item with its price. **¡Ojo!** (*Careful!*) One of the responses will not be used.

_____ 1. aperitivo   a. quince dólares

_____ 2. plato principal   b. ocho dólares

_____ 3. postre   c. treinta dólares

                    d. seis dólares

Un comercial

With a partner, brainstorm and write a MasterCard-like TV ad about something you consider priceless. Then read it to the class. Use as much Spanish as you can.

Aperitivo *Appetizer* Postre *Dessert*

Anuncio de MasterCard

Aperitivo°...

copa de helado: $6

Postre°...

un domingo en familia: no tiene precio

Un domingo en familia...

More activities

vhlcentral   Online activities

 Video

The **Plaza de Mayo** in Buenos Aires, Argentina, is perhaps best known as a place of political protest. Aptly nicknamed **Plaza de Protestas** by the locals, it is the site of weekly demonstrations. Despite this reputation, for many it is also a traditional **plaza**, a spot to escape from the hustle of city life. In warmer months, office workers from neighboring buildings flock to the plaza during lunch hour. **Plaza de Mayo** is also a favorite spot for families, couples, and friends to gather, stroll, or simply sit and chat. Tourists come year-round to take in the iconic surroundings: **Plaza de Mayo** is flanked by the rose-colored presidential palace (**Casa Rosada**), city hall (**municipalidad**), a colonial-era museum (**Cabildo**), and a spectacular cathedral (**Catedral Metropolitana**).

Vocabulario útil	
abrazo	*hug*
¡Cuánto tiempo!	*It's been a long time!*
encuentro	*encounter*
plaza	*city or town square*
¡Qué bueno verte!	*It's great to see you!*
¡Qué suerte verlos!	*How lucky to see you!*

Preparación

Where do you and your friends usually meet? Are there public places where you get together? What activities do you take part in there?

Identificar

Identify the person or people who make(s) each of these statements.

1. ¿Cómo están ustedes?   a. Gonzalo
2. ¡Qué bueno verte!   b. Mariana
3. Bien, ¿y vos?   c. Mark
4. Hola.   d. Silvina
5. ¡Qué suerte verlos!

Encuentros en la plaza

Today we are at the Plaza de Mayo.

People come to walk and get some fresh air...

And children come to play...

Estados Unidos

El país en cifras°

▶ **Población° de los EE.UU.:** 326 millones

▶ **Población de origen hispano:** 57 millones

▶ **País de origen de hispanos en los EE.UU.:**

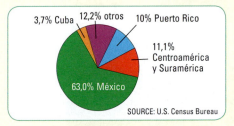

3,7% Cuba · 12,2% otros · 10% Puerto Rico
11,1% Centroamérica y Suramérica
63,0% México

SOURCE: U.S. Census Bureau

▶ **Estados con la mayor° población hispana:**

California 14.800.000
Texas 10.200.000
Florida 4.700.000
Nueva York 3.600.000
Illinois 2.100.000

SOURCE: U.S. Census Bureau

Canadá

El país en cifras

▶ **Población de Canadá:** 36 millones

▶ **Población de origen hispano:** 461.000

▶ **País de origen de hispanos en Canadá:**

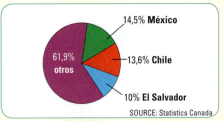

14,5% **México**
13,6% **Chile**
10% **El Salvador**
61,9% **otros**

SOURCE: Statistics Canada

▶ **Ciudades° con la mayor población hispana:**

Montreal, Toronto, Vancouver

en cifras *by the numbers* Población *Population* mayor *largest*
Ciudades *Cities*

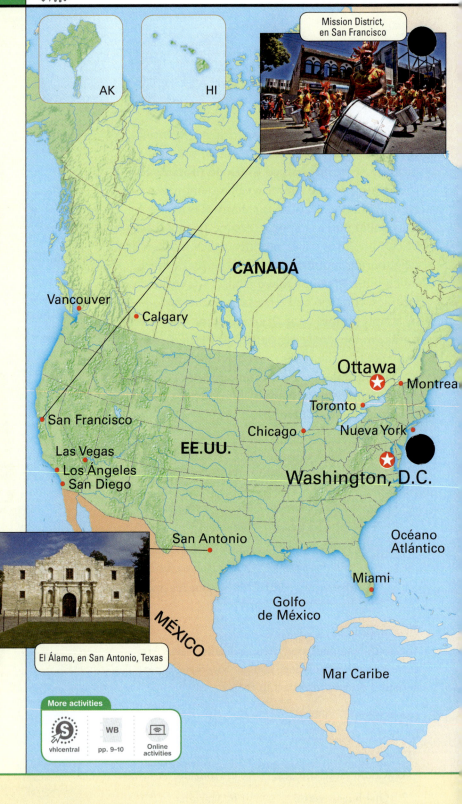

Mission District, en San Francisco

CANADÁ

Vancouver · Calgary

Ottawa · Montreal

Toronto

San Francisco

Las Vegas

Los Ángeles

San Diego

Chicago · Nueva York

EE.UU.

Washington, D.C.

San Antonio

Océano Atlántico

Miami

Golfo de México

MÉXICO

Mar Caribe

El Álamo, en San Antonio, Texas

AK · HI

More activities

 vhlcentral · WB pp. 9–10 · Online activities

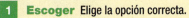

ACTIVIDADES

1 **Escoger** Elige la opción correcta.

1. ¿Cuántos millones de personas de origen hispano hay en los Estados Unidos?
   a. 57   b. 45   c. 36

2. ¿Cuántos millones de hispanos hay en Illinois?
   a. cuatro   b. tres   c. dos

3. ¿De dónde son las enchiladas y los tacos?
   a. Puerto Rico   b. México   c. Cuba

4. ¿Cómo se llama el barrio cubano de Miami?
   a. La Pequeña Habana   b. El Álamo
   c. Mission District

5. ¿Qué hacen (*do*) los puertorriqueños en junio?
   a. una conversación   b. un desfile
   c. una comida

6. ¿Cuántos millones de personas hablan español en los Estados Unidos?
   a. 60   b. 13   c. 43

Comida • **La comida mexicana**

La comida° mexicana es muy popular en los Estados Unidos. Los tacos, las enchiladas, las quesadillas y los frijoles frecuentemente forman parte de las comidas de muchos norteamericanos. También° son populares las variaciones de la comida mexicana en los Estados Unidos: el tex-mex y el cali-mex.

▷ Lugares • **La Pequeña Habana**

La Pequeña Habana° es un barrio° de Miami, Florida, donde viven° muchos cubanoamericanos. Es un lugar° donde se encuentran° las costumbres° de la cultura cubana, los aromas y sabores° de su comida y la música salsa. La Pequeña Habana es una parte de Cuba en los Estados Unidos.

Costumbres • **Desfile puertorriqueño**

Cada junio, desde° 1958 (mil novecientos cincuenta y ocho), los puertorriqueños celebran su cultura con un desfile° en Nueva York. Es un gran espectáculo con carrozas° y música salsa, merengue y hip-hop. Muchos espectadores llevan° la bandera° de Puerto Rico en su ropa° o pintada en la cara°.

▷ Comunidad • **Hispanos en Canadá**

En Canadá viven° muchos hispanos. Toronto y Montreal son las ciudades con mayor población hispana. Muchos de ellos tienen estudios universitarios° y hablan° una de las lenguas° oficiales: inglés o francés°. Los hispanos participan activamente en la vida cotidiana° y profesional de Canadá.

comida *food* También *Also* La Pequeña Habana *Little Havana* barrio *neighborhood* viven *live* lugar *place* se encuentran *are found* costumbres *customs* sabores *flavors* Cada junio desde *Each June since* desfile *parade* con carrozas *with floats* llevan *wear* bandera *flag* ropa *clothing* cara *face* viven *live* tienen estudios universitarios *have a degree* hablan *speak* lenguas *languages* inglés o francés *English or French* vida cotidiana *daily life*

¡Increíble pero cierto!

Después° del inglés, el español es la lengua más hablada° en los EE.UU. Aproximadamente 40 millones de hispanos y 3 millones de personas no hispanas hablan esta lengua en los EE.UU. Hoy, 13% de la población habla español en sus hogares°.

Después *After* hablada *spoken* hogares *homes*

2 ¿Qué aprendiste? Completa las oraciones.

1. Los cuatro estados con las poblaciones hispanas más grandes son California, Texas, Florida y _____.
2. Toronto, Montreal y _____ son las ciudades con más población hispana de Canadá.
3. La Pequeña _____ es un barrio de Miami.
4. Muchos hispanos en Canadá hablan _____ o francés.

3 Describir En parejas, describan la población de origen hispano en los Estados Unidos y en Canadá.

> **modelo**
> Hay quince millones de hispanos en California.

Saludos

Hola.	Hi.
Buenos días.	Good morning.
Buenas tardes.	Good afternoon.
Buenas noches.	Good evening; Good night.

Despedidas

Adiós.	Goodbye.
Nos vemos.	See you.
Hasta luego.	See you later.
Hasta la vista.	See you later.
Hasta pronto.	See you soon.
Hasta mañana.	See you tomorrow.
Saludos a...	Greetings to…
Chau.	Bye.

¿Cómo está?

¿Cómo está usted?	How are you? (form.)
¿Cómo estás?	How are you? (fam.)
¿Qué hay de nuevo?	What's new?
¿Qué pasa?	What's happening?; What's going on?
¿Qué tal?	How are you?; How is it going?
(Muy) bien, gracias.	(Very) well, thanks.
Nada.	Nothing.
No muy bien.	Not very well.
Regular.	So-so; OK.

Expresiones de cortesía

Con permiso.	Pardon me; Excuse me.
De nada.	You're welcome.
Lo siento.	I'm sorry.
(Muchas) gracias.	Thank you (very much); Thanks (a lot).
No hay de qué.	You're welcome.
Perdón.	Pardon me; Excuse me.
por favor	please

Títulos

señor (Sr.); don	Mr.; sir
señora (Sra.); doña	Mrs.; ma'am
señorita (Srta.)	Miss

Presentaciones

¿Cómo se llama usted?	What's your name? (form.)
¿Cómo te llamas?	What's your name? (fam.)
Me llamo...	My name is…
¿Y usted?	And you? (form.)
¿Y tú?	And you? (fam.)
Mucho gusto.	Pleased to meet you.
El gusto es mío.	The pleasure is mine.
Encantado/a.	Delighted; Pleased to meet you.
Igualmente.	Likewise.
Le presento a...	I would like to introduce you to (name). (form.)
Te presento a...	I would like to introduce you to (name). (fam.)
el nombre	name

¿De dónde es?

¿De dónde es usted?	Where are you from? (form.)
¿De dónde eres?	Where are you from? (fam.)
Soy de...	I'm from…

Palabras adicionales

¿cuánto(s)/a(s)?	how much/many?
¿de quién...?	whose…? (sing.)
¿de quiénes...?	whose…? (plural)
(no) hay	there is (not); there are (not)

Sustantivos

el autobús	bus
el chico	boy
la chica	girl
la computadora	computer
la comunidad	community
el/la conductor(a)	driver
la conversación	conversation
la cosa	thing
el cuaderno	notebook
el día	day
el diario	diary
el diccionario	dictionary
la escuela	school
el/la estudiante	student
la foto(grafía)	photograph
el hombre	man
el/la joven	young person
el lápiz	pencil
la lección	lesson
la maleta	suitcase
la mano	hand
el mapa	map
la mujer	woman
la nacionalidad	nationality
el número	number
el país	country
la palabra	word
el/la pasajero/a	passenger
el problema	problem
el/la profesor(a)	teacher
el programa	program
el/la turista	tourist
el video	video

Verbo

ser	to be

Numbers 0–30	See page 16.
Telling time	See pages 24–25.
Expresiones útiles	See page 7.

En la universidad

2

Communicative Goals

You will learn how to:

- Talk about your classes and school life
- Discuss everyday activities
- Ask questions in Spanish
- Describe the location of people and things

🔊 A PRIMERA VISTA

- ¿Hay un chico y una chica en la foto?
- ¿Hay una computadora o dos?
- ¿Son turistas o estudiantes?
- ¿Qué hora es, la una de la mañana o de la tarde?

Hotspots

En la universidad

la biblioteca	*library*
la cafetería	*cafeteria*
la casa	*house; home*
el estadio	*stadium*
el laboratorio	*laboratory*
la librería	*bookstore*
la residencia estudiantil	*dormitory*
la universidad	*university; college*
el/la compañero/a de clase	*classmate*
el/la compañero/a de cuarto	*roommate*
la clase	*class*
el curso	*course*
la especialización	*major*
el examen	*test; exam*
el horario	*schedule*
la prueba	*test; quiz*
el semestre	*semester*
la tarea	*homework*
el trimestre	*trimester; quarter*
la administración de empresas	*business administration*
el arte	*art*
la biología	*biology*
las ciencias	*sciences*
la computación	*computer science*
la contabilidad	*accounting*
la economía	*economics*
el español	*Spanish*
la física	*physics*
la geografía	*geography*
la música	*music*

Variación léxica

pluma ⟷ bolígrafo
pizarra ⟷ pizarrón (*Amér. L.*); tablero (*Col.*)

LAS MATERIAS	COURSES
la historia	*history*
las humanidades	*humanities*
el inglés	*English*
las lenguas extranjeras	*foreign languages*
la literatura	*literature*
las matemáticas	*mathematics*
el periodismo	*journalism*
la psicología	*psychology*
la química	*chemistry*
la sociología	*sociology*

la pizarra

la ventana

la profesora

el marcador

el borrador

la mesa

la pluma

la estudiante

la mochila

el estudiante

el papel

More activities

vhlcentral | LM p. 7 | WB pp. 11–12 | Online activities

el reloj

el mapa

la puerta

la papelera

el escritorio

la silla

el libro

la calculadora

Práctica

1

Indicar Check **sí** if the word you hear is an academic subject or **no** if it's not.

	Sí	No		Sí	No
1.	○	○	5.	○	○
2.	○	○	6.	○	○
3.	○	○	7.	○	○
4.	○	○	8.	○	○

2

¿Cierto o falso? Indicate whether each statement about the drawing is **cierto** or **falso**.

1. _____   5. _____
2. _____   6. _____
3. _____   7. _____
4. _____   8. _____

3

Identificar Identify the word that does not belong in each group.

1. examen • casa • tarea • prueba
2. pizarra • marcador • borrador • librería
3. economía • matemáticas • biblioteca • contabilidad
4. lápiz • cafetería • papel • cuaderno
5. veinte • diez • pluma • treinta
6. conductor • laboratorio • autobús • pasajero

4

Emparejar Match each question with its most logical response.

1. ¿Qué clase es?
2. ¿Quiénes son?
3. ¿Quién es?
4. ¿De dónde es?
5. ¿Cuántos estudiantes hay?
6. ¿A qué hora es la clase de inglés?

a. Hay veinticinco.
b. Es un reloj.
c. Es de Perú.
d. Es la clase de química.
e. Es el señor Bastos.
f. Es a las nueve en punto.
g. Son los profesores.

5

¿Qué clase es? Name the class associated with the subject matter.

> **modelo**
> los elementos, los átomos *Es la clase de química.*

1. Abraham Lincoln, Winston Churchill
2. África, el océano Pacífico
3. Freud, Jung
4. Picasso, Leonardo da Vinci
5. la cultura de España, verbos
6. Hemingway, Shakespeare
7. geometría, calculadora

Los días de la semana

6

¿Qué día es hoy? Complete each statement.

1. Hoy es martes. Mañana es _____. Ayer fue (*Yesterday was*) _____.
2. Ayer fue sábado. Mañana es _____. Hoy es _____.
3. Mañana es viernes. Hoy es _____. Ayer fue _____.
4. Hoy es jueves. Ayer fue _____. Mañana es _____.
5. Ayer fue domingo. Hoy es _____. Mañana es _____.
6. Mañana es lunes. Hoy es _____. Ayer fue _____.

7

Preguntas Answer the questions.

ciencias	geografía	residencia estudiantil
domingo	lenguas extranjeras	siete
especialización	libros	veinticuatro

1. ¿Cuántas horas hay en un día? _____
2. ¿Cuántos días hay en una semana? _____
3. ¿Qué día no hay clases? _____
4. ¿En qué clase hay mapas de Asia y Europa? _____
5. ¿Qué es la administración de empresas? _____
6. ¿Qué son el español y el italiano? _____
7. ¿Qué hay en una mochila? _____
8. ¿Qué son la física y la biología? _____

Comunicación

8 **Horario** Choose three courses from the chart to create your own class schedule, then discuss it with a classmate.

materia	horas	días	profesor(a)
historia	9–10	lunes, miércoles	Prof. Ordóñez
biología	12–1	lunes, jueves	Profa. Dávila
periodismo	2–3	martes, jueves	Profa. Quiñones
matemáticas	2–3	miércoles, jueves	Prof. Jiménez
arte	12–1:30	lunes, miércoles	Prof. Molina

modelo

Estudiante 1: Tomo biología los lunes y jueves, de 12 a 1, con la profesora Dávila.

Estudiante 2: ¿Sí? Yo no tomo biología. Yo tomo arte los lunes y miércoles, de 12 a 1:30, con el profesor Molina.

¡ATENCIÓN!

Use **el** + [*day of the week*] when an activity occurs on a specific day and **los** + [*day of the week*] when an activity occurs regularly.

El lunes tengo un examen.
***On Monday** I have an exam.*

Los lunes y miércoles tomo biología.
***On Mondays and Wednesdays** I take biology.*

•••

Except for **sábados** and **domingos**, the singular and plural forms for days of the week are the same.

AYUDA

tomo *I take*
con *with*

9 **Memoria** Take a good look around your Spanish classroom and then close your eyes. Your partner will ask you questions about the classroom, using these words and other vocabulary. Each person should answer six questions and switch roles every three questions.

escritorio	mapa	pizarra	reloj
estudiante	mesa	profesor(a)	ventana
libro	mochila	puerta	silla

modelo

Estudiante 1: ¿Cuántas ventanas hay?

Estudiante 2: Hay cuatro ventanas.

10 **Nuevos amigos** With a partner, prepare a conversation between two students meeting for the first time. Then act it out for the class.

Estudiante 1		Estudiante 2
Greet your new acquaintance.	→	Introduce yourself.
Find out about him or her.	→	Tell him or her about yourself.
Ask about your partner's class schedule.	→	Compare your schedule to your partner's.
Say nice to meet you and goodbye.	→	Say nice to meet you and goodbye.

¿Qué estudias?

Felipe, Marissa, Juan Carlos y Miguel visitan Chapultepec y hablan de las clases.

PERSONAJES

 MARISSA

 FELIPE

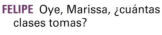 Video

FELIPE Dos boletos, por favor.

EMPLEADO Dos boletos son 64 pesos.

FELIPE Aquí están 100 pesos.

EMPLEADO 100 menos 64 son 36 pesos de cambio.

MIGUEL Marissa, hablas muy bien el español... ¿Y dónde está tu diccionario?

MARISSA En casa de los Díaz. Felipe necesita practicar inglés.

MIGUEL ¡Ay, Maru! Chicos, nos vemos más tarde.

FELIPE Ésta es la Ciudad de México.

FELIPE Oye, Marissa, ¿cuántas clases tomas?

MARISSA Tomo cuatro clases: español, historia, literatura y también geografía. Me gusta mucho la cultura mexicana.

FELIPE Juan Carlos, ¿quién enseña la clase de química este semestre?

JUAN CARLOS El profesor Morales. Ah, ¿por qué tomo química y computación?

FELIPE Porque te gusta la tarea.

JUAN CARLOS

MIGUEL

EMPLEADO

MARU

7

FELIPE Los lunes y los miércoles, economía a las 2:30. Tú tomas computación los martes en la tarde, y química, a ver... Los lunes, los miércoles y los viernes ¿a las 10? ¡Uf!

8

FELIPE Y Miguel, ¿cuándo regresa?

JUAN CARLOS Hoy estudia con Maru.

MARISSA ¿Quién es Maru?

9

MIGUEL ¿Hablas con tu mamá?

MARU Mamá habla. Yo escucho. Es la 1:30.

MIGUEL Ay, lo siento. Juan Carlos y Felipe...

MARU Ay, Felipe.

10

MARU Y ahora, ¿adónde? ¿A la biblioteca?

MIGUEL Sí, pero primero a la librería. Necesito comprar unos libros.

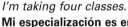
Expresiones útiles

Talking about classes

¿Cuántas clases tomas?
How many classes are you taking?
Tomo cuatro clases.
I'm taking four classes.
Mi especialización es en arqueología.
My major is archeology.
Este año, espero sacar buenas notas y, por supuesto, viajar por el país.
This year, I hope / I'm hoping to get good grades. And, of course, travel through the country.

Talking about likes/dislikes

Me gusta mucho la cultura mexicana.
I like Mexican culture a lot.
Me gustan las ciencias ambientales.
I like environmental science.
Me gusta dibujar.
I like to draw.
¿Te gusta este lugar?
Do you like this place?

Paying for tickets

Dos boletos, por favor.
Two tickets, please.
Dos boletos son sesenta y cuatro pesos.
Two tickets are sixty-four pesos.
Aquí están cien pesos.
Here's a hundred pesos.
Son treinta y seis pesos de cambio.
That's thirty-six pesos change.

Talking about location and direction

¿Dónde está tu diccionario?
Where is your dictionary?
Está en casa de los Díaz.
It's at the Díaz house.
Y ahora, ¿adónde? ¿A la biblioteca?
And now, where to? To the library?
Sí, pero primero a la librería.
Está al lado.
Yes, but first to the bookstore.
It's next door.

More activities

vhlcentral   VM   Online
           pp. 3–4   activities

¿Qué pasó?

1

Escoger Choose the answer that best completes each sentence.

1. Marissa toma (*is taking*) _____ en la universidad.
   a. español, psicología, economía y música   b. historia, inglés, sociología y periodismo
   c. español, historia, literatura y geografía
2. El profesor Morales enseña (*teaches*) _____.
   a. química   b. matemáticas   c. historia
3. Juan Carlos toma química _____.
   a. los miércoles, jueves y viernes   b. los lunes, miércoles y viernes
   c. los lunes, martes y jueves
4. Miguel necesita ir a (*needs to go to*) _____.
   a. la biblioteca   b. la residencia estudiantil   c. la librería

2

Identificar Indicate which person made each statement.

1. ¿Quién es Maru? _____
2. Mamá habla. Yo escucho. _____
3. Sí, tomo química con el profesor Morales.
   _____
4. En clase, me gusta estar cerca de la ventana.
   _____
5. Necesito comprar unos libros. _____
6. Dos boletos, por favor. _____

 MARISSA   **MARU**

 JUAN CARLOS

 MIGUEL   **FELIPE**

> **NOTA CULTURAL**
>
> **Maru** is a shortened version of the name **María Eugenia**. Other popular "combination names" in Spanish are **Juanjo (Juan José)** and **Maite (María Teresa)**.

3

Completar Complete each sentence that is similar to one in the **Fotonovela** with the correct word(s).

Castillo de Chapultepec	estudiar	miércoles
clase	inglés	tarea

1. Marissa, éste es el _____.
2. Felipe tiene (*has*) el diccionario porque (*because*) necesita practicar _____.
3. A Juan Carlos le gusta mucho la _____.
4. Hay clase de economía los lunes y _____.
5. Miguel está con Maru para _____.

> **NOTA CULTURAL**
>
> The **Castillo de Chapultepec** is one of Mexico City's most historic landmarks. Constructed in 1785, it was the residence of emperors and presidents. It has been open to the public since 1944 and now houses the National Museum of History.

4

Preguntas personales Interview a partner.

1. ¿Qué clases tomas en la universidad?
2. ¿Qué clases tomas los martes?
3. ¿Qué clases tomas los viernes?
4. ¿En qué clase hay más chicos?
5. ¿En qué clase hay más chicas?
6. ¿Te gusta la clase de español?

Pronunciación

 Tutorial

Spanish vowels

a   **e**   **i**   **o**   **u**

Spanish vowels are never silent; they are always pronounced in a short, crisp way without the glide sounds used in English.

Álex	**clase**	**nada**	**encantada**

The letter **a** is pronounced like the *a* in *father*, but shorter.

el	**ene**	**mesa**	**elefante**

The letter **e** is pronounced like the *e* in *they*, but shorter.

Inés	**chica**	**tiza**	**señorita**

The letter **i** sounds like the *ee* in *beet*, but shorter.

hola	**con**	**libro**	**don Francisco**

The letter **o** is pronounced like the *o* in *tone*, but shorter.

uno	**regular**	**saludos**	**gusto**

The letter **u** sounds like the *oo* in *room*, but shorter.

Práctica Practice the vowels by saying the names of these places in Spain.

1. Madrid
2. Alicante
3. Tenerife
4. Toledo
5. Barcelona
6. Granada
7. Burgos
8. La Coruña

Oraciones Read the sentences aloud, focusing on the vowels.

1. Hola. Me llamo Ramiro Morgado.
2. Estudio arte en la Universidad de Salamanca.
3. Tomo también literatura y contabilidad.
4. Ay, tengo clase en cinco minutos. ¡Nos vemos!

Refranes Practice the vowels by reading these sayings aloud.

Cada loco con su tema.[2]

Del dicho al hecho hay un gran trecho.[1]

1 *Easier said than done.*
2 *To each his own.*

More activities

vhlcentral   LM p. 8

La elección de una carrera universitaria

Since higher education in the Spanish-speaking world is heavily state-subsidized, tuition is almost free. As a result, public universities see large enrollments. Spanish and Latin American students generally choose their **carrera universitaria** (major) when they're eighteen—which is either the year they enter the university or the year before. In order to enroll, all students must complete a high school degree, known as the **bachillerato**. In countries like Bolivia, Mexico, and Peru, the last year of high school (**colegio***) tends to be specialized in an area of study, such as the arts or natural sciences.

Universidad Central de Venezuela en Caracas

 Students then choose their major according to their area of specialization. Similarly, university-bound students in Argentina focus their studies on their five years of high school. Based on this coursework, Argentine students choose their **carrera**. Finally, in Spain, students choose their major according to the score they receive on the **prueba de aptitud** (skills test or entrance exam).

University graduates receive a **licenciatura**, or bachelor's degree. In Argentina and Chile, a **licenciatura** takes four to six years to complete, and may be considered equivalent to a master's degree. In Peru and Venezuela, a bachelor's degree is a five-year process. Spanish and Colombian **licenciaturas** take four to five years, although some fields, such as medicine, require six or more.

Estudiantes hispanos en los EE.UU.

In the 2015–16 academic year, over 16,500 Mexican students (2% of all international students) studied at U.S. universities. Venezuelans were the second-largest Spanish-speaking group, with over 8,000 students.

*¡Ojo! El colegio is a false cognate. In most countries, it means *high school*, but in some regions it refers to an elementary school. All undergraduate study takes place at **la universidad**.

ACTIVIDADES

1 **¿Cierto o falso?** Indicate whether these statements are **cierto** or **falso**. Correct the false statements.

1. Students in Spanish-speaking countries must pay large amounts of money toward their college tuition.

2. **Carrera** refers to any undergraduate or graduate program that students enroll in to obtain a professional degree.

3. After studying at a **colegio**, students receive their **bachillerato**.

4. Undergraduates study at a **colegio** or an **universidad**.

5. In Latin America and Spain, students usually choose their majors in their second year at the university.

6. In Argentina, students focus their studies in their high school years.

7. In Mexico, the **bachillerato** involves specialized study.

8. In Spain, majors depend on entrance exam scores.

9. Venezuelans complete a **licenciatura** in five years.

10. According to statistics, Venezuelans constitute the third-largest Latin American group studying at U.S. universities.

Clases y exámenes

aprobar	to pass
la asignatura (Esp.)	la clase, la materia
la clase anual	year-long course
el examen parcial	midterm exam
la facultad	department, school
la investigación	research
el profesorado	faculty
reprobar; suspender (Esp.)	to fail
sacar buenas/ malas notas	to get good/ bad grades
tomar apuntes	to take notes

Las universidades hispanas

It is not uncommon for universities in Spain and Latin America to have extremely large student body populations.

- **Universidad de Buenos Aires** (Argentina) 316.000 estudiantes
- **Universidad Autónoma de Santo Domingo** (República Dominicana) 200.000 estudiantes
- **Universidad Complutense de Madrid** (España) 83.000 estudiantes
- **Universidad Central de Venezuela** (Venezuela) 62.600 estudiantes

La Universidad de Salamanca

The University of Salamanca, established in 1218, is the oldest university in Spain. It is located in Salamanca, one of the most spectacular Renaissance cities in Europe. Salamanca is nicknamed **La Ciudad Dorada** (*The Golden City*) for the golden glow of its famous sandstone buildings, and it was declared a UNESCO World Heritage Site in 1988.

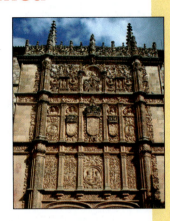

Salamanca is a true college town, as its prosperity and city life depend on and revolve around the university population. Over 32,000 students from all over Spain, as well as abroad, come to study here each year. The school offers over 250 academic programs, as well as renowned Spanish courses

for foreign students. To walk through the university's historic grounds is to follow the footsteps of immortal writers like Miguel de Cervantes and Miguel de Unamuno.

Enrique Iglesias (1975–)
Birthplace: Madrid, Spain

He used the name **Enrique Martínez** on demos to get his first record contract; he wanted to succeed without the help or influence of his famous father, Spanish pop singer Julio Iglesias.

Go to **vhlcentral.com** to find out more about **Enrique Iglesias** and his music.

ACTIVIDADES

2 Comprensión Complete these sentences.
1. The University of Salamanca was established in the year _____.
2. A _____ is a year-long course.
3. Salamanca is called _____.
4. Over 300,000 students attend the _____.
5. An _____ occurs about halfway through a course.

3 La universidad en cifras With a partner, research a Spanish or Latin American university online and find five statistics about that institution (for instance, the total enrollment, majors offered, year it was founded, etc.). Using the information you found, create a dialogue between a prospective student and a university representative. Present your dialogue to the class.

More activities
 vhlcentral Online activities

2.1 Present tense of -ar verbs Tutorial

ANTE TODO In order to talk about activities, you need to use verbs. Verbs express actions or states of being. In English and Spanish, the infinitive is the base form of the verb. In English, the infinitive is preceded by the word *to*: *to study*, *to be*. The infinitive in Spanish is a one-word form and can be recognized by its endings: **-ar**, **-er**, or **-ir**.

-ar verb		*-er* verb		*-ir* verb	
estudiar	*to study*	**comer**	*to eat*	**escribir**	*to write*

▶ In this lesson, you will learn the forms of regular **-ar** verbs.

The verb estudiar (*to study*)

SINGULAR FORMS	yo	estudi**o**	*I study*
	tú	estudi**as**	*you* (fam.) *study*
	Ud./él/ella	estudi**a**	*you* (form.) *study; he/she studies*
PLURAL FORMS	nosotros/as	estudi**amos**	*we study*
	vosotros/as	estudi**áis**	*you* (fam.) *study*
	Uds./ellos/ellas	estudi**an**	*you study; they study*

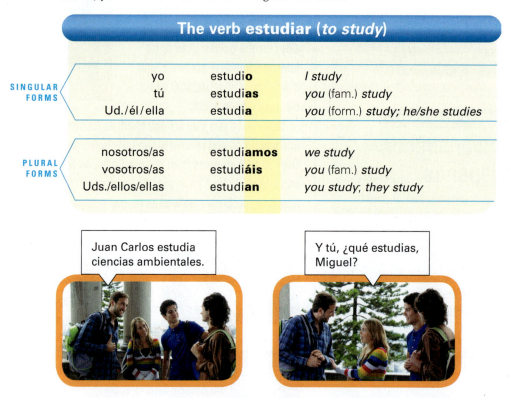

Juan Carlos estudia ciencias ambientales.

Y tú, ¿qué estudias, Miguel?

▶ To create the forms of most regular verbs in Spanish, drop the infinitive endings (**-ar**, **-er**, **-ir**). You then add to the stem the endings that correspond to the different subject pronouns. This diagram will help you visualize verb conjugation.

Conjugation of *-ar* verbs

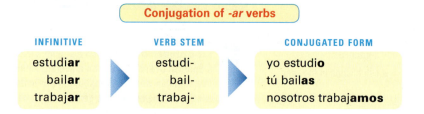

INFINITIVE	VERB STEM	CONJUGATED FORM
estudi**ar**	estudi-	yo estudi**o**
bail**ar**	bail-	tú bail**as**
trabaj**ar**	trabaj-	nosotros trabaj**amos**

Common *-ar* verbs

bailar	to dance	**estudiar**	to study
buscar	to look for	**explicar**	to explain
caminar	to walk	**hablar**	to talk; to speak
cantar	to sing	**llegar**	to arrive
cenar	to have dinner	**llevar**	to carry
comprar	to buy	**mirar**	to look (at); to watch
contestar	to answer	**necesitar (+ *inf.*)**	to need
conversar	to converse, to chat	**practicar**	to practice
desayunar	to have breakfast	**preguntar**	to ask (a question)
descansar	to rest	**preparar**	to prepare
desear (+ *inf.*)	to desire; to wish	**regresar**	to return
dibujar	to draw	**terminar**	to end; to finish
enseñar	to teach	**tomar**	to take; to drink
escuchar	to listen (to)	**trabajar**	to work
esperar (+ *inf.*)	to wait (for); to hope	**viajar**	to travel

▶ **¡Atención!** Unless referring to a person, the Spanish verbs **buscar**, **escuchar**, **esperar**, and **mirar** do not need to be followed by prepositions as they do in English.

Busco la tarea.
I'm looking for the homework.

Espero el autobús.
I'm waiting for the bus.

Escucho la música.
I'm listening to the music.

Miro la pizarra.
I'm looking at the board.

COMPARE & CONTRAST

English uses three sets of forms to talk about the present: (1) the simple present (*Paco works*), (2) the present progressive (*Paco is working*), and (3) the emphatic present (*Paco does work*). In Spanish, the simple present can be used in all three cases.

Paco **trabaja** en la cafetería.

1. *Paco works in the cafeteria.*
2. *Paco is working in the cafeteria.*
3. *Paco does work in the cafeteria.*

In Spanish and English, the present tense is also sometimes used to express future action.

Marina **viaja** a Madrid mañana.

1. *Marina travels to Madrid tomorrow.*
2. *Marina will travel to Madrid tomorrow.*
3. *Marina is traveling to Madrid tomorrow.*

▶ When two verbs are used together with no change of subject, the second verb is generally in the infinitive. To make a sentence negative in Spanish, the word **no** is placed before the conjugated verb. In this case, **no** means *not*.

Deseo hablar con el señor Díaz.
I want to speak with Mr. Díaz.

Alicia **no** desea bailar ahora.
Alicia doesn't want to dance now.

▶ Spanish speakers often omit subject pronouns because the verb endings indicate who the subject is. In Spanish, subject pronouns are used for emphasis, clarification, or contrast.

—¿Qué enseñan?
What do they teach?

—**Ella** enseña arte y **él** enseña física.
She teaches art, and he teaches physics.

—¿Quién desea trabajar hoy?
Who wants to work today?

—**Yo** no deseo trabajar hoy.
I don't want to work today.

The verb **gustar**

▶ **Gustar** is different from other **-ar** verbs. To express your likes and dislikes, use the expression **(no) me gusta** + **el/la** + [*singular noun*] or **(no) me gustan** + **los/las** + [*plural noun*]. Note: You may use the phrase **a mí** for emphasis, but never the subject pronoun **yo**.

Me gusta la música clásica.
I like classical music.

Me gustan las clases de español y biología.
I like Spanish and biology classes.

A mí me gustan las artes.
I like the arts.

A mí no me gusta el programa.
I don't like the program.

▶ To talk about what you like and don't like to do, use **(no) me gusta** + [*infinitive(s)*]. Note that the singular **gusta** is always used, even with more than one infinitive.

No me gusta viajar en autobús.
I don't like to travel by bus.

Me gusta cantar y **bailar**.
I like to sing and dance.

▶ To ask a friend about likes and dislikes, use the pronoun **te** instead of **me**. Note: You may use **a ti** for emphasis, but never the subject pronoun **tú**.

—¿**Te gusta la geografía?**
Do you like geography?

—**Sí, me gusta. Y a ti, ¿te gusta el inglés?**
Yes, I like it. And you, do you like English?

▶ You can use this same structure to talk about other people by using the pronouns **nos**, **le**, and **les**. Unless your instructor tells you otherwise, only the **me** and **te** forms will appear on test materials until **Lección 7**.

Nos gusta dibujar. (nosotros)
We like to draw.

Nos gustan las clases de español e inglés. (nosotros)
We like Spanish class and English class.

No le gusta trabajar. (usted, él, ella)
You don't like to work.
He/She doesn't like to work.

Les gusta el arte. (ustedes, ellos, ellas)
You like art.
They like art.

¡ATENCIÓN!

Note that **gustar** does not behave like other **-ar** verbs. You must study its use carefully and pay attention to prepositions, pronouns, and agreement.

AYUDA

Use the construction **a** + [*name/pronoun*] to clarify to whom you are referring. This construction is not always necessary.
A Gabriela le gusta bailar.
A Sara y a él les gustan los animales.
A mí me gusta viajar.
¿**A ti** te gustan las clases?

CONSULTA

For more on **gustar** and other verbs like it, see **Estructura 7.4**, pp. 246–247.

👐 **¡INTÉNTALO!**   Provide the present tense forms of these verbs.

hablar

1. Yo ____hablo____ español.
2. Ellos _____ español.
3. Inés _____ español.
4. Tú _____ español.
5. Nosotras _____ español.

gustar

1. ___Me gusta___ el café. (a mí)
2. ¿_____ las clases? (a ti)
3. No _____ el café. (a ti)
4. No _____ el café. (a mí)
5. No _____ las clases. (a mí)

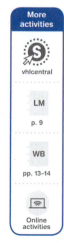

More activities

vhlcentral

LM p. 9

WB pp. 13–14

Online activities

Práctica

1

Completar Complete the conversation with the appropriate forms of the verbs.

JUAN   ¡Hola, Linda! ¿Qué tal las clases?

LINDA   Bien. (1)_____ (tomar) tres clases… química, biología y computación.
Y tú, ¿cuántas clases (2)_____ (tomar)?

JUAN   (3)_____ (tomar) tres también… biología, arte y literatura. El doctor
Cárdenas (4)_____ (enseñar) la clase de biología.

LINDA   ¿Ah, sí? Lily, Alberto y yo (5)_____ (tomar) biología a las diez con la
profesora Garza.

JUAN   ¿(6)_____ (estudiar) mucho ustedes?

LINDA   Sí, nosotros (7)_____ (necesitar) estudiar dos horas todos los días (*every day*).

2

Oraciones Form sentences. Remember to conjugate the verbs and add any other necessary words.

> **modelo**
>
> ustedes / practicar / vocabulario   *Ustedes practican el vocabulario.*

1. ¿preparar (tú) / tarea?
2. clase de español / terminar / once
3. ¿qué / buscar / ustedes?
4. (yo) comprar / calculadora
5. (nosotros) buscar / pluma

3

Gustos Use the information in parentheses to tell what the people like.

> **modelo**
>
> Yo enseño en la universidad. (las clases)   *Me gustan las clases.*

1. Tú deseas mirar cuadros (*paintings*) de Picasso. (el arte)
2. Busco una computadora. (la computación)
3. Tú estudias italiano y español. (las lenguas extranjeras)
4. No descansas los sábados. (cantar y bailar)
5. Soy estudiante de economía. (estudiar)

4

Actividades Get together with a partner and take turns asking each other if you do these activities.
Which activities does your partner like? Which do you both like?

> **modelo**
>
> tomar el autobús
> **Estudiante 1:** ¿Tomas el autobús?
> **Estudiante 2:** Sí, tomo el autobús, pero (*but*) no me gusta./ No, no tomo el autobús.

bailar merengue	escuchar música rock	practicar el español
cantar bien	estudiar física	trabajar en la universidad
dibujar en clase	mirar la televisión	viajar a Europa

Comunicación

5

Describir With a partner, describe what you see using the given verbs. Also ask your partner whether or not he/she likes one of the activities.

> **modelo**
>
> dibujar, escuchar
>
> **Estudiante 1:** La chica dibuja y escucha música.
>   ¿Te gusta dibujar?
> **Estudiante 2:** Sí, me gusta dibujar.

1. desayunar, estudiar, conversar   2. llegar, cantar, bailar

3. trabajar, viajar, llevar   4. mirar, esperar, cenar

6

Charadas In groups of three, play a game of charades using the verbs. For example, if someone is studying, you say "**Estudias**." The first person to guess correctly acts out the next charade.

bailar	cantar	descansar	enseñar	mirar
caminar	conversar	dibujar	escuchar	preguntar

Síntesis

7

Conversación With a partner, prepare a conversation between two friends who have not seen each other on campus lately and want to catch up on things. Mention how you're feeling, what classes you're taking, what days and times you have classes, and which classes you like and don't like.

2.2 Forming questions in Spanish Tutorial

ANTE TODO There are three basic ways to ask questions in Spanish. Can you guess what they are by looking at the photos and photo captions on this page?

Te gusta mucho la tarea, ¿no?

¿Hablas con tu mamá?

¿Estudia Maru?

▶ One way to form a question is to raise the pitch of your voice at the end of a declarative sentence. When writing any question in Spanish, be sure to use an upside-down question mark (¿) at the beginning and a regular question mark (?) at the end of the sentence.

Statement	**Question**
Ustedes trabajan los sábados.	¿Ustedes trabajan los sábados?
You work on Saturdays.	*Do you work on Saturdays?*
Carlota busca un mapa.	¿Carlota busca un mapa?
Carlota is looking for a map.	*Is Carlota looking for a map?*

▶ You can also form a question by inverting the order of the subject and the verb of a declarative statement. The subject may even be placed at the end of the sentence.

Statement	**Question**
SUBJECT VERB	VERB SUBJECT
Ustedes trabajan los sábados.	¿**Trabajan ustedes** los sábados?
You work on Saturdays.	*Do you work on Saturdays?*
SUBJECT VERB	VERB SUBJECT
Carlota regresa a las seis.	¿**Regresa** a las seis **Carlota**?
Carlota returns at six.	*Does Carlota return at six?*

▶ Questions can also be formed by adding the tags **¿no?** or **¿verdad?** at the end of a statement.

Statement	**Question**
Ustedes trabajan los sábados.	Ustedes trabajan los sábados, **¿no?**
You work on Saturdays.	*You work on Saturdays, don't you?*
Carlota regresa a las seis.	Carlota regresa a las seis, **¿verdad?**
Carlota returns at six.	*Carlota returns at six, right?*

Question words

Interrogative words			
¿Adónde?	Where (to)?	**¿De dónde?**	From where?
¿Cómo?	How?	**¿Dónde?**	Where?
¿Cuál?, ¿Cuáles?	Which?; Which one(s)?	**¿Por qué?**	Why?
¿Cuándo?	When?	**¿Qué?**	What?; Which?
¿Cuánto/a?	How much?	**¿Quién?**	Who?
¿Cuántos/as?	How many?	**¿Quiénes?**	Who (plural)?

▶ To ask a question that requires more than a *yes* or *no* answer, use an interrogative word.

¿Cuál de ellos estudia en la biblioteca?
Which of them studies in the library?

¿Adónde caminamos?
Where are we walking (to)?

¿Cuántos estudiantes hablan español?
How many students speak Spanish?

¿Por qué necesitas hablar con ella?
Why do you need to talk to her?

¿Dónde trabaja Ricardo?
Where does Ricardo work?

¿Quién enseña la clase de arte?
Who teaches the art class?

¿Qué clases tomas?
What classes are you taking?

¿Cuánta tarea hay?
How much homework is there?

▶ When you pronounce this type of question, the pitch of your voice falls at the end of the sentence.

¿Cómo llegas a clase?
How do you get to class?

¿Por qué necesitas estudiar?
Why do you need to study?

▶ Notice the difference between **¿por qué?**, which is written as two words and has an accent, and **porque**, which is written as one word without an accent.

¿Por qué estudias español?
Why do you study Spanish?

¡Porque es divertido!
Because it's fun!

▶ In Spanish **no** can mean both *no* and *not*. Therefore, when answering a yes/no question in the negative, you need to use **no** twice.

¿Caminan a la universidad?
Do you walk to the university?

No, **no** caminamos a la universidad.
No, we do not walk to the university.

CONSULTA

You will learn more about the difference between **qué** and **cuál** in **Estructura 9.3**, p. 316.

¡INTÉNTALO! Make questions out of these statements. Use the intonation method and the tag **¿no?** method.

Statement	Intonation	Tag questions
1. Hablas inglés.	¿Hablas inglés?	Hablas inglés, ¿no?
2. Trabajamos mañana.		
3. Raúl estudia mucho.		
4. Ustedes desean bailar.		
5. Enseño a las nueve.		
6. Luz mira la televisión.		

More activities

vhlcentral

LM p. 10

WB pp. 15–16

Online activities

Práctica

1

Preguntas Change these sentences into questions by inverting the word order.

> **modelo**
>
> Ernesto habla con su compañero de clase.
>
> *¿Habla Ernesto con su compañero de clase? /*
> *¿Habla con su compañero de clase Ernesto?*

1. La profesora Cruz prepara la prueba.

2. Sandra y yo necesitamos estudiar.

3. Los chicos practican el vocabulario.

4. Tú trabajas en la biblioteca.

5. Jaime termina la tarea.

2

Más preguntas Change each statement into two questions, using the interrogative words given.

> **modelo**
>
> Ernesto habla bien en la clase de español. (¿quién? ¿dónde?)
>
> *¿Quién habla bien en la clase de español? /*
> *¿Dónde habla bien Ernesto?*

1. Ignacio estudia hoy porque hay un examen el jueves. (¿cuándo? ¿por qué?)

2. Tú trabajas seis horas en la librería. (¿cuántas? ¿dónde?)

3. Los chicos practican el vocabulario en clase. (¿quiénes? ¿qué?)

4. Valeria y Sergio viajan a Barcelona en autobús. (¿adónde? ¿cómo?)

5. Catalina y Susana cenan en la cafetería. (¿quiénes? ¿dónde?)

3

Completar Complete the conversation with the appropriate questions.

IRENE Hola, Manolo. (1)_____

MANOLO Bien, gracias. (2)_____

IRENE Muy bien. (3)_____

MANOLO Son las nueve.

IRENE (4)_____

MANOLO Estudio historia.

IRENE (5)_____

MANOLO Porque hay un examen mañana.

IRENE (6)_____

MANOLO Sí, me gusta mucho la clase.

IRENE (7)_____

MANOLO El profesor Padilla enseña la clase.

IRENE (8)_____

MANOLO No, no tomo psicología este (*this*) semestre.

Comunicación

4

Encuesta Your instructor will give you a worksheet. Change the categories in the first column into questions, then use them to survey your classmates. Find at least one person for each category. Be prepared to report the results of your survey to the class.

5

Un juego In groups of four or five, play a game (**un juego**) of Jeopardy®. Each person has to write two clues. Then take turns reading the clues and guessing the questions. The person who guesses correctly reads the next clue.

Es algo que...	**Es un lugar donde...**	**Es una persona que...**
It's something that...	*It's a place where...*	*It's a person that...*

> **modelo**
>
> **Estudiante 1:** Es un lugar donde estudiamos.
> **Estudiante 2:** ¿Qué es la biblioteca?
>
> **Estudiante 1:** Es algo que escuchamos.
> **Estudiante 2:** ¿Qué es la música?
>
> **Estudiante 1:** Es un director de España.
> **Estudiante 2:** ¿Quién es Pedro Almodóvar?

NOTA CULTURAL

Pedro Almodóvar is an award-winning film director from Spain. His films are full of both humor and melodrama, and their controversial subject matter has often sparked great debate. His film *Hable con ella* won the Oscar for Best Original Screenplay in 2002. His 2006 hit *Volver* was nominated for numerous awards, and won the Best Screenplay and Best Actress award for the entire female cast at the Cannes Film Festival.

6

El nuevo estudiante You are a transfer student and today is your first day of Spanish class. Ask your partner questions to find out all you can about the class, your classmates, and the university. Use the list for ideas. Then switch roles.

biblioteca	curso	librería
cafetería	especialización	residencia estudiantil
clase	examen	tarea

> **modelo**
>
> **Estudiante 1:** Hola, me llamo Samuel. ¿Cómo te llamas?
> **Estudiante 2:** Me llamo Laura.
> **Estudiante 1:** En la universidad hay cursos de ciencias, ¿verdad?
> **Estudiante 2:** Sí, hay clases de biología, química y física.
> **Estudiante 1:** ¿Cuántos exámenes hay en esta clase?
> **Estudiante 2:** Hay dos.

Síntesis

7

Entrevista You are a reporter for the school newspaper. Write five questions about student life at your school and use them to interview two classmates. Be prepared to report your findings to the class.

CONSULTA

To review the forms of **ser**, see **Estructura 1.3**, pp. 19–21.

2.3 Present tense of estar Tutorial

ANTE TODO In **Lección 1**, you learned how to conjugate and use the verb **ser** (*to be*). You will now learn a second verb which means *to be*, the verb **estar**. Although **estar** ends in **-ar**, it does not follow the pattern of regular **-ar** verbs. The **yo** form (**estoy**) is irregular. Also, all forms have an accented **á** except the **yo** and **nosotros/as** forms.

The verb estar (*to be*)		
SINGULAR FORMS		
yo	est**oy**	*I am*
tú	est**ás**	*you* (fam.) *are*
Ud./él/ella	est**á**	*you* (form.) *are; he/she is*
PLURAL FORMS		
nosotros/as	est**amos**	*we are*
vosotros/as	est**áis**	*you* (fam.) *are*
Uds./ellos/ellas	est**án**	*you are; they are*

¡Estamos en Perú!

María está en la biblioteca.

COMPARE & CONTRAST

Compare the uses of the verb **estar** to those of the verb **ser**.

AYUDA

Use **la casa** to express *the house*, but **en casa** to express *at home*.

Uses of *estar*

Location
Estoy en casa.
I am at home.

Marissa **está** al lado de Felipe.
Marissa is next to Felipe.

Health
Juan Carlos **está** enfermo hoy.
Juan Carlos is sick today.

Well-being
—¿Cómo **estás**, Jimena?
How are you, Jimena?

—**Estoy** muy bien, gracias.
I'm very well, thank you.

Uses of *ser*

Identity
Hola, **soy** Maru.
Hello, I'm Maru.

Occupation
Soy estudiante.
I'm a student.

Origin
—¿**Eres** de México?
Are you from Mexico?

—Sí, **soy** de México.
Yes, I'm from Mexico.

Telling time
Son las cuatro.
It's four o'clock.

CONSULTA

To learn more about the difference between **ser** and **estar**, see **Estructura 5.3**, pp. 170–171.

▶ **Estar** is often used with certain prepositions and adverbs to describe the location of a person or an object.

Prepositions and adverbs often used with estar

al lado de	next to	**delante de**	in front of
a la derecha de	to the right of	**detrás de**	behind
a la izquierda de	to the left of	**en**	in; on
allá	over there	**encima de**	on top of
allí	there	**entre**	between
cerca de	near	**lejos de**	far from
con	with	**sin**	without
debajo de	below	**sobre**	on; over

El marcador **está al lado de** la pluma.
The marker is next to the pen.

Los libros **están encima del** escritorio.
The books are on top of the desk.

El laboratorio **está cerca de** la clase.
The lab is near the classroom.

Maribel **está delante de** José.
Maribel is in front of José.

La maleta **está allí**.
The suitcase is there.

El estadio no **está lejos de** la librería.
The stadium isn't far from the bookstore.

El mapa **está entre** la pizarra y la puerta.
The map is between the board and the door.

Los estudiantes **están en** la clase.
The students are in class.

La calculadora **está sobre** la mesa.
The calculator is on the table.

Los turistas **están allá**.
The tourists are over there.

Estamos lejos de casa.

La biblioteca está al lado de la librería.

¡INTÉNTALO! Provide the present tense forms of **estar**.

1. Ustedes _están_ en la clase.
2. José _____ en la biblioteca.
3. Yo _____ bien, gracias.
4. Nosotras _____ en la cafetería.
5. Tú _____ en el laboratorio.
6. Ellas _____ en la clase.
7. Elena _____ en la librería.
8. Ana y yo _____ en la clase.
9. Javier y Maribel _____ en el estadio.
10. ¿Cómo _____ usted?
11. Nosotros _____ en la cafetería.
12. Yo _____ en el laboratorio.
13. Carmen y María _____ enfermas.
14. Tú _____ en la clase.

More activities / vhlcentral / LM p. 11 / WB pp. 17–18 / Online activities

Práctica

1

Completar Complete the conversation with the appropriate forms of **ser** or **estar**.

MAMÁ   Hola, Daniela. ¿Cómo (1)_____?

▶ **DANIELA** Hola, mamá. (2)_____ bien. ¿Dónde (3)_____ papá?
             ¡Ya (*Already*) (4)_____ las ocho de la noche!

MAMÁ   No (5)_____ aquí. (6)_____ en la oficina.

DANIELA Y Andrés y Margarita, ¿dónde (7)_____ ellos?

MAMÁ   (8)_____ en el restaurante La Palma con Martín.

DANIELA ¿Quién (9)_____ Martín?

MAMÁ   (10)_____ un compañero de clase. (11)_____ de México.

DANIELA Ah. Y el restaurante La Palma, ¿dónde (12)_____?

MAMÁ   (13)_____ cerca de la Plaza Mayor, en San Modesto.

DANIELA Gracias, mamá. Voy (*I'm going*) al restaurante. ¡Hasta pronto!

2

Escoger Choose the preposition that best completes each sentence.

1. La pluma está (encima de / detrás de) la mesa.
2. La ventana está (a la izquierda de / debajo de) la puerta.
3. La pizarra está (debajo de / delante de) los estudiantes.
4. Los estudiantes llevan los libros (en / sobre) la mochila.
5. España está (cerca de / lejos de) Puerto Rico.
6. La biblioteca está (sobre / al lado de) la residencia estudiantil.
7. Las sillas están (encima de / detrás de) los escritorios.
8. México está (cerca de / lejos de) los Estados Unidos.

3

La librería Ask the school bookstore clerk (your partner) the location of items in the drawing.

modelo

Estudiante 1: ¿Dónde están las computadoras?
Estudiante 2: Las computadoras están encima de la mesa.

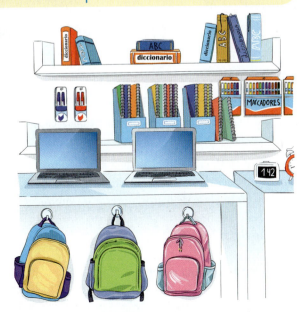

Comunicación

4

¿Dónde estás...? Get together with a partner and take turns asking each other where you normally are at these times.

> **modelo**
>
> lunes / 10:00 a.m.
>
> **Estudiante 1:** ¿Dónde estás los lunes a las diez de la mañana?
>
> **Estudiante 2:** Estoy en la clase de español.

1. sábados / 6:00 a.m.
2. miércoles / 9:15 a.m.
3. lunes / 11:10 a.m.
4. jueves / 12:30 a.m.
5. viernes / 2:25 p.m.
6. martes / 3:50 p.m.
7. jueves / 5:45 p.m.
8. miércoles / 8:20 p.m.

5

La ciudad universitaria You are an exchange student at a Spanish university. Ask a classmate to identify the people for you.

> **modelo**
>
> **Estudiante 1:** ¿Quién es Valeria? ¿Está a la izquierda de la facultad?
>
> **Estudiante 2:** Sí, está a la izquierda de la facultad. Está al lado de David.

Facultad de Filosofía y Letras

David — Valeria — Luis — Andrea — Víctor — Isabel — Prof. Rojas

¡LENGUA VIVA!

La Facultad (*School*) de Filosofía y Letras includes departments such as language, literature, philosophy, history, and linguistics. Fine arts can be studied in la Facultad de Bellas Artes. In Spain, the business school is sometimes called la Facultad de Administración de Empresas. Residencias estudiantiles are referred to as colegios mayores.

Síntesis

6

Entrevista With a partner, take turns asking and answering these questions.

1. ¿Cómo estás?
2. ¿Dónde tomas la clase de inglés/periodismo/física/computación?
3. ¿Dónde está tu (*your*) compañero/a de cuarto ahora?
4. ¿Cuántos estudiantes hay en tu clase de historia/literatura/química/matemáticas?
5. ¿Quién(es) no está(n) en la clase hoy?
6. ¿A qué hora terminan tus clases los lunes?
7. ¿Estudias mucho?
8. ¿Cuántas horas estudias para (*for*) una prueba?

2.4 Numbers 31 and higher   Tutorial

ANTE TODO You have already learned numbers 0–30. Now you will learn the rest of the numbers.

Numbers 31–100

▶ Numbers 31–99 follow the same basic pattern as 21–29.

Numbers 31–100		
31 treinta y uno	**40** cuarenta	**50** cincuenta
32 treinta y dos	**41** cuarenta y uno	**51** cincuenta y uno
33 treinta y tres	**42** cuarenta y dos	**52** cincuenta y dos
34 treinta y cuatro	**43** cuarenta y tres	**60** sesenta
35 treinta y cinco	**44** cuarenta y cuatro	**63** sesenta y tres
36 treinta y seis	**45** cuarenta y cinco	**64** sesenta y cuatro
37 treinta y siete	**46** cuarenta y seis	**70** setenta
38 treinta y ocho	**47** cuarenta y siete	**80** ochenta
39 treinta y nueve	**48** cuarenta y ocho	**90** noventa
	49 cuarenta y nueve	**100** cien, ciento

▶ **Y** is used in most numbers from **31** through **99**. Unlike numbers 21–29, these numbers must be written as three separate words.

Hay **noventa y dos** exámenes.
There are ninety-two exams.

Hay **cuarenta y dos** estudiantes.
There are forty-two students.

Hay cuarenta y siete estudiantes en la clase de geografía.

Cien menos sesenta y cuatro son treinta y seis pesos de cambio.

▶ With numbers that end in **uno** (31, 41, etc.), **uno** becomes **un** before a masculine noun and **una** before a feminine noun.

Hay **treinta y un** chicos.
There are thirty-one guys.

Hay **treinta y una** chicas.
There are thirty-one girls.

▶ **Cien** is used before nouns and in counting. The words **un, una,** and **uno** are never used before **cien** in Spanish. Use **cientos** to say *hundreds.*

Hay **cien** libros y **cien** sillas.
There are one hundred books and one hundred chairs.

¿Cuántos libros hay? **Cientos.**
How many books are there? Hundreds.

Numbers 101 and higher

▶ As shown in the chart, Spanish uses a period to indicate thousands and millions, rather than a comma, as is used in English.

Numbers 101 and higher			
101	ciento uno	1.000	mil
200	doscientos/as	1.100	mil cien
300	trescientos/as	2.000	dos mil
400	cuatrocientos/as	5.000	cinco mil
500	quinientos/as	100.000	cien mil
600	seiscientos/as	200.000	doscientos/as mil
700	setecientos/as	550.000	quinientos/as cincuenta mil
800	ochocientos/as	1.000.000	un millón (de)
900	novecientos/as	8.000.000	ocho millones (de)

▶ Notice that you should use **ciento**, not **cien**, to count numbers over 100.

110 = **ciento diez**   118 = **ciento dieciocho**   150 = **ciento cincuenta**

▶ The numbers 200 through 999 agree in gender with the nouns they modify.

324 plum**as**   3.505 libr**os**
trescient**as** veinticuatro plum**as**   tres mil quinient**os** cinco libr**os**

▶ The word **mil**, which can mean *a thousand* and *one thousand*, is not usually used in the plural form to refer to an exact number, but it can be used to express the idea of *a lot*, *many*, or *thousands*. **Cientos** can also be used to express *hundreds* in this manner.

¡Hay **miles** de personas en el estadio!   Hay **cientos** de libros en la biblioteca.
There are thousands of people   *There are hundreds of books*
in the stadium!   *in the library.*

▶ To express a complex number (including years), string together all of its components.

55.422   cincuenta y cinco mil cuatrocientos veintidós

¡LENGUA VIVA!

In parts of Latin America, you will see a comma instead of a period to indicate thousands and millions.

¡LENGUA VIVA!

In Spanish, years are not expressed as pairs of two-digit numbers as they are in English (1979, *nineteen seventy-nine*): **1776, mil setecientos setenta y seis; 1945, mil novecientos cuarenta y cinco; 2016, dos mil dieciséis.**

¡ATENCIÓN!

When **millón** or **millones** is used before a noun, the word **de** is placed between the two:
1.000.000 hombres = un millón de hombres
12.000.000 casas = doce millones de casas.

More activities

vhlcentral

LM
p. 12

WB
pp. 19–20

Online activities

¡INTÉNTALO!   Write out the Spanish equivalent of each number.

1. **102** _____ *ciento dos* _____
2. **5.000.000** _____
3. **76** _____
4. **201** _____
5. **92** _____
6. **550.300** _____

7. **113** _____
8. **79** _____
9. **235** _____
10. **88** _____
11. **17.123** _____
12. **497** _____

Práctica y Comunicación

1

Baloncesto Provide these basketball scores in Spanish.

1. Ohio State 76, Michigan 65
2. Florida 92, Florida State 104
3. Stanford 83, UCLA 89
4. Duke 115, Virginia 121
5. Princeton 67, Harvard 55
6. Purdue 81, Indiana 78

2

Completar Following the pattern, write out the missing numbers in Spanish.

1. 50, 150, 250 ... 1.050
2. 5.000, 20.000, 35.000 ... 95.000
3. 100.000.000, 90.000.000, 80.000.000 ... 0
4. 100.000, 200.000, 300.000 ... 1.000.000

3

Resolver In pairs, take turns reading the math problems aloud for your partner to solve.

> **modelo**
>
> 200 + 300 =
> **Estudiante 1:** Doscientos más trescientos son...
> **Estudiante 2:** ...quinientos.

AYUDA

+	→	**más**
−	→	**menos**
=	→	**son**

1. 1.000 + 753 =
2. 1.000.000 − 30.000 =
3. 10.000 + 555 =
4. 15 + 150 =
5. 100.000 + 205.000 =
6. 29.000 − 10.000 =

4

Entrevista Find out the phone numbers and e-mail addresses of four classmates.

> **modelo**
>
> **Estudiante 1:** ¿Cuál es tu (your) número de teléfono?
> **Estudiante 2:** Es el 635-19-51.
> **Estudiante 1:** ¿Y tu dirección de correo electrónico?
> **Estudiante 2:** Es a-Smith-arroba-pe-ele-punto-e-de-u. (asmith@pl.edu)

AYUDA

arroba *at* (@)
punto *dot* (.)

Síntesis

5

¿A qué distancia...? Your instructor will give you and a partner incomplete charts that indicate the distances between Madrid and various locations. Fill in the missing information on your chart by asking your partner questions.

> **modelo**
>
> **Estudiante 1:** ¿A qué distancia está Arganda del Rey?
> **Estudiante 2:** Está a veintisiete kilómetros de Madrid.

Recapitulación

Review the grammar concepts you have learned in this lesson by completing these activities.

1 Completar Complete the chart with the correct verb forms. **24 pts.**

yo	tú	nosotros	ellas
compro			
	deseas		
		miramos	
			preguntan

2 Números Write these numbers in Spanish. **16 pts.**

modelo

645: seiscientos cuarenta y cinco

1. **49:** _____
2. **97:** _____
3. **113:** _____
4. **632:** _____
5. **1.781:** _____
6. **3.558:** _____
7. **1.006.015:** _____
8. **67.224.370:** _____

3 Preguntas Write questions for these answers. **12 pts.**

1. —¿_____ Patricia?
   —Patricia es de Colombia.
2. —¿_____ él?
   —Él es mi amigo (*friend*).
3. —¿_____ (tú)?
   —Hablo dos idiomas (*languages*).
4. —¿_____ (ustedes)?
   —Deseamos tomar café.
5. —¿_____?
   —Tomo biología porque me gustan las ciencias.
6. —¿_____?
   —Camilo descansa por las mañanas.

RESUMEN GRAMATICAL

2.1 Present tense of -ar verbs pp. 50–52

estudiar

estudio	estudiamos
estudias	estudiáis
estudia	estudian

The verb gustar

(no) me gusta + el/la + [*singular noun*]

(no) me gustan + los/las + [*plural noun*]

(no) me gusta + [*infinitive(s)*]

Note: You may use **a mí** for emphasis, but never **yo**.

To ask a friend about likes and dislikes, use **te** instead of **me**, but never **tú**.

¿Te gusta la historia?

2.2 Forming questions in Spanish pp. 55–56

► ¿Ustedes trabajan los sábados?
► ¿Trabajan ustedes los sábados?
► Ustedes trabajan los sábados, ¿verdad?/¿no?

Interrogative words

¿Adónde?	¿Cuánto/a?	¿Por qué?
¿Cómo?	¿Cuántos/as?	¿Qué?
¿Cuál(es)?	¿De dónde?	¿Quién(es)?
¿Cuándo?	¿Dónde?	

2.3 Present tense of estar pp. 59–60

► estar: estoy, estás, está, estamos, estáis, están

2.4 Numbers 31 and higher pp. 63–64

31	treinta y uno	101	ciento uno
32	treinta y dos	200	doscientos/as
	(and so on)	500	quinientos/as
40	cuarenta	700	setecientos/as
50	cincuenta	900	novecientos/as
60	sesenta	1.000	mil
70	setenta	2.000	dos mil
80	ochenta	5.100	cinco mil cien
90	noventa	100.000	cien mil
100	cien, ciento	1.000.000	un millón (de)

4 **Al teléfono** Complete this phone conversation with the correct forms of the verb **estar**.

16 pts.

MARÍA TERESA Hola, señora López. (1) ¿ _____ Elisa en casa?

SRA. LÓPEZ Hola, ¿quién es?

MARÍA TERESA Soy María Teresa. Elisa y yo (2) _____ en la misma (*same*) clase de literatura.

SRA. LÓPEZ ¡Ah, María Teresa! ¿Cómo (3) _____ ?

MARÍA TERESA (4) _____ muy bien, gracias. Y usted, ¿cómo (5) _____ ?

SRA. LÓPEZ Bien, gracias. Pues, no, Elisa no (6) _____ en casa. Ella y su hermano (*her brother*) (7) _____ en la Biblioteca Cervantes.

MARÍA TERESA ¿Cervantes?

SRA. LÓPEZ Es la biblioteca que (8) _____ al lado del café Bambú.

MARÍA TERESA ¡Ah, sí! Gracias, señora López.

SRA. LÓPEZ Hasta luego, María Teresa.

5 **¿Qué te gusta?** Write a paragraph of at least five sentences stating what you like and don't like about your university. If possible, explain your likes and dislikes. 32 pts.

> *Me gusta la clase de música porque no hay muchos exámenes. No me gusta cenar en la cafetería...*

6 **Canción** Use the appropriate forms of the verb **gustar** to complete the beginning of a popular song by Manu Chao. 4 EXTRA points!

“ Me _____ los aviones°,
me gustas tú,
me _____ viajar,
me gustas tú,
me gusta la mañana,
me gustas tú. ”

aviones *airplanes*

Lectura

Antes de leer

Estrategia

Predicting content through formats

Recognizing the format of a document can help you to predict its content. For instance, invitations, greeting cards, and classified ads follow an easily identifiable format, which usually gives you a general idea of the information they contain. Look at the text and identify it based on its format.

	lunes	martes	miércoles	jueves	viernes
8:30	biología		biología		biología
9:00		historia		historia	
9:30	inglés		inglés		inglés
10:00					
10:30					
11:00					
12:00					
12:30					
1:00					
2:00	arte		arte		arte

If you guessed that this is a page from a student's schedule, you are correct. You can now infer that the document contains information about a student's weekly schedule, including days, times, and activities.

Cognados

Make a list of the cognates in the text and guess their English meanings. What do cognates reveal about the content of the document?

Examinar el texto

Look at the format of the document entitled *¡Español en Madrid!* What type of text is it? What information do you expect to find in this type of document?

More activities
vhlcentral | Online activities

¡ESPAÑOL EN MADRID!

UAE

Programa de Cursos Intensivos de Español

Universidad Autónoma de España

Después de leer

Correspondencias

Provide the letter of each item in Column B that matches the words in Column A.

A

1. profesores
2. vivienda
3. Madrid
4. número de teléfono
5. Español 2B
6. número de fax

B

a. (34) 91 523 4500
b. (34) 91 524 0210
c. 23 junio–30 julio
d. capital cultural de Europa
e. 16 junio–22 julio
f. especializados en enseñar español como lengua extranjera
g. (34) 91 523 4623
h. familias españolas

Universidad Autónoma de España

Madrid, la capital cultural de Europa, y la UAE te ofrecen cursos intensivos de verano° para aprender° español como nunca antes°.

¿Dónde?
En el campus de la UAE, edificio° de la Facultad de Filosofía y Letras.

¿Quiénes son los profesores?
Son todos hablantes nativos del español y catedráticos° de la UAE especializados en enseñar el español como lengua extranjera.

¿Qué niveles se ofrecen?
Se ofrecen tres niveles° básicos:

1. Español Elemental, A, B y C
2. Español Intermedio, A y B
3. Español Avanzado, A y B

Viviendas
Para estudiantes extranjeros se ofrece vivienda° con familias españolas.

¿Cuándo?
Este verano desde° el 16 de junio hasta el 10 de agosto. Los cursos tienen una duración de 6 semanas.

Cursos	Empieza°	Termina
Español 1A	16 junio	22 julio
Español 1B	23 junio	30 julio
Español 1C	30 junio	10 agosto
Español 2A	16 junio	22 julio
Español 2B	23 junio	30 julio
Español 3A	16 junio	22 julio
Español 3B	23 junio	30 julio

Información
Para mayor información, sirvan comunicarse con la siguiente° oficina:

Universidad Autónoma de España
Programa de Español como Lengua Extranjera
Calle del Valle de Mena 95, 28039 Madrid, España
Tel. (34) 91 523 4500, **Fax** (34) 91 523 4623
www.uae.es

verano *summer* aprender *to learn* nunca antes *never before* edificio *building* catedráticos *professors* niveles *levels* vivienda *housing* desde *from* Empieza *Begins* siguiente *following*

¿Cierto o falso?

Indicate whether each statement is **cierto** or **falso**.
Then correct the false statements.

	Cierto	Falso
1. La Universidad Autónoma de España ofrece (*offers*) cursos intensivos de italiano.	○	○
2. La lengua nativa de los profesores del programa es el inglés.	○	○
3. Los cursos de español son en la Facultad de Ciencias.	○	○
4. Los estudiantes pueden vivir (*can live*) con familias españolas.	○	○

	Cierto	Falso
5. La universidad que ofrece los cursos intensivos está en Salamanca.	○	○
6. Español 3B termina en agosto.	○	○
7. Si deseas información sobre (*about*) los cursos intensivos de español, es posible llamar al (34) 91 523 4500.	○	○
8. Español 1A empieza en julio.	○	○

Escritura

Estrategia
Brainstorming

How do you find ideas to write about? In the early stages of writing, brainstorming can help you generate ideas on a specific topic. You should spend ten to fifteen minutes brainstorming and jotting down any ideas about the topic. Whenever possible, try to write your ideas in Spanish. Express your ideas in single words or phrases, and jot them down in any order. While brainstorming, don't worry about whether your ideas are good or bad. Selecting and organizing ideas should be the second stage of your writing. Remember that the more ideas you write down while you're brainstorming, the more options you'll have to choose from later when you start to organize your ideas.

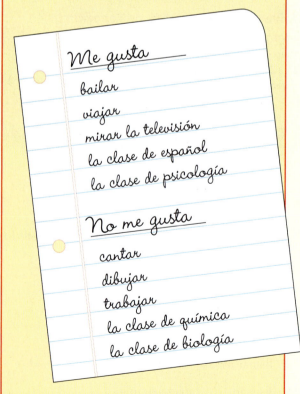

Me gusta

bailar

viajar

mirar la televisión

la clase de español

la clase de psicología

No me gusta

cantar

dibujar

trabajar

la clase de química

la clase de biología

Tema
Una descripción

Write a description of yourself to post in a chat room on a website in order to meet Spanish-speaking people. Include this information in your description:

▶ your name and where you are from, and a photo (optional) of yourself

▶ your major and where you go to school

▶ the courses you are taking

▶ where you work (if you have a job)

▶ some of your likes and dislikes

on   **inicio**   **perfil**

Hola! Me llamo Alicia Roberts. Estudio matemáticas en la Universidad de Toronto.

Escuchar

Antes de escuchar

Estrategia

Listening for cognates

You already know that cognates are words that have similar spellings and meanings in two or more languages: for example, *group* and **grupo** or *stereo* and **estéreo**. Listen for cognates to increase your comprehension of spoken Spanish.

To help you practice this strategy, you will now listen to two sentences. Make a list of all the cognates you hear.

Preparación

Based on the photograph, who do you think Armando and Julia are? What do you think they are talking about?

Ahora escucha

Armando y Julia

Now you are going to hear Armando and Julia's conversation. Make a list of the cognates they use.

Armando	Julia
_____	_____
_____	_____
_____	_____
_____	_____

Based on your knowledge of cognates, decide whether the following statements are **cierto** or **falso.**

	Cierto	Falso
1. Armando y Julia hablan de la familia.	○	○
2. Armando y Julia toman una clase de matemáticas.	○	○
3. Julia toma clases de ciencias.	○	○
4. Armando estudia lenguas extranjeras.	○	○
5. Julia toma una clase de religión.	○	○

Comprensión

Seleccionar

Choose the answer that best completes each sentence.

1. Armando toma _____ clases en la universidad.
   a. cuatro   b. cinco   c. seis
2. Julia toma dos clases de _____.
   a. matemáticas b. lengua   c. ciencias
3. Armando toma italiano y _____.
   a. astronomía   b. japonés   c. geología
4. Armando y Julia estudian _____ los martes y jueves.
   a. filosofía   b. antropología   c. italiano

Preguntas

Answer the questions.

1. ¿Qué clases toma Armando?
   _____

2. ¿Qué clases toma Julia?
   _____

Preguntas personales

1. ¿Cuántas clases tomas tú este semestre?
2. ¿Qué clases tomas este semestre?
3. ¿Qué clases te gustan y qué clases no te gustan?

En pantalla Video

Christmas isn't always in winter. During the months of cold weather and snow in North America, the southern hemisphere enjoys warm weather and longer days. Since Chile's summer lasts from December to February, school vacation coincides with these months. In Chile, the school year starts in early March and finishes toward the end of December.

Vocabulario útil	
quería	I wanted
pedirte	to ask you
te preocupa	it worries you
ahorrar	to save (money)
Navidad	Christmas
aprovecha	take advantage of
nuestras	our
ofertas	offers, deals
calidad	quality
no cuesta	doesn't cost

Preparación

Think about occasions when you normally receive gifts. How do you let your family and friends know what you want? Do you usually get what you want?

¿Qué hay?

For each item, write **sí** if it appears in the TV clip or **no** if it does not.

___ 1. papelera ___ 5. diccionario
___ 2. lápiz ___ 6. cuaderno
___ 3. mesa ___ 7. calculadora
___ 4. computadora ___ 8. ventana

¿Qué quieres?

Write a list of things that you want for your next birthday. Then read it to the class so they know what to get you. Use as much Spanish as you can.

> Lista de cumpleaños°
>
> Quiero°...

cumpleaños *birthday* **Quiero** *I want* **Viejito Pascuero** *Santa Claus (Chile)*

Anuncio de Jumbo

Viejito Pascuero°...

¿Cómo se escribe *mountain bike*?

M... O...

More activities

vhlcentral Online activities

Video

Mexican author and diplomat Octavio Paz (March 31, 1914–April 19, 1998) studied both law and literature at the **Universidad Nacional Autónoma de México** (**UNAM**), but after graduating he immersed himself in the art of writing. An incredibly prolific writer of poetry and essays, Paz solidified his prestige as Mexico's preeminent author with his 1950 book *El laberinto de la soledad*, a fundamental study of Mexican identity. Among the many awards he received in his lifetime are the **Premio Miguel de Cervantes** (1981) and Nobel Prize for Literature (1990). Paz foremost considered himself a poet and affirmed that poetry constitutes "**la religión secreta de la edad° moderna**".

Vocabulario útil

¿Cuál es tu materia favorita?	*What is your favorite subject?*
¿Cuántos años tienes?	*How old are you?*
¿Qué estudias?	*What do you study?*
el/la alumno/a	*student*
la carrera (de medicina)	*(medical) degree program, major*
derecho	*law*
reconocido	*well-known*

Preparación

What is the name of your school or university? What degree program are you in? What classes are you taking this semester?

Emparejar

Match the first part of the sentence with the appropriate ending.

1. En la UNAM no hay
2. México, D.F. es
3. La UNAM es
4. La UNAM ofrece

a. una universidad muy grande.
b. 74 carreras de estudio.
c. residencias estudiantiles.
d. la ciudad más grande (*biggest*) de Hispanoamérica.

Los estudios

①
—¿Qué estudias?
—Ciencias de la comunicación.

②
Estudio derecho en la UNAM.

③
¿Conoces a algún° profesor famoso que dé° clases... en la UNAM?

More activities
vhlcentral — VM pp. 39–40 — Online activities

edad age ¿Conoces a algún...? Do you know any...? que dé that teaches

España

El país en cifras

▶ **Área:** 505.370 km² (kilómetros cuadrados) o 195.124 millas cuadradas°, incluyendo las islas Baleares y las islas Canarias

▶ **Población:** 48.958.000

▶ **Capital:** Madrid—6.199.000

▶ **Ciudades° principales:** Barcelona—5.258.000, Valencia—810.000, Sevilla, Zaragoza

▶ **Moneda°:** euro

▶ **Idiomas°:** español o castellano, catalán, gallego, valenciano, euskera

Regiones lingüísticas

Gallego, Euskera, Catalán, Español, Valenciano

Bandera de España

Españoles célebres

▶ **Miguel de Cervantes,** escritor° (1547–1616)

▶ **Pedro Almodóvar,** director de cine° (1949–)

▶ **Rosa Montero,** escritora y periodista° (1951–)

▶ **Fernando Alonso,** corredor de autos° (1981–)

▶ **Paz Vega,** actriz° (1976–)

▶ **Severo Ochoa,** Premio Nobel de Medicina, 1959; doctor y científico (1905–1993)

millas cuadradas *square miles* Ciudades *Cities* Moneda *Currency* Idiomas *Languages* escritor *writer* cine *film* periodista *reporter* corredor de autos *race car driver* actriz *actress*

La Sagrada Familia en Barcelona

Plaza Mayor en Madrid

Mar Cantábrico — La Coruña — San Sebastián — FRANCIA — ANDORRA — Pirineos — Zaragoza — Río Ebro — Barcelona — Salamanca — ESPAÑA — Menorca — Mallorca — Ibiza — Islas Baleares — PORTUGAL — Madrid — Valencia — Sierra Nevada — Mar Mediterráneo — Sevilla — La costa de Ibiza — Estrecho de Gibraltar — Ceuta — Melilla — MARRUECOS — El baile flamenco

Islas Canarias — La Palma — Tenerife — Gran Canaria — Lanzarote — Gomera — Hierro

More activities — vhlcentral — WB pp. 21–22 — Online activities

ACTIVIDADES

1 **Escoger** Elige las respuestas correctas.

1. ¿Qué celebran las personas cada año en Buñol, Valencia?
   a. el día de la lengua española   b. el festival de *La Tomatina*

2. ¿Quién es Rosa Montero?
   a. una actriz   b. una escritora

3. ¿Cuál es la moneda de España?
   a. el peso   b. el euro

4. ¿Cuáles son algunas de las ciudades más importantes de España?
   a. Barcelona y Valencia   b. Barcelona y La Coruña

5. ¿Quién es el pintor de *Las meninas*?
   a. El Greco   b. Velázquez

6. ¿Quién es un pintor español famoso?
   a. Goya   b. Andrés

Gastronomía • **José Andrés**

José Andrés es un chef español famoso internacionalmente°. Le gusta combinar platos° tradicionales de España con las técnicas de cocina más innovadoras°. Andrés vive° en Washington, DC, y es dueño° de varios restaurantes en los EE.UU. En 2012 la revista° *Time* lo incluyó° en su lista de las "100 personas más influyentes° del mundo". También° ha estado° en el programa *Top Chef*.

Cultura • **La diversidad**

La riqueza° cultural y lingüística de España refleja la combinación de las diversas culturas que han habitado° en su territorio durante siglos°. El español es la lengua oficial del país, pero también son oficiales el catalán, el gallego, el euskera y el valenciano.

Sóc molt fan de la pàgina 335.

Ajuntament de Barcelona

Póster en catalán

▷ Artes • **Velázquez y el Prado**

El Prado, en Madrid, es uno de los museos más famosos del mundo°. En el Prado hay pinturas° importantes de Botticelli, de El Greco y de los españoles Goya y Velázquez. *Las meninas* es la obra° más conocida° de Diego Velázquez, pintor° oficial de la corte real° durante el siglo° XVII.

Las meninas,
Diego Velázquez, 1656

▷ Comida • **La paella**

La paella es uno de los platos más típicos de España.Siempre se prepara° con arroz° y azafrán°, pero hay diferentes recetas°. La paella valenciana, por ejemplo, es de pollo° y conejo°, y la paella marinera es de mariscos°.

internacionalmente *internationally* **platos** *dishes* **más innovadoras** *most innovative* **vive** *lives* **dueño** *owner* **revista** *magazine* **lo incluyó** *included him*
influyentes *influential* **También** *Also* **ha estado** *has been* **riqueza** *richness* **han habitado** *have lived* **durante siglos** *for centuries* **mundo** *world* **pinturas** *paintings*
obra *work* **más conocida** *best-known* **pintor** *painter* **corte real** *royal court* **siglo** *century* **Siempre se prepara** *It is always prepared* **arroz** *rice* **azafrán** *saffron*
recetas *recipes* **pollo** *chicken* **conejo** *rabbit* **mariscos** *seafood*

¡Increíble pero cierto!

En Buñol, un pueblo° de Valencia, la producción de tomates es un recurso económico muy importante. Cada año° se celebra el festival de *La Tomatina*. Durante todo un día°, miles de personas se tiran° tomates. Llegan turistas de todo el país, y se usan varias toneladas° de tomates.

pueblo *town* **Cada año** *Every year* **Durante todo un día** *All day long* **se tiran** *throw at each other*
varias toneladas *many tons*

2 **¿Qué aprendiste?** Completa las oraciones.

1. El chef español _____ es muy famoso.
2. El arroz y el azafrán son ingredientes básicos de la _____.
3. El Prado está en _____.
4. José Andrés vive en _____.
5. El gallego es una de las lenguas oficiales de _____.

3 **Preguntas** En parejas, formen y contesten preguntas sobre las personas y los lugares de la sección **Panorama**.

modelo

Estudiante 1: ¿Dónde está el Prado?
Estudiante 2: Está en Madrid.

La clase y la universidad

el/la compañero/a de clase	classmate
el/la compañero/a de cuarto	roommate
el/la estudiante	student
el/la profesor(a)	teacher
el borrador	eraser
la calculadora	calculator
el escritorio	desk
el libro	book
el mapa	map
el marcador	marker
la mesa	table
la mochila	backpack
el papel	paper
la papelera	wastebasket
la pizarra	whiteboard
la pluma	pen
la puerta	door
el reloj	clock; watch
la silla	seat
la ventana	window
la biblioteca	library
la cafetería	cafeteria
la casa	house; home
el estadio	stadium
el laboratorio	laboratory
la librería	bookstore
la residencia estudiantil	dormitory
la universidad	university; college
la clase	class
el curso, la materia	course
la especialización	major
el examen	test; exam
el horario	schedule
la prueba	test; quiz
el semestre	semester
la tarea	homework
el trimestre	trimester; quarter

Las materias

la administración de empresas	business administration
la arqueología	archeology
el arte	art
la biología	biology
las ciencias	sciences
la computación	computer science
la contabilidad	accounting
la economía	economics
el español	Spanish
la física	physics
la geografía	geography
la historia	history
las humanidades	humanities
el inglés	English
las lenguas extranjeras	foreign languages
la literatura	literature
las matemáticas	mathematics
la música	music
el periodismo	journalism
la psicología	psychology
la química	chemistry
la sociología	sociology

Preposiciones y adverbios

al lado de	next to
a la derecha de	to the right of
a la izquierda de	to the left of
allá	over there
allí	there
cerca de	near
con	with
debajo de	below
delante de	in front of
detrás de	behind
en	in; on
encima de	on top of
entre	between
lejos de	far from
sin	without
sobre	on; over

Palabras adicionales

¿Adónde?	Where (to)?
ahora	now
¿Cuál?, ¿Cuáles?	Which?; Which one(s)?
¿Por qué?	Why?
porque	because

Verbos

bailar	to dance
buscar	to look for
caminar	to walk
cantar	to sing
cenar	to have dinner
comprar	to buy
contestar	to answer
conversar	to converse, to chat
desayunar	to have breakfast
descansar	to rest
desear	to wish; to desire
dibujar	to draw
enseñar	to teach
escuchar la radio/música	to listen (to) the radio/music
esperar (+ *inf.*)	to wait (for); to hope
estar	to be
estudiar	to study
explicar	to explain
gustar	to like
hablar	to talk; to speak
llegar	to arrive
llevar	to carry
mirar	to look (at); to watch
necesitar (+ *inf.*)	to need
practicar	to practice
preguntar	to ask (a question)
preparar	to prepare
regresar	to return
terminar	to end; to finish
tomar	to take; to drink
trabajar	to work
viajar	to travel

Los días de la semana

¿Cuándo?	When?
¿Qué día es hoy?	What day is it?
Hoy es…	Today is…
la semana	week
lunes	Monday
martes	Tuesday
miércoles	Wednesday
jueves	Thursday
viernes	Friday
sábado	Saturday
domingo	Sunday
Numbers 31 and higher	See pages 63–64.
Expresiones útiles	See page 45.

More activities
vhlcentral | LM p. 12

La familia

3

Communicative Goals

You will learn how to:

- Talk about your family and friends
- Describe people and things
- Express possession

👁 A PRIMERA VISTA

- ¿Cuántos chicos hay en la foto?
- ¿Hay una mujer detrás de la chica? ¿Y a la izquierda?
- ¿Hay una cosa en la mano del chico?
- ¿Conversan ellos? ¿Trabajan? ¿Descansan?
- ¿Están en su casa?

La familia

Más vocabulario

los abuelos	grandparents
el/la bisabuelo/a	great-grandfather/ great-grandmother
el/la gemelo/a	twin
el/la hermanastro/a	stepbrother/stepsister
el/la hijastro/a	stepson/stepdaughter
la madrastra	stepmother
el medio hermano/ la media hermana	half-brother/ half-sister
el padrastro	stepfather
los padres	parents
los parientes	relatives
el/la cuñado/a	brother-in-law/ sister-in-law
la nuera	daughter-in-law
el/la suegro/a	father-in-law/ mother-in-law
el yerno	son-in-law
el/la amigo/a	friend
el apellido	last name
la gente	people
el/la muchacho/a	boy/girl
el/la niño/a	child
el/la novio/a	boyfriend/girlfriend
la persona	person
el/la artista	artist
el/la ingeniero/a	engineer
el/la doctor(a), el/la médico/a	doctor; physician
el/la periodista	journalist
el/la programador(a)	computer programmer

Variación léxica

madre ⟷ mamá, mami (colloquial)
padre ⟷ papá, papi (colloquial)
muchacho/a ⟷ chico/a

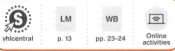

La familia de José Miguel Pérez Santoro

Víctor Miguel Morales Pérez mi sobrino (my nephew) hermano (brother) de Anita

Anita Morales Pérez mi sobrina (my niece) nieta (granddaughter) de mis padres

los hijos (children) de Beatriz Alicia y Felipe

Beatriz Alicia Pérez de Morales mi hermana (sister)

José Miguel Pérez Santoro hijo de Rubén y Mirta

Felipe Morales Zapata esposo (husband) de Beatriz Alicia

Rubén Ernesto Pérez Gómez mi padre (father) esposo de mi madre

Mirta Santoro de Pérez mi madre (mother) hija de Juan y Socorro

Socorro González de Santoro mi abuela (grandmother)

Juan Santoro Sánchez mi abuelo (grandfather)

Héctor Manuel Santoro Gutiérrez
mi primo (*cousin*)
nieto (*grandson*) **de Juan y Socorro**

Carmen Santoro Gutiérrez
mi prima
hija de Ernesto y Marina

Silvia Socorro Santoro Gutiérrez
mi prima (*cousin*)
hija (*daughter*) **de Ernesto y Marina**

Marina Gutiérrez de Santoro
mi tía (*aunt*)
esposa (*wife*) **de Ernesto**

Ernesto Santoro González
mi tío (*uncle*)
hijo (*son*) **de Juan y Socorro**

¡LENGUA VIVA!

In Spanish-speaking countries, it is common for people to go by both their first name and middle name, such as **José Miguel** or **Juan Carlos.** You will learn more about names and naming conventions on p. 86.

Práctica

1 Indicar Write **sí** if the word you hear indicates a family member or **no** if it does not.

1. ____   5. ____
2. ____   6. ____
3. ____   7. ____
4. ____   8. ____

2 Escuchar Indicate whether each statement you hear made by José Miguel Pérez Santoro is **cierto** or **falso**, based on his family tree.

	Cierto	Falso			Cierto	Falso
1.	○	○		5.	○	○
2.	○	○		6.	○	○
3.	○	○		7.	○	○
4.	○	○		8.	○	○

3 Emparejar Match the phrase to the description.

1. Mi hermano programa las computadoras.
2. Son los padres de mi esposo.
3. Es el hijo de mi hermana.
4. Mi tía trabaja en un hospital.
5. Es el hijo de mi madrastra y el hijastro de mi padre.
6. Son los hijos de mis (*my*) tíos.
7. Mi hermanastra enseña en la universidad.
8. Mi primo dibuja y pinta mucho.
9. Es el esposo de mi hija.
10. Mi padre trabaja con planos (*blueprints*).

a. Es médica.
b. Es mi hermanastro.
c. Es programador.
d. Es ingeniero.
e. Son mis suegros.
f. Es mi novio.
g. Es mi padrastro.
h. Son mis primos.
i. Es artista.
j. Es profesora.
k. Es mi sobrino.
l. Es mi yerno.

4 Oraciones Complete each sentence.

abuelo	cuñado	madrastra	nuera
apellidos	gemelas	novia	tío

1. Mi _____ es la esposa de mi hijo.
2. Las muchachas son idénticas porque son _____.
3. El esposo de mi hermana es mi _____.
4. La periodista usa dos _____: Norma *Pardo Alonso.*
5. Es la esposa de mi padre, pero no es mi madre; es mi _____.
6. El padre de mi madre es mi _____.

5

Escoger Complete the description of each photo.

1. La _____ de Sara es grande.

2. Rubén habla con su _____.

3. Maira Díaz es _____.

4. Héctor y Lupita son _____.

5. Irene es _____.

6. Elena Vargas Soto es _____.

6

Definiciones Define these family terms.

> **modelo**
>
> hijastro *Es el hijo de mi esposo/a, pero no es mi hijo.*

1. abuela
2. cuñado
3. suegra
4. primas
5. tío
6. bisabuelo
7. nietos
8. medio hermano

Comunicación

7

Una familia With a classmate, ask each other questions about how each family member is related to Graciela Vargas García.

> **modelo**
> **Estudiante 1:** ¿Quién es Beatriz Pardo de Vargas?
> **Estudiante 2:** Es la abuela de Graciela.

CONSULTA

To see the cities where these family members live, look at the map in **Panorama** on p. 112.

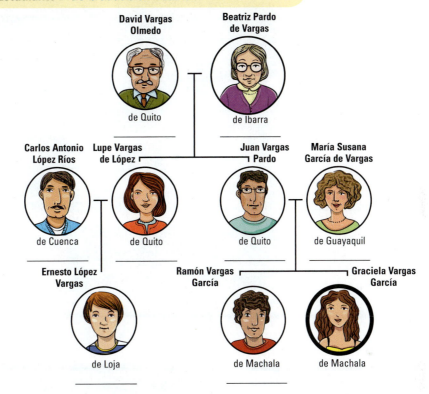

Now take turns asking each other these questions. Then invent three original questions.

1. ¿Cómo se llama el primo de Graciela?
2. ¿Cómo se llama la hija de David y de Beatriz?
3. ¿De dónde es María Susana?
4. ¿De dónde son Ramón y Graciela?
5. ¿Cómo se llama el yerno de David y de Beatriz?
6. ¿De dónde es Carlos Antonio?
7. ¿De dónde es Ernesto?
8. ¿Cuáles son los apellidos del sobrino de Lupe?

8

Preguntas personales With a classmate, take turns asking each other these questions.

1. ¿Cuántas personas hay en tu familia?
2. ¿Cómo se llaman tus padres? ¿De dónde son? ¿Dónde trabajan?
3. ¿Cuántos hermanos tienes? ¿Cómo se llaman? ¿Dónde estudian o trabajan?
4. ¿Cuántos primos tienes? ¿Cuáles son los apellidos de ellos? ¿Cuántos son niños y cuántos son adultos? ¿Hay más chicos o más chicas en tu familia?
5. ¿Eres tío/a? ¿Cómo se llaman tus sobrinos/as? ¿Dónde estudian o trabajan?
6. ¿Quién es tu pariente favorito?
7. ¿Tienes novio/a? ¿Tienes esposo/a? ¿Cómo se llama?

AYUDA

tu, tus *your* (sing., pl.)
mi, mis *my* (sing., pl.)
tienes *you have*
tengo *I have*

Un domingo en familia

Marissa pasa el día en Xochimilco con la familia Díaz.

PERSONAJES

 FELIPE TÍA NAYELI

 Video

JIMENA Hola, tía Nayeli.

TÍA NAYELI ¡Hola, Jimena! ¿Cómo estás?

JIMENA Bien, gracias. Y, ¿dónde están mis primas?

TÍA NAYELI No sé. ¿Dónde están mis hijas? ¡Ah!

MARISSA ¡Qué bonitas son tus hijas! Y ¡qué simpáticas!

MARISSA La verdad, mi familia es pequeña.

SRA. DÍAZ ¿Pequeña? Yo soy hija única. Bueno, y ¿qué más? ¿Tienes novio?

MARISSA No. Tengo mala suerte con los novios.

FELIPE Soy guapo y delgado.

JIMENA Ay, ¡por favor! Eres gordo, antipático y muy feo.

TÍO RAMÓN ¿Tienes una familia grande, Marissa?

MARISSA Tengo dos hermanos mayores, Zack y Jennifer, y un hermano menor, Adam.

MARISSA Tía Nayeli, ¿cuántos años tienen tus hijas?

TÍA NAYELI Marta tiene ocho años y Valentina doce.

JIMENA
 MARTA
 VALENTINA
 SRA. DÍAZ
 TÍO RAMÓN
SR. DÍAZ
MARISSA

SRA. DÍAZ Chicas, ¿compartimos una trajinera?

MARISSA ¡Claro que sí! ¡Qué bonitas son!

SRA. DÍAZ ¿Vienes, Jimena?

JIMENA No, gracias. Tengo que leer.

MARISSA Me gusta mucho este sitio. Tengo ganas de visitar otros lugares en México.

SRA. DÍAZ ¡Debes viajar a Mérida!

TÍA NAYELI ¡Sí, con tus amigos! Debes visitar a Ana María, la hermana de Roberto y de Ramón.

(*La Sra. Díaz habla por teléfono con la tía Ana María.*)

SRA. DÍAZ ¡Qué bien! Excelente. Sí, la próxima semana. Muchísimas gracias.

MARISSA ¡Gracias, Sra. Díaz!
SRA. DÍAZ Tía Ana María.
MARISSA Tía Ana María.
SRA. DÍAZ ¡Un beso, chau!
MARISSA Bye!

Expresiones útiles

Talking about your family

¿Tienes una familia grande?
Do you have a big family?
Tengo dos hermanos mayores y un hermano menor.
I have two older siblings and a younger brother.
La verdad, mi familia es pequeña.
The truth is, my family is small.
¿Pequeña? Yo soy hija única.
Small? I'm an only child.

Describing people

¡Qué bonitas son tus hijas!
Y ¡qué simpáticas!
Your daughters are so pretty!
And so nice!
Soy guapo y delgado.
I'm handsome and slim.
¡Por favor! Eres gordo, antipático y muy feo.
Please! You're fat, unpleasant, and very ugly.

Talking about plans

¿Compartimos una trajinera?
Shall we share a trajinera?
¡Claro que sí! ¡Qué bonitas son!
Of course! They're so pretty!
¿Vienes, Jimena?
Are you coming, Jimena?
No, gracias. Tengo que leer.
No, thanks. I have to read.

Saying how old people are

¿Cuántos años tienen tus hijas?
How old are your daughters?
Marta tiene ocho años y Valentina doce.
Marta is eight and Valentina twelve.

Additional vocabulary

ensayo *essay*
pobrecito/a *poor thing*
próxima *next*
sitio *place*
todavía *still*
trajinera *type of barge*

More activities · vhlcentral · VM pp. 5–6 · Online activities

¿Qué pasó?

1 ¿Cierto o falso? Indicate whether each sentence is **cierto** or **falso**. Correct the false statements.

	Cierto	Falso
1. Marissa dice que (*says that*) tiene una familia grande.	○	○
2. La Sra. Díaz tiene dos hermanos.	○	○
3. Marissa no tiene novio.	○	○
4. Valentina tiene veinte años.	○	○
5. Marissa comparte una trajinera con la Sra. Díaz y la tía Nayeli.	○	○
6. A Marissa le gusta mucho Xochimilco.	○	○

NOTA CULTURAL
Xochimilco is famous for its system of canals and **chinampas**, or artificial islands, which have been used for agricultural purposes since Pre-Hispanic times. In 1987, UNESCO declared **Xochimilco** a World Heritage Site.

2 Identificar Indicate which person says the equivalent of each statement.

1. Felipe es antipático y feo.
2. Mis hermanos se llaman Jennifer, Adam y Zack.
3. ¡Soy un joven muy guapo!
4. Mis hijas tienen ocho y doce años.
5. Me gusta Xochimilco.
6. Ana María es la hermana de Ramón y Roberto.
7. No puedo (*I can't*) compartir una trajinera porque tengo que leer.
8. Tus hijas son bonitas y simpáticas, tía Nayeli.

SRA. DÍAZ   JIMENA

MARISSA   FELIPE

TÍA NAYELI

NOTA CULTURAL
Trajineras are large passenger barges that you can rent in **Xochimilco**. Each boat is named and decorated and has a table and chairs so that passengers can picnic while they ride.

3 Escribir In pairs, choose Marissa, Sra. Díaz, or tía Nayeli and write a brief description of her family. Be creative!

MARISSA   SRA. DÍAZ   TÍA NAYELI

Marissa es de los EE.UU. ¿Cómo es su familia?

La Sra. Díaz es de Cuba. ¿Cómo es su familia?

La tía Nayeli es de México. ¿Cómo es su familia?

4 Conversar With a partner, use these questions to talk about your families.

1. ¿Cuántos años tienes?
2. ¿Tienes una familia grande?
3. ¿Tienes hermanos o hermanas?
4. ¿Cuántos años tiene tu abuelo (tu hermana, tu primo, etc.)?
5. ¿De dónde son tus padres?

AYUDA
Here are some expressions to help you talk about age.
Yo tengo… años.
I am… years old.
Mi abuelo tiene… años.
My grandfather is… years old.

Pronunciación
Diphthongs and linking

 Tutorial

---

hermano   **niña**   **cuñado**

In Spanish, **a**, **e**, and **o** are considered strong vowels. The weak vowels are **i** and **u**.

---

ruido   **parientes**   **periodista**

A diphthong is a combination of two weak vowels or of a strong vowel and a weak vowel. Diphthongs are pronounced as a single syllable.

mi hijo   **una clase excelente**

Two identical vowel sounds that appear together are pronounced like one long vowel.

la abuela

---

con Natalia   **sus sobrinos**   **las sillas**

Two identical consonants together sound like a single consonant.

---

es ingeniera   **mis abuelos**   **sus hijos**

A consonant at the end of a word is linked with the vowel sound at the beginning of the next word.

---

mi hermano   **su esposa**   **nuestro amigo**

A vowel at the end of a word is linked with the vowel sound at the beginning of the next word.

Práctica Say these words aloud, focusing on the diphthongs.

1. historia	5. residencia	9. lenguas
2. nieto	6. prueba	10. estudiar
3. parientes	7. puerta	11. izquierda
4. novia	8. ciencias	12. ecuatoriano

Oraciones Read these sentences aloud to practice diphthongs and linking words.

1. Hola. Me llamo Anita Amaral. Soy del Ecuador.
2. Somos seis en mi familia.
3. Tengo dos hermanos y una hermana.
4. Mi papá es del Ecuador y mi mamá es de España.

Refranes Read these sayings aloud to practice diphthongs and linking sounds.

Cuando una puerta se cierra, otra se abre.[1]

Hablando del rey de Roma, por la puerta se asoma.[2]

1 When one door closes, another opens. 2 Speak of the devil and he will appear.

More activities

vhlcentral   LM   p. 14

¿Cómo te llamas?

In the Spanish-speaking world, it is common to have two last names: one paternal and one maternal. In some cases, the conjunctions **de** or **y** are used to connect the two. For example, in the name **Juan Martínez de Velasco,** *Martínez* is the paternal surname (**el apellido paterno**), and *Velasco* is the maternal surname (**el apellido materno**); **de** simply links the two. This convention of using two last names (**doble apellido**) is a European tradition that Spaniards brought to the Americas. It continues to be practiced in many countries, including Chile, Colombia, Mexico, Peru, and Venezuela. There are exceptions, however. In Argentina, the prevailing custom is for children to inherit only the father's last name.

When a woman marries in a country where two last names are used, legally she retains her two maiden surnames. However, socially she may take her husband's paternal surname in place of her inherited maternal surname. For example, **Mercedes**

Gabriel García Márquez   Mercedes Barcha Pardo

Rodrigo García Barcha

Barcha Pardo, late wife of Colombian writer **Gabriel García Márquez,** might have used the names **Mercedes Barcha García** or **Mercedes Barcha de García** in social situations (although officially her name remained **Mercedes Barcha Pardo**). Adopting a husband's last name for social purposes, though widespread, is only legally recognized in Ecuador and Peru.

Most parents do not break tradition upon naming their children; regardless of the surnames the mother uses, they use the father's first surname followed by the mother's first surname, as in the name **Rodrigo García Barcha**. However, one should note that both surnames come from the grandfathers, and therefore all **apellidos** are effectively paternal.

Hijos en la casa

In Spanish-speaking countries, family and society place very little pressure on young adults to live on their own (**independizarse**), and children often live with their parents well into their thirties. For example, about 60% of Spaniards under 34 years of age live at home with their parents. This delay in moving out is both cultural and economic—lack of job security or low wages coupled with a high cost of living may make it impractical for young adults to live independently before they marry.

ACTIVIDADES

1 **¿Cierto o falso?** Indicate whether these statements are **cierto** or **falso**. Correct the false statements.

1. Most Spanish-speaking people have three last names.

2. Hispanic last names generally consist of the paternal last name followed by the maternal last name.

3. It is common to see **de** or **y** used in a Hispanic last name.

4. Someone from Argentina would most likely have two last names.

5. Generally, married women legally retain two maiden surnames.

6. In social situations, a married woman often uses her husband's last name in place of her inherited paternal surname.

7. Adopting a husband's surname is only legally recognized in Peru and Ecuador.

8. Hispanic last names are effectively a combination of the maternal surnames from the previous generation.

ASÍ SE DICE

Familia y amigos

el/la bisnieto/a	great-grandson/daughter
el/la chamaco/a (Méx.); el/la chamo/a (Ven.); el/la chaval(a) (Esp.); el/la pibe/a (Arg.)	el/la muchacho/a
mi colega (Esp.); mi cuate (Méx.); mi parcero/a (Col.); mi pana (Ven., P. Rico, Rep. Dom.)	my pal; my buddy
la madrina	godmother
el padrino	godfather
el/la tatarabuelo/a	great-great-grandfather/ great-great-grandmother

EL MUNDO HISPANO

Las familias

Although worldwide population trends show a decrease in average family size, households in many Spanish-speaking countries are still larger than their U.S. counterparts.

- **México** 4,0 personas
- **Colombia** 3,4 personas
- **Argentina** 3,6 personas
- **Uruguay** 3,0 personas
- **España** 2,9 personas
- **Estados Unidos** 2,6 personas

PERFIL

Parientes talentosos

Jesse & Joy

Many families have more than one "star" in their midst. **Jesse & Joy** are a brother-and-sister pop music duo from Mexico City. They won a Grammy for Best Latin Pop Album in 2017 for their album *Un besito más*.

One of the world's most famous families has made music a real family affair. Legendary Spanish singer **Julio Iglesias** has recorded albums in 14 different languages and has sold more than 350 million records in a career that spans decades. Following his lead are his sons **Julio Jr.** and **Enrique**, both popular singers in Spain and around the world.

Julio Iglesias

Enrique Iglesias

Julio Iglesias Jr.

CON RITMO HISPANO

Mirella Cesa (1984–)
Birthplace: Guayaquil, Ecuador

Mirella Cesa is known as the "mother of Andipop." Her music is a mix of Latin percussion, Andean instruments, and pop.

Go to **vhlcentral.com** to find out more about **Mirella Cesa** and her music.

ACTIVIDADES

2 Comprensión Complete these sentences.

1. Joy is the _____ of Jesse.
2. In Spanish, your godmother is called _____.
3. Enrique Iglesias is the _____ of Julio Jr.
4. Uruguay's average household has _____ people.
5. If a Venezuelan calls you **mi pana**, you are that person's _____.

3 Una familia famosa Create a genealogical tree of a famous family, using photos or drawings labeled with names and ages. Present the family tree to a classmate and explain who the people are and their relationships to each other.

More activities

vhlcentral

Online activities

3.1 Descriptive adjectives Tutorial

Adjectives are words that describe people, places, and things. In Spanish, descriptive adjectives are used with the verb **ser** to point out characteristics such as nationality, size, color, shape, personality, and appearance.

Forms and agreement of adjectives

COMPARE & CONTRAST

In English, the forms of descriptive adjectives do not change to reflect the gender (masculine/feminine) and number (singular/plural) of the noun or pronoun they describe.

*Juan is **nice**.*   *Elena is **nice**.*   *They are **nice**.*

In Spanish, the forms of descriptive adjectives agree in gender and/or number with the nouns or pronouns they describe.

Juan es simpátic**o**.   Elena es simpátic**a**.   Ellos son simpátic**os**.

▶ Adjectives that end in **-o** have four different forms. The feminine singular is formed by changing the **-o** to **-a**. The plural is formed by adding **-s** to the singular forms.

Masculine		Feminine	
SINGULAR	**PLURAL**	**SINGULAR**	**PLURAL**
el muchach**o** alt**o**	los muchach**os** alt**os**	la muchach**a** alt**a**	las muchach**as** alt**as**

¡Qué bonitas son tus hijas, tía Nayeli!

Felipe es gordo, antipático y muy feo.

▶ Adjectives that end in **-e** or a consonant have the same masculine and feminine forms.

Masculine		Feminine	
SINGULAR	**PLURAL**	**SINGULAR**	**PLURAL**
el chico inteligent**e**	los chicos inteligent**es**	la chica inteligent**e**	las chicas inteligent**es**
el examen difíci**l**	los exámenes difíci**les**	la clase difíci**l**	las clases difíci**les**

▶ Adjectives that end in **-or** are variable in both gender and number.

Masculine		Feminine	
SINGULAR	**PLURAL**	**SINGULAR**	**PLURAL**
el hombre trabajad**or**	los hombres trabajad**ores**	la mujer trabajad**ora**	las mujeres trabajad**oras**

▶ Use the masculine plural form to refer to groups that include males and females.

Manuel es alt**o**.   Lola es alt**a**.   Manuel y Lola son alt**os**.

Common adjectives

alto/a	tall	**gordo/a**	fat	**mucho/a**	much; many; a lot of
antipático/a	unpleasant	**grande**	big		
bajo/a	short (in height)	**guapo/a**	good-looking	**pelirrojo/a**	red-haired
		importante	important	**pequeño/a**	small
bonito/a	pretty	**inteligente**	intelligent	**rubio/a**	blond(e)
bueno/a	good	**interesante**	interesting	**simpático/a**	nice; likeable
delgado/a	thin	**joven**	young	**tonto/a**	foolish
difícil	difficult	**malo/a**	bad	**trabajador(a)**	hard-working
fácil	easy	**mismo/a**	same	**viejo/a**	old
feo/a	ugly	**moreno/a**	brunet(te)		

Adjectives of nationality

▶ Unlike in English, Spanish adjectives of nationality are **not** capitalized. Proper names of countries, however, are capitalized.

Some adjectives of nationality

alemán, alemana	German	**francés, francesa**	French
argentino/a	Argentine	**inglés, inglesa**	English
canadiense	Canadian	**italiano/a**	Italian
chino/a	Chinese	**japonés, japonesa**	Japanese
costarricense	Costa Rican	**mexicano/a**	Mexican
cubano/a	Cuban	**norteamericano/a**	(North) American
ecuatoriano/a	Ecuadorian	**puertorriqueño/a**	Puerto Rican
español(a)	Spanish	**ruso/a**	Russian
estadounidense	from the U.S.		

▶ Adjectives of nationality are formed like other descriptive adjectives. Those that end in **-o** change to **-a** when forming the feminine.

chin**o** ⟶ chin**a**   mexican**o** ⟶ mexican**a**

The plural is formed by adding an **-s** to the masculine or feminine form.

argentin**o** ⟶ argentin**os**   cuban**a** ⟶ cuban**as**

▶ Adjectives of nationality that end in **-e** have only two forms, singular and plural.

canadiens**e** ⟶ canadiens**es**   estadounidens**e** ⟶ estadounidens**es**

▶ To form the feminine of adjectives of nationality that end in a consonant, add **–a**.

alemá**n** ⟶ aleman**a**   españo**l** ⟶ españo**la**
japoné**s** ⟶ japone**sa**   inglé**s** ⟶ ingle**sa**

Position of adjectives

▶ Descriptive adjectives and adjectives of nationality generally follow the nouns they modify.

El niño **rubio** es de España.
The blond boy is from Spain.

La mujer **española** habla inglés.
The Spanish woman speaks English.

▶ Unlike descriptive adjectives, adjectives of quantity precede the modified noun.

Hay **muchos** libros en la biblioteca.
There are many books in the library.

Hablo con **dos** turistas puertorriqueños.
I am talking with two Puerto Rican tourists.

▶ **Bueno/a** and **malo/a** can appear before or after a noun. When placed before a masculine singular noun, the forms are shortened: **bueno ➞ buen; malo ➞ mal**.

Joaquín es un **buen** amigo.
Joaquín es un amigo **bueno**.   ⟶   *Joaquín is a good friend.*

Hoy es un **mal** día.
Hoy es un día **malo**.   ⟶   *Today is a bad day.*

▶ When **grande** appears before a singular noun, it is shortened to **gran**, and the meaning of the word changes: **gran** = *great* and **grande** = *big, large*.

Don Francisco es un **gran** hombre.
Don Francisco is a great man.

La familia de Inés es **grande**.
Inés' family is large.

¡LENGUA VIVA!

Like **bueno** and **grande, santo** (*saint*) is also shortened before masculine nouns (unless they begin with **To-** or **Do-**): **San Francisco, San José** (but: **Santo Tomás, Santo Domingo**). **Santa** is used with names of female saints: **Santa Bárbara, Santa Clara**.

🔗 **¡INTÉNTALO!**   Provide the appropriate forms of the adjectives.

simpático

1. Mi hermano es ___simpático___.
2. La profesora Martínez es _____.
3. Nosotros somos _____.
4. Rosa y Teresa son _____.

difícil

1. La química es ___difícil___.
2. El curso es _____.
3. Las pruebas son _____.
4. Los libros son _____.

alemán

1. Hans es ___alemán___.
2. Marcus y yo somos _____.
3. Mis primas son _____.
4. Mi tía es _____.

guapo

1. Su esposo es ___guapo___.
2. Mis sobrinas son _____.
3. Los padres de ella son _____.
4. Marta es _____.

More activities

vhlcentral

LM
p. 15

WB
pp. 25–26

Online activities

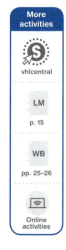

Práctica

1

Emparejar Match the opposites.

A	B
1. guapo	a. delgado
2. alto	b. pequeño
3. joven	c. malo
4. gordo	d. feo
5. moreno	e. viejo
6. grande	f. rubio
7. simpático	g. antipático
	h. bajo

Jorge   Marcos

2

Completar Indicate the nationalities of these people.

1. Penélope Cruz es _____.
▶ 2. Alfonso Cuarón es un gran director de cine de México; es _____.
3. Emma Watson y Daniel Radcliffe son actores _____.
4. Serena Williams y Stephen Curry son _____.
5. Ana de Armas es de La Habana, Cuba; ella es _____.
6. Giorgio Armani es un diseñador de modas (*fashion designer*) _____.
7. Heidi Klum y Michael Fassbender son _____.
8. Ellen Page y Avril Lavigne son _____.

NOTA CULTURAL

Alfonso Cuarón
(1961–) became the
first Mexican winner
of the Best Director
Academy Award for
his film *Gravity* (2013).

3

Describir Describe the family members using as many adjectives as possible.

Josefina Barcos
de Romero

Carlos Romero
Sandoval

Susana Romero
Barcos

Tomás Romero Barcos

Alberto Romero Pereda

1. Susana Romero Barcos es _____.
2. Tomás Romero Barcos es _____.
3. Los dos hermanos son _____.
4. Alberto Romero Pereda es _____.
5. Carlos Romero Sandoval es _____.
6. Josefina Barcos de Romero es _____.
7. Susana y su (*her*) madre son _____.
8. Tomás y su (*his*) padre son _____.

Comunicación

4

¿Cómo es? With a partner, take turns describing each item on the list. Tell your partner whether you agree (**Estoy de acuerdo**) or disagree (**No estoy de acuerdo**) with their descriptions. ◀

> **modelo**
>
> San Francisco
> **Estudiante 1:** San Francisco es una ciudad (city) muy bonita.
> **Estudiante 2:** No estoy de acuerdo. Es muy fea.

1. Nueva York
2. Ryan Gosling
3. las canciones (*songs*) de Taylor Swift
4. el presidente de los Estados Unidos
5. Christopher Nolan
6. la primera dama (*first lady*) de los Estados Unidos
7. el/la profesor(a) de español
8. las personas de Los Ángeles
9. las residencias de mi universidad
10. mi clase de español

AYUDA

Here are some tips to help you complete the descriptions:
- **Ryan Gosling es actor de cine y de televisión.**
- **Taylor Swift es cantante.**
- **Christopher Nolan es director de cine.**

5

Anuncio personal Write a personal ad that describes yourself and your ideal boyfriend, girlfriend, or mate. Then compare your ad with a classmate's. How are you similar and how are you different? Are you looking for the same things in a romantic partner? ◀

AYUDA

casado/a *married*
divorciado/a *divorced*
soltero/a *single; unmarried*

These words and others like them are presented in **Contextos, Lección 9**, p. 302.

★ **SOY ALTA** y bonita.

Soy cubana, de Holguín.
Estudio arte en la universidad.
Busco un chico similar.
Mi novio ideal es alto, inteligente
y muy simpático.

Síntesis

6

Diferencias Your instructor will give you and a partner each a drawing of a family. Describe your version of the drawing to your partner in order to find at least five differences between your picture and your partner's.

> **modelo**
>
> **Estudiante 1:** Susana, la madre, es rubia.
> **Estudiante 2:** No, la madre es morena.

3.2 Possessive adjectives Tutorial

ANTE TODO Possessive adjectives, like descriptive adjectives, are words that are used to qualify people, places, or things. Possessive adjectives express the quality of ownership or possession.

Forms of possessive adjectives

SINGULAR FORMS	PLURAL FORMS	
mi	**mis**	*my*
tu	**tus**	*your* (fam.)
su	**sus**	*his, her, its, your* (form.)
nuestro/a	**nuestros/as**	*our*
vuestro/a	**vuestros/as**	*your* (fam.)
su	**sus**	*their, your*

COMPARE & CONTRAST

In English, possessive adjectives are invariable; that is, they do not agree in gender and number with the nouns they modify. Spanish possessive adjectives, however, do agree in number with the nouns they modify.

my cousin	*my cousins*	*my aunt*	*my aunts*
mi primo	**mis** primos	**mi** tía	**mis** tías

The forms **nuestro** and **vuestro** agree in both gender and number with the nouns they modify.

| nuestr**o** prim**o** | nuestr**os** prim**os** | nuestr**a** tía | nuestr**as** tí**as** |

▶ Possessive adjectives are always placed before the nouns they modify.

—¿Está **tu novio** aquí? —No, **mi novio** está en la biblioteca.
Is your boyfriend here? *No, my boyfriend is in the library.*

▶ Because **su** and **sus** have multiple meanings (*your, his, her, their, its*), you can avoid confusion by using this construction instead: [*article*] + [*noun*] + **de** + [*subject pronoun*].

sus parientes ◀
los parientes **de él/ella** *his/her relatives*
los parientes **de Ud./Uds.** *your relatives*
los parientes **de ellos/ellas** *their relatives*

AYUDA
Look at the context, focusing on nouns and pronouns, to help you determine the meaning of **su(s)**.

More activities

vhlcentral

LM
p. 16

WB
pp. 27–28

Online activities

 ¡INTÉNTALO! Provide the appropriate form of each possessive adjective.

1. Es ___mi___ (*my*) libro.
2. _____ (*My*) familia es ecuatoriana.
3. ____ (*Your*, fam.) esposo es italiano.
4. Es _____ (*her*) reloj.
5. _____ (*Our*) profesor es español.
6. Es _____ (*your*, fam.) mochila.
7. Es _____ (*your*, form.) maleta.
8. ____ (*Their*) sobrina es alemana.

1. ___Sus___ (*Her*) primos son franceses.
2. _____ (*Our*) primos son canadienses.
3. Son _____ (*their*) lápices.
4. _____ (*My*) amigas son inglesas.
5. Son _____ (*our*) plumas.
6. Son _____ (*my*) papeles.
7. _____ (*Their*) nietos son japoneses.
8. Son _____ (*his*) cuadernos.

Práctica

1 **La familia de Manolo** Complete each sentence with the correct possessive adjective. Use the subject of each sentence as a guide.

1. Me llamo Manolo, y _____ (nuestro, mi, sus) hermano es Federico.
2. _____ (Nuestra, Sus, Mis) madre Silvia es profesora y enseña química.
3. Ella admira a _____ (tu, nuestro, sus) estudiantes porque trabajan mucho.
4. Yo estudio en la misma universidad, pero no tomo clases con _____ (mi, nuestras, tus) madre.
5. Federico trabaja en una oficina con _____ (mis, tu, nuestro) padre.
6. _____ (Mi, Su, Tu) oficina está en el centro de la Ciudad de México.
7. Javier y Óscar son _____ (mis, mi, sus) tíos de Oaxaca.
8. ¿Y tú? ¿Cómo es _____ (mi, su, tu) familia?

AYUDA

Remember that possessive adjectives don't agree in number or gender with the owner of an item; they always agree with the item(s) being possessed.

2 **Clarificar** Clarify each sentence with a prepositional phrase. Follow the model.

> **modelo**
>
> Su hermana es muy bonita. (ella)
> **La hermana de ella es muy bonita.**

1. Su casa es muy grande. (ellos) _____
2. Sus padres trabajan en el centro. (ella) _____
3. ¿Cómo se llama su hermano? (ellas) _____
4. Su primo lee los libros. (ellos) _____
5. Maribel es su prima. (ella) _____
6. Sus abuelos son muy simpáticos. (él) _____

3 **¿Dónde está?** With a partner, take turns asking where your belongings are.

> **modelo**
>
> **Estudiante 1:** ¿Dónde está mi mochila?
> **Estudiante 2:** Tu mochila está encima del escritorio.

CONSULTA

For a list of useful prepositions, refer to the table in **Estructura 2.3**, p. 60.

1.

2.

3.

4.

5.

6.

Comunicación

4

Describir With a partner, describe the people and places listed. Make note of any similarities.

> **modelo**
>
> la biblioteca de su universidad
> *La biblioteca de nuestra universidad es muy grande. Hay muchos libros*
> *en la biblioteca. Mis amigos y yo estudiamos en la biblioteca.*

1. tu profesor favorito
2. tu profesora favorita
3. su clase de español
4. la librería de su universidad
5. tus padres
6. tus abuelos
7. tu mejor (*best*) amigo
8. tu mejor amiga
9. su universidad
10. tu país de origen

5

Una familia famosa Assume the identity of a member of a famous family, real or fictional, and write a description of "your" family. Be sure not to use any names! Then, in small groups, take turns reading the descriptions aloud. The other group members may ask follow-up questions to help them identify the famous person.

> **modelo**
>
> **Estudiante 1:** *Soy cantante. Mi padre y mi hermano se llaman Julio.*
> **Estudiante 2:** *¿Eres español?*
> **Estudiante 1:** *Sí.*
> **Estudiante 3:** *¿Eres Enrique Iglesias?*
> **Estudiante 1:** *Sí.*

Síntesis

6

Describe a tu familia Describe your family in several sentences to two classmates (**Mi padre es alto y moreno. Mi madre es delgada y muy bonita. Mis hermanos son...**). They will work together to try to repeat your description (**Su padre es alto y moreno. Su madre...**). If they forget any details, they can ask you questions (**¿Es alto tu hermano?**). Alternate roles until all of you have described your families.

3.3 # Present tense of -er and -ir verbs Tutorial

ANTE TODO   In **Lección 2,** you learned how to form the present tense of regular -ar verbs. You also learned about the importance of verb forms, which change to show who is performing the action. The chart below shows the forms from two other important groups, -er verbs and -ir verbs.

CONSULTA

To review the conjugation of -ar verbs, see **Estructura 2.1**, p. 50.

		comer (to eat)	**escrib**ir (to write)
SINGULAR FORMS	yo	com**o**	escrib**o**
	tú	com**es**	escrib**es**
	Ud./él/ella	com**e**	escrib**e**
PLURAL FORMS	nosotros/as	com**emos**	escrib**imos**
	vosotros/as	com**éis**	escrib**ís**
	Uds./ellos/ellas	com**en**	escrib**en**

Present tense of -er and -ir verbs

▶ **-Er** and **-ir** verbs have very similar endings. Study the preceding chart to detect the patterns that make it easier for you to use them to communicate in Spanish.

Felipe y su tío comen.

Jimena lee.

AYUDA

Here are some tips on learning Spanish verbs:
1) Learn to identify the verb's stem, to which all endings attach.
2) Memorize the endings that go with each verb and verb tense.
3) As often as possible, practice using different forms of each verb in speech and writing.
4) Devote extra time to learning irregular verbs, such as **ser** and **estar**.

▶ Like **-ar** verbs, the **yo** forms of **-er** and **-ir** verbs end in **-o.**

Yo com**o**.   Yo escrib**o**.

▶ Except for the **yo** form, all of the verb endings for **-er** verbs begin with **-e**.

-es	-emos	-en
-e	-éis	

▶ **-Er** and **-ir** verbs have the exact same endings, except in the **nosotros/as** and **vosotros/as** forms.

nosotros ◀ com**emos**   escrib**imos**

vosotros ◀ com**éis**   escrib**ís**

Common -er and -ir verbs

-er verbs		-ir verbs	
aprender (a + *inf.*)	*to learn*	abrir	*to open*
beber	*to drink*	asistir (a)	*to attend*
comer	*to eat*	compartir	*to share*
comprender	*to understand*	decidir (+ *inf.*)	*to decide*
correr	*to run*	describir	*to describe*
creer (en)	*to believe (in)*	escribir	*to write*
deber (+ *inf.*)	*should*	recibir	*to receive*
leer	*to read*	vivir	*to live*

Ellos **corren** en el parque.

Ella **escribe** en su diario.

¡INTÉNTALO! Provide the appropriate present tense forms of these verbs.

correr
1. Graciela ___corre___.
2. Tú _____.
3. Yo _____.
4. Sara y Ana _____.
5. Usted _____.
6. Marcos y yo _____.
7. La gente _____.
8. Ustedes _____.

abrir
1. Ellos ___abren___ la puerta.
2. Carolina _____ la maleta.
3. Yo _____ las ventanas.
4. Usted _____ el cuaderno.
5. Nosotras _____ los libros.
6. Tú _____ la ventana.
7. Ustedes _____ las maletas.
8. Los muchachos _____ los cuadernos.

aprender
1. Él ___aprende___ español.
2. Maribel y yo _____ inglés.
3. Tú _____ japonés.
4. Mi hijo _____ chino.
5. Tú y tu hermanastra _____ francés.
6. Yo _____ alemán.
7. Usted _____ inglés.
8. Nosotros _____ italiano.

More activities

vhlcentral

LM
p. 17

WB
pp. 29–30

Online activities

Práctica

1

Completar   Complete Susana's sentences about her family with the correct forms of the verbs. One of the verbs will remain in the infinitive.

1. Mi familia y yo _____ (vivir) en Mérida, Yucatán.
2. Tengo muchos libros. Me gusta _____ (leer).
3. Mi hermano Alfredo es muy inteligente. Alfredo _____ (asistir) a clases los lunes, miércoles y viernes.
4. Los martes y jueves Alfredo y yo _____ (correr) en el Parque del Centenario.
5. Mis padres _____ (comer) mucha lasaña los domingos y se quedan dormidos (*they fall asleep*).
6. Yo _____ (creer) que (*that*) mis padres deben comer menos (*less*).

2

Oraciones   Form complete sentences by adding any other necessary elements.

> **modelo**
>
> yo / correr / amigos / lunes y miércoles
> *Yo corro con mis amigos los lunes y miércoles.*

1. Manuela / asistir / clase / yoga
2. Isabel y yo / leer / biblioteca
3. Sofía y Roberto / aprender / hablar / inglés
4. Eugenio / abrir / correo electrónico (*e-mail*)
5. tú / comer / cafetería / universidad
6. mi novia y yo / compartir / libro de historia

3

Consejos   In pairs, say what Mario and/or his family members are doing or should do to adjust to living in Japan for a year to learn Japanese. Then, create one more sentence using a verb not on the list.

> **modelo**
>
> recibir libros / deber practicar japonés
> **Estudiante 1:** *Mario y su esposa reciben muchos libros en japonés.*
> **Estudiante 2:** *Los hijos deben practicar japonés.*

aprender japonés	decidir explorar el país
asistir a clases	escribir listas de palabras en japonés
beber sake	leer novelas japonesas
deber comer cosas nuevas	vivir con una familia japonesa

Comunicación

4

Entrevista In pairs, use these questions to interview each other.

1. ¿Dónde comes al mediodía? ¿Comes mucho?
2. ¿Cuándo asistes a tus clases?
3. ¿Cuál es tu clase favorita? ¿Por qué?
4. ¿Dónde vives?
5. ¿Con quién vives?
6. ¿Qué cursos debes tomar el próximo (*next*) semestre?
7. ¿Recibes muchos mensajes de texto (*text messages*)? ¿De quién(es)?
8. ¿Crees en fantasmas (*ghosts*)?

5

¿Acción o descripción? In small groups, take turns choosing a verb. Then choose to act out the verb or give a description. The other members of the group will say what you are doing. Be creative!

abrir (un libro, una puerta, una mochila)

aprender (a bailar, a hablar francés, a dibujar)

asistir (a una clase de yoga, a un concierto de rock, a una clase interesante)

beber (agua, Coca-Cola)

comer (pasta, un sándwich, pizza)

compartir (un libro, un sándwich)

correr (en el parque, en un maratón)

escribir (una composición, un mensaje de texto [*text message*], con lápiz)

leer (una carta [*letter*] de amor, un mensaje electrónico [*e-mail message*], un periódico [*newspaper*])

recibir un regalo (*gift*)

¿?

modelo

Estudiante 1: (*pantomimes typing on a keyboard*)
Estudiante 2: ¿Escribes un mensaje electrónico?
Estudiante 1: Sí.

modelo

Estudiante 1: Soy estudiante y tomo muchas clases. Vivo en Roma.
Estudiante 2: ¿Comes pasta?
Estudiante 1: No, no como pasta.
Estudiante 3: ¿Aprendes a hablar italiano?
Estudiante 1: ¡Sí!

Síntesis

6

Horario Your instructor will give you and a partner incomplete versions of Alicia's schedule. Fill in the missing information on the schedule by talking to your partner.

3.4 Present tense of **tener** and **venir** Tutorial

ANTE TODO The verbs **tener** (*to have*) and **venir** (*to come*) are among the most frequently used in Spanish. Because most of their forms are irregular, you will have to learn each one individually.

		tener	**ven**ir
SINGULAR FORMS	yo	ten**go**	ven**go**
	tú	tien**es**	vien**es**
	Ud./él/ella	tien**e**	vien**e**
PLURAL FORMS	nosotros/as	ten**emos**	ven**imos**
	vosotros/as	ten**éis**	ven**ís**
	Uds./ellos/ellas	tien**en**	vien**en**

The verbs **tener** and **venir**

▶ The endings are the same as those of regular **-er** and **-ir** verbs, except for the **yo** forms, which are irregular: **tengo, vengo.**

▶ In the **tú, Ud.,** and **Uds.** forms, the **e** of the stem changes to **ie,** as shown below.

INFINITIVE	VERB STEM	VERB FORM
tener ⟶	ten- ⟶	tú ti**e**nes
		Ud./él/ella ti**e**ne
		Uds./ellos/ellas ti**e**nen
venir ⟶	ven- ⟶	tú vi**e**nes
		Ud./él/ella vi**e**ne
		Uds./ellos/ellas vi**e**nen

¿Tienes una familia grande, Marissa?

No, tengo una familia pequeña.

▶ Only the **nosotros** and **vosotros** forms are regular. Compare them to the forms of **comer** and **escribir** that you learned on page 96.

	tener	**comer**	**venir**	**escribir**
nosotros/as	ten**emos**	com**emos**	ven**imos**	escrib**imos**
vosotros/as	ten**éis**	com**éis**	ven**ís**	escrib**ís**

▶ In certain idiomatic or set expressions in Spanish, you use the construction **tener** + [*noun*] to express *to be* + [*adjective*]. This chart contains a list of the most common expressions with **tener**.

Expressions with tener

tener... años	*to be... years old*	**tener (mucha) prisa**	*to be in a (big) hurry*
tener (mucho) calor	*to be (very) hot*	**tener razón**	*to be right*
tener (mucho) cuidado	*to be (very) careful*	**no tener razón**	*to be wrong*
tener (mucho) frío	*to be (very) cold*	**tener (mucha) sed**	*to be (very) thirsty*
tener (mucha) hambre	*to be (very) hungry*	**tener (mucho) sueño**	*to be (very) sleepy*
tener (mucho) miedo (de)	*to be (very) afraid/ scared (of)*	**tener (mucha) suerte**	*to be (very) lucky*

—¿**Tienen** hambre ustedes?
Are you hungry?

—Sí, y **tenemos** sed también.
Yes, and we're thirsty, too.

▶ To express an obligation, use **tener que** (*to have to*) + [*infinitive*].

—¿Qué **tienes que** estudiar hoy?
What do you have to study today?

—**Tengo que** estudiar biología.
I have to study biology.

▶ To ask people if they feel like doing something, use **tener ganas de** (*to feel like*) + [*infinitive*].

—¿**Tienes ganas de** comer?
Do you feel like eating?

—No, **tengo ganas de** dormir.
No, I feel like sleeping.

miciudad.com
Usted tiene que visitarnos.

More activities

vhlcentral

LM
p. 18

WB
pp. 31–32

Online activities

 ¡INTÉNTALO! Provide the appropriate forms of **tener** and **venir**.

tener

1. Ellos ___tienen___ dos hermanos.
2. Nosotros _____ diez tíos.
3. El artista _____ tres primos.
4. Yo _____ una hermana.
5. Eva y Diana _____ un sobrino.
6. Usted _____ cinco nietos.
7. Tú _____ dos hermanastras.
8. Ustedes _____ cuatro hijos.
9. Ella _____ una hija.

venir

1. Mis padres ___vienen___ de México.
2. Yo _____ de Francia.
3. Nosotras _____ de Cuba.
4. Pepe _____ de Italia.
5. Tú _____ de España.
6. Ustedes _____ de Canadá.
7. Alfonso y yo _____ de Portugal.
8. Ellos _____ de Alemania.
9. Usted _____ de Venezuela.

Práctica

1

Emparejar Match the items to the most appropriate expressions with **tener**. Then, come up with a new item that corresponds with the leftover expression in column B.

A	B
1. el Polo Norte	a. tener calor
2. una sauna	b. tener sed
3. una dieta	c. tener frío
4. un abuelo	d. tener razón
5. la comida salada (*salty food*)	e. tener ganas de
6. una persona muy inteligente	f. tener hambre
	g. tener 75 años

2

Completar Complete the sentences with the correct forms of **tener** or **venir**.

1. Hoy nosotros _____ una reunión familiar (*family reunion*).
2. Todos mis parientes _____, excepto mi tío Manolo y su esposa.
3. Ellos no _____ ganas de venir porque viven en Portoviejo.
4. Yo _____ en autobús de la Universidad de Quito.
5. Mi prima Susana y su novio no _____ hasta las ocho porque ella _____ que trabajar.
6. En las fiestas, mi hermana siempre (*always*) _____ muy tarde (*late*).
7. Nosotros _____ mucha suerte porque las reuniones son divertidas (*fun*).
8. Mi madre cree que mis sobrinos son muy simpáticos. Creo que ella _____ razón.

3

Describir Describe what these people are doing or feeling using an expression with **tener**.

1. _____ 2. _____ 3. _____

4. _____ 5. _____ 6. _____

Comunicación

4

¿Sí o no? Indicate whether these statements apply to you by checking either **Sí** or **No**.

	Sí	No
1. Mi padre tiene 50 años.	○	○
2. Mis amigos vienen a mi casa todos los días (*every day*).	○	○
3. Vengo a la universidad los martes.	○	○
4. Tengo hambre.	○	○
5. Tengo dos computadoras.	○	○
6. Tengo sed.	○	○
7. Tengo que estudiar los domingos.	○	○
8. Tengo una familia grande.	○	○

Now interview a classmate by transforming each statement into a question.

> **modelo**
>
> **Estudiante 1:** ¿Tiene tu padre 50 años?
> **Estudiante 2:** No, no tiene 50 años. Tiene 65.

5

Preguntas Get together with a classmate and ask each other these questions.

1. ¿Tienes que estudiar hoy?
2. ¿Cuántos años tienes? ¿Y tus hermanos/as?
3. ¿Cuándo vienes a la clase de español?
4. ¿Cuándo vienen tus amigos a tu casa, apartamento o residencia estudiantil?
5. ¿De qué tienes miedo? ¿Por qué?
6. ¿Qué tienes ganas de hacer esta noche (*tonight*)?

6

Conversación Use an expression with **tener** to hint at what's on your mind. Your partner will ask questions to find out why you feel that way. If your partner cannot guess what's on your mind after three attempts, tell him/her. Then switch roles.

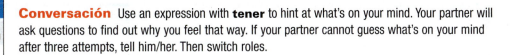

estar cerca/lejos de la ventana   no beber/desayunar/descansar
hablar/cantar en público   tener una clase/un examen/buenos amigos

> **modelo**
>
> **Estudiante 1:** Tengo miedo.
> **Estudiante 2:** ¿Tienes que hablar en público?
> **Estudiante 1:** No.
> **Estudiante 2:** ¿Tienes un examen hoy?
> **Estudiante 1:** Sí, y no tengo tiempo para estudiar.

Síntesis

7

Minidrama Act out this situation with a partner: you are introducing your boyfriend/girlfriend to your extended family. To avoid any surprises before you go, talk about who is coming and what each family member is like. Switch roles.

Recapitulación

Review the grammar concepts you have learned in this lesson by completing these activities.

1 Adjetivos
Complete each phrase with the appropriate adjective. Make all necessary changes. **12 pts.**

antipático	interesante	mexicano
difícil	joven	moreno

1. Mi tía es _____. Vive en Guadalajara.
2. Mi primo no es rubio, es _____.
3. Mi novio cree que la clase no es fácil; es _____.
4. Los libros son _____; me gustan mucho.
5. Mis hermanos son _____; no tienen muchos amigos.
6. Las gemelas tienen quince años. Son _____.

2 Completar
For each set of sentences, provide the appropriate form of the verb **tener** and the possessive adjective. Follow the model. **24 pts.**

> **modelo**
> Él *tiene* un libro. Es *su* libro.

1. Esteban y Julio _____ una tía. Es _____ tía.
2. Yo _____ muchos amigos. Son _____ amigos.
3. Tú _____ tres primas. Son _____ primas.
4. María y tú _____ un hermano. Es _____ hermano.
5. Nosotras _____ unas mochilas. Son _____ mochilas.
6. Usted _____ dos sobrinos. Son _____ sobrinos.

3 Oraciones
Arrange the words in the correct order to form complete logical sentences. **¡Ojo!** Don't forget to conjugate the verbs. **10 pts.**

1. libros / unos / tener / interesantes / tú / muy
   _____
2. dos / leer / fáciles / compañera / tu / lecciones
   _____
3. mi / francés / ser / amigo / buen / Hugo
   _____
4. ser / simpáticas / dos / personas / nosotras
   _____
5. a / clases / menores / mismas / sus / asistir / hermanos / las
   _____

RESUMEN GRAMATICAL

3.1 Descriptive adjectives   *pp. 88–90*

Forms and agreement of adjectives

Masculine		Feminine	
Singular	Plural	Singular	Plural
alto	altos	alta	altas
inteligente	inteligentes	inteligente	inteligentes
trabajador	trabajadores	trabajadora	trabajadoras

▶ Descriptive adjectives follow the noun:
  el chico rubio

▶ Adjectives of nationality also follow the noun:
  la mujer española

▶ Adjectives of quantity precede the noun:
  muchos libros, dos turistas

▶ When placed before a masculine singular noun, these adjectives are shortened.

  bueno → buen   malo → mal

▶ When placed before a singular noun, **grande** is shortened to **gran**.

3.2 Possessive adjectives   *p. 93*

Singular		Plural	
mi	nuestro/a	mis	nuestros/as
tu	vuestro/a	tus	vuestros/as
su	su	sus	sus

3.3 Present tense of -er and -ir verbs   *pp. 96–97*

com**er**		escrib**ir**	
como	comemos	escribo	escribimos
comes	coméis	escribes	escribís
come	comen	escribe	escriben

3.4 Present tense of tener and venir   *pp. 100–101*

tener		venir	
tengo	tenemos	vengo	venimos
tienes	tenéis	vienes	venís
tiene	tienen	viene	vienen

4 **Carta** Complete this letter with the correct forms of the appropriate verbs. `20 pts.`

abrir	correr	recibir
asistir	creer	tener
compartir	escribir	venir
comprender	leer	vivir

Hola, Ángel:

¿Qué tal? (Yo) (1) _____ esta carta (this letter) en la biblioteca. Todos los días (2) _____ aquí y (3) _____ un buen libro. Yo (4) _____ que es importante leer por diversión. Mi compañero de apartamento no (5) _____ por qué me gusta leer. Él sólo (6) _____ los libros de texto. Pero nosotros (7) _____ unos intereses. Por ejemplo, los dos somos atléticos; por las mañanas nosotros (8) _____. También nos gustan las ciencias; por las tardes (9) _____ a nuestra clase de biología. Y tú, ¿cómo estás? ¿(Tú) (10) _____ mucho trabajo (work)?

5 **Su familia** Write a brief description of a friend's family. Describe the family members using vocabulary and structures from this lesson. Write at least five sentences. `34 pts.`

modelo

La familia de mi amiga Gabriela es grande. Ella tiene tres hermanos y una hermana. Su hermana mayor es periodista...

6 **Proverbio** Complete this proverb with the correct forms of the verbs. `4 EXTRA points!`

" Dos andares° _____ (tener) el dinero°,
_____ (venir) despacio°
y se va° ligero°. "

andares *speeds* dinero *money* despacio *slowly*
se va *it leaves* ligero *quickly*

Lectura

Antes de leer

Estrategia

Guessing meaning from context

As you read in Spanish, you'll often come across words you haven't learned. You can guess what they mean by looking at the surrounding words and sentences. Look at the following text and guess what **tía abuela** means, based on the context.

¡Hola, Claudia!
¿Qué hay de nuevo?
¿Sabes qué? Ayer fui a ver a mi tía abuela, la hermana de mi abuela. Tiene 85 años, pero es muy independiente. Vive en un apartamento en Quito con su prima Lorena, quien también tiene 85 años.

If you guessed *great-aunt*, you are correct, and you can conclude from this word and the format clues that this is a letter about someone's visit with his or her great-aunt.

Examinar el texto

Quickly read through the paragraphs and find two or three words you don't know. Using the context as your guide, guess what these words mean. Then glance at the paragraphs where these words appear and try to predict what the paragraphs are about.

Examinar el formato

Look at the format of the reading. What clues do the captions, photos, and layout give you about its content?

Gente··· Las familias

1. Me llamo Armando y tengo setenta años, pero no me considero viejo. Tengo seis nietas y un nieto. Vivo con mi hija y tengo la oportunidad de pasar mucho tiempo con ella y con mi nieto. Por las tardes salgo a pasear° por el parque con él y por la noche le leo cuentos°.

Armando. Tiene seis nietas y un nieto.

2. Mi prima Victoria y yo nos llevamos muy bien. Estudiamos juntas° en la universidad y compartimos un apartamento. Ella es muy inteligente y me ayuda° con los estudios. Además°, es muy simpática y generosa. Si necesito cualquier° cosa, ¡ella me la compra!

Diana. Vive con su prima.

3. Me llamo Ramona y soy paraguaya, aunque° ahora vivo en los Estados Unidos. Tengo tres hijos, uno de nueve años, uno de doce y el mayor de quince. Es difícil a veces, pero mi esposo y yo tratamos° de ayudarlos y comprenderlos siempre°.

Ramona. Sus hijos son muy importantes para ella.

4. Tengo mucha suerte. Aunque mis padres están divorciados, tengo una familia muy unida. Tengo dos hermanos y dos hermanas. Me gusta hablar y salir a fiestas con ellos. Ahora tengo novio en la universidad y él no conoce a mis hermanos. ¡Espero que se lleven bien!

Ana María. Su familia es muy unida.

5. Antes quería° tener hermanos, pero ya no° es tan importante. Ser hijo único tiene muchas

ventajas°: no tengo que compartir mis cosas con hermanos, no hay discusiones° y, como soy nieto único también, ¡mis abuelos piensan° que soy perfecto!

Fernando.
Es hijo único.

6. Como soy joven todavía°, no tengo ni esposa ni hijos. Pero tengo un sobrino, el hijo de mi hermano, que es muy especial para mí. Se llama Benjamín y tiene diez años. Es un muchacho muy simpático. Siempre tiene hambre y por lo tanto vamos° frecuentemente a comer hamburguesas. Nos gusta también ir al cine° a ver películas de acción.
Hablamos de todo. ¡Creo que ser tío es mejor que ser padre!

Santiago. Cree que ser tío es divertido.

salgo a pasear *I go take a walk* cuentos *stories* juntas *together*
e ayuda *she helps me* Además *Besides* cualquier *any* aunque *although*
tamos *we try* siempre *always* quería *I wanted* ya no *no longer*
ventajas *advantages* discusiones *arguments* piensan *think* todavía *still*
vamos *we go* ir al cine *to go to the movies*

Después de leer

Emparejar
Glance at the paragraphs and see how these words and phrases are used in context. Then find their English equivalents.

A
1. me la compra
2. nos llevamos bien
3. no conoce
4. películas
5. mejor que
6. el mayor

B
a. the oldest
b. movies
c. the youngest
d. buys it for me
e. borrows it from me
f. we see each other
g. doesn't know
h. we get along
i. portraits
j. better than

Seleccionar
Choose the sentence that best summarizes each paragraph.

1. Párrafo 1
   a. Me gusta mucho ser abuelo.
   b. No hablo mucho con mi nieto.
   c. No tengo nietos.

2. Párrafo 2
   a. Mi prima es antipática.
   b. Mi prima no es muy trabajadora.
   c. Mi prima y yo somos muy buenas amigas.

3. Párrafo 3
   a. Tener hijos es un gran sacrificio, pero es muy bonito también.
   b. No comprendo a mis hijos.
   c. Mi esposo y yo no tenemos hijos.

4. Párrafo 4
   a. No hablo mucho con mis hermanos.
   b. Comparto mis cosas con mis hermanos.
   c. Mis hermanos y yo somos como (*like*) amigos.

5. Párrafo 5
   a. Me gusta ser hijo único.
   b. Tengo hermanos y hermanas.
   c. Vivo con mis abuelos.

6. Párrafo 6
   a. Mi sobrino tiene diez años.
   b. Me gusta mucho ser tío.
   c. Mi esposa y yo no tenemos hijos.

Escritura

Estrategia

Using idea maps

How do you organize ideas for a first draft? Often, the organization of ideas represents the most challenging part of the process. Idea maps are useful for organizing pertinent information. Here is an example of an idea map you can use:

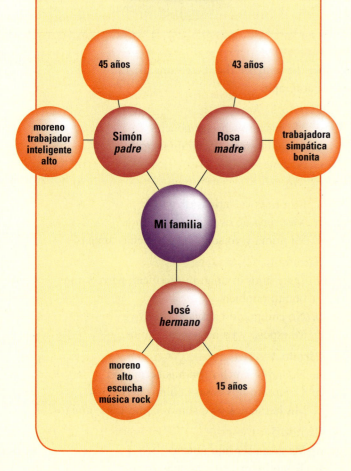

MAPA DE IDEAS

- 45 años
- 43 años
- moreno trabajador inteligente alto
- **Simón** *padre*
- **Rosa** *madre*
- trabajadora simpática bonita
- **Mi familia**
- **José** *hermano*
- moreno alto escucha música rock
- 15 años

Tema

Escribir un mensaje electrónico

A friend you met in a chat room for Spanish speakers wants to know about your family. Using some of the verbs and adjectives you have learned in this lesson, write a brief e-mail describing your family or an imaginary family, including:

▶ Names and relationships

▶ Physical characteristics

▶ Hobbies and interests

Here are some useful expressions for writing an e-mail or letter in Spanish:

Salutations

Estimado/a Julio/Julia:	*Dear Julio/Julia,*
Querido/a Miguel/Ana María:	*Dear Miguel/Ana María,*

Closings

Un abrazo,	*A hug,*
Abrazos,	*Hugs,*
Cariños,	*Much love,*
¡Hasta pronto!	*See you soon!*
¡Hasta la próxima semana!	*See you next week!*

Escuchar
Antes de escuchar

Estrategia
Asking for repetition/ Replaying the recording

Sometimes it is difficult to understand what people say, especially in a noisy environment. During a conversation, you can ask someone to repeat by saying **¿Cómo?** (*What?*) or **¿Perdón?** (*Pardon me?*). In class, you can ask your teacher to repeat by saying **Repita, por favor** (*Repeat, please*). If you don't understand a recorded activity, you can simply replay it.

To help you practice this strategy, you will listen to a short paragraph. Ask your professor to repeat it or replay the recording, and then summarize what you heard.

Preparación

Based on the photograph, where do you think Cristina and Laura are?

Ahora escucha

Adjetivos

Now you are going to hear Laura and Cristina's conversation. Use **R** to indicate which adjectives describe Cristina's boyfriend, Rafael. Use **E** for adjectives that describe Laura's boyfriend, Esteban. Some adjectives will not be used.

___ rubio	___ interesante
___ feo	___ antipático
___ alto	___ inteligente
___ trabajador	___ moreno
___ un poco gordo	___ viejo

Comprensión

Identificar

Which person would make each statement: Cristina or Laura?

	Cristina	Laura
1. Mi novio habla sólo de fútbol y de béisbol.	○	○
2. Tengo un novio muy interesante y simpático.	○	○
3. Mi novio es alto y moreno.	○	○
4. Mi novio trabaja mucho.	○	○
5. Mi amiga no tiene buena suerte con los muchachos.	○	○
6. El novio de mi amiga es un poco gordo, pero guapo.	○	○

¿Cierto o falso?

Indicate whether each sentence is **cierto** or **falso**, then correct the false statements.

	Cierto	Falso
1. Esteban es un chico interesante y simpático.	○	○
2. Laura tiene mala suerte con los chicos.	○	○
3. Rafael es muy interesante.	○	○
4. Laura y su novio hablan de muchas cosas.	○	○

En pantalla Video

With over 440 million native Spanish speakers worldwide and the number growing due to an increasing popularity in learning Spanish, it is not uncommon to hear words that end in **-ito(a)** used not only to denote small size (for example, **niñita** and **pequeñito**), but also to express affection (for example, **abuelita** and **papito**). These words are called diminutives. The use of diminutives can vary by country and region; in some places the diminutive endings **-ico(a)**, **-illo(a)**, and **-uelo(a)** are more commonly used than **-ito(a)**.

Vocabulario útil	
cerraremos	we will close
conjuntito	little outfit
par de zapatitos	little pair of shoes
piecitos	little feet
saquito	little coat
¿Te falta mucho?	Are you almost done?

Preparación

Do you like shopping or spending time in malls? Do you prefer buying things for yourself or for others?

Completar

Complete the sentences.

comprar	hija	regresar
esposo	prisa	zapatitos

1. Marcos es el _____ de Claudia.
2. Claudia compra _____ y otras cosas.
3. Marcos y Claudia tienen una _____.
4. Claudia tiene _____ porque debe _____ pronto a casa.
5. Claudia necesita _____ algo para la beba en diez minutos.

Descripción

Write descriptions of the characters. Then compare your descriptions with a partner's.

¡Un saquito te compró° mamá!

Un par de zapatitos...

Tengo que buscar algo° para la beba, si no, Marcos me mata°.

More activities

vhlcentral   Online activities

compró *bought* algo *something* me mata *is going to kill me*

 Video

If a Spanish-speaking friend told you he was going to a **reunión familiar,** what type of event would you picture? Most likely, your friend would not be referring to an annual event reuniting family members from far-flung cities. In Hispanic culture, family gatherings are much more frequent and relaxed, and thus do not require intensive planning or juggling of schedules. Some families gather every Sunday afternoon to enjoy a leisurely meal; others may prefer to hold get-togethers on a Saturday evening, with food, music, and dancing. In any case, gatherings tend to be laid-back events in which family members spend hours chatting, sharing stories, and telling jokes.

Vocabulario útil

el Día de la Madre	Mother's Day
estamos celebrando	we are celebrating
familia grande y feliz	a big, happy family
familia numerosa	a large family
hacer (algo) juntos	to do (something) together
el patio interior	courtyard
pelear	to fight
reuniones familiares	family gatherings, reunions

Preparación

What is a "typical family" like where you live? Is there such a thing? What members of a family usually live together?

Completar

Complete this paragraph with the correct options.

Los Valdivieso y los Bolaños son dos ejemplos de familias en Ecuador. Los Valdivieso son una familia (1) _____ (difícil/numerosa). Viven en una casa (2) _____ (grande/buena). En el patio, hacen (*they do*) muchas reuniones (3) _____ (familiares/con amigos). Los Bolaños son una familia pequeña. Ellos comen ( ) _____ (separados/juntos) y preparan canelazo, una bebida (*drink*) típica ecuatoriana.

tan *so*

La familia

—Érica, ¿y cómo se llaman tus padres?
—Mi mamá, Lorena y mi papá, Miguel.

¡Qué familia tan° grande tiene!

Te presento a la familia Bolaños.

Ecuador

El país en cifras

▶ **Área:** 283.560 km² (109.483 millas²), *incluyendo las islas Galápagos, aproximadamente el área de Colorado*

▶ **Población:** 16.290.00

▶ **Capital:** Quito—1.726.000

▶ **Ciudades° principales:** Guayaquil—2.709.000, Cuenca, Machala, Portoviejo

▶ **Moneda:** dólar estadounidense

▶ **Idiomas:** español (oficial), quichua
La lengua oficial de Ecuador es el español, pero también se hablan° otras° lenguas en el país. Aproximadamente unos 4.000.000 de ecuatorianos hablan lenguas indígenas; la mayoría° de ellos habla quichua. El quichua es el dialecto ecuatoriano del quechua, la lengua de los incas.

Bandera de Ecuador

Ecuatorianos célebres

▶ **Francisco Eugenio de Santa Cruz y Espejo,** médico, periodista y patriota (1747–1795)

▶ **Juan León Mera,** novelista (1832–1894)

▶ **Eduardo Kingman,** pintor° (1913–1997)

▶ **Rosalía Arteaga,** abogada°, política y ex vicepresidenta (1956–)

▶ **Iván Vallejo Ricaurte,** montañista (1959–)

Ciudades *cities* se hablan *are spoken* otras *other* mayoría *majority* pintor *painter* abogada *lawyer*

Las islas Galápagos

ESTADOS UNIDOS
OCÉANO PACÍFICO
OCÉANO ATLÁNTICO
ECUADOR
AMÉRICA DEL SUR

COLOMBIA

Indígena del Amazonas

Río Esmeraldas

Ibarra

Quito ⭐

Volcán Cotopaxi

Río Napo

Portoviejo

Volcán Tungurahua

Río Daule

Río Pastaza

Guayaquil

Cordillera de los Andes

Volcán Chimborazo

Océano Pacífico

Cuenca

Muchos indígenas de Ecuador hablan quichua.

Machala

Loja

La ciudad de Quito y la cordillera de los Andes

Catedral de Guayaquil

PERÚ

More activities
vhlcentral   WB pp. 33–34   Online activities

ACTIVIDADES

1   **Seleccionar** Escoge la respuesta correcta.

1. ¿Por qué es famoso Oswaldo Guayasamín?
   a. por ser escultor y muralista
   b. por estudiar la evolución de las especies

2. ¿Por qué son famosas las islas Galápagos?
   a. por el monumento la Mitad del Mundo
   b. por las tortugas gigantes

3. ¿Quién es Juan León Mera?
   a. un ingeniero
   b. un novelista

4. Además del español, ¿cuál es la lengua más popular en Ecuador?
   a. el alemán
   b. el quichua

5. ¿Cuál es la moneda oficial de Ecuador?
   a. el dólar estadounidense
   b. el peso ecuatoriano

⊳ Lugares • Las islas Galápagos

Muchas personas vienen de lejos a visitar las islas Galápagos porque son un verdadero tesoro° ecológico. Aquí Charles Darwin estudió° las especies que inspiraron° sus ideas sobre la evolución. Como las Galápagos están lejos del continente, sus plantas y animales son únicos. Las islas son famosas por sus tortugas° gigantes.

Artes • Oswaldo Guayasamín

Oswaldo Guayasamín fue° uno de los artistas latinoamericanos más famosos del mundo. Fue escultor° y muralista. Su expresivo estilo viene del cubismo y sus temas preferidos son la injusticia y la pobreza° sufridas° por los indígenas de su país.

Deportes • El *trekking*

El sistema montañoso de los Andes cruza° y divide Ecuador en varias regiones. La Sierra,que tiene volcanes, grandes valles y una variedad increíble de plantas y animales, es perfecta para el *trekking*. Muchos turistas visitan Ecuador cada° año para hacer° *trekking* y escalar montañas°.

⊳ Lugares • Latitud 0

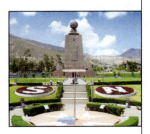

Hay un monumento en Ecuador, a unos 22 kilómetros (14 millas) de Quito, donde los visitantes están en el hemisferio norte y el hemisferio sur a la vez°. Este monumento se llama la Mitad del Mundo° y es un destino turístico muy popular.

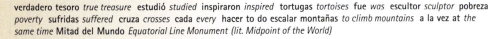

verdadero tesoro *true treasure* estudió *studied* inspiraron *inspired* tortugas *tortoises* fue *was* escultor *sculptor* pobreza *poverty* sufridas *suffered* cruza *crosses* cada *every* hacer *to do* escalar montañas *to climb mountains* a la vez *at the same time* Mitad del Mundo *Equatorial Line Monument (lit. Midpoint of the World)*

¡Increíble pero cierto!

El volcán Cotopaxi, situado a unos 50 kilómetros al sur° de Quito, es considerado uno de los volcanes activos más altos del mundo°. Tiene una altura de 5.897 metros (19.340 pies°). Es dos veces más alto que° el monte Santa Elena (2.550 metros o 9.215 pies) en el estado de Washington.

sur *south* mundo *world* pies *feet* dos veces más alto que *twice as tall as*

2 **¿Qué aprendiste?** Completa las oraciones.

1. La ciudad más grande (*biggest*) de Ecuador es _____.
2. La capital de Ecuador es _____.
3. Unos 4.000.000 de ecuatorianos hablan _____.
4. Un monumento muy popular es _____.
5. La Sierra es un lugar perfecto para el _____.

3 **Conversar** En parejas, describan uno de los lugares más importantes de Ecuador y expliquen por qué creen que es interesante.

 modelo

La Mitad del Mundo es un lugar fantástico. Es interesante porque...

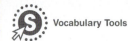
La familia

el/la abuelo/a	grandfather/grandmother
los abuelos	grandparents
el apellido	last name
el/la bisabuelo/a	great-grandfather/great-grandmother
el/la cuñado/a	brother-in-law/sister-in-law
el/la esposo/a	husband/wife; spouse
la familia	family
el/la gemelo/a	twin
el/la hermanastro/a	stepbrother/stepsister
el/la hermano/a	brother/sister
el/la hijastro/a	stepson/stepdaughter
el/la hijo/a	son/daughter
los hijos	children
la madrastra	stepmother
la madre	mother
el/la medio/a hermano/a	half-brother/half-sister
el/la nieto/a	grandson/granddaughter
la nuera	daughter-in-law
el padrastro	stepfather
el padre	father
los padres	parents
los parientes	relatives
el/la primo/a	cousin
el/la sobrino/a	nephew/niece
el/la suegro/a	father-in-law/mother-in-law
el/la tío/a	uncle/aunt
el yerno	son-in-law

Otras personas

el/la amigo/a	friend
la gente	people
el/la muchacho/a	boy/girl
el/la niño/a	child
el/la novio/a	boyfriend/girlfriend
la persona	person

Profesiones

el/la artista	artist
el/la doctor(a), el/la médico/a	doctor; physician
el/la ingeniero/a	engineer
el/la periodista	journalist
el/la programador(a)	computer programmer

Adjetivos

alto/a	tall
antipático/a	unpleasant
bajo/a	short (in height)
bonito/a	pretty
buen, bueno/a	good
delgado/a	thin
difícil	difficult
fácil	easy
feo/a	ugly
gordo/a	fat
grande	big
guapo/a	good-looking
importante	important
inteligente	intelligent
interesante	interesting
joven (sing.), jóvenes (pl.)	young
mal, malo/a	bad
mismo/a	same
moreno/a	brunet(te)
mucho/a	much; many; a lot of
pelirrojo/a	red-haired
pequeño/a	small
rubio/a	blond(e)
simpático/a	nice; likeable
tonto/a	foolish
trabajador(a)	hard-working
viejo/a	old

Nacionalidades

alemán, alemana	German
argentino/a	Argentine
canadiense	Canadian
chino/a	Chinese
costarricense	Costa Rican
cubano/a	Cuban
ecuatoriano/a	Ecuadorian
español(a)	Spanish
estadounidense	from the U.S.
francés, francesa	French
inglés, inglesa	English
italiano/a	Italian
japonés, japonesa	Japanese
mexicano/a	Mexican
norteamericano/a	(North) American
puertorriqueño/a	Puerto Rican
ruso/a	Russian

Verbos

abrir	to open
aprender (a + inf.)	to learn
asistir (a)	to attend
beber	to drink
comer	to eat
compartir	to share
comprender	to understand
correr	to run
creer (en)	to believe (in)
deber (+ inf.)	should
decidir (+ inf.)	to decide
describir	to describe
escribir	to write
leer	to read
recibir	to receive
tener	to have
venir	to come
vivir	to live

Possessive adjectives	See page 93.
Expressions with *tener*	See page 101.
Expresiones útiles	See page 83.

Los pasatiempos

4

🔍 A PRIMERA VISTA

- ¿Es esta persona una atleta o una artista?
- ¿Tiene cuidado?
- ¿Es vieja? ¿Es delgada?
- ¿Tiene frío o calor?

Los pasatiempos

Más vocabulario

el baloncesto	basketball
el béisbol	baseball
el ciclismo	cycling
el esquí (acuático)	(water) skiing
el fútbol americano	football
el hockey	hockey
la natación	swimming
el equipo	team
el parque	park
el partido	game; match
la piscina	swimming pool
la plaza	city or town square
bucear	to scuba dive
escalar montañas (f., pl.)	to climb mountains
esquiar	to ski
ganar	to win
ir de excursión	to go on a hike
nadar	to swim
patinar	to skate
practicar deportes (m., pl.)	to play sports
visitar monumentos (m., pl.)	to visit monuments
escribir una carta/ un mensaje electrónico	to write a letter/ an e-mail
leer el correo electrónico	to read e-mail
leer el periódico	to read the newspaper
deportivo/a	sports-related

Variación léxica

piscina	⟷	pileta (*Arg.*); alberca (*Méx.*)
baloncesto	⟷	básquetbol (*Amér. L.*)
béisbol	⟷	pelota (*P. Rico, Rep. Dom.*)

PARQUE MUNICIPAL

Pasean. (pasear)

Pasea en bicicleta. (pasear)

Lee una revista. (leer)

el fútbol

el vóleibol

la pelota

el jugador

la jugadora

el tenis

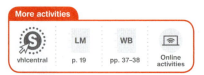

el golf

Anda en patineta.
(andar)

Toma el sol.
(tomar)

Práctica

1 **Indicar** Write **sí** if each activity you hear requires a ball or **no** if does not.

1. ____   5. ____
2. ____   6. ____
3. ____   7. ____
4. ____   8. ____

2 **Escuchar** Indicate the activity that best corresponds to each statement you hear.

A	B

1. _____   a. leer el correo electrónico
2. _____   b. tomar el sol
3. _____   c. ir de excursión
4. _____   d. ir a un partido de fútbol americano
5. _____   e. escribir una carta
6. _____   f. practicar muchos deportes
           g. nadar
           h. pasear en bicicleta

3 **¿Cierto o falso?** Indicate whether each statement is **cierto** or **falso** based on the illustration.

	Cierto	Falso
1. Una persona pasea en bicicleta.	○	○
2. Hay un partido de baloncesto.	○	○
3. Las personas viejas esquían.	○	○
4. Hay dos jugadores de vóleibol.	○	○
5. Dos niñas tienen una pelota.	○	○
6. Una mujer lee el periódico.	○	○
7. Hay un equipo de hockey.	○	○
8. Un chico anda en patineta.	○	○

4 **Clasificar** Fill in the chart with as many terms from **Contextos** as you can.

Actividades	Deportes	Personas
_____	_____	_____
_____	_____	_____
_____	_____	_____
_____	_____	_____
_____	_____	_____
_____	_____	_____

En el centro

el gimnasio
el museo
el café
el restaurante
el cine

Más vocabulario

la diversión	fun activity; entertainment; recreation
el fin de semana	weekend
el pasatiempo	pastime; hobby
los ratos libres	spare (free) time
el videojuego	video game
la iglesia	church
el lugar	place
ver películas (f., pl.)	to watch movies
favorito/a	favorite

5

Identificar Identify the place where these activities would take place.

modelo
Esquiamos. **Es una montaña.**

1. Tomamos una limonada.
2. Vemos una película.
3. Practicamos deportes.
4. Hay muchos monumentos.
5. Comemos tacos y fajitas.
6. Nadamos y tomamos el sol.
7. Hay mucho tráfico.
8. Miramos pinturas (*paintings*) de Diego Rivera y Frida Kahlo.

6

Preguntar Ask a classmate what he or she does in the places mentioned. Your classmate will respond using one of the verbs.

modelo
una plaza
Estudiante 1: ¿Qué haces (*do you do*) cuando estás en una plaza?
Estudiante 2: Camino por la plaza y miro a las personas.

beber	escalar	mirar	practicar
caminar	escribir	nadar	tomar
correr	leer	patinar	visitar

1. una biblioteca
2. las montañas
3. un café
4. una piscina
5. un estadio
6. un parque
7. una plaza
8. un museo

Comunicación

7

Crucigrama Your instructor will give you and your partner an incomplete crossword puzzle. Yours has the words your partner needs and vice versa. In order to complete the puzzle, take turns giving each other clues, using definitions, examples, and phrases.

> **modelo**
> **2 horizontal:** Es un deporte que practicamos en la piscina.
> **6 vertical:** Es un mensaje que escribimos con lápiz o con pluma.

8

Entrevista In pairs, take turns asking and answering these questions.

1. ¿Hay un café cerca de la universidad? ¿Dónde está?
2. ¿Cuál es tu restaurante favorito?
3. ¿Te gusta viajar y visitar monumentos? ¿Por qué?
4. ¿Te gusta ir al cine los fines de semana?
5. ¿Cuáles son tus películas favoritas?
6. ¿Te gusta practicar deportes?
7. ¿Cuáles son tus deportes favoritos? ¿Por qué?
8. ¿Cuáles son tus pasatiempos favoritos?

CONSULTA
To review expressions with **gustar**, see **Estructura 2.1**, p. 52.

9

Conversación Work with a partner to prepare a short conversation about pastimes.

| ¿a qué hora? | ¿con quién(es)? | ¿dónde? |
| ¿cómo? | ¿cuándo? | ¿qué? |

> **modelo**
> **Estudiante 1:** ¿Cuándo patinas?
> **Estudiante 2:** Patino los domingos. Y tú, ¿patinas?
> **Estudiante 1:** No, no me gusta patinar. Me gusta practicar el béisbol.

10

Pasatiempos In pairs, tell each other what pastimes three of your friends and family members enjoy. Be prepared to share with the class any pastimes you noticed they have in common.

> **modelo**
> **Estudiante 1:** Mi hermana pasea mucho en bicicleta, pero mis padres practican la natación. Mi hermano no nada, pero visita muchos museos.
> **Estudiante 2:** Mi primo lee muchas revistas, pero no practica muchos deportes. Mis tíos esquían y practican el golf...

Fútbol, cenotes y mole

Maru, Miguel, Jimena y Marissa visitan un cenote, mientras Felipe y Juan Carlos van a un partido de fútbol.

MIGUEL

PABLO

Video

MIGUEL Buenos días a todos.

TÍA ANA MARÍA Hola, Miguel. Maru, ¿qué van a hacer hoy?

MARU Miguel y yo vamos a llevar a Marissa a un cenote.

MARISSA ¿No vamos a nadar? ¿Qué es un cenote?

MIGUEL Sí, sí vamos a nadar. Un cenote... difícil de explicar. Es una piscina natural en un hueco profundo.

MARU ¡Ya vas a ver! Seguro que te va a gustar.

(unos minutos después)

EDUARDO Hay un partido de fútbol en el parque. ¿Quieren ir conmigo?

PABLO Y conmigo. Si no consigo más jugadores, nuestro equipo va a perder.

ANA MARÍA Marissa, ¿qué te gusta hacer? ¿Escalar montañas? ¿Ir de excursión?

MARISSA Sí, me gusta ir de excursión y practicar el esquí acuático. Y usted, ¿qué prefiere hacer en sus ratos libres?

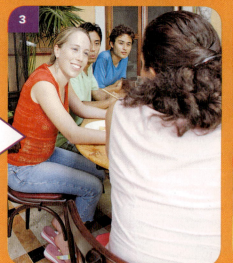

PABLO Mi mamá tiene muchos pasatiempos y actividades.

EDUARDO Sí. Ella nada y juega al tenis y al golf.

PABLO Va al cine y a los museos.

ANA MARÍA Sí, salgo mucho los fines de semana.

FELIPE ¿Recuerdas el restaurante del mole?

EDUARDO ¿Qué restaurante?

JIMENA El mole de mi tía Ana María es mi favorito.

MARU Chicos, ya es hora. ¡Vamos!

ANA MARÍA

MARU

MARISSA

EDUARDO

FELIPE

JUAN CARLOS

JIMENA

DON GUILLERMO

7

(*más tarde, en el parque*)

PABLO No puede ser. ¡Cinco a uno!

FELIPE ¡Vamos a jugar! Si perdemos, compramos el almuerzo. Y si ganamos...

EDUARDO ¡Empezamos!

8

(*mientras tanto, en el cenote*)

MARISSA ¿Hay muchos cenotes en México?

MIGUEL Sólo en la península de Yucatán.

MARISSA ¡Vamos a nadar!

9

(*Los chicos visitan a don Guillermo, un vendedor de paletas heladas.*)

JUAN CARLOS Don Guillermo, ¿dónde podemos conseguir un buen mole?

FELIPE Eduardo y Pablo van a pagar el almuerzo. Y yo voy a pedir un montón de comida.

10

FELIPE Sí, éste es el restaurante. Recuerdo la comida.

EDUARDO Oye, Pablo... No tengo...

PABLO No te preocupes, hermanito.

FELIPE ¿Qué buscas? (*muestra la cartera de Pablo*) ¿Esto?

More activities

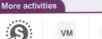

vhlcentral   VM pp. 7–8   Online activities

Expresiones útiles

Making invitations

Hay un partido de fútbol en el parque. ¿Quieren ir conmigo?
There's a soccer game in the park. Do you want to come with me?

¡Yo puedo jugar!
I can play!

Mmm... no quiero.
Hmm... I don't want to.

Lo siento, pero no puedo.
I'm sorry, but I can't.

¡Vamos a nadar!
Let's go swimming!

Sí, vamos.
Yes, let's go.

Making plans

¿Qué van a hacer hoy?
What are you going to do today?

Vamos a llevar a Marissa a un cenote.
We are taking Marissa to a cenote.

Vamos a comprar unas paletas heladas.
We're going to buy some popsicles.

Vamos a jugar. Si perdemos, compramos el almuerzo.
Let's play. If we lose, we'll buy lunch.

Talking about pastimes

¿Qué te gusta hacer? ¿Escalar montañas? ¿Ir de excursión?
What do you like to do? Mountain climbing? Hiking?

Sí, me gusta ir de excursión y practicar esquí acuático.
Yes, I like hiking and water skiing.

Y usted, ¿qué prefiere hacer en sus ratos libres?
And you, what do you like to do in your free time?

Salgo mucho los fines de semana.
I go out a lot on the weekends.

Voy al cine y a los museos.
I go to the movies and to museums.

Additional vocabulary

el/la aficionado/a *fan*
la cartera *wallet*   **el hueco** *hole*
un montón de *a lot of*

¿Qué pasó?

1 **Escoger** Choose the answer that best completes each sentence.

1. Marissa, Maru y Miguel desean _____.
   a. nadar b. correr por el parque c. leer el periódico

2. A Marissa le gusta _____.
   a. el tenis b. el vóleibol c. ir de excursión y practicar esquí acuático

3. A la tía Ana María le gusta _____.
   a. jugar al hockey b. nadar y jugar al tenis y al golf c. hacer ciclismo

4. Pablo y Eduardo pierden el partido de _____.
   a. fútbol b. béisbol c. baloncesto

5. Juan Carlos y Felipe desean _____.
   a. patinar b. esquiar c. comer mole

NOTA CULTURAL

Mole is a typical sauce in Mexican cuisine. It is made from pumpkin seeds, chile, and chocolate, and it is usually served with chicken, beef, or pork. To learn more about **mole**, go to page 272.

2 **Identificar** Identify the person who made each statement.

1. ¿Qué es un cenote? _____

2. Mi mamá tiene muchos pasatiempos y actividades. _____

3. Yo voy a pedir un montón de comida. _____

4. Hay un partido de fútbol en el parque. ¿Quieren ir conmigo? _____

5. Sí, salgo mucho los fines de semana. _____

MARISSA
FELIPE
PABLO
EDUARDO
TÍA ANA MARÍA

NOTA CULTURAL

Cenotes are deep, freshwater sinkholes found in caves throughout the Yucatán peninsula. They were formed in prehistoric times by the erosion and collapse of cave walls. The Mayan civilization considered the **cenotes** sacred, and performed rituals there. Today, they are popular destinations for swimming and diving.

3 **Preguntas** Answer the questions.

1. ¿Qué van a hacer Miguel y Maru?

2. ¿Adónde van Felipe y Juan Carlos mientras sus amigos van al cenote?

3. ¿Quién gana el partido de fútbol?

4. ¿Quiénes van al cenote con Maru y Miguel?

4 **Conversación** With a partner, prepare a conversation in which you talk about pastimes and invite each other to do some activity together. Use these expressions and also look at **Expresiones útiles** on the previous page.

¿A qué hora? *(At) What time?*
contigo *with you*
¿Dónde? *Where?*
No puedo porque... *I can't because...*
Nos vemos a las siete. *See you at seven.*

▶ ¿Eres aficionado/a a...?
▶ ¿Te gusta...?
▶ ¿Por qué no...?
▶ ¿Quieres... conmigo?
▶ ¿Qué vas a hacer esta noche?

Pronunciación

Tutorial

Word stress and accent marks

pe-**lí**-cu-la	e-**di**-fi-**cio**	ver	**yo**

Every Spanish syllable contains at least one vowel. When two vowels are joined in the same syllable they form a **diphthong***. A **monosyllable** is a word formed by a single syllable.

bi-blio-**te**-ca	vi-si-**tar**	**par**-que	**fút**-bol

The syllable of a Spanish word that is pronounced most emphatically is the "stressed" syllable.

pe-**lo**-ta	pis-**ci**-na	**ra**-tos	**ha**-blan

Words that end in **n, s,** or a **vowel** are usually stressed on the next-to-last syllable.

na-ta-**ción**	pa-**pá**	in-**glés**	Jo-**sé**

If words that end in **n, s,** or a **vowel** are stressed on the last syllable, they must carry an accent mark on the stressed syllable.

bai-**lar**	es-pa-**ñol**	u-ni-ver-si-**dad**	tra-ba-ja-**dor**

Words that do not end in **n, s,** or a **vowel** are usually stressed on the last syllable.

béis-bol	**lá**-piz	**ár**-bol	**Gó**-mez

If words that do not end in **n, s,** or a **vowel** are stressed on the next-to-last syllable, they must carry an accent mark on the stressed syllable.

The two vowels that form a diphthong are either both weak or one is weak and the other is strong.

Práctica Pronounce each word, stressing the correct syllable. Then give the word stress rule for each word.

1. profesor
2. Puebla
3. ¿Cuántos?
4. Mazatlán
5. examen
6. ¿Cómo?
7. niños
8. Guadalajara
9. programador
10. México
11. están
12. geografía

Oraciones Read the conversation aloud to practice word stress.

MARINA Hola, Carlos. ¿Qué tal?
CARLOS Bien. Oye, ¿a qué hora es el partido de fútbol?
MARINA Creo que es a las siete.
CARLOS ¿Quieres ir?
MARINA Lo siento, pero no puedo. Tengo que estudiar biología.

Refranes Read these sayings aloud to practice word stress.

En la unión está la fuerza.[2]

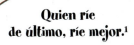

Quien ríe de último, ríe mejor.[1]

More activities

vhlcentral

LM p. 20

1 He who laughs last, laughs best. 2 United we stand.

Real Madrid y Barça: rivalidad total

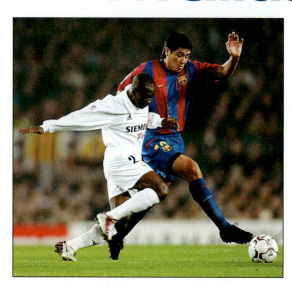

Soccer in Spain is a force to be reckoned with, and no two teams draw more attention than **Real Madrid** and the **Fútbol Club Barcelona.** Whether the venue is Madrid's **Santiago Bernabéu** or Barcelona's **Camp Nou,** the two cities shut down for the showdown, paralyzed by **fútbol** fever. A ticket to the actual game is always the hottest ticket in town.

The rivalry between **Real Madrid** and **Barça** is about more than soccer. As the two biggest, most powerful cities in Spain, Barcelona and Madrid are constantly compared to one another and have a natural rivalry. There is also a political component to the dynamic. Barcelona, with its distinct language and culture, has long struggled for increased autonomy from Madrid's centralized government. Under Francisco Franco's rule (1939–1975), when repression of the Catalan identity was at its height, a game between **Real Madrid** and **FC Barcelona** was wrapped up with all the symbolism of the regime versus the resistance, even though both teams suffered casualties in Spain's civil war and the subsequent Franco dictatorship.

Although the dictatorship is long over, the momentum of all those decades of competition still transforms both cities into a frenzied, tense panic leading up to the game. Once the final score is announced, one of those cities is transformed again, this time into the best party in the country.

Rivalidades del fútbol

Argentina: Boca Juniors vs. River Plate

México: Águilas del América vs. Chivas del Guadalajara

Chile: Colo Colo vs. Universidad de Chile

Guatemala: Comunicaciones vs. Municipal

Uruguay: Peñarol vs. Nacional

Colombia: Millonarios vs. Independiente Santa Fe

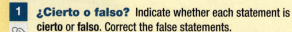
ACTIVIDADES

1 **¿Cierto o falso?** Indicate whether each statement is **cierto** or **falso**. Correct the false statements.

1. People from Spain don't like soccer.
2. Madrid and Barcelona are the most important cities in Spain.
3. Santiago Bernabéu is a stadium in Barcelona.
4. The rivalry between Real Madrid and FC Barcelona is not only in soccer.
5. Barcelona has resisted Madrid's centralized government.
6. Only the FC Barcelona team was affected by the civil war.
7. During Franco's regime, the Catalan culture thrived.
8. There are many famous rivalries between soccer teams in the Spanish-speaking world.
9. River Plate is a popular team from Argentina.
10. Comunicaciones and Peñarol are famous rivals in Guatemala.

Los deportes

el/la árbitro/a	referee
el/la atleta	athlete
la bola; el balón	la pelota
el campeón/ la campeona	champion
la carrera	race
competir	to compete
empatar	to tie
la medalla	medal
el/la mejor	the best
mundial	worldwide
el torneo	tournament

Atletas importantes

World-renowned Hispanic athletes:

- **Rafael Nadal** (España) has won 20 Grand Slam singles titles and the 2008 Olympic gold medal in singles tennis.

- **Lionel Andrés Messi** (Argentina) is one of the world's top soccer players. He plays for **FC Barcelona** and for the Argentine national team.

- **Mireia Belmonte García** (España) won two silver medals in swimming at the 2012 Olympics. She also won a gold and a bronze at the 2016 Olympics.

- **Lorena Ochoa** (México) was the top-ranked female golfer in the world when she retired in 2010 at the age of 28. She still hosts an LPGA golf tournament every year.

Miguel Cabrera y Paola Espinosa

Miguel Cabrera, considered one of the best hitters in baseball, now plays first base for the Detroit Tigers. Born in Venezuela in 1983, he made his Major League debut at the age of 20. Cabrera has been selected for both the National League and American League All-Star Teams. In 2012, he became the first player since 1967 to win the Triple Crown.

Mexican diver **Paola Milagros Espinosa Sánchez**, born in 1986, has competed in four Olympics (2004, 2008, 2012, and 2016). She and her partner Tatiana Ortiz took home a bronze medal in 2008. In 2012, she won a silver medal with partner Alejandra Orozco. She won three gold medals at the Pan American Games in 2007 and again in 2011; in 2015 she won two.

Maná (1987–)
Place of origin: Guadalajara, Mexico

Maná has sold over 40 million copies of its 21 albums worldwide, which makes it the most successful and one of the most influential Latin American rock bands of all time.

Go to **vhlcentral.com** to find out more about **Maná**.

2 Comprensión Write the name of the athlete described in each sentence.

1. Es un jugador de fútbol de Argentina. _____
2. Es una mujer que practica el golf. _____
3. Es un jugador de béisbol de Venezuela. _____
4. Es una mujer mexicana que practica un deporte en la piscina. _____

3 ¿Quién es? Write a short paragraph describing an athlete that you like, but do not mention his/her name. What does he/she look like? What sport does he/she play? Where does he/she live? Read your description to the class to see if they can guess who it is.

More activities

vhlcentral

Online activities

4.1 Present tense of ir Tutorial

ANTE TODO The verb **ir** (*to go*) is irregular in the present tense. Note that, except for the **yo** form (**voy**) and the lack of a written accent on the **vosotros** form (**vais**), the endings are the same as those for regular present tense -**ar** verbs.

The verb ir (*to go*)

Singular forms		Plural forms	
yo	**voy**	nosotros/as	**vamos**
tú	**vas**	vosotros/as	**vais**
Ud./él/ella	**va**	Uds./ellos/ellas	**van**

▶ **Ir** is often used with the preposition **a** (*to*). If **a** is followed by the definite article **el**, they combine to form the contraction **al**. If **a** is followed by the other definite articles (**la, las, los**), there is no contraction.

a + el = al

Voy **al** parque con Juan.
I'm going to the park with Juan.

Mis amigos van **a las** montañas.
My friends are going to the mountains.

▶ The construction **ir a** + [*infinitive*] is used to talk about actions that are going to happen in the future. It is equivalent to the English *to be going* + [*infinitive*].

Va a leer el periódico.
He is going to read the newspaper.

Van a pasear por el pueblo.
They are going to walk around town.

¡Voy a ir con ellos!

Ella va al cine y a los museos.

▶ **Vamos a** + [*infinitive*] can also express the idea of *let's* (*do something*).

Vamos a pasear.
Let's take a walk.

¡**Vamos a** comer!
Let's eat!

CONSULTA

To review the contraction **de + el**, see **Estructura 1.3**, pp. 20–21.

AYUDA

When asking a question that contains a form of the verb **ir**, remember to use **adónde**:

¿Adónde vas?
(To) Where are you going?

More activities

vhlcentral

LM
p. 21

WB
pp. 39–40

Online activities

¡INTÉNTALO! Provide the present tense forms of **ir**.

1. Ellos ___van___.
2. Yo _____.
3. Tu novio _____.
4. Tú _____.
5. Mi prima y yo _____.
6. Adela _____.
7. Ustedes _____.
8. Nosotros _____.
9. Usted _____.
10. Ellas _____.
11. Miguel _____.
12. Nosotras _____.

Práctica

1 ¿Adónde van? Tell where the people are going.

> **modelo**
>
> los chicos / el parque Los chicos van al parque.

1. la señora Castillo / el centro
2. las hermanas Gómez / la piscina
3. yo / el Museo de Arte Moderno
4. tu tío y tu papá / el partido de fútbol
5. nosotros / el restaurante Miramar

2 ¿Qué van a hacer? Use **ir a** + [*infinitive*] to say that these people are also going to do the same activities tomorrow.

> **modelo**
>
> Ellas nadan en la piscina. Van a nadar en la piscina mañana también.

1. Sara lee una revista.
2. Yo practico deportes.
3. Paseamos con nuestros amigos.
4. Tú tomas el sol.
5. Ustedes van de excursión.

3 Preguntas With a partner, take turns asking and answering questions about where the people are going and what they are going to do there.

> **modelo**
>
> **Estudiante 1:** ¿Adónde va Estela?
> **Estudiante 2:** Va a la librería.
> **Estudiante 1:** Va a comprar un libro.

Estela

1. ustedes

2. mi amigo

3. los estudiantes

4. tú

5. la profesora Torres

6. Álex y Miguel

Comunicación

4

Situaciones Work with a partner and say where you and your friends go in these situations.

1. Cuando deseo descansar…
2. Cuando mi novio/a tiene que estudiar…
3. Si deseo hablar con mis amigos…
4. Cuando mis amigos y yo tenemos hambre…
5. En mis ratos libres…
6. Cuando mis amigos desean esquiar…
7. Si estoy de vacaciones…
8. Si tengo ganas de leer…

5

Encuesta Your instructor will give you a worksheet. Walk around the class and ask your classmates if they are going to do these activities today. Find one person to answer **Sí** and one to answer **No** for each item and note their names on the worksheet in the appropriate column.

> **modelo**
>
> **Tú:** ¿Vas a leer el periódico hoy?
> **Ana:** Sí, voy a leer el periódico hoy.
> **Luis:** No, no voy a leer el periódico hoy.

Actividades	Sí	No
1. comer en un restaurante chino		
2. leer el periódico	Ana	Luis
3. escribir un mensaje electrónico		
4. correr 20 kilómetros		
5. ver una película de terror		
6. pasear en bicicleta		

6

Entrevista Talk to two classmates in order to find out where they are going and what they are going to do on their next vacation.

> **modelo**
>
> **Estudiante 1:** ¿Adónde vas de vacaciones (*on vacation*)?
> **Estudiante 2:** Voy a Guadalajara con mis amigos.
> **Estudiante 3:** ¿Y qué van a hacer (*to do*) ustedes en Guadalajara?
> **Estudiante 2:** Vamos a visitar unos monumentos y museos. ¿Y tú?

Síntesis

7

Planes Make a schedule of your activities for the weekend. Then, share with a partner.

▶ For each day, list at least three things you have to do.
▶ For each day, list at least two things you will do for fun.
▶ Tell a classmate what your weekend schedule is like. He or she will write down what you say.
▶ Switch roles to see if you have any plans in common.
▶ Take turns asking each other to participate in some of the activities you listed.

4.2 Stem-changing verbs: e→ie, o→ue

Tutorial

ANTE TODO
Stem-changing verbs deviate from the normal pattern of regular verbs. When stem-changing verbs are conjugated, they have a vowel change in the last syllable of the stem.

CONSULTA

To review the present tense of regular -ar verbs, see **Estructura 2.1**, p. 50.

•••

To review the present tense of regular -er and -ir verbs, see **Estructura 3.3**, p. 96.

INFINITIVE	VERB STEM	STEM CHANGE	CONJUGATED FORM
empezar volver	empez- volv-	empiez- vuelv-	empiezo vuelvo

▶ In many verbs, such as **empezar** (*to begin*), the stem vowel changes from **e** to **ie**. Note that the **nosotros/as** and **vosotros/as** forms don't have a stem change.

The verb empezar (e:ie) (*to begin*)

Singular forms		Plural forms	
yo	empiezo	nosotros/as	empezamos
tú	empiezas	vosotros/as	empezáis
Ud./él/ella	empieza	Uds./ellos/ellas	empiezan

Los chicos empiezan a hablar de su visita al cenote.

Ellos vuelven a comer en el restaurante.

▶ In many other verbs, such as **volver** (*to return*), the stem vowel changes from **o** to **ue**. The **nosotros/as** and **vosotros/as** forms have no stem change.

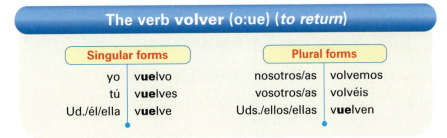

The verb volver (o:ue) (*to return*)

Singular forms		Plural forms	
yo	vuelvo	nosotros/as	volvemos
tú	vuelves	vosotros/as	volvéis
Ud./él/ella	vuelve	Uds./ellos/ellas	vuelven

▶ To help you identify stem-changing verbs, they will appear as follows throughout the text:

empezar (e:ie), volver (o:ue)

Common stem-changing verbs

e:ie		o:ue	
cerrar	to close	almorzar	to have lunch
comenzar (a + *inf.*)	to begin	contar	to count; to tell
empezar (a + *inf.*)	to begin	dormir	to sleep
entender	to understand	encontrar	to find
pensar	to think	mostrar	to show
perder	to lose; to miss	poder (+ *inf.*)	to be able to; can
preferir (+ *inf.*)	to prefer	recordar	to remember
querer (+ *inf.*)	to want; to love	volver	to return

¡LENGUA VIVA!

The verb **perder** can mean *to lose* or *to miss*, in the sense of "to miss a train."

Siempre pierdo mis llaves.
I always lose my keys.

Es importante no perder el autobús.
It's important not to miss the bus.

▶ **Jugar** (*to play a sport or a game*) is the only Spanish verb that has a **u:ue** stem change. **Jugar** is followed by **a** + [*definite article*] when the name of a sport or game is mentioned.

Ella juega al tenis y al golf.

Los chicos juegan al fútbol.

▶ **Comenzar** and **empezar** require the preposition **a** when they are followed by an infinitive.

Comienzan a jugar a las siete.
They begin playing at seven.

Ana **empieza a** escribir una postal.
Ana is starting to write a postcard.

▶ **Pensar** + [*infinitive*] means *to plan* or *to intend to do something*. **Pensar en** means *to think about someone* or *something*.

¿Piensan ir al gimnasio?
Are you planning to go to the gym?

¿En qué **piensas?**
What are you thinking about?

¡INTÉNTALO!   Provide the present tense forms of these verbs.

cerrar (e:ie)

1. Ustedes ___cierran___.
2. Ella _____.
3. Nosotras _____.
4. Mi hermano _____.
5. Yo _____.
6. Usted _____.
7. Los chicos _____.
8. Tú _____.

dormir (o:ue)

1. Mi abuela no ___duerme___.
2. Yo no _____.
3. Mis hijos no _____.
4. Tú no _____.
5. Usted no _____.
6. Nosotros no _____.
7. Él no _____.
8. Ustedes no _____.

More activities

vhlcentral

LM
p. 22

WB
pp. 41–42

Online activities

Práctica

1

Completar Complete this conversation with the appropriate forms of the verbs. Then act it out with a partner.

PABLO Óscar, voy al centro ahora.

ÓSCAR ¿A qué hora (1)_____ (pensar) volver? El partido de fútbol (2)_____ (empezar) a las dos.

PABLO (3)_____ (volver) a la una. (4)_____ (querer) ver el partido.

ÓSCAR (5)¿_____ (recordar) que (*that*) nuestro equipo es muy bueno? (6)¡_____ (poder) ganar!

PABLO No, (7)_____ (pensar) que va a (8)_____ (perder). Los jugadores de Guadalajara son salvajes (*wild*) cuando (9)_____ (jugar).

2

Preferencias With a partner, take turns asking and answering questions about what these people want to do.

> **modelo**
>
> Guillermo: estudiar / pasear en bicicleta
>
> **Estudiante 1:** ¿Quiere estudiar Guillermo?
>
> **Estudiante 2:** No, prefiere pasear en bicicleta.

1. tú: trabajar / dormir

▶ 2. ustedes: mirar la televisión / jugar al dominó

3. Elisa: ver una película / leer una revista

4. tú: comer en la cafetería / ir a un restaurante

5. tus amigos: ir de excursión / descansar

6. María y su hermana: tomar el sol / practicar el esquí acuático

3

Describir Use the verbs to describe what these people are doing.

almorzar	cerrar	contar	dormir	jugar	mostrar

1. yo

2. las niñas

3. Pedro

4. tú

5. nosotros

6. Teresa

Comunicación

4 **Frecuencia** In pairs, take turns using the verbs from the list and other stem-changing verbs you know to tell your partner which activities you do daily (**todos los días**), which you do once a month (**una vez al mes**), and which you do once a year (**una vez al año**). Record your partner's responses in the chart so that you can report back to the class.

> **modelo**
>
> **Estudiante 1:** Yo recuerdo a mi familia todos los días.
> **Estudiante 2:** Yo pierdo uno de mis libros una vez al año.

cerrar	perder
dormir	poder
empezar	preferir
encontrar	querer
jugar	recordar
¿?	¿?

todos los días	una vez al mes	una vez al año

5 **En la televisión** In pairs, write a conversation between two siblings arguing about what to watch on TV. Be creative and be prepared to act out your conversation for the class.

> **modelo**
>
> **Hermano:** Podemos ver la Copa Mundial.
> **Hermana:** ¡No, no quiero ver la Copa Mundial! Prefiero ver...

NOTA CULTURAL

Iker Casillas Fernández was a famous goalkeeper for **Real Madrid**. A native of Madrid, he is among the best goalkeepers of his generation.

Síntesis

6 **Situación** Your instructor will give you and your partner each a partially illustrated itinerary of a city tour. Complete the itineraries by asking each other questions using the verbs in the captions and vocabulary you have learned.

> **modelo**
>
> **Estudiante 1:** Por la mañana, empiezan en el café.
> **Estudiante 2:** Y luego...

4.3 Stem-changing verbs: e→i   Tutorial

ANTE TODO You've already seen that many verbs in Spanish change their stem vowel when conjugated. There is a third kind of stem-vowel change in some verbs, such as **pedir** (*to ask for; to request*). In these verbs, the stressed vowel in the stem changes from **e** to **i**, as shown in the diagram.

INFINITIVE	VERB STEM	STEM CHANGE	CONJUGATED FORM
pedir	ped-	pid-	pido

▶ As with other stem-changing verbs you have learned, there is no stem change in the **nosotros/as** or **vosotros/as** forms in the present tense.

The verb pedir (e:i) (*to ask for; to request*)

Singular forms		Plural forms	
yo	pido	nosotros/as	pedimos
tú	pides	vosotros/as	pedís
Ud./él/ella	pide	Uds./ellos/ellas	piden

▶ To help you identify verbs with the **e:i** stem change, they will appear as follows throughout the text:

pedir (e:i)

▶ These are the most common **e:i** stem-changing verbs:

conseguir	**decir**	**repetir**	**seguir**
to get; to obtain	*to say; to tell*	*to repeat*	*to follow; to continue; to keep (doing something)*

Pido favores cuando es necesario.
I ask for favors when it's necessary.

Javier **dice** la verdad.
Javier is telling the truth.

Sigue con su tarea.
He continues with his homework.

Consiguen ver buenas películas.
They get to see good movies.

▶ **¡Atención!** The verb **decir** is irregular in its **yo** form: **yo digo.**

▶ The **yo** forms of **seguir** and **conseguir** have a spelling change in addition to the stem change **e:i.**

Sigo su plan.
I'm following their plan.

Consigo novelas en la librería.
I get novels at the bookstore.

¡INTÉNTALO! Provide the correct forms of the verbs.

repetir (e:i)
1. Arturo y Eva _repiten_.
2. Nosotros _____.
3. Yo _____.
4. Julia _____.
5. Sofía y yo _____.

decir (e:i)
1. Yo _digo_.
2. Él _____.
3. Tú _____.
4. Ellas _____.
5. Usted _____.

seguir (e:i)
1. Yo _sigo_.
2. Los chicos _____.
3. Tú _____.
4. Nosotros _____.
5. Usted _____.

Práctica

1

Completar Complete these sentences with the correct form of the verb.

1. Cuando mi familia pasea por la ciudad, mi madre siempre (*always*) va a un café y _____ (pedir) una soda.
2. Pero mi padre _____ (decir) que perdemos mucho tiempo. Tiene prisa por llegar al Bosque de Chapultepec.
3. Mi padre tiene suerte, porque él siempre _____ (conseguir) lo que (*that which*) desea.
4. Cuando llegamos al parque, mis hermanos y yo _____ (seguir) conversando (*talking*) con nuestros padres.
5. Mis padres siempre _____ (repetir) la misma cosa: "Nosotros tomamos el sol aquí sin ustedes".
6. Yo siempre _____ (pedir) permiso para volver a casa un poco más tarde porque me gusta mucho el parque.

NOTA CULTURAL

A popular weekend destination for residents and tourists, **el Bosque de Chapultepec** is a beautiful park located in Mexico City. It occupies over 1.5 square miles and includes lakes, wooded areas, several museums, and a botanical garden. You may recognize this park from **Fotonovela, Lección 2.**

2

Combinar Combine words from the two columns to create sentences about yourself and people you know.

> **modelo**
>
> Mi hermana consigue libros en Internet.

A	B
yo	nunca (*never*) pedir perdón
mi compañero/a de cuarto	(no) pedir muchos favores
mi mejor (*best*) amigo/a	nunca seguir las instrucciones
mi familia	siempre seguir las instrucciones
mis amigos/as	repetir el vocabulario
mis amigos/as y yo	conseguir libros en Internet
mis padres	poder hablar dos lenguas
mi hermano/a	dormir hasta el mediodía
mi profesor(a) de español	siempre perder sus libros

CONSULTA

To review possessive adjectives, see **Estructura 3.2**, p. 93.

3

Opiniones In pairs, take turns guessing how your partner completed the sentences from **Actividad 2**. If you guess incorrectly, your partner must supply the correct answer.

> **modelo**
>
> **Estudiante 1:** Creo que tus padres consiguen libros en Internet.
> **Estudiante 2:** ¡No! Mi hermana consigue libros en Internet.

4

¿Quién? Your instructor will give you a worksheet. Talk to your classmates until you find one person who does each of the activities. Use **e:ie**, **o:ue**, and **e:i** stem-changing verbs.

> **modelo**
>
> **Tú:** ¿Pides consejos con frecuencia?
> **Maira:** No, no pido consejos con frecuencia.
> **Tú:** ¿Pides consejos con frecuencia?
> **Lucas:** Sí, pido consejos con frecuencia.

Comunicación

5

Las películas Use these questions to interview a classmate.

1. ¿Prefieres las películas románticas, las películas de acción o las películas de terror? ¿Por qué?
2. ¿Dónde consigues información sobre (*about*) cine y televisión?
3. ¿Dónde consigues las entradas (*tickets*) para ver una película?
4. Para decidir qué películas vas a ver, ¿sigues las recomendaciones de los críticos de cine? ¿Qué dicen los críticos en general?
5. ¿Qué cines en tu comunidad muestran las mejores (*best*) películas?
6. ¿Vas a ver una película esta semana? ¿A qué hora empieza la película?

Síntesis

6

El cine In pairs, first scan the ad and jot down all the stem-changing verbs. Then answer the questions.

1. ¿Qué palabras indican que *Dunkirk* es una película dramática?
2. ¿Cómo está el personaje (*character*) del póster? ¿Qué quiere hacer?
3. ¿Te gustan las películas como ésta (*this one*)? ¿Por qué?
4. Describe tu película favorita con los verbos de la **Lección 4**.

Una de las mejores películas del año

Dunkerque: un momento decisivo de la Segunda Guerra Mundial

Cuando los nazis comienzan a controlar toda Francia, las fuerzas aliadas no pierden la esperanza. Sólo quieren cumplir su misión: evacuar las tropas de Dunkerque y seguir luchando por la libertad de Europa.

¿Consiguen escapar? ¿Vuelven a Inglaterra?

Una película dramática de acción histórica, con actuación y efectos especiales espectaculares. Escrita y dirigida por Christopher Nolan.

4.4 Verbs with irregular yo forms

Tutorial

ANTE TODO In Spanish, several verbs have irregular **yo** forms in the present tense. You have already seen three verbs with the **-go** ending in the **yo** form: **decir → digo**, **tener → tengo**, and **venir → vengo**.

▶ Here are some common expressions with **decir**.

decir la verdad
to tell the truth

decir mentiras
to tell lies

decir que
to say that

decir la respuesta
to say the answer

▶ The verb **hacer** is often used to ask questions about what someone does. Note that when answering, **hacer** is frequently replaced with another, more specific action verb.

Verbs with irregular yo forms

	hacer (to do; to make)	**poner** (to put; to place)	**salir** (to leave)	**suponer** (to suppose)	**traer** (to bring)
SINGULAR FORMS	**hago**	**pongo**	**salgo**	**supongo**	**traigo**
	haces	pones	sales	supones	traes
	hace	pone	sale	supone	trae
PLURAL FORMS	hacemos	ponemos	salimos	suponemos	traemos
	hacéis	ponéis	salís	suponéis	traéis
	hacen	ponen	salen	suponen	traen

Salgo mucho los fines de semana.

Yo no salgo, yo hago la tarea y veo películas en la televisión.

▶ **Poner** can also mean *to turn on* a household appliance.

Carlos **pone** la radio.
Carlos turns on the radio.

María **pone** la televisión.
María turns on the television.

▶ **Salir de** is used to indicate that someone is leaving a particular place.

Hoy **salgo del** hospital.
Today I leave the hospital.

Sale de la clase a las cuatro.
He leaves class at four.

▶ **Salir para** is used to indicate someone's destination.

> Mañana **salgo para** México.   Hoy **salen para** España.
> *Tomorrow I leave for Mexico.*   *Today they leave for Spain.*

▶ **Salir con** means *to leave with someone* or *something*, or *to date someone.*

> Alberto **sale con** su mochila.   Margarita **sale con** Guillermo.
> *Alberto is leaving with his backpack.* *Margarita is going out with Guillermo.*

The verbs **ver** and **oír**

▶ The verb **ver** (*to see*) has an irregular **yo** form. The other forms of **ver** are regular.

The verb ver (*to see*)

Singular forms		Plural forms	
yo	**veo**	nosotros/as	vemos
tú	ves	vosotros/as	veis
Ud./él/ella	ve	Uds./ellos/ellas	ven

▶ The verb **oír** (*to hear*) has an irregular **yo** form and the spelling change **i:y** in the **tú**, **usted/él/ella**, and **ustedes/ellos/ellas** forms. The **nosotros/as** and **vosotros/as** forms have an accent mark.

The verb oír (*to hear*)

Singular forms		Plural forms	
yo	**oigo**	nosotros/as	oímos
tú	oyes	vosotros/as	oís
Ud./él/ella	oye	Uds./ellos/ellas	oyen

▶ While most commonly translated as *to hear*, **oír** is also used in contexts where the verb *to listen* would be used in English.

> **Oigo** a unas personas en la otra sala.   ¿**Oyes** la radio por la mañana?
> *I hear some people in the other room.*   *Do you listen to the radio in the morning?*

More activities

vhlcentral

LM
p. 24

WB
pp. 45–46

Online activities

∞ **¡INTÉNTALO!** Provide the correct forms of these verbs.

1. salir   Isabel ___*sale*___.   Nosotros _____.   Yo _____.
2. ver   Yo _____.   Ustedes _____.   Tú _____.
3. poner   Rita y yo _____.   Yo _____.   Los niños _____.
4. traer   Ellas _____.   Yo _____.   Tú _____.
5. oír   Él _____.   Nosotros _____.   Yo _____.
6. hacer   Yo _____.   Tú _____.   Usted _____.
7. suponer   Yo _____.   Mi amigo _____.   Nosotras _____.

Práctica

1

Completar Complete this conversation with the correct forms of the verbs. Then act it out with a partner.

ERNESTO David, ¿qué (1)_____ (hacer) hoy?

DAVID Ahora estudio biología, pero esta noche (2)_____ (salir) con Luisa. Vamos al cine. Los críticos (3)_____ (decir) que la nueva (*new*) película de Almodóvar es buena.

ERNESTO ¿Y Diana? ¿Qué (4)_____ (hacer) ella?

DAVID (5)_____ (salir) a comer con sus padres.

ERNESTO ¿Qué (6)_____ (hacer) Andrés y Javier?

DAVID Tienen que (7)_____ (hacer) las maletas. (8)_____ (salir) para Monterrey mañana.

ERNESTO Pues, ¿qué (9)_____ (hacer) yo?

DAVID Yo (10)_____ (suponer) que puedes estudiar o (11)_____ (ver) la televisión.

ERNESTO No quiero estudiar. Mejor (12)_____ (poner) la televisión. Mi programa favorito empieza en unos minutos.

2

Oraciones Form sentences using verbs from **Estructura 4.4**.

> **modelo**
> tú / _____ / cosas / en / su lugar / antes de (*before*) / salir
> **Tú pones las cosas en su lugar antes de salir.**

1. mis amigos / _____ / conmigo / centro
2. yo / no / _____ / muchas películas
3. Alberto / _____ / música del café Pasatiempos
4. tú / _____ / mentiras / pero / yo _____ / verdad
5. domingo / nosotros / _____ / mucha / tarea
6. si / yo / _____ / que / yo / querer / ir / cine / mis amigos / ir / también

3

Describir Use the verbs from **Estructura 4.4** to describe what these people are doing.

1. Fernán

2. el estudiante

3. los aficionados

4. nosotros

5. la señora Vargas

6. yo

Comunicación

4

Tu rutina In pairs, take turns asking each other these questions.

1. ¿Qué traes a clase?
2. ¿A qué hora sales de tu residencia estudiantil o de tu casa por la mañana? ¿A qué hora sale tu compañero/a de cuarto?
3. ¿Dónde pones tus libros cuando regresas de clase?
   ¿Siempre (*Always*) pones tus cosas en su lugar?
4. ¿Oyes música cuando estudias?
5. ¿Ves películas en casa o prefieres ir al cine?
6. ¿Haces mucha tarea los fines de semana?
7. ¿Sales con tus amigos los fines de semana? ¿A qué hora? ¿Qué hacen?
8. ¿Te gusta ver deportes en la televisión o prefieres ver otros programas? ¿Cuáles?

5

Charadas In groups, play a game of charades. Each person should think of two phrases containing the verbs **hacer, oír, poner, salir, traer,** or **ver**. The first person to guess correctly acts out the next charade.

6

Entrevista You are doing a market research report on lifestyles. Interview a classmate to find out when he or she goes out with these people and what they do for entertainment.

▶ los/las amigos/as
▶ el/la novio/a
▶ el/la esposo/a
▶ la familia

Síntesis

7

Situación With a partner, prepare a conversation between two roommates.

Estudiante 1	Estudiante 2
Ask your partner what he or she is doing.	→ Tell your partner that you are watching TV.
Say what you suppose he or she is watching.	→ Say that you like the show _____. Ask if he or she wants to watch.
Say no, because you are going out with friends, and tell where you are going.	→ Say you think it's a good idea, and ask what your partner and his or her friends are doing there.
Say what you are going to do, and ask your partner whether he or she wants to come along.	→ Say no and tell your partner what you prefer to do.

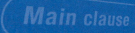

Recapitulación

Review the grammar concepts you have learned in this lesson by completing these activities.

1 **Completar** Complete the chart with the correct verb forms. **30 pts.**

Infinitive	yo	nosotros/as	ellos/as
	vuelvo		
comenzar		comenzamos	
		hacemos	hacen
ir			
	juego		
repetir			repiten

2 **Un día típico** Complete the paragraph with the correct forms of the appropriate verbs. **20 pts.**

almorzar	ir	salir
cerrar	jugar	seguir
empezar	mostrar	ver
hacer	querer	volver

¡Hola! Me llamo Cecilia y vivo en Puerto Vallarta, México. ¿Cómo es un día típico en mi vida (*life*)? Por la mañana bebo café con mis padres y juntos (*together*) (1) _____ las noticias (*news*) en la televisión. A las siete y media, (*yo*) (2) _____ de mi casa y tomo el autobús. Me gusta llegar temprano (*early*) a la universidad porque siempre (*always*) (3) _____ a mis amigos en la cafetería. Tomamos café y planeamos lo que (4) _____ hacer cada (*each*) día. A las ocho y cuarto, mi amiga Sandra y yo (5) _____ al laboratorio de lenguas. La clase de francés (6) _____ a las ocho y media. ¡Es mi clase favorita! A las doce y media (*yo*) (7) _____ en la cafetería con mis amigos. Después (*Afterward*), yo (8) _____ con mis clases. Por las tardes, mis amigos (9) _____ a sus casas, pero yo (10) _____ al vóleibol con mi amigo Tomás.

RESUMEN GRAMATICAL

4.1 **Present tense of ir** *p. 126*

yo	voy	nos.	vamos
tú	vas	vos.	vais
él	va	ellas	van

▶ ir a + [*infinitive*] = *to be going* + [*infinitive*]

▶ a + el = al

▶ vamos a + [*infinitive*] = *let's* (*do something*)

4.2 **Stem-changing verbs e:ie, o:ue, u:ue** *pp. 129–130*

	empezar	volver	jugar
yo	empiezo	vuelvo	juego
tú	empiezas	vuelves	juegas
él	empieza	vuelve	juega
nos.	empezamos	volvemos	jugamos
vos.	empezáis	volvéis	jugáis
ellas	empiezan	vuelven	juegan

▶ Other e:ie verbs: **cerrar, comenzar, entender, pensar, perder, preferir, querer**

▶ Other o:ue verbs: **almorzar, contar, dormir, encontrar, mostrar, poder, recordar**

4.3 **Stem-changing verbs e:i** *p. 133*

		pedir	
yo	pido	nos.	pedimos
tú	pides	vos.	pedís
él	pide	ellas	piden

▶ Other e:i verbs: **conseguir, decir, repetir, seguir**

4.4 **Verbs with irregular yo forms** *pp. 136–137*

hacer	poner	salir	suponer	traer
hago	pongo	salgo	supongo	traigo

▶ ver: **veo,** ves, ve, vemos, veis, ven

▶ oír: **oigo,** oyes, oye, oímos, oís, oyen

3 **Oraciones** Arrange the cues in the correct order to form complete sentences. Make all necessary changes. `14 pts.`

1. tarea / los / hacer / sábados / nosotros / la
   _____

2. en / pizza / Andrés / una / restaurante / el / pedir
   _____

3. a / ? / museo / ir / ¿ / el / (tú)
   _____

4. de / oír / amigos / bien / los / no / Elena
   _____

5. libros / traer / yo / clase / mis / a
   _____

6. película / ver / en / Jorge y Carlos / pensar / cine / una / el
   _____

7. unos / escribir / Mariana / electrónicos / querer / mensajes
   _____

4 **Escribir** Write a short paragraph about what you do on a typical day. Use at least six of the verbs you have learned in this lesson. You can use the paragraph on the opposite page (**Actividad 2**) as a model. `36 pts.`

Un día típico

Hola, me llamo Julia y vivo en Vancouver, Canadá. Por la mañana, yo...

5 **Rima** Complete the rhyme with the correct forms of the appropriate verbs. `4 EXTRA points!`

contar	poder
oír	suponer

❝ Si no _____ dormir
y el sueño deseas,
lo vas a conseguir
si _____ ovejas°. ❞

ovejas *sheep*

Lectura

Antes de leer

Estrategia

Predicting content from visuals

When you are reading in Spanish, be sure to look for visual clues that will orient you as to the content and purpose of what you are reading. Photos and illustrations, for example, will often give you a good idea of the main points that the reading covers. You may also encounter very helpful visuals that are used to summarize large amounts of data in a way that is easy to comprehend; these include bar graphs, pie charts, flow charts, lists of percentages, and other sorts of diagrams.

Examinar el texto

Take a quick look at the visual elements of the magazine article in order to generate a list of ideas about its content. Then compare your list with a classmate's. Are they the same or are they different? Discuss your lists and make any changes needed to produce a final list of ideas.

Contestar

Read the list of ideas you wrote in **Examinar el texto**, and look again at the visual elements of the magazine article. Then answer the questions.

1. Who is the woman in the photo, and what is her role?
2. What is the article about?
3. What is the subject of the pie chart?
4. What is the subject of the bar graph?

por María Úrsula Echevarría

El fútbol es el deporte más popular en el mundo° hispano, según° una encuesta° reciente realizada entre jóvenes universitarios. Mucha gente practica este deporte y tiene un equipo de fútbol favorito. Cada cuatro años se realiza la Copa Mundial°. Argentina y Uruguay han ganado° este campeonato° más de una vez°. Los aficionados siguen los partidos de fútbol en casa por tele y en muchos otros lugares como bares, restaurantes, estadios y clubes deportivos. Los jóvenes juegan al fútbol con sus amigos en parques y gimnasios.

Países hispanos en campeonatos mundiales de fútbol (1930–2018)

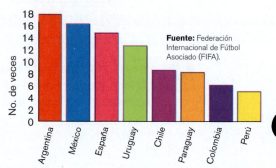

Fuente: Federación Internacional de Fútbol Asociado (FIFA).

Pero, por supuesto°, en los países de habla hispana también hay otros deportes populares. ¿Qué deporte sigue al fútbol en estos países? Bueno, ¡depende del país y de otros factores!

Después de leer

Evaluación y predicción

Which of the following sporting events would be most popular among the college students surveyed? Rate them from one (most popular) to five (least popular). Which would be the most popular at your college or university?

_____ 1. la Copa Mundial de Fútbol

_____ 2. los Juegos Olímpicos

_____ 3. el Campeonato de Wimbledon

_____ 4. la Serie Mundial de Béisbol

_____ 5. el Tour de Francia

No sólo el fútbol

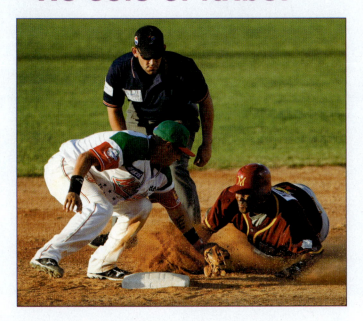

En Colombia, el béisbol también es muy popular después del fútbol, aunque° esto varía según la región del país. En la costa del norte de Colombia, el béisbol es una pasión. Y el ciclismo también es un deporte que los colombianos siguen con mucho interés.

Donde el béisbol es más popular

En los países del Caribe, el béisbol es el deporte predominante. Éste es el caso en Puerto Rico, Cuba y la República Dominicana. Los niños empiezan a jugar cuando son muy pequeños. En Puerto Rico y la República Dominicana, la gente también quiere participar en otros deportes, como el baloncesto, o ver los partidos en la tele. Y para los espectadores aficionados del Caribe, el boxeo es número dos.

Donde el fútbol es más popular

En México, el béisbol es el segundo° deporte más popular después° del fútbol. Pero en Argentina, después del fútbol, el rugby tiene mucha importancia. En Perú a la gente le gusta mucho ver partidos de vóleibol. ¿Y en España? Muchas personas prefieren el baloncesto, el tenis y el ciclismo.

Deportes más populares

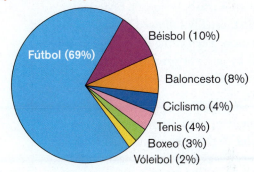

Fútbol (69%)
Béisbol (10%)
Baloncesto (8%)
Ciclismo (4%)
Tenis (4%)
Boxeo (3%)
Vóleibol (2%)

mundo *world* según *according to* encuesta *survey* se realiza la Copa Mundial *the World Cup is held* han ganado *have won* campeonato *championship* más de una vez *more than once* por supuesto *of course* segundo *second* después *after* aunque *although*

¿Cierto o falso?

Indicate whether each sentence is **cierto** or **falso**, then correct the false statements.

	Cierto	Falso
1. El vóleibol es el segundo deporte más popular en México.	○	○
2. En España a la gente le gustan varios deportes como el baloncesto y el ciclismo.	○	○
3. En la costa del norte de Colombia, el tenis es una pasión.	○	○
4. En el Caribe, el deporte más popular es el béisbol.	○	○

Preguntas

Answer these questions.

1. ¿Dónde ven el fútbol los aficionados? Y tú, ¿cómo ves tus deportes favoritos?
2. ¿Te gusta el fútbol? ¿Por qué?
3. ¿Miras la Copa Mundial en la televisión?
4. ¿Qué deportes miras en la televisión?
5. En tu opinión, ¿cuáles son los tres deportes más populares en tu universidad? ¿En tu comunidad? ¿En tu país?
6. ¿Practicas deportes en tus ratos libres?

Escritura

Estrategia
Using a dictionary

A common mistake made by beginning language learners is to embrace the dictionary as the ultimate resource for reading, writing, and speaking. While it is true that the dictionary is a useful tool that can provide valuable information about vocabulary, using the dictionary correctly requires that you understand the elements of each entry.

If you glance at a Spanish-English dictionary, you will notice that its format is similar to that of an English dictionary. The word is listed first, usually followed by its pronunciation. Then come the definitions, organized by parts of speech. Sometimes the most frequently used definitions are listed first.

To find the best word for your needs, you should refer to the abbreviations and the explanatory notes that appear next to the entries. For example, imagine that you are writing about your pastimes. You want to write, "I want to buy a new racket for my match tomorrow," but you don't know the Spanish word for "racket." In the dictionary, you may find an entry like this:

> **racket** *s* **1**. alboroto; **2**. raqueta (*dep.*)

The abbreviation key at the front of the dictionary says that *s* corresponds to **sustantivo** (*noun*). Then, the first word you see is **alboroto**. The definition of **alboroto** is *noise* or *racket*, so **alboroto** is probably not the word you're looking for. The second word is **raqueta**, followed by the abbreviation *dep.*, which stands for **deportes**. This indicates that the word **raqueta** is the best choice for your needs.

Tema
 Escribir un folleto

Choose one topic to write a brochure.

1. You are the head of the Homecoming Committee at your school this year. Create a pamphlet that lists events for Friday night, Saturday, and Sunday. Include a brief description of each event and its time and location. Include activities for different age groups, since some alumni will bring their families.

2. You are on the Freshman Student Orientation Committee and are in charge of creating a pamphlet for new students that describes the sports offered at your school. Write the flyer and include activities for both men and women.

3. You work for the Chamber of Commerce in your community. It is your job to market your community to potential residents. Write a brief pamphlet that describes the recreational opportunities your community provides, the areas where the activities take place, and the costs, if any. Be sure to include activities that will appeal to singles as well as couples and families; you should include activities for all age groups and for both men and women.

Escuchar
Antes de escuchar

> ### Estrategia
> **Listening for the gist**
>
> Listening for the general idea, or gist, can help you follow what someone is saying even if you can't hear or understand some of the words. When you listen for the gist, you simply try to capture the essence of what you hear without focusing on individual words.
>
> To help you practice this strategy, you will listen to a paragraph made up of three sentences. Jot down a brief summary of what you hear.

Preparación

Based on the photo, what do you think Anabela is like? Do you and Anabela have similar interests?

Ahora escucha

Pasatiempos favoritos

You will hear first José talking, then Anabela. As you listen, check off each person's favorite activities.

Pasatiempos favoritos de José

1. _____ leer el correo electrónico
2. _____ jugar al béisbol
3. _____ ver películas de acción
4. _____ ir al café
5. _____ ir a partidos de béisbol
6. _____ ver películas románticas
7. _____ dormir la siesta
8. _____ escribir mensajes electrónicos

Pasatiempos favoritos de Anabela

9. _____ esquiar
10. _____ nadar
11. _____ practicar el ciclismo
12. _____ jugar al golf
13. _____ jugar al baloncesto
14. _____ ir a ver partidos de tenis
15. _____ escalar montañas
16. _____ ver televisión

Comprensión

Preguntas

Answer these questions about José's and Anabela's pastimes.

1. ¿Quién practica más deportes?
2. ¿Quién piensa que es importante descansar?
3. ¿A qué deporte es aficionado José?
4. ¿Por qué Anabela no practica el baloncesto?
5. ¿Qué películas le gustan a la novia de José?
6. ¿Cuál es el deporte favorito de Anabela?

Seleccionar

Which person do these statements best describe?

1. Le gusta practicar deportes.
2. Prefiere las películas de acción.
3. Le gustan las computadoras.
4. Le gusta nadar.
5. Siempre (*Always*) duerme una siesta por la tarde.
6. Quiere ir de vacaciones a las montañas.

En pantalla 🅢 Video

BMX, skateboarding, surfing, and other extreme sports are passions for many young men and women who, in search of speed and adrenaline, make their bikes and boards the center of their lives. Communities around the world are responding to the demand for extreme sports by constructing bike and skate parks, and Spanish-speaking countries are no exception. The UCI BMX World Championship was held in Medellín in 2016. Colombian Olympic Gold Medalist Mariana Pajón has won gold at the games three times (2011, 2014, 2016).

Vocabulario útil	
andar	to go
bici	bike
callejón	alley
campeonato	championship
conocer	to be acquainted with
molar	to be cool
rampas	ramps

Preparación

What role do sports play in your life? Which sports do you enjoy? Why?

🔗 Comprensión

Indicate whether each statement is **cierto** or **falso**.

	Cierto	Falso
1. A Diego le gusta la bici.	○	○
2. Sarini cree que patinar es un arte.	○	○
3. Pequesaurio prefiere la patineta.	○	○
4. A Pequesaurio le gusta la rampa.	○	○

👥 Conversación

With a partner, discuss these questions in Spanish.

1. ¿Qué deportes se pueden practicar fácilmente en tu comunidad? ¿Qué deportes son fomentados (*encouraged*) en tu comunidad?

2. ¿Cuál es la diferencia entre un deporte y un juego? ¿Cuál es la diferencia entre un deporte y un deporte extremo?

Me quedo con la bici *I'll stick with the bike*

Ejes

Patino por pasión más que por otra cosa.

Es un deporte también, pero creo que es un arte.

A mí me gusta la bici y me quedo con la bici°.

Video

The rivalry between the teams **Real Madrid** and **FC Barcelona** is perhaps the fiercest in all of soccer—just imagine if they occupied the same city! Well, each team also has competing clubs within its respective city: Spain's capital has the **Club Atlético de Madrid**, and Barcelona is home to **Espanyol**. In fact, across the Spanish-speaking world, it is common for a city to have more than one professional team, often with strikingly dissimilar origins, identity, and fan base. For example, in Bogotá, the **Millonarios** were so named for the large sums spent on players, while the **Santa Fe** team is one of the most traditional in Colombian soccer. **River Plate** and **Boca Juniors**, who enjoy a famous rivalry, are just two of twenty-four clubs in Buenos Aires—the city with the most professional soccer teams in the world.

Vocabulario útil

afición	*fans*
celebran	*they celebrate*
preferido/a	*favorite*
rivalidad	*rivalry*
se junta con	*it's tied up with*

Preparación

What is the most popular sport at your school? What teams are your rivals? How do students celebrate a win?

Escoger

Select the correct answer.

1. Un partido entre el Barça y el Real Madrid es un _____ (deporte/evento) importante en toda España.

2. Los aficionados _____ (miran/celebran) las victorias de sus equipos en las calles (*streets*).

3. La rivalidad entre el Real Madrid y el Barça está relacionada con la _____ (religión/política).

¡Fútbol en España!

(Hay mucha afición al fútbol en España.)

¿Y cuál es vuestro jugador favorito?

—**¿Y quién va a ganar?**
—**El Real Madrid.**

Video

México

El país en cifras

▶ **Área:** 1.972.550 km² (761.603 millas²), *casi° tres veces° el área de Texas*

La situación geográfica de México, al sur° de los Estados Unidos, ha influido en° la economía y la sociedad de los dos países. Una de las consecuencias es la emigración de la población mexicana al país vecino°. Hoy día, más de 34 millones de personas de ascendencia mexicana viven en los Estados Unidos.

▶ **Población:** 124.574.000

▶ **Capital:** Ciudad de México (y su área metropolitana)—20.999.000

▶ **Ciudades principales:** Guadalajara —4.843.000, Monterrey—4.513.000, Puebla—2.984.000, Ciudad Juárez—1.391.000

▶ **Moneda:** peso mexicano

▶ **Idiomas:** español (oficial), náhuatl, otras lenguas indígenas

Bandera de México

Mexicanos célebres

▶ **Benito Juárez,** héroe nacional (1806–1872)

▶ **Octavio Paz,** poeta (1914–1998)

▶ **Elena Poniatowska,** periodista y escritora (1932–)

▶ **Mario Molina,** Premio Nobel de Química, 1995; químico (1943–)

▶ **Paulina Rubio,** cantante (1971–)

casi *almost* veces *times* sur *south* ha influido en *has influenced* vecino *neighboring*

Cabo San Lucas

ESTADOS UNIDOS

Autorretrato con collar de espinas, 1940, Frida Kahlo

Ciudad Juárez

Río Grande

Río Bravo del Norte

Golfo de California

Baja California

Sierra Madre Oriental

Sierra Madre Occidental

ESTADOS UNIDOS

MÉXICO

OCÉANO ATLÁNTICO

OCÉANO PACÍFICO

AMÉRICA DEL SUR

Monterrey

Ciudad de México

Puerto Vallarta

Guadalajara

Puebla

Acapulco

Océano Pacífico

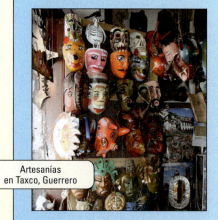
Artesanías en Taxco, Guerrero

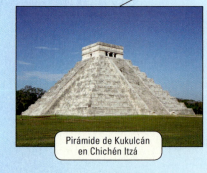
Pirámide de Kukulcán en Chichén Itzá

More activities

vhlcentral

WB pp. 47–48

Online activities

ACTIVIDADES

1 **¿Cierto o falso?** Indica si lo que dice cada oración es **cierto** o **falso**.

1. México está en América del Sur.
2. La moneda de México es el dólar estadounidense.
3. Mario Molina tiene un Premio Nobel de Química.
4. Cabo San Lucas es una iglesia mexicana.
5. Encuentras artesanías en Taxco.
6. Muchos inmigrantes y turistas van a la Ciudad de México.
7. Uno puede ver obras de Frida Kahlo en el Museo de Arte Moderno de la Ciudad de México.
8. Tenochtitlán, la capital azteca, es la Ciudad de México hoy día.
9. Zacatecas es una ciudad principal de México.
10. Cada año, el dos de noviembre, los mexicanos ponen flores en los cementerios.

Ciudades • Ciudad de México

La Ciudad de México, fundada° en 1525, también es conocida como el D.F. o el Distrito Federal. Muchos turistas e inmigrantes vienen a la ciudad porque es el centro cultural y económico del país. El crecimiento° de la población es de los más altos° del mundo. La población de la Ciudad de México es mayor que la de ciudades como Nueva York, Madrid o París.

Artes • Diego Rivera y Frida Kahlo

Frida Kahlo y Diego Rivera eran° artistas mexicanos muy famosos. Se casaron° en 1929. Los dos se interesaron° en las condiciones sociales de la gente indígena de su país. Puedes ver algunas° de sus obras° en el Museo de Arte Moderno de la Ciudad de México.

▷ Historia • Los aztecas

Los aztecas dominaron° en México del siglo° XIV al siglo XVI. Sus canales, puentes° y pirámides con templos religiosos eran muy importantes. El fin del imperio azteca comenzó° con la llegada° de los españoles en 1519, pero la presencia azteca sigue hoy. La Ciudad de México está situada en la capital azteca de Tenochtitlán, y muchos turistas van a visitar sus ruinas.

▷ Economía • La plata

México es el mayor productor de plata° del mundo°. Estados como Zacatecas y Durango tienen ciudades fundadas cerca de los más grandes yacimientos° de plata del país. Estas ciudades fueron° en la época colonial unas de las más ricas e importantes. Hoy en día, aún° conservan mucho de su encanto° y esplendor.

Golfo de México

Península de Yucatán

Bahía de Campeche

Mérida

Cancún

Veracruz

Istmo de Tehuantepec

BELICE

GUATEMALA

fundada *founded* crecimiento *growth* más altos *highest* eran *were* Se casaron *They got married* se interesaron *were interested* algunas *some* obras *works* dominaron *dominated* siglo *century* puentes *bridges* comenzó *started* llegada *arrival* plata *silver* mundo *world* yacimientos *deposits* fueron *were* aún *still* encanto *charm*

¡Increíble pero cierto!

Cada dos de noviembre los cementerios de México se llenan de luz°, música y flores°. El Día de Muertos° no es un evento triste; es una fiesta en honor a las personas muertas. En ese día, los mexicanos se ríen° de la muerte°, lo cual se refleja° en detalles como las calaveras de azúcar° y el pan° de muerto (pan en forma de huesos°).

se llenan de luz *get filled with light* flores *flowers* Muertos *Dead* se ríen *laugh* muerte *death* lo cual se refleja *which is reflected* calaveras de azúcar *sugar skulls* pan *bread* huesos *bones*

---

2 **¿Qué aprendiste?** Contesta las preguntas.

1. ¿Qué lenguas hablan los mexicanos?

2. ¿En qué se interesaron Frida Kahlo y Diego Rivera?

3. Nombra algunas de las estructuras de la arquitectura azteca.

4. ¿Qué estados de México tienen los mayores yacimientos de plata?

3 **Turistas** En parejas, imaginen que viajan a México. Hablen de las cosas que quieren ver y hacer allí.

modelo

Estudiante 1: *Quiero ir a Chichén Itzá.*

Estudiante 2: *Sí. Quiero ver la pirámide de Kukulcán.*

Pasatiempos

andar en patineta	*to skateboard*
bucear	*to scuba dive*
escalar montañas (*f., pl.*)	*to climb mountains*
escribir una carta	*to write a letter*
escribir un mensaje electrónico	*to write an e-mail*
esquiar	*to ski*
ganar	*to win*
ir de excursión	*to go on a hike*
leer el correo electrónico	*to read e-mail*
leer un periódico	*to read a newspaper*
leer una revista	*to read a magazine*
nadar	*to swim*
pasear	*to take a walk*
pasear en bicicleta	*to ride a bicycle*
patinar	*to skate*
practicar deportes (*m., pl.*)	*to play sports*
tomar el sol	*to sunbathe*
ver películas (*f., pl.*)	*to watch movies*
visitar monumentos (*m., pl.*)	*to visit monuments*
la diversión	*fun activity; entertainment; recreation*
el fin de semana	*weekend*
el pasatiempo	*pastime; hobby*
los ratos libres	*spare (free) time*
el videojuego	*video game*

Deportes

el baloncesto	*basketball*
el béisbol	*baseball*
el ciclismo	*cycling*
el equipo	*team*
el esquí (acuático)	*(water) skiing*
el fútbol	*soccer*
el fútbol americano	*football*
el golf	*golf*
el hockey	*hockey*
el/la jugador(a)	*player*
la natación	*swimming*
el partido	*game; match*
la pelota	*ball*
el tenis	*tennis*
el vóleibol	*volleyball*

Adjetivos

deportivo/a	*sports-related*
favorito/a	*favorite*

Lugares

el café	*café*
el centro	*downtown*
el cine	*movie theater*
el gimnasio	*gymnasium*
la iglesia	*church*
el lugar	*place*
el museo	*museum*
el parque	*park*
la piscina	*swimming pool*
la plaza	*city or town square*
el restaurante	*restaurant*

Verbos

almorzar (o:ue)	*to have lunch*
cerrar (e:ie)	*to close*
comenzar (e:ie)	*to begin*
conseguir (e:i)	*to get; to obtain*
contar (o:ue)	*to count; to tell*
decir (e:i)	*to say; to tell*
dormir (o:ue)	*to sleep*
empezar (e:ie)	*to begin*
encontrar (o:ue)	*to find*
entender (e:ie)	*to understand*
hacer	*to do; to make*
ir	*to go*
jugar (u:ue)	*to play (a sport or a game)*
mostrar (o:ue)	*to show*
oír	*to hear*
pedir (e:i)	*to ask for; to request*
pensar (e:ie)	*to think*
pensar (+ *inf.*)	*to intend*
pensar en	*to think about*
perder (e:ie)	*to lose; to miss*
poder (o:ue)	*to be able to; can*
poner	*to put; to place*
preferir (e:ie)	*to prefer*
querer (e:ie)	*to want; to love*
recordar (o:ue)	*to remember*
repetir (e:i)	*to repeat*
salir	*to leave*
seguir (e:i)	*to follow; to continue*
suponer	*to suppose*
traer	*to bring*
ver	*to see*
volver (o:ue)	*to return*

Decir expressions	*See page 136.*
Expresiones útiles	*See page 121.*

Las vacaciones

5

Communicative Goals

You will learn how to:

- Discuss and plan a vacation
- Describe a hotel
- Talk about how you feel
- Talk about the seasons and the weather

👓 A PRIMERA VISTA
- ¿La persona es vieja o joven?
- ¿Lleva una pelota o una mochila?
- ¿Pasea o ve una película? ¿Anda en patineta o va de excursión?
- ¿Es posible nadar en este lugar?

Las vacaciones

Más vocabulario

la cama	bed
la habitación individual, doble	single, double room
la llave	key
el piso	floor (of a building)
la planta baja	ground floor
el campo	countryside
el paisaje	landscape
la estación de autobuses, del metro, de tren	bus, subway, train station
el/la inspector(a) de aduanas	customs inspector
la llegada	arrival
el pasaje (de ida y vuelta)	(round-trip) ticket
el pasaporte	passport
la salida	departure; exit
la tabla de (wind)surf	surfboard/sailboard
acampar	to camp
confirmar una reservación	to confirm a reservation
estar de vacaciones	to be on vacation
hacer las maletas	to pack (one's suitcases)
hacer un viaje	to take a trip
hacer (wind)surf	to (wind)surf
ir de compras	to go shopping
ir de vacaciones	to go on vacation
ir en autobús (m.), auto(móvil) (m.), motocicleta (f.)	to go by bus, car, motorcycle
jugar a las cartas	to play cards

Variación léxica

automóvil	⟷	coche (*Esp.*), carro (*Amér. L.*)
autobús	⟷	camión (*Méx.*), guagua (*Caribe*)
motocicleta	⟷	moto (*coloquial*)

More activities

 vhlcentral   **LM** p. 25   **WB** pp. 49–50   Online activities

el aeropuerto

el avión

el autobús

el viajero

Monta a caballo. (montar)

Saca/Toma fotos. (sacar, tomar)

la playa

Hace surf. (hacer)

la tabla de surf

Va en barco. (ir)

el mar

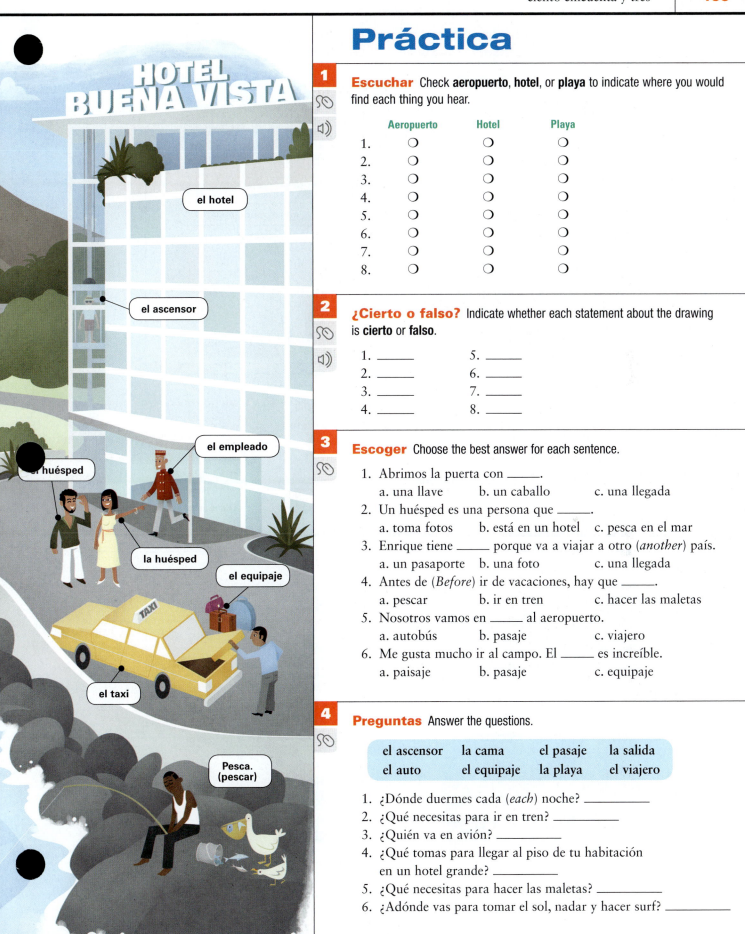

HOTEL BUENA VISTA

el hotel

el ascensor

el empleado

el huésped

la huésped

el equipaje

TAXI

el taxi

Pesca. (pescar)

Práctica

1 **Escuchar** Check **aeropuerto**, **hotel**, or **playa** to indicate where you would find each thing you hear.

	Aeropuerto	Hotel	Playa
1.	○	○	○
2.	○	○	○
3.	○	○	○
4.	○	○	○
5.	○	○	○
6.	○	○	○
7.	○	○	○
8.	○	○	○

2 **¿Cierto o falso?** Indicate whether each statement about the drawing is **cierto** or **falso**.

1. _____   5. _____
2. _____   6. _____
3. _____   7. _____
4. _____   8. _____

3 **Escoger** Choose the best answer for each sentence.

1. Abrimos la puerta con _____.
   a. una llave   b. un caballo   c. una llegada
2. Un huésped es una persona que _____.
   a. toma fotos   b. está en un hotel   c. pesca en el mar
3. Enrique tiene _____ porque va a viajar a otro (*another*) país.
   a. un pasaporte   b. una foto   c. una llegada
4. Antes de (*Before*) ir de vacaciones, hay que _____.
   a. pescar   b. ir en tren   c. hacer las maletas
5. Nosotros vamos en _____ al aeropuerto.
   a. autobús   b. pasaje   c. viajero
6. Me gusta mucho ir al campo. El _____ es increíble.
   a. paisaje   b. pasaje   c. equipaje

4 **Preguntas** Answer the questions.

el ascensor	la cama	el pasaje	la salida
el auto	el equipaje	la playa	el viajero

1. ¿Dónde duermes cada (*each*) noche? _____
2. ¿Qué necesitas para ir en tren? _____
3. ¿Quién va en avión? _____
4. ¿Qué tomas para llegar al piso de tu habitación en un hotel grande? _____
5. ¿Qué necesitas para hacer las maletas? _____
6. ¿Adónde vas para tomar el sol, nadar y hacer surf? _____

Las estaciones y los meses del año

el invierno: diciembre, enero, febrero

la primavera: marzo, abril, mayo

el verano: junio, julio, agosto

el otoño: septiembre, octubre, noviembre

—**¿Cuál es la fecha de hoy?**   *What is today's date?*
—**Es el primero de octubre.**   *It's the first of October.*
—**Es el dos de marzo.**   *It's March 2ⁿᵈ.*
—**Es el diez de noviembre.**   *It's November 10ᵗʰ.*

Más vocabulario

Está (muy) nublado.	*It's (very) cloudy.*
Hace fresco.	*It's cool.*
Hace (mucho) sol.	*It's (very) sunny.*
Hace (mucho) viento.	*It's (very) windy.*

El tiempo

—**¿Qué tiempo hace?**   *How's the weather?*
—**Hace buen/mal tiempo.**   *The weather is good/bad.*

Hace (mucho) calor.
It's (very) hot.

Hace (mucho) frío.
It's (very) cold.

Llueve. (llover o:ue)
It's raining.
Está lloviendo.
It's raining.

Nieva. (nevar e:ie)
It's snowing.
Está nevando.
It's snowing.

5

El Hotel Regis Label the floors of the hotel.

Números ordinales	
primer *(before a masculine singular noun)*, **primero/a**	*first*
segundo/a	*second*
tercer *(before a masculine singular noun)*, **tercero/a**	*third*
cuarto/a	*fourth*
quinto/a	*fifth*
sexto/a	*sixth*
séptimo/a	*seventh*
octavo/a	*eighth*
noveno/a	*ninth*
décimo/a	*tenth*

a. _____ piso
b. _____ piso
c. _____ piso
d. _____ piso
e. _____ piso
f. _____ piso
g. _____ piso
h. _____ baja

6

Contestar In pairs, take turns asking each other these questions. Use the illustrations on the previous page to answer the questions about the seasons.

> **modelo**
>
> **Estudiante 1:** ¿Cuál es el primer mes de la primavera?
> **Estudiante 2:** marzo

1. ¿Cuál es el primer mes del invierno?
2. ¿Cuál es el tercer mes del otoño?
3. ¿Cuál es el segundo mes de la primavera?
4. ¿Cuál es el primer mes del año?
5. ¿Cuál es el octavo mes del año?
6. ¿Cuál es el quinto mes del año?
7. ¿Cuál es el décimo mes del año?
8. ¿Cuál es el segundo mes del verano?
9. ¿Cuál es el tercer mes del invierno?
10. ¿Cuál es el sexto mes del año?

7

Las estaciones Name the season that applies to the description.

1. Las clases terminan.
2. Vamos a la playa.
3. Nieva mucho.
4. Acampamos.
5. Las clases empiezan.
6. Llueve mucho.
7. Hace mucho calor.
8. Esquiamos.
9. el entrenamiento (*training*) de béisbol
10. el Día de Acción de Gracias (*Thanksgiving*)

8

¿Cuál es la fecha? Give the dates for these holidays.

> **modelo**
>
> el día de San Valentín   14 de febrero

1. el día de Halloween
2. el día de San Patricio
3. el primer día de verano
4. el Año Nuevo
5. mi cumpleaños (*birthday*)
6. mi día de fiesta favorito

9 **Seleccionar** Choose the word or phrase that best completes each sentence.

1. A mis padres les gusta ir a Yucatán porque (hace sol, nieva).
2. Mis amigos van a esquiar si (nieva, está nublado).
3. Mi primo de Kansas dice que durante (*during*) un tornado, hace mucho (sol, viento).
4. Tomo el sol cuando (hace calor, llueve).
5. Nosotros vamos a ver una película si hace (buen, mal) tiempo.
6. Mi hermana prefiere correr cuando (hace mucho calor, hace fresco).
7. Mi padre no quiere jugar al golf si (hace fresco, llueve).
8. Mis tíos van de excursión si hace (buen, mal) tiempo.
9. Cuando hace mucho (sol, frío), tomo chocolate caliente (*hot*).
10. Hoy mi sobrino va al parque porque (está lloviendo, hace buen tiempo).

10 **El clima** With a partner, take turns asking and answering questions about the weather and temperatures in these cities.

> **modelo**
>
> **Estudiante 1:** ¿Qué tiempo hace hoy en Nueva York?
> **Estudiante 2:** Hace frío y hace viento.
> **Estudiante 1:** ¿Cuál es la temperatura máxima?
> **Estudiante 2:** Treinta y un grados (*degrees*).
> **Estudiante 1:** ¿Y la temperatura mínima?
> **Estudiante 2:** Diez grados.

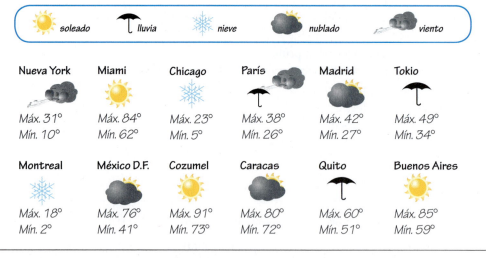

soleado   lluvia   nieve   nublado   viento

Nueva York
Máx. 31°
Mín. 10°

Miami
Máx. 84°
Mín. 62°

Chicago
Máx. 23°
Mín. 5°

París
Máx. 38°
Mín. 26°

Madrid
Máx. 42°
Mín. 27°

Tokio
Máx. 49°
Mín. 34°

Montreal
Máx. 18°
Mín. 2°

México D.F.
Máx. 76°
Mín. 41°

Cozumel
Máx. 91°
Mín. 73°

Caracas
Máx. 80°
Mín. 72°

Quito
Máx. 60°
Mín. 51°

Buenos Aires
Máx. 85°
Mín. 59°

11 **Completar** Complete these sentences with your own ideas.

1. Cuando hace sol, yo…
2. Cuando llueve, mis amigos y yo…
3. Cuando hace calor, mi familia…
4. Cuando hace viento, la gente…
5. Cuando hace frío, yo…
6. Cuando hace mal tiempo, mis amigos…
7. Cuando nieva, muchas personas…
8. Cuando está nublado, mis amigos y yo…
9. Cuando hace fresco, mis padres…
10. Cuando hace buen tiempo, mis amigos…

NOTA CULTURAL

In most Spanish-speaking countries, temperatures are given in degrees Celsius. Use these formulas to convert between **grados centígrados** and **grados Fahrenheit**.

degrees C × 9 ÷ 5 + 32 = degrees F

degrees F - 32 × 5 ÷ 9 = degrees C

CONSULTA

Calor and **frío** can apply to both weather and people. Use **hacer** to describe weather conditions or climate.

Hace frío en Santiago. *It's cold in Santiago.*

Use **tener** to refer to people.

El viajero tiene frío. *The traveler is cold.*

See **Estructura 3.4**, p. 101.

Comunicación

12

Preguntas personales In pairs, ask each other these questions.

1. ¿Cuál es la fecha de hoy? ¿Qué estación es?
2. ¿Te gusta esta estación? ¿Por qué?
3. ¿Qué estación prefieres? ¿Por qué?
4. ¿Prefieres el mar o las montañas? ¿La playa o el campo? ¿Por qué?
5. Cuando haces un viaje, ¿qué te gusta hacer y ver?
6. ¿Piensas ir de vacaciones este verano? ¿Adónde quieres ir? ¿Por qué?
7. ¿Qué deseas ver y qué lugares quieres visitar?
8. ¿Cómo te gusta viajar? ¿En avión? ¿En motocicleta...?

13

Encuesta Your instructor will give you a worksheet. How does the weather affect what you do? Walk around the class and ask your classmates what they prefer or like to do in the weather conditions given. Note their responses on your worksheet. Make sure to personalize your survey by adding a few original questions.

14

La reservación In pairs, prepare a conversation between a hotel receptionist and a tourist calling to make a reservation. Read only the information that pertains to you. Then role-play the situation.

Turista

Vas a viajar a Yucatán con un amigo. Llegan a Cancún el 23 de febrero y necesitan una habitación con baño privado para cuatro noches. Ustedes quieren descansar y prefieren una habitación con vista (view) al mar. Averigua (Find out) toda la información que necesitas (el costo, cuántas camas, etc.) y decide si quieres hacer la reservación o no.

Empleado/a

Trabajas en la recepción del Hotel Oceanía en Cancún. Para el mes de febrero, sólo quedan (remain) dos habitaciones: una individual ($168/noche) en el primer piso y una doble ($134/noche) en el quinto piso que tiene descuento porque no hay ascensor. Todas las habitaciones tienen baño privado y vista (view) a la piscina.

15

Minidrama With two or three classmates, prepare a skit about people who are on vacation or are planning a vacation. The skit should take place in one of these locations.

- la playa
- una casa
- un aeropuerto, una estación de tren/autobuses
- un hotel
- el campo

Síntesis

16

Un viaje You are planning a trip to Mexico and have many questions about your itinerary on which your partner, a travel agent, will advise you. Your instructor will give you and your partner each a sheet with different instructions for acting out the roles.

¡Vamos a la playa!

Los seis amigos hacen un viaje a la playa.

 Video

TÍA ANA MARÍA ¿Están listos para su viaje a la playa?

TODOS Sí.

TÍA ANA MARÍA Excelente... ¡A la estación de autobuses!

MARU ¿Dónde está Miguel?

FELIPE Yo lo traigo.

(se escucha un grito de Miguel)

FELIPE Ya está listo. Y tal vez enojado. Ahorita vamos.

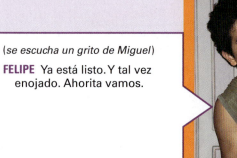

EMPLEADO Bienvenidas. ¿En qué puedo servirles?

MARU Hola. Tenemos una reservación para seis personas para esta noche.

EMPLEADO ¿A nombre de quién?

JIMENA ¿Díaz? ¿López? No estoy segura.

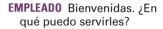

EMPLEADO No encuentro su nombre. Ah, no, ahora sí lo veo, aquí está. Díaz. Dos habitaciones en el primer piso para seis huéspedes.

FELIPE No está nada mal el hotel, ¿verdad? Limpio, cómodo... ¡Oye, Miguel! ¿Todavía estás enojado conmigo? *(a Juan Carlos)* Miguel está de mal humor. No me habla.

JUAN CARLOS ¿Todavía?

EMPLEADO Aquí están las llaves de sus habitaciones.

MARU Gracias. Una cosa más. Mi novio y yo queremos hacer windsurf, pero no tenemos tablas.

EMPLEADO El botones las puede conseguir para ustedes.

MARISSA **JIMENA** **MARU** **MIGUEL** **MAITE FUENTES** **ANA MARÍA** **EMPLEADO**

7

JUAN CARLOS ¿Qué hace este libro aquí? ¿Estás estudiando en la playa?

JIMENA Sí, es que tengo un examen la próxima semana.

8

JUAN CARLOS Ay, Jimena. ¡No! ¿Vamos a nadar?

JIMENA Bueno, como estudiar es tan aburrido y el tiempo está tan bonito...

MARISSA Yo estoy un poco cansada. ¿Y tú? ¿Por qué no estás nadando?

FELIPE Es por causa de Miguel.

9

10

MARISSA Hmm, estoy confundida.

FELIPE Esta mañana. ¡Sigue enojado conmigo!

MARISSA No puede seguir enojado tanto tiempo.

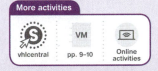

More activities

vhlcentral   VM pp. 9–10   Online activities

Expresiones útiles

Talking with hotel personnel

¿En qué puedo servirles?
How can I help you?
Tenemos una reservación.
We have a reservation.
¿A nombre de quién?
In whose name?
¿Quizás López? ¿Tal vez Díaz?
Maybe López? Maybe Díaz?
Ahora lo veo, aquí está. Díaz.
Now I see it. Here it is. Díaz.
Dos habitaciones en el primer piso para seis huéspedes.
Two rooms on the first floor for six guests.
Aquí están las llaves.
Here are the keys.

Describing a hotel

No está nada mal el hotel.
The hotel isn't bad at all.
Todo está tan limpio y cómodo.
Everything is so clean and comfortable.
Es excelente/estupendo/fabuloso/ fenomenal/increíble/magnífico/ maravilloso/perfecto.
It's excellent/stupendous/fabulous/ phenomenal/incredible/magnificent/ marvelous/perfect.

Talking about how you feel

Yo estoy un poco cansado/a.
I am a little tired.
Estoy confundido/a. *I'm confused.*
Todavía estoy/Sigo enojado/a contigo.
I'm still angry with you.

Additional vocabulary

afuera *outside*
amable *nice; friendly*
el balde *bucket*
el/la botones *bellhop*
la crema de afeitar
shaving cream
el frente (frío) *(cold) front*
el grito *scream*
la temporada *period of time*
entonces *so, then*
es igual *it's the same*

¿Qué pasó?

1

Completar Complete these sentences.

aburrido	botones	la llave
el aeropuerto	la estación de autobuses	montar a caballo
amable	habitaciones	reservación

1. Los amigos van a _____ para ir a la playa.
2. La _____ del hotel está a nombre de los Díaz.
3. Los amigos tienen dos _____ para seis personas.
4. El _____ puede conseguir tablas de windsurf para Maru.
5. Jimena dice que estudiar en vacaciones es muy _____.

CONSULTA

The meaning of some adjectives, such as **aburrido**, changes depending on whether they are used with **ser** or **estar**. See **Estructura 5.3**, pp. 170–171.

2

Identificar Identify the person who made each statement.

1. Aquí están las llaves de sus habitaciones. El botones puede llevar su equipaje al primer piso.
2. ¿Qué hace este libro aquí? ¿Estás estudiando en la playa?
3. Tenemos una reservación para seis personas para esta noche.
4. Miguel está de mal humor. No me habla.
5. ¿Están listos para su viaje a la playa?

EMPLEADO   MARU

FELIPE

JUAN CARLOS   TÍA ANA MARÍA

3

Ordenar Place these events in the correct order.

_____ a. El empleado busca la reservación.
_____ b. Marissa dice que está confundida.
_____ c. Los amigos están listos para ir a la playa.
_____ d. El empleado da (*gives*) las llaves de las habitaciones a las chicas.
_____ e. Miguel grita (*screams*).

4

Conversar With a partner, create a conversation between a hotel employee and a guest in Mexico.

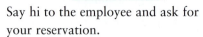

Huésped	Empleado/a
Say hi to the employee and ask for your reservation.	→ Tell the guest that you can't find his/her reservation.
Tell the employee that the reservation is in your name.	→ Tell him/her that you found the reservation and that it's for a double room.
Tell the employee that the hotel is very clean and comfortable.	→ Say that you agree with the guest, welcome him/her, and give him/her the keys.

Pronunciación

Tutorial

Spanish b and v

bueno	**v**ólei**b**ol	**bi**blioteca	**vi**vir

There is no difference in pronunciation between the Spanish letters **b** and **v**. However, each letter can be pronounced two different ways, depending on which letters appear next to them.

bonito	**v**iajar	ta**mb**ién	i**nv**estigar

B and **v** are pronounced like the English hard *b* when they appear either as the first letter of a word, at the beginning of a phrase, or after **m** or **n**.

de**b**er	no**v**io	a**b**ril	cer**v**eza

In all other positions, **b** and **v** have a softer pronunciation, which has no equivalent in English. Unlike the hard **b**, which is produced by tightly closing the lips and stopping the flow of air, the soft **b** is produced by keeping the lips slightly open.

bola	**v**ela	Cari**b**e	decli**v**e

In both pronunciations, there is no difference in sound between **b** and **v**. The English *v* sound, produced by friction between the upper teeth and lower lip, does not exist in Spanish. Instead, the soft **b** comes from friction between the two lips.

Verónica y su esposo canta**n b**oleros.

When **b** or **v** begins a word, its pronunciation depends on the previous word. At the beginning of a phrase or after a word that ends in **m** or **n**, it is pronounced as a hard **b**.

Benito   es d**e B**oquerón   per**o v**ive   e**n V**ictoria.

Words that begin with **b** or **v** are pronounced with a soft **b** if they appear immediately after a word that ends in a vowel or any consonant other than **m** or **n**.

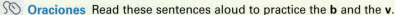

Práctica Read these words aloud to practice the **b** and the **v**.

1. hablamos		4. van		7. doble		10. nublado
2. trabajar		5. contabilidad		8. novia		11. llave
3. botones		6. bien		9. béisbol		12. invierno

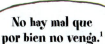
No hay mal que por bien no venga.[1]

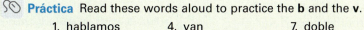

Oraciones Read these sentences aloud to practice the **b** and the **v**.

1. Vamos a Guaynabo en autobús.
2. Voy de vacaciones a la Isla Culebra.
3. Tengo una habitación individual en el octavo piso.
4. Víctor y Eva van en avión al Caribe.
5. La planta baja es bonita también.
6. ¿Qué vamos a ver en Bayamón?
7. Beatriz, la novia de Víctor, es de Arecibo, Puerto Rico.

Refranes Read these sayings aloud to practice the **b** and the **v**.

Hombre prevenido vale por dos.[2]

More activities

vhlcentral

LM
p. 26

El Viejo San Juan

San Juan, the capital of Puerto Rico, was founded by Juan Ponce de León in 1508. The original settlement was called **Caparra**. In 1521 the name was formally changed to **San Juan Bautista°** de Puerto Rico. The city has served as the island's capital ever since. The oldest part of the capital, known as **el Viejo San Juan**, is an international tourist destination. Many Caribbean cruise ships make stops there.

El Viejo San Juan is most famous for its Spanish colonial architecture, which according to strict regulations can neither be altered nor demolished. Furthermore, all new construction must maintain the integrity of the Spanish colonial style.

Visitors flock to this historic site to stroll the colonial **callejones°**, tour monuments such as the **Casa Blanca** and the fortress known as **El Morro**, and enjoy the climate of **la Isla del Encanto°**.

El Viejo San Juan was added to the U.S. National Register of Historic Places in 1966, and in 1983 it was designated a World Heritage Site by UNESCO.

In 2017, Hurricane María severely damaged parts of the old city, causing a disruption to tourism. In time, the people of the city cleaned up and repaired. As one reporter put it, "Old San Juan has already survived 500 hurricane seasons. It will survive this one, too!"

Plaza de Armas

San Juan Bautista *Saint John the Baptist* callejones *narrow lanes, alleyways* la Isla del Encanto *the Isle of Enchantment (nickname for Puerto Rico)*

Sitios históricos del Viejo San Juan

- **Plaza de Armas:** the main public square in el Viejo San Juan
- **Catedral Metropolitana Basílica de San Juan Bautista:** the second oldest cathedral in the Western Hemisphere
- **El Morro** and **Castillo de San Cristóbal:** forts built to protect the city and San Juan Bay
- **Casa Blanca:** historic house and museum, residence of Ponce de León's family from 1521 to the mid-18th century

ACTIVIDADES

1 ¿Cierto o falso? Indicate whether these statements are **cierto** or **falso**. Correct the false statements.

1. **Caparra** was the name of the original settlement.
2. Puerto Rico's capital is named after a saint.
3. To protect its historic sites, most of **el Viejo San Juan** is off-limits to the public.
4. The buildings in **el Viejo San Juan** maintain a Spanish colonial architectural style.
5. The city is culturally important in the United States but not internationally.
6. Hurricane María completely spared **el Viejo San Juan**.
7. **El Viejo San Juan** does not have a main public square.
8. The second oldest cathedral in the Americas is in San Juan.
9. **El Castillo de San Cristóbal** was principally a colonial trading post.
10. You can visit Ponce de León's family home in **el Viejo San Juan**.

ASÍ SE DICE

Viajes y turismo

el asiento del medio, del pasillo, de la ventanilla	*center, aisle, window seat*
el itinerario	*itinerary*
media pensión	*breakfast and one meal included*
el ómnibus *(Perú)*	**el autobús**
pensión completa	*all meals included*
el puente	*long weekend (lit., bridge)*

EL MUNDO HISPANO

Destinos populares

- **Las playas del Parque Nacional Manuel Antonio** (Costa Rica) ofrecen° la oportunidad de nadar y luego caminar por el bosque tropical°.

- **Teotihuacán** (México) Desde antes de la época° de los aztecas, aquí se celebra el equinoccio de primavera en la Pirámide del Sol.

- **Puerto Chicama** (Perú), con sus olas° de cuatro kilómetros de largo°, es un destino para surfistas expertos.

- **Tikal** (Guatemala) Aquí puedes ver las maravillas de la selva° y ruinas de la civilización maya.

- **Las playas de Rincón** (Puerto Rico) Son ideales para descansar y observar ballenas°.

ofrecen *offer* bosque tropical *rain forest*
Desde antes de la época *Since before the time* olas *waves*
de largo *in length* selva *jungle* ballenas *whales*

PERFIL

Punta del Este

One of South America's largest and most fashionable beach resort towns is Uruguay's **Punta del Este**, a narrow strip of land containing twenty miles of pristine beaches. Its peninsular shape gives it two very different seascapes. **La Playa Mansa**, facing the bay and therefore the more protected side, has calm waters. Here, people practice water sports like swimming, water skiing, windsurfing, and diving. **La Playa Brava**, facing the east, receives the Atlantic Ocean's powerful, wave-producing winds, making it popular for surfing, body boarding, and kite surfing. Besides the beaches, posh shopping, and world-famous nightlife, **Punta** offers its 620,000 yearly visitors yacht and fishing clubs, golf courses, and excursions to observe sea lions at the **Isla de Lobos** nature reserve.

CON RITMO HISPANO

Luis Fonsi (1978–)
Birthplace: San Juan, Puerto Rico

He has released ten albums and worked with artists such as Christina Aguilera, David Bisbal, Laura Pausini, and Juan Luis Guerra. His song "Despacito," featuring Daddy Yankee, was an international hit.

Go to **vhlcentral.com** to find out more about **Luis Fonsi** and his music.

ACTIVIDADES

2 **Comprensión** Complete the sentences.

1. En las playas de Rincón puedes ver _____.
2. Cerca de 620.000 turistas visitan _____ cada año.
3. En el avión pides un _____ si te gusta ver el paisaje.
4. En Punta del Este, la gente prefiere nadar en la Playa _____.
5. El _____ es un medio de transporte en Perú.

3 **De vacaciones** Spring break is coming up, and you want to go on a short vacation with some friends. Working in a small group, decide which of the locations featured on these pages best suits the group's likes and interests. Come to an agreement about how you will get there, where you prefer to stay and for how long, and what each of you will do during free time.

More activities

vhlcentral

Online activities

5.1 Estar with conditions and emotions

CONSULTA

To review the present tense of **estar**, see **Estructura 2.3**, p. 59.

• • •

To review the present tense of **ser**, see **Estructura 1.3**, p. 20.

ANTE TODO As you learned in **Lecciones 1** and **2**, the verb **estar** is used to talk about how you feel and to say where people, places, and things are located. **Estar** is also used with adjectives to talk about certain emotional and physical conditions.

▶ Use **estar** with adjectives to describe the physical condition of places and things.

La habitación **está** sucia.
The room is dirty.

La puerta **está** cerrada.
The door is closed.

▶ Use **estar** with adjectives to describe how people feel, both mentally and physically.

Yo estoy cansada.

¿Están listos para su viaje?

▶ **¡Atención!** Two important expressions with **estar** that you can use to talk about conditions and emotions are **estar de buen humor** (*to be in a good mood*) and **estar de mal humor** (*to be in a bad mood*).

Adjectives that describe emotions and conditions

abierto/a	open	**contento/a**	content	**listo/a**	ready
aburrido/a	bored	**desordenado/a**	disorderly	**nervioso/a**	nervous
alegre	happy	**enamorado/a (de)**	in love (with)	**ocupado/a**	busy
avergonzado/a	embarrassed			**ordenado/a**	orderly
cansado/a	tired	**enojado/a**	angry	**preocupado/a (por)**	worried (about)
cerrado/a	closed	**equivocado/a**	wrong	**seguro/a**	sure
cómodo/a	comfortable	**feliz**	happy	**sucio/a**	dirty
confundido/a	confused	**limpio/a**	clean	**triste**	sad

¡INTÉNTALO! Provide the present tense forms of **estar**, and choose which adjective best completes the sentence.

1. La biblioteca ___está___ (cerrada / nerviosa) los domingos por la noche. *cerrada*
2. Nosotros _____ muy (ocupados / equivocados) todos los lunes.
3. Ellas _____ (alegres / confundidas) porque tienen vacaciones.
4. Javier _____ (enamorado / ordenado) de Maribel.
5. Yo _____ (nerviosa / abierta) por el viaje.
6. Diana _____ (enojada / limpia) con su novio.
7. La habitación siempre _____ (ordenada / segura) cuando vienen sus padres.
8. Ustedes no comprenden; _____ (equivocados / tristes).

More activities

vhlcentral

LM p. 27

WB pp. 51–52

Online activities
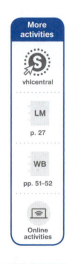

Práctica y Comunicación

1

¿Cómo están? In the first blank of each statement made by Martín, fill in the correct form of **estar**. In the second blank, fill in the adjective that best fits the context.

1. Yo _____ un poco _____ porque tengo un examen mañana.
2. Mis hermanos Juan y José salen de la casa a las cinco de la mañana. Por la noche, siempre _____ muy _____.
3. Mi hermana Patricia _____ muy _____ porque mañana va a hacer una excursión al campo.
4. Mi amigo Ramiro _____ _____; su novia se llama Adela.
5. Mi papá y sus colegas _____ muy _____ hoy. ¡Hay mucho trabajo!
6. Patricia y yo _____ un poco _____ por ellos porque trabajan mucho.
7. Mi amiga Mónica _____ un poco _____ porque su novio no puede salir esta noche.
8. Esta clase no es muy interesante. ¿Tú _____ _____ también?

2

Describir Describe these people and places.

1. Anabela

2. Juan y Luisa

3. la habitación de Teresa

4. César

3

Situaciones With a partner, use **estar** to talk about how you feel in these situations.

1. Cuando hace sol...
2. Cuando tomas un examen...
3. Cuando viajas en avión...
4. Cuando estás en la clase de español...
5. Cuando ves una película con tu actor/actriz favorito/a...

4

En la tele In small groups, imagine that you are a family that stars on a reality TV show. You are vacationing together, but the trip isn't going well for everyone. Write the script of a scene from the show and then act it out. Use at least six adjectives from the previous page and be creative!

modelo

Papá: ¿Por qué estás enojada, María Rosa? El hotel es muy bonito y las habitaciones están limpias.

Mamá: ¡Pero mira, Roberto! Las maletas de Elisa están abiertas y, como siempre, sus cosas están muy desordenadas.

5.2 The present progressive Tutorial

ANTE TODO   Both Spanish and English use the present progressive, which consists of the present tense of the verb *to be* and the present participle of another verb (the *-ing* form in English).

Las chicas están hablando con el empleado del hotel.

¿Estás estudiando en la playa?

▶ Form the present progressive with the present tense of **estar** and a present participle.

FORM OF **ESTAR** + PRESENT PARTICIPLE		FORM OF **ESTAR** + PRESENT PARTICIPLE	
Estoy	**pescando.**	**Estamos**	**comiendo.**
I am	*fishing.*	*We are*	*eating.*

▶ The present participle of regular **-ar**, **-er**, and **-ir** verbs is formed as follows:

INFINITIVE	STEM	ENDING	PRESENT PARTICIPLE
hablar	habl-	**-ando**	habl**ando**
comer	com-	**-iendo**	com**iendo**
escribir	escrib-	**-iendo**	escrib**iendo**

▶ **¡Atención!** When the stem of an **-er** or **-ir** verb ends in a vowel, the present participle ends in **-yendo**.

INFINITIVE	STEM	ENDING	PRESENT PARTICIPLE
leer	le-	**-yendo**	le**yendo**
oír	o-	**-yendo**	o**yendo**
traer	tra-	**-yendo**	tra**yendo**

▶ **Ir**, **poder**, and **venir** have irregular present participles (**yendo**, **pudiendo**, **viniendo**). Several other verbs have irregular present participles that you will need to learn.

▶ **-Ir** stem-changing verbs have a stem change in the present participle.

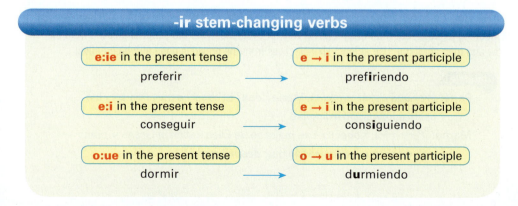

-ir stem-changing verbs

e:ie in the present tense	**e → i** in the present participle
preferir	prefi**r**iendo

e:i in the present tense	**e → i** in the present participle
conseguir	cons**i**guiendo

o:ue in the present tense	**o → u** in the present participle
dormir	d**u**rmiendo

COMPARE & CONTRAST

The use of the present progressive is much more restricted in Spanish than in English. In Spanish, the present progressive is mainly used to emphasize that an action is in progress at the time of speaking.

> Maru **está escuchando** música latina **ahora mismo**.
> *Maru is listening to Latin music right now.*

> Felipe y su amigo **todavía están jugando** al fútbol.
> *Felipe and his friend are still playing soccer.*

In English, the present progressive is often used to talk about situations and actions that occur over an extended period of time or in the future. In Spanish, the simple present tense is often used instead.

> Xavier **estudia** computación este semestre.
> *Xavier is studying computer science this semester.*

> Marissa **sale** mañana para los Estados Unidos.
> *Marissa is leaving tomorrow for the United States.*

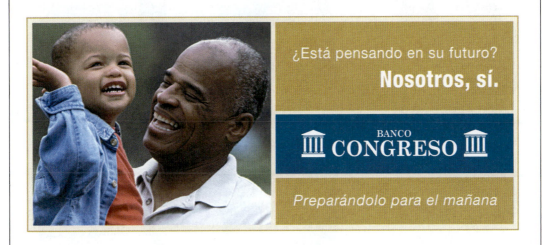

¿Está pensando en su futuro?
Nosotros, sí.

BANCO CONGRESO

Preparándolo para el mañana

More activities

vhlcentral

LM p. 28

WB p. 53

Online activities

¡INTÉNTALO! Create complete sentences by putting the verbs in the present progressive.

1. mis amigos / descansar en la playa *Mis amigos están descansando en la playa.*
2. nosotros / practicar deportes _____
3. Carmen / comer en casa _____
4. yo / leer el periódico _____
5. nuestro equipo / ganar el partido _____
6. él / pensar comprar una bicicleta _____
7. ustedes / jugar a las cartas _____
8. Marcela / leer el correo electrónico _____
9. José y Francisco / dormir _____
10. yo / preparar sándwiches _____
11. Carlos / tomar fotos _____
12. ¿dormir / tú? _____

Práctica

1

Completar Use the present progressive of the verb to complete Alfredo's description of what everyone in his class is doing to prepare for a trip to Puerto Rico.

1. Yo _____ (investigar) la situación política de la isla (*island*).
2. Marta y José Luis _____ (buscar) información sobre San Juan en Internet.
3. La esposa del profesor _____ (hacer) las maletas.
4. Enrique y yo _____ (leer) un correo electrónico de nuestro amigo puertorriqueño.
5. Javier _____ (aprender) mucho sobre la cultura puertorriqueña.
6. Y tú _____ (practicar) el español, ¿verdad?

2

¿Qué están haciendo? Complete María's description of what she and her friends are doing right now as they vacation in Puerto Rico.

CONSULTA

For more information about Puerto Rico, see **Panorama**, pp. 186–187.

1. Alejandro y Rebeca

2. Javier

3. Yo

4. Celia y yo

5. Samuel

6. Lorenzo

3

Personajes famosos Say what these celebrities are doing right now.

AYUDA

Isabel Allende: **novelas**

Rachael Ray: **televisión, negocios** (*business*)

James Cameron: **cine**

Venus y Serena Williams: **tenis**

José Altuve: **béisbol**

Daymé Arocena: **canciones**

Kevin Durant: **baloncesto**

Las Rockettes de Nueva York: **baile**

> **modelo**
>
> Shakira
>
> *Shakira está cantando una canción ahora mismo.*

A		B	
Isabel Allende	Daymé Arocena	bailar	hacer
Rachael Ray	Kevin Durant	cantar	jugar
James Cameron	Las Rockettes de	correr	preparar
Venus y Serena	Nueva York	escribir	¿?
Williams	¿?	hablar	¿?
José Altuve	¿?		

Comunicación

4

Preguntar With a partner, take turns asking each other what you are doing at these times.

> **modelo**
> 8:00 a.m.
> **Estudiante 1:** ¡Hola, Andrés! Son las ocho de la mañana. ¿Qué estás haciendo?
> **Estudiante 2:** Estoy desayunando.

1. 5:00 a.m.   3. 11:00 a.m.   5. 2:00 p.m.   7. 9:00 p.m.
2. 9:30 a.m.   4. 12:00 p.m.   6. 5:00 p.m.   8. 11:30 p.m.

5

Describir Work with a partner and use the present progressive to describe what is going on in this Spanish beach scene.

NOTA CULTURAL

Nearly 70 million tourists travel to Spain every year, many of them drawn by the warm climate and beautiful coasts. Tourists wanting a beach vacation go mostly to the **Costa del Sol** or the Balearic Islands, in the Mediterranean.

6

Conversar With a partner, prepare a phone conversation between two babysitters. Be creative and add further comments.

Estudiante 1	**Estudiante 2**
Say hello and ask what the kids are doing.	Say hello and tell your partner that two of your kids are doing their homework. Then ask what the kids at his/her house are doing.
Tell your partner that two of your kids are running and dancing in the house.	Tell your partner that one of the kids is reading.
Tell your partner that you are tired and that two of your kids are watching TV and eating pizza.	Tell your partner that one of the kids is sleeping.
Tell your partner you have to go; the kids are playing soccer in the house.	Say goodbye and good luck (**¡Buena suerte!**).

Síntesis

7

¿Qué están haciendo? A group of classmates is traveling to San Juan, Puerto Rico, for a week-long Spanish immersion program. In order for the participants to be on time for their flight, you and your partner must locate them. Your instructor will give you each a handout to help you complete this task.

5.3 Ser and estar Tutorial

ANTE TODO You have already learned that **ser** and **estar** both mean *to be* but are used for different purposes. These charts summarize the key differences in usage between **ser** and **estar**.

Uses of ser

1. Nationality and place of origin	Juan Carlos **es** argentino. **Es** de Buenos Aires.
2. Profession or occupation	Adela **es** inspectora de aduanas. Francisco **es** médico.
3. Characteristics of people and things . . .	José y Clara **son** simpáticos. El clima de Puerto Rico **es** agradable.
4. Generalizations	¡**Es** fabuloso viajar! **Es** difícil estudiar a la una de la mañana.
5. Possession	**Es** la pluma de Jimena. **Son** las llaves del señor Díaz.
6. What something is made of	La bicicleta **es** de metal. Los pasajes **son** de papel.
7. Time and date	Hoy **es** martes. **Son** las dos. Hoy **es** el primero de julio.
8. Where or when an event takes place . .	El partido **es** en el estadio Santa Fe. La conferencia **es** a las siete.

Ellos son mis amigos.

Miguel está enojado conmigo.

Uses of estar

1. Location or spatial relationships	El aeropuerto **está** lejos de la ciudad. Tu habitación **está** en el tercer piso.
2. Health	¿Cómo **estás**? **Estoy** bien, gracias.
3. Physical states and conditions	El profesor **está** ocupado. Las ventanas **están** abiertas.
4. Emotional states	Marissa **está** feliz hoy. **Estoy** muy enojado con Maru.
5. Certain weather expressions	**Está** lloviendo. **Está** nublado.
6. Ongoing actions (progressive tenses) . .	**Estamos** estudiando para un examen. Ana **está** leyendo una novela.

Ser and estar with adjectives

▶ With many descriptive adjectives, **ser** and **estar** can both be used, but the meaning will change.

Juan **es** delgado.
Juan is thin.

Ana **es** nerviosa.
Ana is a nervous person.

Juan **está** más delgado hoy.
Juan looks thinner today.

Ana **está** nerviosa por el examen.
Ana is nervous because of the exam.

▶ In the examples above, the statements with **ser** are general observations about the inherent qualities of Juan and Ana. The statements with **estar** describe conditions that are variable.

▶ Here are some adjectives that change in meaning when used with **ser** and **estar**.

With ser	**With estar**
El chico **es listo**.	El chico **está listo**.
The boy is smart.	*The boy is ready.*
La profesora **es mala**.	La profesora **está mala**.
The professor is bad.	*The professor is sick.*
Jaime **es aburrido**.	Jaime **está aburrido**.
Jaime is boring.	*Jaime is bored.*
Las peras **son verdes**.	Las peras **están verdes**.
Pears are green.	*The pears are not ripe.*
El gato **es muy vivo**.	El gato **está vivo**.
The cat is very clever.	*The cat is alive.*
Iván **es un hombre seguro**.	Iván no **está seguro**.
Iván is a confident man.	*Iván is not sure.*

¡ATENCIÓN!

When referring to objects, **ser seguro/a** means *to be safe.*
El puente es seguro.
The bridge is safe.

¡INTÉNTALO! Form complete sentences by using the correct form of **ser** or **estar** and making any other necessary changes.

1. Alejandra / cansado
   Alejandra está cansada.

2. ellos / pelirrojo

3. yo / la clase de español

4. Carmen / alto

5. película / a las once

6. hoy / viernes

7. Romeo y Julieta / enamorado

8. Antonio / médico

9. nosotras / enojado

10. libros / de Ana

11. Mariana y Juan / estudiando

12. partido de baloncesto / gimnasio

More activities

vhlcentral

LM
p. 29

WB
pp. 54–55

Online activities

Práctica

1 **¿Ser o estar?** Indicate whether each adjective takes **ser** or **estar**. **¡Ojo!** Three of them can take both verbs.

	ser	estar		ser	estar
1. canadiense	○	○	5. enojada	○	○
2. delgada	○	○	6. seguro	○	○
3. enamorado	○	○	7. importante	○	○
4. lista	○	○	8. avergonzada	○	○

2 **Completar** Complete this conversation with the appropriate forms of **ser** and **estar**.

EDUARDO ¡Hola, Ceci! ¿Cómo (1)_____?

CECILIA Hola, Eduardo. Bien, gracias. ¡Qué guapo (2)_____ hoy!

EDUARDO Gracias. (3)_____ muy amable. Oye, ¿qué (4)_____ haciendo? (5)¿_____ ocupada?

CECILIA No, sólo le (6)_____ escribiendo una carta a mi prima Pilar.

EDUARDO ¿De dónde (7)_____ ella?

CECILIA Pilar (8)_____ de Ecuador. Su papá (9)_____ médico en Quito. Pero ahora Pilar y su familia (10)_____ de vacaciones en Ponce, Puerto Rico.

EDUARDO Y… ¿cómo (11)_____ Pilar?

CECILIA (12)_____ muy lista. Y también (13)_____ alta, rubia y muy bonita.

3 **En el parque** With a partner, take turns describing the people in the drawing. Your descriptions should answer the questions.

1. ¿Quiénes son?
2. ¿Dónde están?
3. ¿Cómo son?
4. ¿Cómo están?
5. ¿Qué están haciendo?
6. ¿Qué estación es?
7. ¿Qué tiempo hace?
8. ¿Quiénes están de vacaciones?

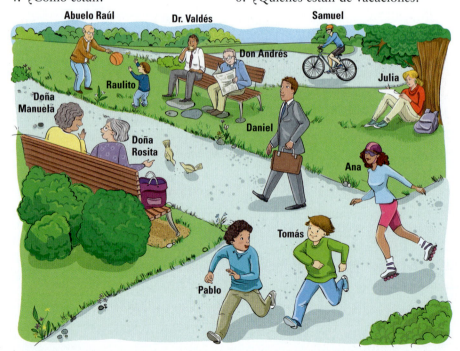

Comunicación

4

Describir With a classmate, take turns describing these people. Mention where they are from, what they are like, how they are feeling, and what they are doing right now.

> **modelo**
>
> tu compañero/a de cuarto
>
> *Mi compañera de cuarto es de San Juan, Puerto Rico. Es muy inteligente.*
> *Está cansada pero está estudiando porque tiene un examen.*

1. tu mejor (*best*) amigo/a
2. tu actor/actriz favorito/a
3. tu profesor(a) favorito/a
4. tu novio/a o esposo/a
5. tus abuelos
6. tus padres

5

Adivinar Get together with a partner and take turns describing a celebrity. Don't mention the celebrity's name. Can your partner guess who you are describing?

- descripción física
- cómo está ahora
- origen
- dónde está ahora
- qué está haciendo ahora
- profesión u ocupación

6

En el aeropuerto In groups of three, take turns assuming the identity of a character from this drawing. Your partners will ask you questions using **ser** and **estar** until they figure out who you are.

> **modelo**
>
> **Estudiante 3:** ¿Dónde estás?
> **Estudiante 1:** Estoy cerca de la puerta.
> **Estudiante 2:** ¿Qué estás haciendo?
> **Estudiante 1:** Estoy escuchando a otra persona.
> **Estudiante 3:** ¿Eres uno de los pasajeros?
> **Estudiante 1:** No, soy empleado del aeropuerto.
> **Estudiante 2:** ¿Eres Camilo?

Síntesis

7

Conversación With a partner, role-play a conversation between two airline passengers seated next to each other.

5.4 Direct object nouns and pronouns

 Tutorial

SUBJECT	VERB	DIRECT OBJECT NOUN
Juan Carlos y Jimena	están tomando	fotos.
Juan Carlos and Jimena	*are taking*	*photos.*

▶ A direct object noun receives the action of the verb directly and generally follows the verb. In the example above, the direct object noun answers the question *What are Juan Carlos and Jimena taking?*

▶ When a direct object noun in Spanish is a person or a pet, it is preceded by the word **a**. This is called the personal **a**; there is no English equivalent for this construction.

Mariela mira **a** Carlos.
Mariela is watching Carlos.

Mariela mira televisión.
Mariela is watching TV.

▶ In the first sentence above, the personal **a** is required because the direct object is a person. In the second sentence, the personal **a** is not required because the direct object is a thing, not a person.

No tenemos tablas de windsurf.

Miguel no me perdona.

El botones las puede conseguir para ustedes.

▶ Direct object pronouns are words that replace direct object nouns. Like English, Spanish uses a direct object pronoun to avoid repeating a noun already mentioned.

	DIRECT OBJECT		DIRECT OBJECT PRONOUN	
Maribel hace	las maletas.	Maribel	las	hace.
Felipe compra	el sombrero.	Felipe	lo	compra.
Vicky tiene	la llave.	Vicky	la	tiene.

Direct object pronouns

SINGULAR		PLURAL	
me	*me*	**nos**	*us*
te	*you* (fam.)	**os**	*you* (fam.)
lo	*you* (m., form.)	**los**	*you* (m.)
	him; it (m.)		*them* (m.)
la	*you* (f., form.)	**las**	*you* (f.)
	her; it (f.)		*them* (f.)

▶ In affirmative sentences, direct object pronouns generally appear before the conjugated verb. In negative sentences, the pronoun is placed between the word **no** and the verb.

Adela practica **el tenis.**
Adela **lo** practica.

Gabriela no tiene **las llaves.**
Gabriela **no las** tiene.

Carmen compra **los pasajes.**
Carmen **los** compra.

Diego no hace **las maletas.**
Diego **no las** hace.

▶ When the verb is an infinitive construction, such as **ir a** + [*infinitive*], the direct object pronoun can be placed before the conjugated form or attached to the infinitive.

Ellos van a escribir **unas postales.**
⟨ Ellos **las** van a escribir.
Ellos van a escribir**las.**

Lidia quiere ver **una película.**
⟨ Lidia **la** quiere ver.
Lidia quiere ver**la.**

▶ When the verb is in the present progressive, the direct object pronoun can be placed before the conjugated form or attached to the present participle. **¡Atención!** When a direct object pronoun is attached to the present participle, an accent mark is added to maintain the proper stress.

CONSULTA

To learn more about accents, see **Lección 4**, **Pronunciación**, p. 123, **Lección 10, Ortografía**, p. 339, and **Lección 11**, **Ortografía**, p. 375.

Gerardo está leyendo **la lección.**
⟨ Gerardo **la** está leyendo.
Gerardo está leyéndo**la.**

Toni está mirando **el partido.**
⟨ Toni **lo** está mirando.
Toni está mirándo**lo.**

 **¡INTÉNTALO!**   Choose the correct direct object pronoun for each sentence.

1. Tienes el libro de español. *c*
   a. La tienes. b. Los tienes. c. Lo tienes.
2. Marcos busca la llave.
   a. Me busca. b. La busca. c. Las busca.
3. El artista quiere dibujar a Luisa y a su mamá.
   a. Quiere dibujarme. b. Quiere dibujarla. c. Quiere dibujarlas.
4. Voy a ver el partido de baloncesto.
   a. Voy a verlo. b. Voy a verte. c. Voy a vernos.
5. Puedo oír a Gerardo y a Miguel.
   a. Puedo oírte. b. Puedo oírlos. c. Puedo oírlo.
6. Rita me lleva al aeropuerto y también lleva a Tomás.
   a. Nos lleva. b. Las lleva. c. Te lleva.
7. Quieren estudiar la gramática.
   a. Quieren estudiarnos. b. Quieren estudiarlo. c. Quieren estudiarla.
8. ¿Practicas los verbos irregulares?
   a. ¿Los practicas? b. ¿Las practicas? c. ¿Lo practicas?
9. Ignacio ve la película.
   a. La ve. b. Lo ve. c. Las ve.
10. Sandra va a invitar a Mario a la excursión. También me va a invitar a mí.
    a. Los va a invitar. b. Lo va a invitar. c. Nos va a invitar.

More activities

vhlcentral

LM p. 30

WB p. 56

Online activities

Práctica

1

Simplificar Describe preparations for a class trip to Costa Rica by changing the direct object nouns into direct object pronouns.

> **modelo**
>
> La profesora Vega tiene su pasaporte.
> *La profesora Vega lo tiene.*

1. Nosotros leemos los folletos (*brochures*).
2. Gustavo y Héctor confirman las reservaciones.
3. Ana María estudia el mapa.
4. Yo aprendo los nombres de los monumentos de San José.
5. Alicia escucha a la profesora.
6. Miguel escribe las instrucciones para ir al hotel.
7. Esteban busca el pasaje.
8. Nosotros planeamos una excursión.

2

Vacaciones Restate Ramón's thoughts about his trip to San Juan more succinctly using direct object pronouns.

> **modelo**
>
> Quiero hacer una excursión.
> *Quiero hacerla./La quiero hacer.*

1. Marcos está pidiendo el folleto turístico.
2. Necesitamos llevar los pasaportes.
3. Voy a hacer mi maleta.
4. Javier debe llamar a sus padres.
5. Ellos desean visitar el Viejo San Juan.
6. Puedo llamar a Javier por la mañana.
7. Prefiero llevar mi cámara.
8. No queremos perder nuestras reservaciones de hotel.

3

¿Quién? Answer the questions about the Garza family's trip to Puerto Rico. Use direct object pronouns in your answers.

> **modelo**
>
> ¿Quién hace las reservaciones para el hotel? (el Sr. Garza)
> *El Sr. Garza las hace.*

1. ¿Quién compra los pasajes para el vuelo (*flight*)? (la Sra. Garza)
2. ¿Quién tiene que hacer las maletas de los niños? (María)
3. ¿Quién compra un mapa de Puerto Rico? (Antonio)
4. ¿Quién va a confirmar las reservaciones de hotel? (la Sra. Garza)
5. ¿Quién busca la cámara? (María)
6. ¿Quiénes buscan los pasaportes? (Antonio y María)

Comunicación

4

Entrevista Take turns asking and answering these questions with a classmate. Be sure to use direct object pronouns in your responses.

1. ¿Ves mucho la televisión?
2. ¿Cuándo vas a ver tu programa favorito?
3. ¿Quién prepara la comida (*food*) en tu casa?
4. ¿Te visita mucho tu familia?
5. ¿Visitas mucho a tus abuelos?
6. ¿Nos entienden nuestros padres a nosotros?
7. ¿Cuándo ves a tus amigos/as?
8. ¿Cuándo te llaman tus amigos/as?

5

Los pasajeros Get together with a partner and take turns asking each other questions about the drawing. Use the verbs and direct object pronouns.

AYUDA

For travel-related vocabulary, see **Contextos**, pp. 152–153.

▶ **modelo**

Estudiante 1: ¿Quién está leyendo el libro?
Estudiante 2: Susana lo está leyendo./Susana está leyéndolo.

buscar	escuchar	llevar	tener	¿?
encontrar	leer	mirar	traer	

Síntesis

6

Adivinanzas In pairs, take turns describing a person, place, or thing for your partner to guess. Each of you should give at least five descriptions.

modelo

Estudiante 1: Lo uso para (*I use it to*) escribir en mi cuaderno.
 No es muy grande y tiene borrador. ¿Qué es?
Estudiante 2: ¿Es un lápiz?
Estudiante 1: ¡Sí!

Recapitulación

SUBJECT → Javier   CONJUGATED FORM   empiezo   Main clause   Dudan

Review the grammar concepts you have learned in this lesson by completing these activities.

1   **Completar** Complete the chart with the correct present participle of these verbs. **16 pts.**

Infinitive	Present participle	Infinitive	Present participle
hacer		estar	
acampar		ser	
tener		vivir	
venir		estudiar	

2   **Vacaciones en París** Complete this paragraph with the correct form of **ser** or **estar**. **24 pts.**

Hoy (1) _____ (es/está) el 3 de julio y voy a París por tres semanas. (Yo) (2) _____ (Soy/Estoy) muy feliz porque voy a ver a mi mejor amiga. Ella (3) _____ (es/está) de Puerto Rico, pero ahora (4) _____ (es/está) viviendo en París. También (yo) (5) _____ (soy/estoy) un poco nerviosa porque (6) _____ (es/está) mi primer viaje a Francia. El vuelo (*flight*) (7) _____ (es/está) hoy por la tarde, pero ahora (8) _____ (es/está) lloviendo. Por eso (9) _____ (somos/estamos) preocupadas, porque probablemente el avión va a salir tarde. Mi equipaje ya (10) _____ (es/está) listo. (11) _____ (Es/Está) tarde y me tengo que ir. ¡Va a (12) _____ (ser/estar) un viaje fenomenal!

3   **¿Qué hacen?** Respond to these questions by indicating what people do with the items mentioned. Use direct object pronouns. **10 pts.**

> **modelo**
> ¿Qué hacen ellos con la película? (ver)
> La ven.

1. ¿Qué haces tú con el libro de viajes? (leer) _____
2. ¿Qué hacen los turistas en la ciudad? (explorar) _____
3. ¿Qué hace el botones con el equipaje? (llevar) _____
4. ¿Qué hace la agente con las reservaciones? (confirmar) _____
5. ¿Qué hacen ustedes con los pasaportes? (mostrar) _____

RESUMEN GRAMATICAL

5.1   **Estar with conditions and emotions**   *p. 164*

► Yo est**oy** aburrido/a, feliz, nervioso/a.

► El cuarto est**á** desordenado, limpio, ordenado.

► Estos libros est**án** abiertos, cerrados, sucios.

5.2   **The present progressive**   *pp. 166–167*

► The present progressive is formed with the present tense of **estar** plus the present participle.

Forming the present participle

infinitive	stem	ending	present participle
hablar	habl-	-ando	habl**ando**
comer	com-	-iendo	com**iendo**
escribir	escrib-	-iendo	escrib**iendo**

-ir stem-changing verbs

	infinitive	present participle
e:ie	preferir	pref**i**riendo
e:i	conseguir	cons**i**guiendo
o:ue	dormir	d**u**rmiendo

► Irregular present participles: **yendo (ir), pudiendo (poder), viniendo (venir)**

5.3   **Ser and estar**   *pp. 170–171*

► Uses of **ser**: nationality, origin, profession or occupation, characteristics, generalizations, possession, what something is made of, time and date, time and place of events

► Uses of **estar**: location, health, physical states and conditions, emotional states, weather expressions, ongoing actions

► Many adjectives can be used with both **ser** and **estar**, but the meaning of the adjectives will change.

Juan **es** delgado.	Juan **está** más delgado hoy.
Juan is thin.	*Juan looks thinner today.*

5.4 **Direct object nouns and pronouns** *pp. 174–175*

Direct object pronouns

Singular		Plural	
me	lo	nos	los
te	la	os	las

In affirmative sentences:
Adela practica **el tenis**. → Adela **lo** practica.

In negative sentences: Adela **no lo** practica.

With an infinitive:
Adela **lo** va a practicar./Adela va a practicar**lo**.

With the present progressive:
Adela **lo** está practicando./Adela está practicándo**lo**.

4 **Opuestos** Complete these sentences with the appropriate form of the verb **estar** and an antonym for the underlined adjective. **10 pts.**

> **modelo**
> Mis respuestas están <u>bien</u>, pero las de Susana *están mal*.

1. Las tiendas están <u>abiertas</u>, pero la estación del metro _____ _____.
2. No me gustan las habitaciones <u>desordenadas</u>. Incluso (*Even*) mi habitación de hotel _____ _____.
3. Nosotras estamos <u>tristes</u> cuando trabajamos. Hoy comienzan las vacaciones y _____ _____.
4. En esta ciudad los autobuses están <u>sucios</u>, pero los taxis _____ _____.
5. —El avión sale a las 5:30, ¿verdad? —No, estás <u>confundida</u>. Yo _____ _____ de que el avión sale a las 5:00.

5 **En la playa** Describe what these people are doing. Complete the sentences using the present progressive tense. **8 pts.**

1. El Sr. Camacho _____.
2. Felicia _____.
3. Ana _____.
4. Nosotros _____.

6 **Antes del viaje** Write a paragraph of at least six sentences describing the time right before you go on a trip. Say how you feel and what you are doing. You can use **Actividad 2** as a model. **32 pts.**

> **modelo**
> Hoy es viernes, 27 de octubre. Estoy en mi habitación...

7 **Refrán** Complete this Spanish saying by filling in the missing present participles. Refer to the translation and the drawing. **4 EXTRA points!**

¡LA CIUDAD ESTÁ MUY SUCIA!

66 Se consigue más _____ que _____. **99**

(You can accomplish more by doing than by saying.)

 Audio: Reading

Lectura

Antes de leer

Examinar el texto

Scan the reading selection for cognates and write down a few of them.

1. _____   4. _____
2. _____   5. _____
3. _____   6. _____

Based on the cognates you found, what do you think this document is about?

_____

Preguntas

Read these questions. Then scan the document again to look for answers.

1. What is the format of the reading selection?

   _____

2. Which place is the document about?

   _____

3. What are some of the visual cues this document provides? What do they tell you about the content of the document?

   _____

4. Who produced the document, and what do you think it is for?

   _____

More activities

vhlcentral

Online activities

Turismo ecológico en Puerto Rico

Hotel Vistahermosa

~ Lajas, Puerto Rico ~

- 40 habitaciones individuales
- 15 habitaciones dobles
- Teléfono / TV por cable / Internet
- Aire acondicionado
- Restaurante (Bar)
- Piscina
- Área de juegos
- Cajero automático°

El hotel está situado en Playa Grande, un pequeño pueblo de pescadores del mar Caribe. Es el lugar perfecto para el viajero que viene de vacaciones. Las playas son seguras y limpias, ideales para tomar el sol, descansar, tomar fotografías y nadar. Está abierto los 365 días del año. Hay una rebaja° especial para estudiantes universitarios.

DIRECCIÓN: Playa Grande 406, Lajas, PR 00667, cerca del Parque Nacional Foresta.

Cajero automático *ATM*   rebaja *discount*

Atracciones cercanas

Playa Grande ¿Busca la playa perfecta? Playa Grande es la playa que está buscando. Usted puede pescar, sacar fotos, nadar y pasear en bicicleta. Playa Grande es un paraíso para el turista que quiere practicar deportes acuáticos. El lugar es bonito e interesante y usted va a tener muchas oportunidades para descansar y disfrutar en familia.

Valle Niebla Ir de excursión, tomar café, montar a caballo, caminar, hacer picnics. Más de cien lugares para acampar.

Bahía Fosforescente Sacar fotos, salidas de noche, excursión en barco. Una maravillosa experiencia llena de luz°.

Arrecifes de Coral Sacar fotos, bucear, explorar. Es un lugar único en el Caribe.

Playa Vieja Tomar el sol, pasear en bicicleta, jugar a las cartas, escuchar música. Ideal para la familia.

Parque Nacional Foresta Sacar fotos, visitar el Museo de Arte Nativo. Reserva Mundial de la Biosfera.

Santuario de las Aves Sacar fotos, observar aves°, seguir rutas de excursión.

llena de luz *full of light* **aves** *birds*

Después de leer

Listas

Which amenities of Hotel Vistahermosa would most interest these potential guests? Explain your choices.

1. dos padres con un hijo de seis años y una hija de ocho años

   _____

2. un hombre y una mujer en su luna de miel (*honeymoon*)

   _____

3. una persona en un viaje de negocios (*business trip*)

   _____

Conversaciones

With a partner, take turns asking each other these questions.

1. ¿Quieres visitar el Hotel Vistahermosa? ¿Por qué?
2. Tienes tiempo de visitar sólo tres de las atracciones turísticas que están cerca del hotel. ¿Cuáles vas a visitar? ¿Por qué?
3. ¿Qué prefieres hacer en Valle Niebla? ¿En Playa Vieja? ¿En el Parque Nacional Foresta?

Situaciones

You have just arrived at Hotel Vistahermosa. Your partner is the concierge. Use the phrases to express your interests and ask for suggestions about where to go.

1. montar a caballo
2. bucear
3. pasear en bicicleta
4. pescar
5. observar aves

Contestar

Answer these questions.

1. ¿Quieres visitar Puerto Rico? Explica tu respuesta.

   _____

2. ¿Adónde quieres ir de vacaciones el verano que viene? Explica tu respuesta.

   _____

Escritura

Estrategia

Making an outline

When we write to share information, an outline can serve to separate topics and subtopics, providing a framework for the presentation of data. Consider the following excerpt from an outline of the tourist brochure on pages 180–181.

IV. Descripción del sitio (con foto)
  A. Playa Grande
    1. Playas seguras y limpias
    2. Ideal para tomar el sol, descansar, tomar fotografías, nadar
  B. El hotel
    1. Abierto los 365 días del año
    2. Rebaja para estudiantes universitarios

Mapa de ideas

Idea maps can be used to create outlines. The major sections of an idea map correspond to the Roman numerals in an outline. The minor idea map sections correspond to the outline's capital letters, and so on. Examine the idea map that led to the outline above.

Tema

Escribir un folleto

Write a tourist brochure for a hotel or resort you have visited. If you wish, you may write about an imaginary location. You may want to include some of this information in your brochure:

▶ the name of the hotel or resort
▶ phone and fax numbers that tourists can use to make contact
▶ the hotel website that tourists can consult
▶ an e-mail address that tourists can use to request information
▶ a description of the exterior of the hotel or resort
▶ a description of the interior of the hotel or resort, including facilities and amenities
▶ a description of the surrounding area, including its climate
▶ a listing of nearby scenic natural attractions
▶ a listing of nearby cultural attractions
▶ a listing of recreational activities that tourists can pursue in the vicinity of the hotel or resort

Escuchar
Antes de escuchar

Estrategia
Listening for key words

By listening for key words or phrases, you can identify the subject and main ideas of what you hear, as well as some of the details.

To practice this strategy, you will now listen to a short paragraph. As you listen, jot down the key words that help you identify the subject of the paragraph and its main ideas.

Preparación
Based on the illustration, who do you think Hernán Jiménez is, and what is he doing? What key words might you listen for to help you understand what he is saying?

Ahora escucha

El pronóstico del tiempo
Now you are going to listen to a weather report by Hernán Jiménez. Note which phrases are correct according to the key words and phrases you hear.

Santo Domingo
1. hace sol
2. va a hacer frío
3. una mañana de mal tiempo
4. va a estar nublado
5. buena tarde para tomar el sol
6. buena mañana para la playa

San Francisco de Macorís
1. hace frío
2. hace sol
3. va a nevar
4. va a llover
5. hace calor
6. mal día para excursiones

Comprensión

¿Cierto o falso?
Indicate whether each statement is **cierto** or **falso**, based on the weather report. Correct the false statements.

1. Según el meteorólogo, la temperatura en Santo Domingo es de 26 grados.
2. La temperatura máxima en Santo Domingo hoy va a ser de 30 grados.
3. Está lloviendo ahora en Santo Domingo.
4. En San Francisco de Macorís la temperatura mínima de hoy va a ser de 20 grados.
5. Va a llover mucho hoy en San Francisco de Macorís.

Preguntas
Answer these questions about the weather report.
1. ¿Hace viento en Santo Domingo ahora?
2. ¿Está nublado en Santo Domingo ahora?
3. ¿Está nevando ahora en San Francisco de Macorís?
4. ¿Qué tiempo hace en San Francisco de Macorís?

En pantalla

 Video

Known as the "Crossroads of the Americas," Panama is a Central American country that borders Colombia in the southeast and Costa Rica in the northwest. The Panama Canal bridges the Atlantic and Pacific Oceans. Panama boasts an amazing variety of flora and fauna with over 900 different bird species, as well as rivers, mountains, rain forests, and hiking trails both near and far from urban areas. Visitors can enjoy an array of water sports as well as culturally diverse activities in fairly moderate temperatures, ranging from 75° to 90°F, year-round.

Vocabulario útil	
a nadie le viene mal	doesn't hurt anyone
aventura	adventure
estrellas	stars
redes	(social) networks

Preparación

Where do you like to go on vacation? What do you like to do there?

¿Qué hacen?

Check **sí** if the activity is shown in the ad or **no** if it's not.

	Sí	No
1. bucear	○	○
2. acampar	○	○
3. pescar	○	○
4. hacer surf	○	○
5. escalar montañas	○	○
6. nadar en una piscina	○	○
7. ir de excursión	○	○
8. montar a caballo	○	○

Conversación

With a partner, take turns asking each other these questions.

1. ¿Quieres ir de vacaciones a Panamá? Explica tu respuesta.

2. ¿Qué prefieres: la montaña o la playa?

3. ¿Qué deportes o actividades del anuncio te gusta practicar?

cortada *cut through* ríos *rivers* trochas *narrow paths* senderos *trails*
Deja atrás *Leave behind*

Autoridad de Turismo de **Panamá**

Tu Panamá está cortada° por ríos°, trochas° y senderos°...

Deja atrás° la ciudad.

Nos vemos en el camino.

Video

Between 1438 and 1533, when the vast and powerful Incan Empire was at its height, the Incas built an elaborate network of **caminos** (*trails*) that traversed the Andes Mountains and converged on the empire's capital, Cuzco. Today, hundreds of thousands of tourists come to Peru annually to walk the surviving trails and enjoy the spectacular scenery. The most popular trail, **el Camino Inca**, leads from Cuzco to **Intipunku** (*Sun Gate*), the entrance to the ancient mountain city of Machu Picchu.

Vocabulario útil

ciudadela	*citadel*
de cultivo	*farming*
el/la guía	*guide*
maravilla	*wonder*
quechua	*Quechua (indigenous Peruvian)*
sector (urbano)	*(urban) sector*

Preparación

Have you ever visited an archeological or historic site? Where? Why did you go there?

Completar

Complete these sentences. Make the necessary changes.

1. Las ruinas de Machu Picchu son una antigua _____ inca.

2. La ciudadela estaba (*was*) dividida en tres sectores: _____ , religioso y de cultivo.

3. Cada año los _____ reciben a cientos de turistas de diferentes países.

4. Hoy en día, la cultura _____ está presente en las comunidades andinas (*Andean*) de Perú.

¡Vacaciones en Perú!

Machu Picchu [...] se encuentra aislada sobre° esta montaña...

... siempre he querido° venir [...] Me encantan° las civilizaciones antiguas°.

Somos una familia francesa [...] Perú es un país muy, muy bonito de verdad.

se encuentra aislada sobre *it is isolated on* siempre he querido *I have always wanted* Me encantan *I love* antiguas *ancient*

Video

Puerto Rico

El país en cifras

▸ **Área:** 8.959 km² (3.459 millas²)
  menor° que el área de Connecticut
▸ **Población:** 3.351.000
*Puerto Rico es una de las islas más
densamente pobladas° del mundo. Más
de la mitad de la población vive en
San Juan, la capital.*
▸ **Capital:** San Juan—2.463.000
▸ **Ciudades principales:** Arecibo, Bayamón,
  Fajardo, Mayagüez, Ponce
▸ **Moneda:** dólar estadounidense
▸ **Idiomas:** español (oficial); inglés (oficial)
*Aproximadamente la cuarta parte de la población
puertorriqueña habla inglés, pero en las zonas
turísticas este porcentaje es mucho más alto. El uso
del inglés es obligatorio para documentos federales.*

Bandera
de Puerto Rico

Puertorriqueños célebres

▸ **Raúl Juliá,** actor (1940–1994)
▸ **Roberto Clemente,** beisbolista
  (1934–1972)
▸ **Julia de Burgos,** escritora
  (1914–1953)
▸ **Benicio del Toro,** actor y productor
  (1967–)
▸ **Rosie Pérez,** actriz y bailarina
  (1964–)
▸ **José Rivera,** dramaturgo y guionista (1955–)

menor *less* pobladas *populated*

Playa en San Juan

Faro en Arecibo

Océano Atlántico

Arecibo

San Juan ⭐

Bayamón

Río Grande de Añasco

Mayagüez

Cordillera Central

Sierra de Cavey

Ponce

Iglesia en Ponce

Mar Caribe

Universidad de Puerto Rico
en Mayagüez

OCÉANO
ATLÁNTICO

PUERTO RICO

OCÉANO
PACÍFICO

More activities

| vhlcentral | WB pp. 57–58 | Online activities |

ACTIVIDADES

1 **¿Cierto o falso?** Indica si lo que dice cada oración es **cierto** o **falso**.

1. Benicio del Toro es un beisbolista puertorriqueño.
2. María es un famoso río de Puerto Rico.
3. La salsa es un estilo musical que nace en el barrio latino de Nueva York.
4. En el Observatorio de Arecibo es posible estudiar el arte y la arquitectura de Puerto Rico.

5. El Morro, hoy en día, es un museo que recibe muchos turistas.
6. Los puertorriqueños son ciudadanos estadounidenses desde 1898.
7. Felipe Rodríguez es un músico famoso de Nueva York.
8. Más de la mitad (*half*) de la población de Puerto Rico vive en la capital.

Lugares • **El Morro**

El Morro es una fortaleza que se construyó para proteger° la bahía° de San Juan desde principios del siglo° XVI hasta principios del siglo XX. Hoy día muchos turistas visitan este lugar, convertido en un museo. Es el sitio más fotografiado de Puerto Rico. La arquitectura de la fortaleza es impresionante. Tiene misteriosos túneles, oscuras mazmorras° y vistas fabulosas de la bahía.

▷ Artes • **Salsa**

La salsa, un estilo musical de origen puertorriqueño y cubano, nació° en el barrio latino de la ciudad de Nueva York. Dos de los músicos de salsa más famosos son Tito Puente y Willie Colón, los dos de Nueva York. Las estrellas° de la salsa en Puerto Rico son Felipe Rodríguez y Héctor Lavoe. Hoy en día, Puerto Rico es el centro internacional de este estilo musical. El Gran Combo de Puerto Rico es una de las orquestas de salsa más famosas del mundo°.

Río Loíza

Isla de Culebra

Fajardo

Isla de Vieques

▷ Ciencias • **El Observatorio de Arecibo**

El Observatorio de Arecibo tiene uno de los radiotelescopios más grandes del mundo. Gracias a este telescopio, los científicos° pueden estudiar las propiedades de la Tierra°, la Luna° y otros cuerpos celestes. También pueden analizar fenómenos celestiales como los quasares y pulsares, y detectar emisiones de radio de otras galaxias, en busca de inteligencia extraterrestre.

Historia • **Relación con los Estados Unidos**

Puerto Rico pasó a ser° parte de los Estados Unidos después de° la guerra° de 1898 y se hizo° un estado libre asociado en 1952. Los puertorriqueños, ciudadanos° estadounidenses desde° 1917, tienen representación política en el Congreso, pero sólo pueden participar en las elecciones presidenciales si viven en los Estados Unidos continentales. En el referendo de 2017, los puertorriqueños votaron° "sí" a favor de convertirse° en el estado 51 de los Estados Unidos. Sin embargo, la decisión final depende del Congreso estadounidense.

proteger *protect* bahía *bay* siglo *century* mazmorras *dungeons* nació *was born* estrellas *stars* mundo *world* científicos *scientists* Tierra *Earth* Luna *Moon* pasó a ser *became* después de *after* guerra *war* se hizo *became* ciudadanos *citizens* desde *since* votaron *voted* convertirse *to become*

¡Increíble pero cierto!

El 20 de septiembre de 2017, el huracán María atravesó° Puerto Rico. Pasó° a sólo 25 millas de San Juan, a una velocidad° de 155 millas por hora. María afectó° a toda la población. Miles de personas perdieron° sus casas y, además, quedaron incomunicadas° por la falta de energía eléctrica°.

atravesó *crossed* Pasó *It passed* velocidad *speed* afectó *affected* perdieron *lost* quedaron incomunicadas *were cut off* falta de energía eléctrica *lack of electrical power*

---

2 **¿Qué aprendiste?** Responde a cada pregunta.

1. ¿Cuál es la moneda de Puerto Rico?

2. ¿Qué idiomas se hablan (*are spoken*) en Puerto Rico?

3. ¿Cuál es el sitio más fotografiado de Puerto Rico?

4. ¿Qué es el Gran Combo?

3 **Adivinanzas** Describe dos lugares o personas de Puerto Rico a un(a) compañero/a. Cada uno/a debe adivinar (*guess*) qué está describiendo el/la otro/a.

modelo

Estudiante 1: Es un cantante de salsa.

Estudiante 2: ¿Es Héctor Lavoe?

Estudiante 1: Sí.

Los viajes y las vacaciones

acampar	*to camp*
confirmar una reservación	*to confirm a reservation*
estar de vacaciones (*f. pl.*)	*to be on vacation*
hacer las maletas	*to pack (one's suitcases)*
hacer un viaje	*to take a trip*
hacer (wind)surf	*to (wind)surf*
ir de compras (*f. pl.*)	*to go shopping*
ir de vacaciones	*to go on vacation*
ir en autobús (*m.*), auto(móvil) (*m.*), avión (*m.*), barco (*m.*), moto(cicleta) (*f.*), taxi (*m.*)	*to go by bus, car, plane, boat, motorcycle, taxi*
jugar a las cartas	*to play cards*
montar a caballo (*m.*)	*to ride a horse*
pescar	*to fish*
sacar/tomar fotos (*f. pl.*)	*to take photos*
el/la inspector(a) de aduanas	*customs inspector*
el/la viajero/a	*traveler*
el aeropuerto	*airport*
el campo	*countryside*
el equipaje	*luggage*
la estación de autobuses, del metro, de tren	*bus, subway, train station*
la llegada	*arrival*
el mar	*sea*
el paisaje	*landscape*
el pasaje (de ida y vuelta)	*(round-trip) ticket*
el pasaporte	*passport*
la playa	*beach*
la salida	*departure; exit*
la tabla de (wind)surf	*surfboard/sailboard*

El hotel

el ascensor	*elevator*
la cama	*bed*
el/la empleado/a	*employee*
la habitación individual, doble	*single, double room*
el hotel	*hotel*
el/la huésped	*guest*
la llave	*key*
el piso	*floor (of a building)*
la planta baja	*ground floor*

Adjetivos

abierto/a	*open*
aburrido/a	*bored; boring*
alegre	*happy*
amable	*nice; friendly*
avergonzado/a	*embarrassed*
cansado/a	*tired*
cerrado/a	*closed*
cómodo/a	*comfortable*
confundido/a	*confused*
contento/a	*content*
desordenado/a	*disorderly*
enamorado/a (de)	*in love (with)*
enojado/a	*angry*
equivocado/a	*wrong*
feliz	*happy*
limpio/a	*clean*
listo/a	*ready; smart*
nervioso/a	*nervous*
ocupado/a	*busy*
ordenado/a	*orderly*
preocupado/a (por)	*worried (about)*
seguro/a	*sure; safe; confident*
sucio/a	*dirty*
triste	*sad*

Los números ordinales

primer, primero/a	*first*
segundo/a	*second*
tercer, tercero/a	*third*
cuarto/a	*fourth*
quinto/a	*fifth*
sexto/a	*sixth*
séptimo/a	*seventh*
octavo/a	*eighth*
noveno/a	*ninth*
décimo/a	*tenth*

Palabras adicionales

ahora mismo	*right now*
el año	*year*
¿Cuál es la fecha (de hoy)?	*What is the date (today)?*
de buen/mal humor	*in a good/bad mood*
la estación	*season*
el mes	*month*
todavía	*yet; still*

Seasons, months, and dates	*See page 154.*
Weather expressions	*See page 154.*
Direct object pronouns	*See page 174.*
Expresiones útiles	*See page 159.*

¡De compras!

Communicative Goals

You will learn how to:

- **Talk about and describe clothing**
- **Express preferences in a store**
- **Negotiate and pay for items you buy**

🔊 A PRIMERA VISTA

- ¿Está buscando algo la chica?
- ¿Hace las maletas o va de compras?
- ¿Está de buen o mal humor?
- ¿Es rubia o morena?

Hotspots

¡De compras!

Más vocabulario

el abrigo	coat
los calcetines (el calcetín)	sock(s)
el cinturón	belt
las gafas (de sol)	(sun)glasses
los guantes	gloves
el impermeable	raincoat
las medias	pantyhose; stockings
la ropa	clothes
la ropa interior	underwear
el traje	suit
los zapatos de tenis	sneakers
el regalo	gift
el almacén	department store
el centro comercial	shopping mall
el mercado (al aire libre)	(open-air) market
el precio (fijo)	(fixed; set) price
la rebaja	sale
la tarjeta de débito	debit card
la tienda	store
comprar en línea	to buy online
costar (o:ue)	to cost
gastar	to spend (money)
pagar	to pay
regatear	to bargain
vender	to sell
hacer juego (con)	to match (with)
llevar	to wear; to take
usar	to wear; to use

Variación léxica

calcetines	⟷	medias (Amér. L.)
cinturón	⟷	correa (Col., Venez.)
gafas/lentes	⟷	espejuelos (Cuba, P.R.), anteojos (Arg., Chile)
zapatos de tenis	⟷	zapatillas de deporte (Esp.), zapatillas (Arg., Perú)

el traje de baño

el vestido

la dependienta/ la vendedora

el dependiente/ el vendedor

el dinero en efectivo

la tarjeta de crédito

la bolsa

la caja

el suéter

la cartera

los pantalones cortos

los (blue)jeans

las sandalias

los zapatos

la clienta

el cliente

Práctica

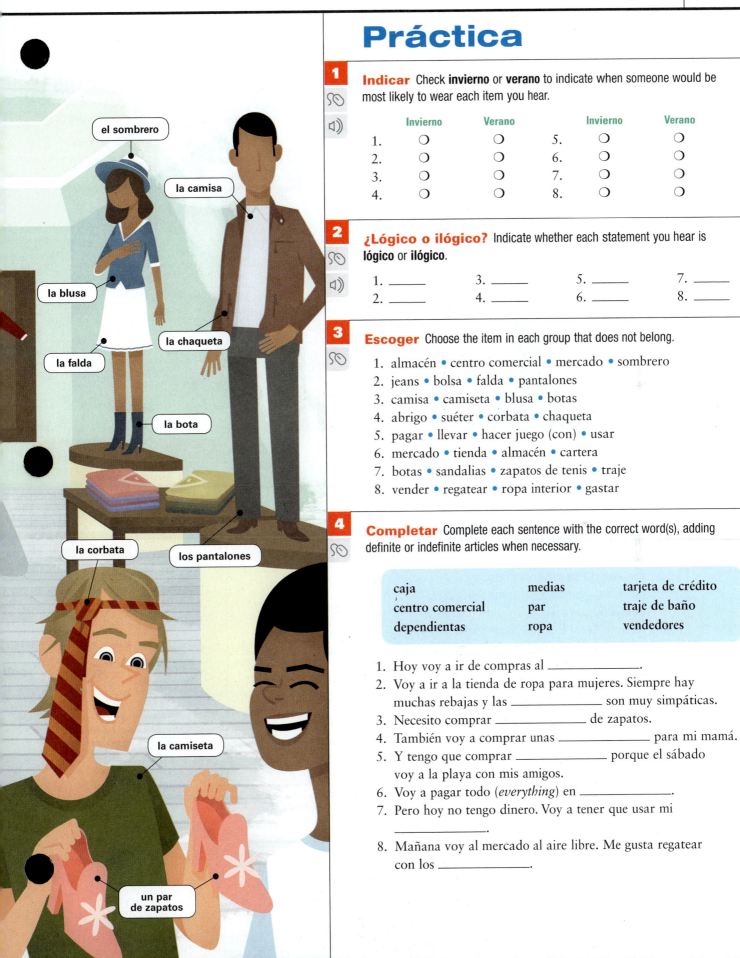

el sombrero

la camisa

la blusa

la chaqueta

la falda

la bota

la corbata

los pantalones

la camiseta

un par
de zapatos

1 **Indicar** Check **invierno** or **verano** to indicate when someone would be most likely to wear each item you hear.

	Invierno	Verano		Invierno	Verano
1.	○	○	5.	○	○
2.	○	○	6.	○	○
3.	○	○	7.	○	○
4.	○	○	8.	○	○

2 **¿Lógico o ilógico?** Indicate whether each statement you hear is **lógico** or **ilógico**.

1. _____   3. _____   5. _____   7. _____
2. _____   4. _____   6. _____   8. _____

3 **Escoger** Choose the item in each group that does not belong.

1. almacén • centro comercial • mercado • sombrero
2. jeans • bolsa • falda • pantalones
3. camisa • camiseta • blusa • botas
4. abrigo • suéter • corbata • chaqueta
5. pagar • llevar • hacer juego (con) • usar
6. mercado • tienda • almacén • cartera
7. botas • sandalias • zapatos de tenis • traje
8. vender • regatear • ropa interior • gastar

4 **Completar** Complete each sentence with the correct word(s), adding definite or indefinite articles when necessary.

caja	medias	tarjeta de crédito
centro comercial	par	traje de baño
dependientas	ropa	vendedores

1. Hoy voy a ir de compras al _____.
2. Voy a ir a la tienda de ropa para mujeres. Siempre hay muchas rebajas y las _____ son muy simpáticas.
3. Necesito comprar _____ de zapatos.
4. También voy a comprar unas _____ para mi mamá.
5. Y tengo que comprar _____ porque el sábado voy a la playa con mis amigos.
6. Voy a pagar todo (*everything*) en _____.
7. Pero hoy no tengo dinero. Voy a tener que usar mi _____.
8. Mañana voy al mercado al aire libre. Me gusta regatear con los _____.

Los colores

amarillo/a   azul   gris

anaranjado/a   blanco/a   marrón, café

morado/a   verde

negro/a   rojo/a   rosado/a

¡LENGUA VIVA!

The names of colors vary throughout the Spanish-speaking world. For example, in some countries, **anaranjado/a** may be referred to as **naranja**, **morado/a** as **púrpura**, and **rojo/a** as **colorado/a**.

Other terms that will prove helpful include **claro** (*light*) and **oscuro** (*dark*): **azul claro, azul oscuro.**

5

Contrastes Complete each phrase with the opposite of the underlined word.

1. un vestido <u>corto</u> • una falda…
2. unas vendedoras <u>malas</u> • unos dependientes…
3. una corbata <u>barata</u> • unas camisas…
4. un hombre muy <u>pobre</u> • una mujer muy…
5. una cartera <u>nueva</u> • un cinturón…
6. unos trajes <u>hermosos</u> • unos jeans…
7. unos calcetines <u>blancos</u> • unas medias…
8. un impermeable <u>caro</u> • unos suéteres…

Adjetivos

barato/a	*cheap*
bueno/a	*good*
cada	*each*
caro/a	*expensive*
corto/a	*short (in length)*
elegante	*elegant*
hermoso/a	*beautiful*
largo/a	*long*
loco/a	*crazy*
nuevo/a	*new*
otro/a	*other; another*
pobre	*poor*
rico/a	*rich*

6

Preguntas Answer these questions with a classmate.

modelo

¿De qué color es el flamenco (*flamingo*)?
Es rosado.

1. ¿De qué color es la nieve?
2. ¿De qué color es el océano Atlántico?
3. ¿De qué color es la casa donde vive el presidente de los EE.UU.?
4. ¿De qué color es la bandera (*flag*) de Canadá?
5. ¿De qué color es el sol?
6. ¿De qué color es la pelota de baloncesto?
7. ¿De qué color es el dólar de los EE.UU.?
8. ¿De qué color es la cebra (*zebra*)?

CONSULTA

Like other adjectives you have seen, color words must agree in gender and number with the nouns they modify.

Ex: **las camisas verdes, el vestido amarillo.**

For a review of descriptive adjectives, see **Estructura 3.1,** pp. 88–89.

Comunicación

7

Las maletas With a classmate, answer these questions about the drawings.

1. ¿Qué hay al lado de la maleta de Carmela?

2. ¿Qué hay en la maleta?

3. ¿De qué color son las sandalias? ¿Y la camiseta?

4. ¿Adónde va Carmela?

▶ 5. ¿Qué tiempo va a hacer?

6. ¿Qué hay al lado de la maleta de Pepe?

7. ¿Qué hay en la maleta?

8. ¿De qué color es el suéter? ¿Y los pantalones?

▶ 9. ¿Qué va a hacer Pepe en Bariloche?

10. ¿Qué tiempo va a hacer?

CONSULTA

To review weather, see **Lección 5, Contextos**, p. 154.

NOTA CULTURAL

Bariloche is a popular resort for skiing in South America. Located in Argentina's Patagonia region, the town is also known for its chocolate factories and its beautiful lakes, mountains, and forests.

8

El viaje You are going on vacation with two classmates. Pick a destination and then draw three suitcases. Write in each one what clothing each person is taking. Present your drawings to the rest of the class, answering these questions.

- ¿Adónde van?
- ¿Qué tiempo va a hacer allí?
- ¿Qué van a hacer allí?
- ¿Qué hay en sus maletas?
- ¿De qué color es la ropa que llevan?

9

Preferencias Take turns asking and answering these questions with a classmate.

1. ¿Adónde vas a comprar ropa? ¿Por qué?
2. ¿Qué tipo de ropa prefieres? ¿Por qué?
3. ¿Cuáles son tus colores favoritos?
4. En tu opinión, ¿es importante comprar ropa nueva frecuentemente? ¿Por qué?
5. ¿Gastas mucho dinero en ropa cada mes? ¿Buscas rebajas?
6. ¿Regateas cuando compras ropa? ¿Usas tarjetas de crédito?
7. ¿Cómo prefieres pagar? ¿Con dinero en efectivo? ¿Con tarjeta de crédito o débito?
8. ¿Prefieres ir de compras o comprar en línea? ¿Por qué?

En el mercado

Los chicos van de compras al mercado. ¿Quién hizo la mejor compra?

PERSONAJES

 FELIPE

 JUAN CARLOS

 Video

MARISSA Oigan, vamos al mercado.

JUAN CARLOS ¡Sí! Los chicos en un equipo y las chicas en otro.

FELIPE Tenemos dos horas para ir de compras.

MARU Y don Guillermo decide quién gana.

JIMENA Esta falda azul es muy elegante.

MARISSA ¡Sí! Además, este color está de moda.

MARU Éste rojo es de algodón.

(*Las chicas encuentran unas bolsas.*)

VENDEDOR Ésta de rayas cuesta 190 pesos, ésta 120 pesos y ésta 220 pesos.

MARISSA ¿Me das aquella blusa rosada? Me parece que hace juego con esta falda, ¿no? ¿No tienen otras tallas?

JIMENA Sí, aquí. ¿Qué talla usas?

MARISSA Uso talla 4.

JIMENA La encontré. ¡Qué ropa más bonita!

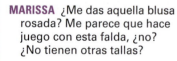

(*En otra parte del mercado*)

FELIPE Juan Carlos compró una camisa de muy buena calidad.

MIGUEL (*a la vendedora*) ¿Puedo ver ésos, por favor?

VENDEDORA Sí, señor. Le doy un muy buen precio.

VENDEDOR Son 530 por las tres bolsas. Pero como ustedes son tan bonitas, son 500 pesos.

MARU Señor, no somos turistas ricas. Somos estudiantes pobres.

VENDEDOR Bueno, son 480 pesos.

MARISSA   **JIMENA**   **MARU**   **MIGUEL**   **DON GUILLERMO**   **VENDEDORA**   **VENDEDOR**

7

JUAN CARLOS Miren, mi nueva camisa. Elegante, ¿verdad?

FELIPE A ver, Juan Carlos... te queda bien.

8

MARU ¿Qué compraste?

MIGUEL Sólo esto.

MARU ¡Qué bonitos aretes! Gracias, mi amor.

9

JUAN CARLOS Y ustedes, ¿qué compraron?

JIMENA Bolsas.

MARU Acabamos de comprar tres bolsas por sólo 480 pesos. ¡Una ganga!

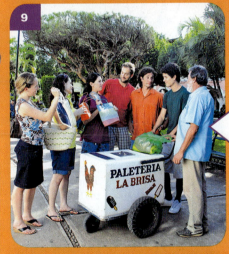

10

FELIPE Don Guillermo, usted tiene que decidir quién gana. ¿Los chicos o las chicas?

DON GUILLERMO El ganador es... Miguel. ¡Porque no compró nada para él, sino para su novia!

Expresiones útiles

Talking about clothing

¡Qué ropa más bonita!
What nice clothing!

Esta falda azul es muy elegante.
This blue skirt is very elegant.

Está de moda.
It's in style.

Éste rojo es de algodón/lana.
This red one is cotton/wool.

Ésta de rayas/lunares/cuadros es de seda.
This striped / polka-dotted / plaid one is silk.

Es de muy buena calidad.
It's very good quality.

¿Qué talla usas/llevas?
What size do you wear?

Uso/Llevo talla 4.
I wear a size 4.

¿Qué número calza?
What size shoe do you wear?

Yo calzo siete.
I wear a size seven.

Te queda bien.
That looks good on you.

Negotiating a price

¿Cuánto cuesta?
How much does it cost?

Demasiado caro/a.
Too expensive.

Es una ganga.
It's a bargain.

Saying what you bought

¿Qué compraste?/¿Qué compró usted?
What did you buy?

Sólo compré esto.
I only bought this.

¡Qué bonitos aretes!
What beautiful earrings!

Y ustedes, ¿qué compraron?
And you guys, what did you buy?

Additional vocabulary

híjole *wow*

More activities

vhlcentral   VM pp. 11–12   Online activities

¿Qué pasó?

1 ¿Cierto o falso?
Indicate whether each sentence is **cierto** or **falso**. Correct the false statements.

	Cierto	Falso
1. Jimena dice que la falda azul no es elegante.	○	○
2. Juan Carlos compra una camisa.	○	○
3. Marissa dice que el azul es un color que está de moda.	○	○
4. Miguel compra unas sandalias para Maru.	○	○

2 Identificar
Provide the first initial of the person who says the equivalent of each statement.

____ 1. Gracias por los aretes.
____ 2. Te queda muy bien esa camisa, Juan Carlos.
____ 3. No podemos pagar 500, señor, eso es muy caro.
____ 4. ¿Qué talla necesitas, Marissa?
____ 5. Esta falda me gusta mucho, el color azul es muy elegante.
____ 6. ¿Ganan los chicos o las chicas?

MARU

FELIPE

JIMENA

3 Completar
Answer the questions.

1. ¿Qué talla usa Marissa?
2. ¿Cuánto les pide el vendedor por las tres bolsas?
3. ¿Cuál es el precio que pagan las tres amigas por las bolsas?
4. ¿Qué dice Juan Carlos sobre su nueva camisa?
5. ¿Quién ganó al hacer las compras? ¿Por qué?

4 Conversar
With a partner, role-play a conversation between a customer and a salesperson in an open-air market. Use these expressions and also look at **Expresiones útiles** on the previous page.

¿Qué desea?	Estoy buscando...	Prefiero el/la rojo/a.
What would you like?	*I'm looking for...*	*I prefer the red one.*

Cliente/a

Say good afternoon.

Explain that you are looking for a particular item of clothing.

Discuss colors and sizes.

Ask for the price and begin bargaining.

Settle on a price and purchase the item.

Vendedor(a)

Greet the customer and ask what he/she would like.

Show him/her some items and ask what he/she prefers.

Discuss colors and sizes.

Tell him/her a price. Negotiate a price.

Accept a price and say thank you.

Pronunciación
The consonants **d** and **t**

Tutorial

¿Dónde? **vender** **nadar** **verdad**

Like **b** and **v**, the Spanish **d** can have a hard sound or a soft sound, depending on which letters appear next to it.

Don **dinero** **tienda** **falda**

At the beginning of a phrase and after **n** or **l**, the letter **d** is pronounced with a hard sound. This sound is similar to the English *d* in *dog*, but a little softer and duller. The tongue should touch the back of the upper teeth, not the roof of the mouth.

---

medias **verde** **vestido** **huésped**

In all other positions, **d** has a soft sound. It is similar to the English *th* in *there*, but a little softer.

Don Diego no tiene el diccionario

When **d** begins a word, its pronunciation depends on the previous word. At the beginning of a phrase or after a word that ends in **n** or **l**, it is pronounced as a hard **d**.

Doña Dolores es de la capital

Words that begin with **d** are pronounced with a soft **d** if they appear immediately after a word that ends in a vowel or any consonant other than **n** or **l**.

---

traje **pantalones** **tarjeta** **tienda**

When pronouncing the Spanish **t**, the tongue should touch the back of the upper teeth, not the roof of the mouth. Unlike the English *t*, no air is expelled from the mouth.

Práctica Read these phrases aloud to practice the **d** and the **t**.

1. Hasta pronto.
2. De nada.
3. Mucho gusto.
4. Lo siento.
5. No hay de qué.
6. ¿De dónde es usted?
7. ¡Todos a bordo!
8. No puedo.
9. Es estupendo.
10. No tengo computadora.
11. ¿Cuándo vienen?
12. Son las tres y media.

Oraciones Read these sentences aloud to practice the **d** and the **t**.

1. Don Teodoro tiene una tienda en un almacén en La Habana.
2. Don Teodoro vende muchos trajes, vestidos y zapatos todos los días.
3. Un día un turista, Federico Machado, entra en la tienda para comprar un par de botas.
4. Federico regatea con don Teodoro y compra las botas y también un par de sandalias.

Refranes Read these sayings aloud to practice the **d** and the **t**.

En la variedad está el gusto.[1]

Aunque la mona se vista de seda, mona se queda.[2]

1 *Variety is the spice of life.* 2 *You can't make a silk purse out of a sow's ear.*

Los mercados
al aire libre

Mercados al aire libre are an integral part of commerce and culture in the Spanish-speaking world. Whether they take place daily or weekly, these markets are an important forum where tourists, locals, and vendors interact. People come to the marketplace to shop, socialize, taste local foods, and watch street performers. Wandering from one **puesto** (*stand*) to the next, one can browse for fresh fruits and vegetables, clothing, CDs and DVDs, and **artesanías** (*crafts*). Some markets offer a mix of products, while others specialize in food, fashion, or used merchandise, such as antiques and books.

When shoppers see an item they like, they can bargain with the vendor. Friendly bargaining is an expected ritual and may result in a significantly lower price. When selling food, vendors may give the customer a little extra of what they purchase; this free addition is known as **la ñapa.**

Many open-air markets are also tourist attractions. The market in Otavalo, Ecuador, is world-famous and has taken place every Saturday since pre-Incan times. This market is well-known for the colorful textiles woven by the **otavaleños**, the indigenous people of the area. One can also find leather goods and wood carvings from nearby towns. Another popular market is **El Rastro**, held every Sunday in Madrid, Spain. Sellers set up **puestos** along the streets to display their wares, which range from local artwork and antiques to inexpensive clothing and electronics.

Mercado de Otavalo

Otros mercados famosos

Mercado	Lugar	Productos
Feria Artesanal de Recoleta	Buenos Aires, Argentina	artesanías
Mercado Central	Santiago, Chile	mariscos°, pescado°, frutas, verduras°
Tianguis Cultural del Chopo	Ciudad de México, México	ropa, música, revistas, libros, arte, artesanías
El mercado de Chichicastenango	Chichicastenango, Guatemala	frutas y verduras, flores°, cerámica, textiles

mariscos *seafood* pescado *fish* verduras *vegetables* flores *flowers*

1 **¿Cierto o falso?** Indicate whether these statements are **cierto** or **falso**. Correct the false statements.

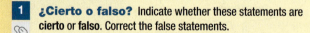

1. Generally, open-air markets specialize in one type of goods.
2. Bargaining is commonplace at outdoor markets.
3. Only new goods can be found at open-air markets.
4. A Spaniard in search of antiques could search at **El Rastro.**
5. If you are in Guatemala and want to buy ceramics, you can go to Chichicastenango.
6. A **ñapa** is a tax on open-air market goods.
7. The **otavaleños** weave colorful textiles to sell on Saturdays.
8. Santiago's **Mercado Central** is known for books and music.

ASÍ SE DICE

La ropa

la chamarra (Méx.)	la chaqueta
de manga corta/larga	*short/long-sleeved*
los mahones (P. Rico); el pantalón de mezclilla (Méx.); los tejanos (Esp.); los vaqueros (Arg., Cuba, Esp., Uru.)	los bluejeans
la marca	*brand*
la playera (Méx.); la remera (Arg.)	la camiseta

EL MUNDO HISPANO

Diseñadores de moda

- **Adolfo Domínguez** (España) Su ropa tiene un estilo minimalista y práctico. Usa telas° naturales y cómodas en sus diseños.

- **Silvia Tcherassi** (Colombia) Los colores vivos y las líneas asimétricas de sus vestidos y trajes muestran influencias tropicales.

- **Óscar de la Renta** (República Dominicana) Diseñó ropa opulenta para la mujer clásica.

- **Narciso Rodríguez** (EE.UU.) En sus diseños delicados y finos predominan los colores blanco y negro. Hizo° el vestido de boda° de Carolyn Bessette Kennedy. También diseñó varios vestidos para Michelle Obama.

telas *fabrics* Hizo *He made* de boda *wedding*

PERFIL

Carolina Herrera

In 1980, at the urging of some friends, **Carolina Herrera** created a fashion collection as a "test." The Venezuelan designer received such a favorable response that within one year she moved her family from Caracas to New York City and created her own label, Carolina Herrera, Ltd.

"I love elegance and intricacy, but whether it is in a piece of clothing or a fragrance, the intricacy must appear as simplicity," Herrera once stated. She quickly found that many sophisticated women

agreed; from the start, her sleek and glamorous designs have been in constant demand. Over the years, Herrera has grown her brand into a veritable fashion empire that encompasses her fashion and bridal collections, cosmetics, perfume, and accessories that are sold around the globe.

CON RITMO HISPANO

Gente de Zona (2000–)
Place of origin: Havana, Cuba

This duo, consisting of Alexander Delgado and Randy Malcolm Martínez, gained worldwide recognition thanks to the song "Bailando," in collaboration with Enrique Iglesias.

Go to **vhlcentral.com** to find out more about **Gente de Zona** and their music.

ACTIVIDADES

2 **Comprensión** Complete these sentences.

1. Adolfo Domínguez usa telas _____ y _____ en su ropa.
2. Si hace fresco en el D.F., puedes llevar una _____.
3. La diseñadora _____ hace ropa, perfumes y más.
4. La ropa de _____ muestra influencias tropicales.
5. Los _____ son una ropa casual en Puerto Rico.

3 **Mi ropa favorita** Write a brief description of your favorite article of clothing. Mention what store it is from, the brand, colors, fabric, style, and any other information. Then get together with a small group, collect the descriptions, and take turns reading them aloud at random. Can the rest of the group guess whose favorite piece of clothing is being described?

More activities

vhlcentral

Online activities

6.1 Saber and conocer Tutorial

ANTE TODO Spanish has two verbs that mean *to know*: **saber** and **conocer**. They cannot be used interchangeably. Note the irregular **yo** forms.

The verbs saber and conocer

		saber *(to know)*	**conocer** *(to know)*
SINGULAR FORMS	yo	**sé**	**conozco**
	tú	**sabes**	**conoces**
	Ud./él/ella	**sabe**	**conoce**
PLURAL FORMS	nosotros/as	**sabemos**	**conocemos**
	vosotros/as	**sabéis**	**conocéis**
	Uds./ellos/ellas	**saben**	**conocen**

▶ **Saber** means *to know a fact or piece(s) of information* or *to know how to do something.*

> No **sé** tu número de teléfono.
> *I don't know your phone number.*

> Mi hermana **sabe** hablar francés.
> *My sister knows how to speak French.*

▶ **Conocer** means *to know* or *be familiar/acquainted* with a person, place, or thing.

> ¿**Conoces** la ciudad de Nueva York?
> *Do you know New York City?*

> No **conozco** a tu amigo Esteban.
> *I don't know your friend Esteban.*

▶ When the direct object of **conocer** is a person or pet, the personal **a** is used.

> ¿Conoces La Habana?   *but*   ¿Conoces **a** Celia Cruz?
> *Do you know Havana?*   *Do you know Celia Cruz?*

▶ **¡Atención!** **Parecer** (*to seem*) and **ofrecer** (*to offer*) are conjugated like **conocer**.

▶ **¡Atención!** **Conducir** (*to drive*) and **traducir** (*to translate*) also have an irregular **yo** form, but since they are **-ir** verbs, they are conjugated differently from **conocer**.

conducir	**conduzco**, conduces, conduce, condu**cimos**, condu**cís**, conducen
traducir	**traduzco**, traduces, traduce, tradu**cimos**, tradu**cís**, traducen

NOTA CULTURAL

Cuban singer **Celia Cruz** (1925–2003), known as the "Queen of Salsa," recorded many albums over her long career. Adored by her fans, she was famous for her colorful and lively on-stage performances.

¡INTÉNTALO! Provide the appropriate forms of these verbs.

saber

1. José no _sabe_ la hora.
2. Sara y yo _____ jugar al tenis.
3. ¿Por qué no _____ tú estos verbos?
4. Mis padres _____ hablar japonés.
5. Yo _____ a qué hora es la clase.
6. Nosotros _____ muchas cosas.
7. Mi hermano no _____ nadar.
8. Usted no _____ dónde vivo.

conocer

1. Usted y yo _conocemos_ bien Miami.
2. ¿Tú _____ a mi amigo Manuel?
3. Sergio y Taydé _____ mi pueblo.
4. Yo _____ muy bien el centro.
5. Emiliano _____ a mis padres.
6. ¿Ustedes _____ la tienda Gigante?
7. Nosotras _____ una playa hermosa.
8. ¿Usted _____ a mi profesora?

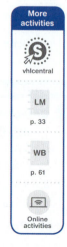

More activities

vhlcentral

LM p. 33

WB p. 61

Online activities

Práctica y Comunicación

1

Completar Indicate the correct verb for each sentence.

1. —¿(Conocen/Saben) ustedes dónde está el estadio? —No, no lo (conocemos/sabemos).
2. Mis hermanos (conocen/saben) conducir, pero yo no (sé/conozco).
3. —¿(Conoces/Sabes) a Lady Gaga? —Bueno, (sé/conozco) quién es, pero no la (conozco/sé).
4. Mi profesora (sabe/conoce) Cuba y también (conoce/sabe) bailar salsa.

2

Combinar Combine elements from each column to create sentences.

 A　　 **B**　　 **C**

A	B	C
Shakira	(no) conocer	Jimmy Kimmel
los Yankees	(no) saber	cantar y bailar
el primer ministro		La Habana Vieja
de Canadá		muchas personas importantes
mis amigos y yo		hablar dos lenguas extranjeras
tú		jugar al béisbol

3

Preguntas In pairs, ask each other these questions. Answer with complete sentences.

1. ¿Conoces a un(a) cantante famoso/a? ¿Te gusta cómo canta?
2. En tu familia, ¿quién sabe cantar bien? ¿Tu opinión es objetiva?
3. Y tú, ¿conduces bien o mal? ¿Y tus amigos?
4. Si un(a) amigo/a no conduce muy bien, ¿le ofreces crítica constructiva?
5. ¿Cómo parece estar el/la profesor(a) hoy? ¿Y tus compañeros de clase?

4

Entrevista Jot down three things you know how to do, three people you know, and three places you are familiar with. Then, in a small group, find out what you have in common.

 modelo
Estudiante 1: ¿Conocen ustedes a David Lomas?
Estudiante 2: Sí, conozco a David. Vivimos en la misma residencia estudiantil.
Estudiante 3: No, no lo conozco. ¿Cómo es?

5

Anuncio In groups, answer these questions about the ad.

1. Busquen ejemplos de los verbos **saber** y **conocer.**
2. ¿Qué saben del Centro Comercial Málaga?
3. ¿Qué pueden hacer en el Centro Comercial Málaga?
4. ¿Conocen otros centros comerciales similares? ¿Cómo se llaman? ¿Dónde están?
5. ¿Conocen un centro comercial en otro país? ¿Cómo es?

6.2 Indirect object pronouns Tutorial

ANTE TODO In **Lección 5**, you learned that a direct object receives the action of the verb directly. In contrast, an indirect object receives the action of the verb indirectly.

SUBJECT	I.O. PRONOUN	VERB	DIRECT OBJECT	INDIRECT OBJECT
Roberto	**le**	presta	cien pesos	**a Luisa**.
Roberto		*lends*	*100 pesos*	*to Luisa.*

An indirect object is a noun or pronoun that answers the question *to whom* or *for whom* an action is done. In the preceding example, the indirect object answers this question: **¿A quién le presta Roberto cien pesos?** *To whom does Roberto lend 100 pesos?*

Indirect object pronouns

Singular forms		Plural forms	
me	(to, for) *me*	**nos**	(to, for) *us*
te	(to, for) *you* (fam.)	**os**	(to, for) *you* (fam.)
le	(to, for) *you* (form.)	**les**	(to, for) *you*
	(to, for) *him; her*		(to, for) *them*

▶ **¡Atención!** The forms of indirect object pronouns for the first and second persons (**me, te, nos, os**) are the same as the direct object pronouns. Indirect object pronouns agree in number with the corresponding nouns, but not in gender.

Acabo de mostrarles que sí sabemos regatear.

Bueno, le doy un descuento.

Using indirect object pronouns

▶ Spanish speakers commonly use both an indirect object pronoun and the noun to which it refers in the same sentence. This is done to emphasize and clarify to whom the pronoun refers.

I.O. PRONOUN		INDIRECT OBJECT	I.O. PRONOUN		INDIRECT OBJECT

Ella **le** vende la ropa **a Elena**.   **Les** prestamos el dinero **a Inés y a Álex**.

▶ Indirect object pronouns are also used without the indirect object noun when the person for whom the action is being done is known.

Ana **le** presta la falda **a Elena**.   También **le** presta unos jeans.
Ana lends her skirt to Elena.   *She also lends her a pair of jeans.*

▶ Indirect object pronouns are usually placed before the conjugated form of the verb. In negative sentences the pronoun is placed between **no** and the conjugated verb.

CONSULTA

For more information on accents, see **Lección 4, Pronunciación**, p. 123, **Lección 10, Ortografía**, p. 339, and **Lección 11, Ortografía**, p. 375.

> Martín **me** compra un regalo.
> *Martín is buying me a gift.*

> Eva **no me** escribe cartas.
> *Eva doesn't write me letters.*

▶ When a conjugated verb is followed by an infinitive or the present progressive, the indirect object pronoun may be placed before the conjugated verb or attached to the infinitive or present participle. **¡Atención!** When an indirect object pronoun is attached to a present participle, an accent mark is added to maintain the proper stress.

> Él no quiere **pagarte**./
> Él no **te** quiere pagar.
> *He does not want to pay you.*

> Él está **escribiéndole** una postal a ella./
> Él **le** está escribiendo una postal a ella.
> *He is writing a postcard to her.*

▶ Because the indirect object pronouns **le** and **les** have multiple meanings, Spanish speakers often clarify to whom the pronouns refer with the preposition **a** + [*pronoun*] or **a** + [*noun*].

UNCLARIFIED STATEMENTS	CLARIFIED STATEMENTS
Yo **le** compro un abrigo.	Yo **le** compro un abrigo **a usted/él/ella**.
Ella **le** describe un libro.	Ella **le** describe un libro **a Juan**.

UNCLARIFIED STATEMENTS	CLARIFIED STATEMENTS
Él **les** vende unos sombreros.	Él **les** vende unos sombreros **a ustedes/ellos/ellas**.
Ellos **les** hablan muy claro.	Ellos **les** hablan muy claro **a los clientes**.

▶ The irregular verbs **dar** (*to give*) and **decir** (*to say; to tell*) are often used with indirect object pronouns.

The verbs dar and decir

Singular forms	dar	decir	Plural forms	dar	decir
yo	**doy**	**digo**	nosotros/as	**damos**	**decimos**
tú	**das**	**dices**	vosotros/as	**dais**	**decís**
Ud./él/ella	**da**	**dice**	Uds./ellos/ellas	**dan**	**dicen**

Me dan una fiesta cada año.
They give (throw) me a party every year.

Te digo la verdad.
I'm telling you the truth.

Voy a **darle** consejos.
I'm going to give her advice.

No **les digo** mentiras a mis padres.
I don't tell lies to my parents.

More activities

S
vhlcentral

LM
p. 34

WB
pp. 62–63

Online activities

¡INTÉNTALO! Provide the correct indirect object pronoun for each sentence.

1. Juan ___le___ quiere dar un regalo. (*to Elena*)
2. María _____ prepara un café. (*for us*)
3. Beatriz y Felipe _____ escriben desde (*from*) Cuba. (*to me*)
4. Los vendedores _____ venden ropa. (*to you, fam. sing.*)
5. Marta y yo _____ compramos unos guantes. (*for them*)
6. La dependienta _____ muestra los guantes. (*to us*)

Práctica

1

Completar Fill in the blanks with the correct pronouns to complete Mónica's description of her family's holiday shopping.

1. Juan y yo _____ damos una blusa a nuestra hermana Gisela.
2. Mi tía _____ da a nosotros una mesa para la casa.
3. Mis padres _____ dan un traje nuevo a mí.
4. A mi mamá yo _____ doy un par de guantes negros.
5. A mi profesora _____ doy dos libros de José Martí.
6. Juan _____ da un regalo a mis padres.
7. Gisela _____ da dos corbatas a su novio.
8. Y a ti, yo _____ doy un regalo también. ¿Quieres verlo?

2

En La Habana Describe what happens on Pascual's trip to Cuba.

1. yo / preparar el almuerzo (*lunch*) / (ti)

2. él / comprar / libros / (sus hijos) / Plaza de Armas

3. ellos / cantar / canción / (mí)

4. él / explicar cómo llegar / (conductor)

5. mi novia / sacar / foto / (nosotros)

6. el guía (*guide*) / mostrar / catedral de San Cristóbal / (ustedes)

3

Combinar Use an item from each column and an indirect object pronoun to create logical sentences.

> **modelo**
>
> Mis padres les dan regalos a mis primos.

A	B	C	D
yo	comprar	mensajes electrónicos	mí
el dependiente	dar	corbata	ustedes
el profesor Arce	decir	dinero en efectivo	clienta
la vendedora	escribir	tarea	novia
mis padres	explicar	problemas	primos
tú	pagar	regalos	ti
nosotros/as	prestar	ropa	nosotros
¿?	vender	¿?	¿?

NOTA CULTURAL

Cuban writer and patriot **José Martí** (1853–1895) was born in **La Habana Vieja**, the old colonial center of Havana. Founded by Spanish explorers in the early 1500s, Havana, along with San Juan, Puerto Rico, served as a major stopping point for Spaniards traveling to Mexico and South America.

NOTA CULTURAL

La Habana Vieja, Cuba, is the site of another well-known outdoor market. Located in the **Plaza de la Catedral**, it is a place where Cuban painters, artists, and sculptors sell their work, and other vendors offer handmade crafts and clothing.

Comunicación

4

Preguntas In pairs, take turns asking and answering to/for whom you do these activities.

> cantar canciones de amor (*love songs*)   escribir mensajes electrónicos
> comprar ropa   mostrar fotos de un viaje
> dar una fiesta   pedir dinero
> decir mentiras   preparar comida (*food*) mexicana

> **modelo**
> escribir mensajes electrónicos
> **Estudiante 1:** ¿A quién le escribes mensajes electrónicos?
> **Estudiante 2:** Le escribo mensajes electrónicos a mi hermano.

5

¡Somos ricos! You and your classmates chipped in on a lottery ticket and you won! Now you want to spend money on your loved ones. In groups of three, discuss what each person is buying for family and friends.

> **modelo**
> **Estudiante 1:** Quiero comprarle un vestido de Carolina Herrera a mi madre.
> **Estudiante 2:** Y yo voy a darles un automóvil nuevo a mis padres.
> **Estudiante 3:** Voy a comprarles una casa a mis padres, pero a mis amigos no les voy a dar nada.

6

Entrevista Use these questions to interview a classmate.

1. ¿Qué tiendas, almacenes o centros comerciales prefieres?
2. ¿A quién le compras regalos cuando hay rebajas?
3. ¿A quién le prestas dinero cuando lo necesita?
4. Quiero ir de compras. ¿Cuánto dinero me puedes prestar?
5. ¿Te dan tus padres su tarjeta de crédito cuando vas de compras?

Síntesis

7

Minidrama In groups of three, take turns playing the roles of two shoppers and a clerk in a clothing store. The shoppers should talk about the articles of clothing they are looking for and for whom they are buying the clothes. The clerk should recommend several items based on the shoppers' descriptions. Use these expressions and also look at **Expresiones útiles** on page 195.

> Me queda grande/pequeño.   ¿Está en rebaja?
> *It's big/small on me.*   *Is it on sale?*
> ¿Tiene otro color?   También estoy buscando...
> *Do you have another color?*   *I'm also looking for...*

6.3 Preterite tense of regular verbs

 Tutorial

ANTE TODO   In order to talk about events in the past, Spanish uses two simple tenses: the preterite and the imperfect. In this lesson, you will learn how to form the preterite tense, which is used to express actions or states completed in the past.

Preterite of regular -ar, -er, and -ir verbs

		-ar verbs **comprar**	-er verbs **vender**	-ir verbs **escribir**
SINGULAR FORMS	yo	compr**é** *I bought*	vend**í** *I sold*	escrib**í** *I wrote*
	tú	compr**aste**	vend**iste**	escrib**iste**
	Ud./él/ella	compr**ó**	vend**ió**	escrib**ió**
PLURAL FORMS	nosotros/as	compr**amos**	vend**imos**	escrib**imos**
	vosotros/as	compr**asteis**	vend**isteis**	escrib**isteis**
	Uds./ellos/ellas	compr**aron**	vend**ieron**	escrib**ieron**

▶ **¡Atención!** The **yo** and **Ud./él/ella** forms of all three conjugations have written accents on the last syllable to show that it is stressed.

▶ As the chart shows, the endings for regular **-er** and **-ir** verbs are identical in the preterite.

¿Qué compraste?

Compré estos aretes.

▶ Note that the **nosotros/as** forms of regular **-ar** and **-ir** verbs in the preterite are identical to the present tense forms. Context will help you determine which tense is being used.

En invierno **compramos** ropa.
In the winter, we buy clothes.

Anoche **compramos** unos zapatos.
Last night we bought some shoes.

CONSULTA

There are a few high-frequency irregular verbs in the preterite. You will learn more about them in **Estructura 9.1**, p. 310.

▶ **-Ar** and **-er** verbs that have a stem change in the present tense are regular in the preterite. They do *not* have a stem change.

	PRESENT	PRETERITE
cerrar (e:ie)	La tienda **cierra** a las seis.	La tienda **cerró** a las seis.
volver (o:ue)	Carlitos **vuelve** tarde.	Carlitos **volvió** tarde.
jugar (u:ue)	Él **juega** al fútbol.	Él **jugó** al fútbol.

▶ **¡Atención!** **-Ir** verbs that have a stem change in the present tense also have a stem change in the preterite.

CONSULTA

You will learn about the preterite of **-ir** stem-changing verbs in **Estructura 8.1**, p. 274.

▶ Verbs that end in **-car**, **-gar**, and **-zar** have a spelling change in the first person singular (**yo** form) in the preterite.

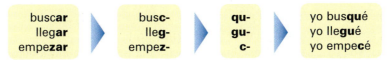

buscar		busc-		qu-		yo busqué
llegar		lleg-		gu-		yo llegué
empezar		empez-		c-		yo empecé

▶ Except for the **yo** form, all other forms of **-car**, **-gar**, and **-zar** verbs are regular in the preterite.

▶ Three other verbs—**creer**, **leer**, and **oír**—have spelling changes in the preterite. The **i** of the verb endings of **creer**, **leer**, and **oír** carries an accent in the **yo**, **tú**, **nosotros/as**, and **vosotros/as** forms, and changes to **y** in the **Ud./él/ella** and **Uds./ellos/ellas** forms.

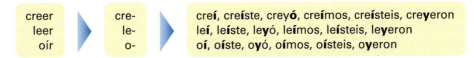

creer		cre-		creí, creíste, creyó, creímos, creísteis, creyeron
leer		le-		leí, leíste, leyó, leímos, leísteis, leyeron
oír		o-		oí, oíste, oyó, oímos, oísteis, oyeron

▶ **Ver** is regular in the preterite, but none of its forms has an accent.

ver ⟶ vi, viste, vio, vimos, visteis, vieron

Words commonly used with the preterite

anoche	last night	pasado/a (*adj.*)	last; past
anteayer	the day before yesterday	el año pasado	last year
		la semana pasada	last week
ayer	yesterday	una vez	once
de repente	suddenly	dos veces	twice
desde... hasta...	from... until...	ya	already

Ayer llegué a Santiago de Cuba.
Yesterday I arrived in Santiago de Cuba.

Anoche oí un ruido extraño.
Last night I heard a strange noise.

▶ **Acabar de** + [*infinitive*] is used to say that something has just occurred. Note that **acabar** is in the present tense in this construction.

Acabo de comprar una falda.
I just bought a skirt.

Acabas de ir de compras.
You just went shopping.

More activities

vhlcentral

LM
p. 35

WB
pp. 64–65

Online activities

¡INTÉNTALO! Provide the appropriate preterite forms of the verbs.

	comer	salir	comenzar	leer
1. ellas	comieron	salieron	comenzaron	leyeron
2. tú	_____	_____	_____	_____
3. yo	_____	_____	_____	_____
4. nosotros	_____	_____	_____	_____
5. usted	_____	_____	_____	_____

Práctica

1

Completar Complete each sentence by choosing the correct verb and putting it in the preterite.

1. El viernes a las cuatro de la tarde, la profesora Mora _____ (asistir, costar, usar) a una reunión (*meeting*) de profesores.
2. A la una, yo _____ (llegar, bucear, llevar) a la tienda con mis amigos.
3. Mis amigos y yo _____ (comprar, regatear, gastar) dos o tres cosas.
4. Yo _____ (costar, comprar, escribir) unos pantalones negros y mi amigo Mateo _____ (gastar, pasear, comprar) una camisa azul.
5. Después, nosotros _____ (llevar, vivir, comer) cerca de un mercado.
6. A las tres, Pepe _____ (hablar, pasear, nadar) con su novia por teléfono.
7. El sábado por la tarde, mi mamá _____ (escribir, beber, vivir) una carta.
8. El domingo mi tía _____ (decidir, salir, escribir) comprarme un traje.
9. A las cuatro de la tarde, mi tía _____ (beber, salir, encontrar) el traje y después nosotras _____ (acabar, ver, salir) una película.

2

Preguntas Ask a partner if he/she did these activities. Your partner will respond that he/she already did or has just done them. Take turns asking and answering.

> **modelo**
>
> leer la lección
> **Estudiante 1:** ¿Leíste la lección?
> **Estudiante 2:** Sí, ya la leí./Sí, acabo de leerla.

1. lavar (*to wash*) la ropa
2. escribir el mensaje electrónico
3. oír las noticias (*news*)
4. comprar pantalones cortos
5. practicar los verbos
6. pagar la cuenta (*bill*)
7. empezar la composición
8. ver la película *Diarios de motocicleta*

3

¿Cuándo? Use the time expressions to talk about when you and others did the activities.

anoche	anteayer	el mes pasado	una vez
ayer	la semana pasada	el año pasado	dos veces

1. mi compañero/a de cuarto: llegar tarde (*late*) a clase
2. mi mejor (*best*) amigo/a: salir con un(a) chico/a guapo/a
3. mis padres: ver una película
4. yo: llevar un traje/vestido
5. el presidente/primer ministro de mi país: asistir a una conferencia internacional
6. mis amigos y yo: comer en un restaurante
7. ¿?: comprar algo (*something*) bueno, bonito y barato

Comunicación

4

Ayer Jot down at what time you did these activities yesterday. Then get together with a classmate and find out at what time he or she did these activities.

1. desayunar
2. empezar la primera clase
3. almorzar
4. ver a un(a) amigo/a
5. salir de clase
6. volver a la residencia/casa

5

Las vacaciones Get together with a partner and use the pictures to tell him or her about your vacation with friends.

6

El fin de semana Your instructor will give you and your partner different incomplete charts about what four employees at **Almacén Gigante** did last weekend. After you fill out the chart based on each other's information, you will fill out the final column about your partner.

Síntesis

7

Conversación Get together with a partner and have a conversation about what you did last week using the verbs. Don't forget to include school activities, shopping, and pastimes.

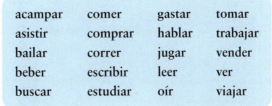

acampar	comer	gastar	tomar
asistir	comprar	hablar	trabajar
bailar	correr	jugar	vender
beber	escribir	leer	ver
buscar	estudiar	oír	viajar

6.4 Demonstrative adjectives and pronouns

Demonstrative adjectives

Tutorial

ANTE TODO In Spanish, as in English, demonstrative adjectives are words that "demonstrate" or "point out" nouns. Demonstrative adjectives precede the nouns they modify and, like other Spanish adjectives you have studied, agree with them in gender and number. Observe these examples and then study the chart.

esta camisa	**ese** vendedor	**aquellos** zapatos
this shirt	*that salesman*	*those shoes (over there)*

Demonstrative adjectives

Singular		Plural		
MASCULINE	FEMININE	MASCULINE	FEMININE	
este	**esta**	**estos**	**estas**	*this; these*
ese	**esa**	**esos**	**esas**	*that; those*
aquel	**aquella**	**aquellos**	**aquellas**	*that; those (over there)*

▶ There are three sets of demonstrative adjectives. To determine which one to use, you must establish the relationship between the speaker and the noun(s) being pointed out.

▶ The demonstrative adjectives **este**, **esta**, **estos**, and **estas** are used to point out things that are close to the speaker and the listener.

Me gustan estos zapatos.

▶ The demonstrative adjectives **ese**, **esa**, **esos**, and **esas** are used to point out things that are not close in space and time to the speaker. They may, however, be close to the listener.

Prefiero esos zapatos.

▶ The demonstrative adjectives **aquel**, **aquella**, **aquellos**, and **aquellas** are used to point out things that are far away from the speaker and the listener.

Aquel auto es de mi hermana.

Demonstrative pronouns

▶ Demonstrative pronouns are identical to their corresponding demonstrative adjectives, with the exception that they traditionally carry an accent mark on the stressed vowel. The **Real Academia** no longer requires this accent, but it is still used.

Demonstrative pronouns			
Singular		**Plural**	
MASCULINE	FEMININE	MASCULINE	FEMININE
éste	ésta	éstos	éstas
ése	ésa	ésos	ésas
aquél	aquélla	aquéllos	aquéllas

—¿Quieres comprar **este suéter**?
Do you want to buy this sweater?

—No, no quiero **éste**. Quiero **ése**.
No, I don't want this one. I want that one.

—¿Vas a leer **estas revistas**?
Are you going to read these magazines?

—Sí, voy a leer **éstas**. También voy a leer **aquéllas**.
Yes, I'm going to read these. I'll also read those (over there).

▶ **¡Atención!** Like demonstrative adjectives, demonstrative pronouns agree in gender and number with the corresponding noun.

    Este libro es de Pablito.   **Éstos** son de Juana.

▶ There are three neuter demonstrative pronouns: **esto**, **eso**, and **aquello**. These forms refer to unidentified or unspecified things, situations, ideas, and concepts. They do not change in gender or number and never carry an accent mark.

—¿Qué es **esto**?
What's this?

—**Eso** es interesante.
That's interesting.

—**Aquello** es bonito.
That's pretty.

More activities

vhlcentral

LM
p. 36

WB
pp. 66–68

Online activities

¡INTÉNTALO!   Provide the correct form of the demonstrative adjective for these nouns.

1. la falda / este   *esta falda*
2. los países / aquel _____
3. los estudiantes / este _____
4. la ventana / ese _____

5. el chico / aquel _____
6. los periodistas / ese _____
7. las sandalias / este _____
8. las chicas / aquel _____

Práctica

1

Cambiar Make the singular sentences plural and the plural sentences singular.

> **modelo**
>
> Estas camisas son blancas.
> Esta camisa es blanca.

1. Aquellos sombreros son muy elegantes.
2. Ese abrigo es muy caro.
3. Estos cinturones son hermosos.
4. ¿Quieres ir a aquel almacén?
5. Estas faldas son muy cortas.
6. Esos precios son muy buenos.
7. Esas blusas son baratas.
8. Esta corbata hace juego con mi traje.

2

Completar Complete the sentences with the correct demonstrative pronouns.

1. Esta guayabera es bonita, pero prefiero _____. (*that one*)
2. Estas corbatas rojas son muy bonitas, pero _____ son fabulosas. (*those*)
3. No me gustan esos zapatos. Voy a comprar _____. (*these*)
4. ¿Vas a comprar ese traje o _____? (*this one*)
5. Estos cinturones cuestan demasiado. Prefiero _____. (*those over there*)
6. ¿Te gustan esas botas o _____? (*these*)
7. Esa bolsa roja es bonita, pero prefiero _____. (*that one over there*)
8. ¿Prefieres estos pantalones o _____? (*those*)
9. No voy a comprar estas botas; voy a comprar _____. (*those over there*)
10. Me gusta este vestido, pero voy a comprar _____. (*that one*)
11. Me gusta ese almacén, pero _____ es mejor (*better*). (*that one over there*)
12. Esa blusa es bonita, pero cuesta demasiado. Voy a comprar _____. (*this one*)

3

Describir With your partner, look for two items in the classroom that are one of these colors: **amarillo, azul, blanco, marrón, negro, verde, rojo.** Take turns pointing them out to each other, first using demonstrative adjectives, and then demonstrative pronouns.

> **modelo**
>
> azul
> **Estudiante 1:** Esta silla es azul. Aquella mochila es azul.
> **Estudiante 2:** Ésta es azul. Aquélla es azul.

Now use demonstrative adjectives and pronouns to discuss the colors of your classmates' clothing. One of you can ask a question about an article of clothing, using the wrong color. Your partner will correct you and point out that color somewhere else in the room.

> **modelo**
>
> **Estudiante 1:** ¿Esa camisa es negra?
> **Estudiante 2:** No, ésa es azul. Aquélla es negra.

Comunicación

4   **Conversación** With a classmate, use demonstrative adjectives and pronouns to ask each other questions about the people around you.

¿A qué hora…?	¿Cuántos años tiene(n)…?
¿Cómo es/son...?	¿De dónde es/son...?
¿Cómo se llama...?	¿De quién es/son...?
¿Cuándo…?	¿Qué clases toma(n)…?

> **modelo**
>
> **Estudiante 1:** ¿Cómo se llama esa chica?
> **Estudiante 2:** Se llama Rebeca.
> **Estudiante 1:** ¿A qué hora llegó aquel chico a la clase?
> **Estudiante 2:** A las nueve.

5   **En una tienda** You and a classmate are in Madrid shopping at Zara. Study the floor plan, then have a conversation about your surroundings. Use demonstrative adjectives and pronouns.

> **modelo**
>
> **Estudiante 1:** Me gusta este suéter gris.
> **Estudiante 2:** Yo prefiero aquella chaqueta azul.

Hombres — chaquetas — suéteres — camisas — camisetas — botas — pantalones cortos — pantalones — **Estudiante 1**

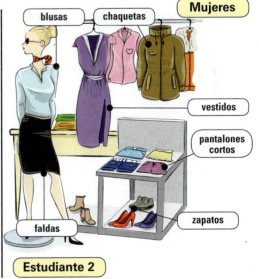

blusas — chaquetas — Mujeres — vestidos — pantalones cortos — faldas — zapatos — **Estudiante 2**

Síntesis

6   **Diferencias** Your instructor will give you and a partner each a drawing of a store. They are almost identical, but not quite. Use demonstrative adjectives and pronouns to find seven differences.

> **modelo**
>
> **Estudiante 1:** Aquellas gafas de sol son feas, ¿verdad?
> **Estudiante 2:** No. Aquellas gafas de sol son hermosas.

Recapitulación

SUBJECT
Javier
CONJUGATED FORM
empiezo
Main clause
Dudan

Review the grammar concepts you have learned in this lesson by completing these activities.

1 **Completar** Complete the chart with the correct preterite or infinitive form of the verbs. `30 pts.`

Infinitive	yo	ella	ellos
			tomaron
		abrió	
comprender			
	leí		
pagar			

2 **En la tienda** Complete the conversation with demonstrative adjectives and pronouns. `14 pts.`

CLIENTE Buenos días, señorita. Deseo comprar (1) _____ corbata.

VENDEDORA Muy bien, señor. ¿No le interesa mirar (2) _____ trajes que están allá? Hay unos que hacen juego con la corbata.

CLIENTE (3) _____ de allá son de lana, ¿no? Prefiero ver (4) _____ traje marrón que está detrás de usted.

VENDEDORA Estupendo. Como puede ver, es de seda. Cuesta seiscientos cincuenta dólares.

CLIENTE Ah… eh… no, creo que sólo voy a comprar la corbata, gracias.

VENDEDORA Bueno… si busca algo más económico, hay rebaja en (5) _____ sombreros de allá. Cuestan sólo treinta dólares.

CLIENTE ¡Magnífico! Me gusta (6) _____, el blanco que está hasta arriba (*at the top*). Y quiero pagar todo con (7) _____ tarjeta.

VENDEDORA Sí, señor. Ahora mismo le traigo el sombrero.

RESUMEN GRAMATICAL

6.1 **Saber and conocer**   *p. 200*

saber	conocer
sé	conozco
sabes	conoces
sabe	conoce
sabemos	conocemos
sabéis	conocéis
saben	conocen

▶ **saber** = to know facts/how to do something

▶ **conocer** = to know a person, place, or thing

6.2 **Indirect object pronouns**   *pp. 202–203*

Indirect object pronouns

Singular	Plural
me	nos
te	os
le	les

▶ **dar** = **doy**, das, da, damos, dais, dan

▶ **decir (e:i)** = **digo**, dices, dice, decimos, decís, dicen

6.3 **Preterite tense of regular verbs**   *pp. 206–207*

comprar	vender	escribir
compré	vendí	escribí
compraste	vendiste	escribiste
compró	vendió	escribió
compramos	vendimos	escribimos
comprasteis	vendisteis	escribisteis
compraron	vendieron	escribieron

Verbs with spelling changes in the preterite

▶ -car: buscar → yo busqué

▶ -gar: llegar → yo llegué

▶ -zar: empezar → yo empecé

▶ creer: creí, creíste, creyó, creímos, creísteis, creyeron

▶ leer: leí, leíste, leyó, leímos, leísteis, leyeron

▶ oír: oí, oíste, oyó, oímos, oísteis, oyeron

▶ ver: vi, viste, vio, vimos, visteis, vieron

6.4   Demonstrative adjectives and pronouns   *pp. 210–211*

Demonstrative adjectives

Singular		Plural	
Masc.	Fem.	Masc.	Fem.
este	esta	estos	estas
ese	esa	esos	esas
aquel	aquella	aquellos	aquellas

Demonstrative pronouns

Singular		Plural	
Masc.	Fem.	Masc.	Fem.
éste	ésta	éstos	éstas
ése	ésa	ésos	ésas
aquél	aquélla	aquéllos	aquéllas

3 ¿Saber o conocer? Complete each dialogue with the correct form of **saber** or **conocer.** **20 pts.**

1. —¿Qué _____ hacer tú?
   —(Yo) _____ jugar al fútbol.
2. —¿_____ tú esta tienda de ropa?
   —No, (yo) no la _____. ¿Es buena?
3. —¿Tus padres no _____ a tu novio?
   —No, ¡ellos no _____ que tengo novio!
4. —Mi compañero de cuarto todavía no me _____ bien.
   —Y tú, ¿lo quieres _____ a él?
5. —¿_____ ustedes dónde está el mercado?
   —No, nosotros no _____ bien esta ciudad.

4 Oraciones Form complete sentences using the information provided. Use indirect object pronouns and the present tense of the verbs. **10 pts.**

1. Javier / prestar / el abrigo / a Maripili

   _____

2. nosotros / vender / ropa / a los clientes

   _____

3. el vendedor / traer / las camisetas / a mis amigos y a mí

   _____

4. yo / querer dar / consejos / a ti

   _____

5. ¿tú / ir a comprar / un regalo / a mí?

   _____

5 Mi última compra Write a short paragraph describing the last time you went shopping. Use at least four verbs in the preterite tense. **26 pts.**

> *modelo*
> El viernes pasado, busqué unos zapatos en el centro comercial...

6 Poema Write the missing words to complete the excerpt from the poem *Romance sonámbulo* by Federico García Lorca. **4 EXTRA points!**

> " Verde que _____ quiero verde.
> Verde viento. Verdes ramas°.
> El barco sobre la mar
> y el caballo en la montaña, [...]
> Verde que te quiero _____ (*green*). "

ramas *branches*

Lectura

Antes de leer

 **Examinar el texto**

Look at the format of the reading selection. How is it organized? What does the organization of the document tell you about its content?

Buscar cognados

Scan the reading selection to locate at least five cognates. Based on the cognates, what do you think the reading selection is about?

1. _____   4. _____
2. _____   5. _____
3. _____

The reading selection is about _____.

Impresiones generales

Now skim the reading selection to understand its general meaning. Jot down your impressions. What new information did you learn about the document by skimming it? Based on all the information you now have, answer these questions in Spanish.

1. Who created this document?
2. What is its purpose?
3. Who is its intended audience?

 More activities — vhlcentral · Online activities

---

Corona — http://corona.cl

¡Corona tiene las ofertas más locas del verano!

La tienda más elegante de la ciudad con precios increíbles

niños | **mujeres** | casa | baño | equipaje

Faldas largas
ROPA BONITA
Algodón. De distintos colores
Talla mediana
Precio especial: 8.000 pesos

Blusas de seda
BAMBÚ
De cuadros y de lunares
Ahora: 21.000 pesos
40% de rebaja

Vestido de algodón
PANAMÁ
Colores blanco, azul y verde
Ahora: 18.000 pesos
30% de rebaja

Accesorios
BELLEZA
Cinturones, gafas de sol, sombreros, medias
Diversos estilos
Todos con un 40% de rebaja

Carteras
ELEGANCIA
Colores anaranjado, blanco, rosado y amarillo
Ahora: 15.000 pesos
50% de rebaja

Sandalias de playa
GINO
Números del 35 al 38
A sólo 12.000 pesos
50% de descuento

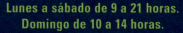
Lunes a sábado de 9 a 21 horas.
Domingo de 10 a 14 horas.

Real° Liquidación°

¡Grandes rebajas!

¡La rebaja está de moda en Corona!

y con la tarjeta de crédito más conveniente del mercado.

bebé | **hombres** | jardín | joyas | electrónica

Chaquetas
CASINO
Microfibra. Colores negro, café y gris
Tallas: P, M, G, XG
Ahora: 22.500 pesos

Traje inglés
GALES
Modelos originales
Ahora: 105.000 pesos
30% de rebaja

Pantalones
OCÉANO
Colores negro, gris y café
Ahora: 11.500 pesos
30% de rebaja

Accesorios
GUAPO
Gafas de sol, corbatas, cinturones, calcetines
Diversos estilos
Todos con un 40% de rebaja

Zapatos
COLOR
Italianos y franceses
Números del 40 al 45
A sólo 20.000 pesos

Ropa interior
ATLÁNTICO
Tallas: P, M, G
Colores blanco, negro y gris
40% de rebaja

Real *Royal* Liquidación *Clearance sale*

Por la compra de 40.000 pesos, puede llevar un regalo gratis.

- Un hermoso cinturón de mujer
- Un par de calcetines
- Una corbata de seda
- Una bolsa para la playa
- Una mochila
- Unas medias

Después de leer

Completar

Complete this paragraph with the correct forms of the words.

almacén	hacer juego	tarjeta de crédito
caro	increíble	tienda
dinero	pantalones	verano
falda	rebaja	zapato

En este anuncio, el _____ Corona anuncia la liquidación de _____ con grandes _____. Con muy poco _____ usted puede conseguir ropa fina y elegante. Si no tiene dinero en efectivo, puede utilizar su _____ y pagar luego. Para el hombre con gustos refinados, hay _____ importados de París y Roma. La señora elegante puede encontrar blusas de seda que _____ con todo tipo de _____ o _____. Los precios de esta liquidación son realmente _____.

¿Cierto o falso?

Indicate whether each statement is **cierto** or **falso**. Correct the false statements.

1. Hay sandalias de playa.
2. Las corbatas tienen una rebaja del 30%.
3. El almacén Corona tiene un departamento de zapatos.
4. Normalmente las sandalias cuestan 22.000 pesos.
5. Cuando gastas 30.000 pesos en la tienda, llevas un regalo gratis.
6. Tienen carteras amarillas.

Preguntas

In pairs, take turns asking and answering these questions.

1. Imagina que vas a ir a la tienda Corona. ¿Qué departamentos vas a visitar? ¿El departamento de ropa para mujeres, el departamento de ropa para hombres…?
2. ¿Qué vas a buscar en Corona?
3. ¿Hay tiendas similares a la tienda Corona en tu pueblo o ciudad? ¿Cómo se llaman? ¿Tienen muchas gangas?

Escritura

Estrategia

How to report an interview

There are several ways to prepare a written report about an interview. For example, you can transcribe the interview verbatim, you can simply summarize it, or you can summarize it but quote the speakers occasionally. In any event, the report should begin with an interesting title and a brief introduction, which may include the five Ws (*what, where, when, who, why*) and the H (*how*) of the interview. The report should end with an interesting conclusion. Note that when you transcribe dialogue in Spanish, you should pay careful attention to format and punctuation.

Writing dialogue in Spanish

- If you need to transcribe an interview verbatim, you can use speakers' names to indicate a change of speaker.

  CARMELA ¿Qué compraste? ¿Encontraste muchas gangas?

  ROBERTO Sí, muchas. Compré un suéter, una camisa y dos corbatas. Y tú, ¿qué compraste?

  CARMELA Una blusa y una falda muy bonitas. ¿Cuánto costó tu camisa?

  ROBERTO Sólo diez dólares. ¿Cuánto costó tu blusa?

  CARMELA Veinte dólares.

- You can also use a dash (*raya*) to mark the beginning of each speaker's words.

  —¿Qué compraste?

  —Un suéter y una camisa muy bonitos. Y tú, ¿encontraste muchas gangas?

  —Sí... compré dos blusas, tres camisetas y un par de zapatos.

  —¡A ver!

Tema

Escribe un informe

Write a report for the school newspaper about an interview you conducted with a student about his or her shopping habits and clothing preferences. First, brainstorm a list of interview questions. Then conduct the interview using the questions as a guide, but feel free to ask other questions as they occur to you.

Examples of questions:

- ¿Cuándo vas de compras?
- ¿Adónde vas de compras?
- ¿Con quién vas de compras?
- ¿Qué tiendas, almacenes o centros comerciales prefieres?
- ¿Compras ropa de catálogos o en línea?
- ¿Prefieres comprar ropa cara o barata? ¿Por qué? ¿Te gusta buscar gangas?
- ¿Qué ropa llevas cuando vas a clase?
- ¿Qué ropa llevas cuando sales a bailar?
- ¿Qué ropa llevas cuando practicas un deporte?
- ¿Cuáles son tus colores favoritos? ¿Compras mucha ropa de esos colores?
- ¿Les das ropa a tu familia o a tus amigos/as?

Escuchar

Antes de escuchar

Estrategia
Listening for linguistic cues

You can enhance your listening comprehension by listening for specific linguistic cues. For example, if you listen for the endings of conjugated verbs, or for familiar constructions, such as **acabar de** + [*infinitive*] or **ir a** + [*infinitive*], you can find out whether an event already took place, is taking place now, or will take place in the future. Verb endings also give clues about who is participating in the action.

 To practice listening for linguistic cues, you will now listen to four sentences. As you listen, note whether each sentence refers to a past, present, or future action. Also jot down the subject of each sentence.

Preparación
Based on the photograph, what do you think Marisol has recently done? What do you think Marisol and Alicia are talking about? What else can you guess about their conversation from the visual clues in the photograph?

Ahora escucha

La ropa
Now you are going to hear Marisol and Alicia's conversation. Make a list of the clothing items that each person mentions. Then put a check mark after the item if the person actually purchased it.

Marisol	Alicia
1. _____	1. _____
2. _____	2. _____
3. _____	3. _____
4. _____	4. _____

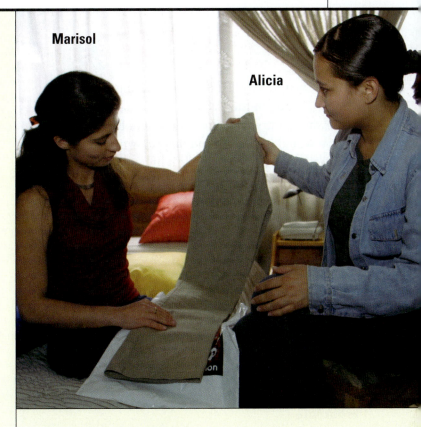

Marisol

Alicia

Comprensión

¿Cierto o falso?
Indicate whether each statement is **cierto** or **falso.** Then correct the false statements.

1. Marisol y Alicia acaban de ir de compras juntas (*together*).
2. Marisol va a comprar unos pantalones y una blusa mañana.
3. Marisol compró una blusa de cuadros.
4. Alicia compró unos zapatos nuevos hoy.
5. Alicia y Marisol van a ir al café.
6. Marisol gastó todo el dinero de la semana en ropa nueva.

Preguntas
Discuss the following questions with a classmate.

1. ¿Crees que Alicia y Marisol son buenas amigas? ¿Por qué?
2. ¿Cuál de las dos estudiantes es más ahorradora (*frugal*)? ¿Por qué?
3. ¿Crees que a Alicia le gusta la ropa que Marisol compró?
4. ¿Crees que la moda es importante para Alicia? ¿Para Marisol? ¿Por qué?
5. ¿Es importante para ti estar a la moda? ¿Por qué?

En pantalla Video

Juguettos, first established in Villena (Comunidad de Valencia), Spain, in the 1980s, now has chain stores all over the country. Juguettos offers both brand-name toys you would recognize (and maybe own) and those that specifically cater to a child's life and cultural experiences in Spain. But children's toys, like their imaginations, are very similar throughout the world. Indeed, the company declares it has founded its own "country," el País de Siempre Jugar.

Vocabulario útil	
copionas	*copycats*
despistado/a	*distracted*
sean	*they may be*
pidan	*they may ask for*

Preparación

¿Cómo eres? Escribe tres adjetivos que te describan. ¿Qué actividades ilustran (*illustrate*) tu personalidad?

Emparejar

Match the personality trait with its visual representation in the ad.

____ 1. valiente

____ 2. galáctico/a

____ 3. artista

____ 4. generoso/a

____ 5. intrépido/a

    a. Tienen una batalla (*battle*) imaginaria.

    b. Le compra juguetes a su mascota (*pet*).

    c. Está en un cartón con forma de nave espacial (*spaceship*).

    d. Hacen música con parte de una basurera (*trashcan*).

    e. Imagina que puede volar (*fly*).

Conversación

Answer these questions with a classmate.

    1. ¿Por qué es importante la imaginación en la vida de los niños?

    2. ¿Qué importancia tiene la imaginación en la vida de los adultos?

Anuncio de Juguettos

1 Me lo pido.

2 Me pido éste, éste.

3 ¿Te lo pido?

More activities

vhlcentral   Online activities

S Video

Comprar en los mercados

In the Spanish-speaking world, most city dwellers shop at large supermarkets and little stores that specialize in just one item, such as a butcher shop (**carnicería**), vegetable market (**verdulería**), perfume shop (**perfumería**), or hat shop (**sombrerería**). In small towns where supermarkets are less common, many people rely exclusively on specialty shops. This requires shopping more frequently—often every day or every other day for perishable items—but also means that the foods they consume are fresher and the goods are usually locally produced. Each neighborhood generally has its own shops, so people don't have to walk far to find fresh bread (at a **panadería**) for the midday meal.

Trescientos colones.

Vocabulario útil

colones (pl.)	currency from Costa Rica
¿Cuánto vale?	¿Cuánto cuesta?
descuento	discount
disculpe	excuse me
¿Dónde queda...?	Where is... located?
los helados	ice cream
el regateo	bargaining

... pero me hace un buen descuento.

Preparación

Have you ever been to an open-air market? What did you buy? Have you ever negotiated a price? What did you say?

¿Cierto o falso?

Indicate whether each statement is **cierto** or **falso**.

	Cierto	Falso
1. Randy lleva una camiseta verde.	○	○
2. El Mercado de Guadalupe está abierto cada domingo.	○	○
3. Randy regatea cuando compra papayas.	○	○
4. El Mercado Central es un mercado al aire libre.	○	○
5. Venden zapatos en el Mercado Central.	○	○

¿Qué compran en el Mercado Central?

More activities

S vhlcentral   VM pp. 47–48   Online activities

🔄 Video

Cuba

El país en cifras

▸ **Área:** 110.860 km² (42.803 millas²), *aproximadamente el área de Pensilvania*

▸ **Población:** 11.147.400

▸ **Capital:** La Habana—2.137.000

La Habana Vieja fue declarada° Patrimonio° Cultural de la Humanidad por la UNESCO en 1982. Este distrito es uno de los lugares más fascinantes de Cuba. En la Plaza de Armas, se puede visitar el majestuoso Palacio de Capitanes Generales, que ahora es un museo. En la calle° Obispo, frecuentada por el autor Ernest Hemingway, hay hermosos cafés, clubes nocturnos y tiendas elegantes.

▸ **Ciudades principales:** Santiago de Cuba, Camagüey, Holguín, Guantánamo

▸ **Moneda:** peso cubano

▸ **Idiomas:** español (oficial)

Bandera de Cuba

Cubanos célebres

▸ **Carlos Finlay,** doctor y científico (1833–1915)

▸ **José Martí,** político y poeta (1853–1895)

▸ **Fidel Castro,** ex primer ministro, ex comandante en jefe° de las fuerzas armadas (1926–2016)

▸ **Zoé Valdés,** escritora (1959–)

▸ **Ibrahim Ferrer,** músico (1927–2005)

▸ **Carlos Acosta,** bailarín (1973–)

fue declarada *was declared* Patrimonio *Heritage* calle *street*
comandante en jefe *commander in chief*

Golfo de México

ESTADOS UNIDOS

Gran Teatro de La Habana

Océano Atlántico

Los coco taxis son un medio de transporte cubano muy popular.

Plaza del Capitolio

La Habana

Cordillera de Guaniguánico

Isla de la Juventud

ESTADOS UNIDOS

CUBA

OCÉANO ATLÁNTICO

OCÉANO PACÍFICO

AMÉRICA DEL SUR

Mar Caribe

Camagüey

La música es parte esencial de la vida en Cuba.

More activities

🔄 vhlcentral | WB pp. 69–70 | 📶 Online activities

ACTIVIDADES

1 Completar Completa las oraciones con la información correcta.

1. La moneda oficial de Cuba es el _____ .

2. _____ es una escritora cubana.

3. _____ es Patrimonio Cultural de la Humanidad desde 1982.

4. El ave más pequeña del mundo es _____ y está en Cuba.

5. El Palacio de Capitanes Generales es actualmente un _____ .

6. En la calle _____ encontramos cafés y tiendas elegantes.

7. Los _____ son un medio de transporte muy popular en Cuba.

8. Alicia Alonso es una _____ cubana muy famosa.

▷ Baile • **Ballet Nacional de Cuba**

La bailarina Alicia Alonso (1920–2019) fundó el Ballet Nacional de Cuba en 1948, después de° convertirse en una estrella° internacional en el Ballet de Nueva York y en Broadway. El Ballet Nacional de Cuba es famoso en todo el mundo por su creatividad y perfección técnica.

▷ Economía • **La caña de azúcar y el tabaco**

La caña de azúcar° es el producto agrícola° que más se cultiva en la isla y su exportación es muy importante para la economía del país. El tabaco, que se usa para fabricar los famosos puros° cubanos, es otro cultivo° de mucha importancia.

Gente • **Población**

La población cubana tiene raíces° muy heterogéneas. La inmigración a la isla fue determinante° desde la colonia hasta mediados° del siglo° XX. Los cubanos de hoy son descendientes de africanos, europeos, chinos y antillanos, entre otros.

Música • **Buena Vista Social Club**

En 1997 nace° el fenómeno musical conocido como *Buena Vista Social Club*. Este proyecto reúne° a un grupo de importantes músicos de Cuba, la mayoría´ ya mayores, con una larga trayectoria interpretando canciones clásicas del son° cubano. Ese mismo año ganaron un *Grammy*. Hoy en día estos músicos son conocidos en todo el mundo, y personas de todas las edades bailan al ritmo° de su música.

després de *after* estrella *star* caña de azúcar *sugar cane* agrícola *farming* puros *cigars* cultivo *crop* raíces *roots* determinante *deciding* mediados *halfway through* siglo *century* nace *is born* reúne *gets together* son *Cuban musical genre* ritmo *rhythm*

Holguín
Santiago de Cuba
Guantánamo
Sierra Maestra

¡Increíble pero cierto!

Pequeño y liviano°, el colibrí abeja° de Cuba es una de las más de 320 especies de colibrí y es también el ave° más pequeña del mundo°. Menores que muchos insectos, estas aves minúsculas miden° 5 centímetros y pesan° sólo 1,95 gramos.

liviano *light* colibrí abeja *bee hummingbird* ave *bird* mundo *world* miden *measure* pesan *weigh*

---

2 **¿Qué aprendiste?** Responde a las preguntas.

1. ¿Qué autor está asociado con La Habana Vieja?
2. ¿Por qué es famoso el Ballet Nacional de Cuba?
3. ¿Cuáles son los dos cultivos más importantes para la economía cubana?
4. ¿En qué año ganó un *Grammy* el disco *Buena Vista Social Club*?

3 **Conversar** En parejas, háganse preguntas sobre lo que saben y conocen sobre Cuba.

modelo

Estudiante 1: *¿Sabes cuál es la capital de Cuba?*

Estudiante 2: *Sí, es La Habana.*

La ropa

el abrigo	coat
los (blue)jeans	jeans
la blusa	blouse
la bolsa	purse; bag
la bota	boot
los calcetines (el calcetín)	sock(s)
la camisa	shirt
la camiseta	t-shirt
la cartera	wallet
la chaqueta	jacket
el cinturón	belt
la corbata	tie
la falda	skirt
las gafas (de sol)	(sun)glasses
los guantes	gloves
el impermeable	raincoat
las medias	pantyhose; stockings
los pantalones	pants
los pantalones cortos	shorts
la ropa	clothes
la ropa interior	underwear
las sandalias	sandals
el sombrero	hat
el suéter	sweater
el traje	suit
el traje de baño	bathing suit
el vestido	dress
los zapatos de tenis	sneakers

Verbos

conducir	to drive
conocer	to know; to be acquainted with
dar	to give
ofrecer	to offer
parecer	to seem
saber	to know; to know how
traducir	to translate

Ir de compras

el almacén	department store
la caja	cash register
el centro comercial	shopping mall
el/la cliente/a	customer
el/la dependiente/a	clerk
el dinero	money
(en) efectivo	cash
el mercado (al aire libre)	(open-air) market
un par (de zapatos)	a pair (of shoes)
el precio (fijo)	(fixed; set) price
la rebaja	sale
el regalo	gift
la tarjeta de crédito	credit card
la tarjeta de débito	debit card
la tienda	store
el/la vendedor(a)	salesperson
comprar en línea	to buy online
costar (o:ue)	to cost
gastar	to spend (money)
hacer juego (con)	to match (with)
llevar	to wear; to take
pagar	to pay
regatear	to bargain
usar	to wear; to use
vender	to sell

Adjetivos

barato/a	cheap
bueno/a	good
cada	each
caro/a	expensive
corto/a	short (in length)
elegante	elegant
hermoso/a	beautiful
largo/a	long
loco/a	crazy
nuevo/a	new
otro/a	other; another
pobre	poor
rico/a	rich

Los colores

el color	color
amarillo/a	yellow
anaranjado/a	orange
azul	blue
blanco/a	white
gris	gray
marrón, café	brown
morado/a	purple
negro/a	black
rojo/a	red
rosado/a	pink
verde	green

Palabras adicionales

acabar de (+ inf.)	to have just done something
anoche	last night
anteayer	the day before yesterday
ayer	yesterday
de repente	suddenly
desde	from
dos veces	twice
hasta	until
pasado/a (adj.)	last; past
el año pasado	last year
la semana pasada	last week
prestar	to lend; to loan
una vez	once
ya	already

Indirect object pronouns	See page 202.
Demonstrative adjectives and pronouns	See page 210.
Expresiones útiles	See page 195.

Consulta

Plan de escritura

① Ideas y organización

Begin by organizing your writing materials. If you prefer to write by hand, you may want to have a few spare pens and pencils on hand, as well as an eraser or correction fluid. If you prefer to use a word-processing program, make sure you know how to type Spanish accent marks, the **tilde**, and Spanish punctuation marks. Then make a list of the resources you can consult while writing. Finally, make a list of the basic ideas you want to cover. Beside each idea, jot down a few Spanish words and phrases you may want to use while writing.

② Primer borrador

Write your first draft, using the resources and ideas you gathered in **Ideas y organización.**

③ Comentario

Exchange papers with a classmate and comment on each other's work, using these questions as a guide. Begin by mentioning what you like about your classmate's writing.

a. How can your classmate make his or her writing clearer, more logical, or more organized?

b. What suggestions do you have for making the writing more interesting or complete?

c. Do you see any spelling or grammatical errors?

④ Redacción

Revise your first draft, keeping in mind your classmate's comments. Also, incorporate any new information you may have. Before handing in the final version, review your work using these guidelines:

a. Make sure each verb agrees with its subject. Then check the gender and number of each article, noun, and adjective.

b. Check your spelling and punctuation.

c. Consult your **Anotaciones para mejorar la escritura** (see description below) to avoid repetition of previous errors.

⑤ Evaluación y progreso

You may want to share what you've written with a classmate, a small group, or the entire class. After your instructor has returned your paper, review the comments and corrections. On a separate sheet of paper, write the heading **Anotaciones para mejorar** (*Notes for improving*) **la escritura** and list your most common errors. Place this list and your corrected document in your writing portfolio (**Carpeta de trabajos**) and consult it from time to time to gauge your progress.

Spanish Terms for Direction Lines and Classroom Use

Below is a list of useful terms that you might hear your instructor say in class. It also includes Spanish terms that appear in the direction lines of your textbook.

En las instrucciones *In direction lines*

Cambia/Cambien...	*Change...*
Camina/Caminen por la clase.	*Walk around the classroom.*
Ciertas o falsas	*True or false*
Cierto o falso	*True or false*
Circula/Circulen por la clase.	*Walk around the classroom.*
Completa las oraciones de una manera lógica.	*Complete the sentences logically.*
Con un(a) compañero/a...	*With a classmate...*
Contesta las preguntas.	*Answer the questions.*
Corrige las oraciones falsas.	*Correct the false statements.*
Cuenta/Cuenten...	*Tell...*
Di/Digan...	*Say...*
Discute/Discutan...	*Discuss...*
En grupos...	*In groups...*
En parejas...	*In pairs...*
Entrevista...	*Interview...*
Escúchala	*Listen to it*
Forma oraciones completas.	*Create/Make complete sentences.*
Háganse preguntas.	*Ask each other questions.*
Haz el papel de...	*Play the role of...*
Haz los cambios necesarios.	*Make the necessary changes.*
Indica/Indiquen si las oraciones...	*Indicate if the sentences...*
Intercambia/Intercambien...	*Exchange...*
Lee/Lean en voz alta.	*Read aloud.*
Pon/Pongan...	*Put...*
... que mejor completa...	*...that best completes...*
Reúnete...	*Get together...*
... se da/dan como ejemplo.	*...is/are given as a model.*
Toma nota...	*Take note...*
Tomen apuntes.	*Take notes.*
Túrnense...	*Take turns...*

Palabras útiles *Useful words*

la adivinanza	*riddle*
el anuncio	*advertisement/ad*
los apuntes	*notes*
el borrador	*draft*
la canción	*song*
la concordancia	*agreement*
el contenido	*contents*
el cortometraje	*short film*
eficaz	*efficient; effective*
la encuesta	*survey*
el equipo	*team*
el esquema	*outline*
el folleto	*brochure*
las frases	*phrases*
la hoja de actividades	*activity sheet/handout*
la hoja de papel	*piece of paper*
la información errónea	*incorrect information*
el/la lector(a)	*reader*
la lectura	*reading*
las oraciones	*sentences*
la ortografía	*spelling*
el papel	*role*
el párrafo	*paragraph*
el paso	*step*
la(s) persona(s) descrita(s)	*the person (people) described*
la pista	*clue*
por ejemplo	*for example*
el propósito	*purpose*
los recursos	*resources*
el reportaje	*report*
los resultados	*results*
según	*according to*
siguiente	*following*
la sugerencia	*suggestion*
el sustantivo	*noun*
el tema	*topic*
último	*last*
el último recurso	*last resort*

Verbos útiles *Useful verbs*

adivinar	*to guess*
anotar	*to jot down*
añadir	*to add*
apoyar	*to support*
averiguar	*to find out*
cambiar	*to change*
combinar	*to combine*
compartir	*to share*
comprobar (o:ue)	*to check*
contestar	*to answer*
corregir (e:i)	*to correct*
crear	*to create*
devolver (o:ue)	*to return*
doblar	*to fold*
dramatizar	*to act out*
elegir (e:i)	*to choose/select*
emparejar	*to match*
entrevistar	*to interview*
escoger	*to choose*
identificar	*to identify*
incluir	*to include*
informar	*to report*
intentar	*to try*
intercambiar	*to exchange*
investigar	*to research*
marcar	*to mark*
preguntar	*to ask*
recordar (o:ue)	*to remember*
responder	*to answer*
revisar	*to revise*
seguir (e:i)	*to follow*
seleccionar	*to select*
subrayar	*to underline*
traducir	*to translate*
tratar de	*to be about*

Expresiones útiles *Useful expressions*

Ahora mismo.	*Right away.*
¿Cómo no?	*But of course.*
¿Cómo se dice _____ en español?	*How do you say _____ in Spanish?*
¿Cómo se escribe _____?	*How do you spell _____?*
¿Comprende(n)?	*Do you understand?*
Con gusto.	*With pleasure.*
Con permiso.	*Excuse me.*
De acuerdo.	*Okay.*
De nada.	*You're welcome.*
¿De veras?	*Really?*
¿En qué página estamos?	*What page are we on?*
¿En serio?	*Seriously?*
Enseguida.	*Right away.*
hoy día	*nowadays*
Más despacio, por favor.	*Slower, please.*
Muchas gracias.	*Thanks a lot.*
No entiendo.	*I don't understand.*
No hay de qué.	*Don't mention it.*
No importa.	*No problem./It doesn't matter.*
¡No me digas!	*You don't say!*
No sé.	*I don't know.*
¡Ojalá!	*Hopefully!*
Perdone.	*Pardon me.*
Por favor.	*Please.*
Por supuesto.	*Of course.*
¡Qué bien!	*Great!*
¡Qué gracioso!	*How funny!*
¡Qué pena!	*What a shame/pity!*
¿Qué significa _____?	*What does _____ mean?*
Repite, por favor.	*Please repeat.*
Tengo una pregunta.	*I have a question.*
¿Tiene(n) alguna pregunta?	*Do you have any questions?*
Vaya(n) a la página dos.	*Go to page 2.*

Glossary of Grammatical Terms

ADJECTIVE A word that modifies, or describes, a noun or pronoun.

muchos libros
many books

un hombre **rico**
*a **rich** man*

las mujeres **altas**
*the **tall** women*

Demonstrative adjective An adjective that specifies which noun a speaker is referring to.

esta fiesta
this party

ese chico
that boy

aquellas flores
those flowers

Possessive adjective An adjective that indicates ownership or possession.

mi mejor vestido
my best dress

Éste es **mi** hermano.
*This is **my** brother.*

Stressed possessive adjective A possessive adjective that emphasizes the owner or possessor.

Es un libro **mío.**
*It's **my** book./It's a book **of mine.***

Es amiga **tuya**; yo no la conozco.
*She's a friend **of yours**; I don't know her.*

ADVERB A word that modifies, or describes, a verb, adjective, or other adverb.

Pancho escribe **rápidamente.**
*Pancho writes **quickly.***

Este cuadro es **muy** bonito.
*This picture is **very** pretty.*

ARTICLE A word that points out a noun in either a specific or a non-specific way.

Definite article An article that points out a noun in a specific way.

el libro
the book

la maleta
the suitcase

los diccionarios
the dictionaries

las palabras
the words

Indefinite article An article that points out a noun in a general, non-specific way.

un lápiz
a pencil

una computadora
a computer

unos pájaros
some birds

unas escuelas
some schools

CLAUSE A group of words that contains both a conjugated verb and a subject, either expressed or implied.

Main (or Independent) clause A clause that can stand alone as a complete sentence.

Pienso ir a cenar pronto.
I plan to go to dinner soon.

Subordinate (or Dependent) clause A clause that does not express a complete thought and therefore cannot stand alone as a sentence.

Trabajo en la cafetería **porque necesito dinero para la escuela.**
*I work in the cafeteria **because I need money for school.***

COMPARATIVE A construction used with an adjective or adverb to express a comparison between two people, places, or things.

Este programa es **más interesante que** el otro.
*This program is **more interesting than** the other one.*

Tomás no es **tan alto como** Alberto.
*Tomás is not **as tall as** Alberto.*

CONJUGATION A set of the forms of a verb for a specific tense or mood or the process by which these verb forms are presented.

Preterite conjugation of **cantar:**

cant**é**	cant**amos**
cant**aste**	cant**asteis**
cant**ó**	cant**aron**

CONJUNCTION A word used to connect words, clauses, or phrases.

Susana es de Cuba **y** Pedro es de España.
*Susana is from Cuba **and** Pedro is from Spain.*

No quiero estudiar **pero** tengo que hacerlo.
*I don't want to study, **but** I have to.*

CONTRACTION The joining of two words into one. The only contractions in Spanish are **al** and **del**.

Mi hermano fue **al** concierto ayer.
*My brother went **to the** concert yesterday.*

Saqué dinero **del** banco.
*I took money **from the** bank.*

DIRECT OBJECT A noun or pronoun that directly receives the action of the verb.

Tomás lee **el libro.**   **La** pagó ayer.
*Tomás reads **the book.***   *She paid **it** yesterday.*

GENDER The grammatical categorizing of certain kinds of words, such as nouns and pronouns, as masculine, feminine, or neuter.

Masculine
articles **el, un**
pronouns **él, lo, mío, éste, ése, aquél**
adjective **simpático**

Feminine
articles **la, una**
pronouns **ella, la, mía, ésta, ésa, aquélla**
adjective **simpática**

IMPERSONAL EXPRESSION A third-person expression with no expressed or specific subject.

Es muy importante.   **Llueve** mucho.
It's very important.   *It's raining hard.*

Aquí **se habla** español.
*Spanish **is spoken** here.*

INDIRECT OBJECT A noun or pronoun that receives the action of the verb indirectly; the object, often a living being, to or for whom an action is performed.

Eduardo **le** dio un libro **a Linda.**
*Eduardo gave a book **to Linda.***

La profesora **me** puso una C en el examen.
*The professor gave **me** a C on the test.*

INFINITIVE The basic form of a verb. Infinitives in Spanish end in **-ar**, **-er**, or **-ir**.

hablar   correr   abrir
to speak   *to run*   *to open*

INTERROGATIVE An adjective, adverb, or pronoun used to ask a question.

¿**Quién** habla?   ¿**Cuántos** compraste?
Who is speaking?   *How many did you buy?*

¿**Qué** piensas hacer hoy?
What do you plan to do today?

INVERSION Changing the word order of a sentence, often to form a question.

Statement: Elena pagó la cuenta del restaurante.

Inversion: ¿Pagó Elena la cuenta del restaurante?

MOOD A grammatical distinction of verbs that indicates whether the verb is intended to make a statement or command or to express a doubt, emotion, or condition contrary to fact.

Imperative mood Verb forms used to make commands.

Di la verdad.   **Caminen** ustedes conmigo.
Tell the truth.   *Walk with me.*

¡**Comamos** ahora!
Let's eat now!

Indicative mood Verb forms used to state facts, actions, and states considered to be real.

Sé que **tienes** el dinero.
I know that you have the money.

Subjunctive mood Verb forms used principally in subordinate (dependent) clauses to express wishes, desires, emotions, doubts, and certain conditions, such as contrary-to-fact situations.

Prefieren que **hables** en español.
*They prefer that **you speak** in Spanish.*

Dudo que Luis **tenga** el dinero necesario.
*I doubt that Luis **has** the necessary money.*

NOUN A word that identifies people, animals, places, things, and ideas.

hombre   gato
man   *cat*

México   casa
Mexico   *house*

libertad   libro
freedom   *book*

NUMBER A grammatical term that refers to singular or plural. Nouns in Spanish and English have number. Other parts of a sentence, such as adjectives, articles, and verbs, can also have number.

Singular	Plural
una cosa	**unas** cosas
a thing	*some things*
el profesor	**los** profesores
the professor	*the professors*

NUMBERS Words that represent amounts.

Cardinal numbers Words that show specific amounts.

cinco minutos
five minutes

el año **dos mil veintitrés**
the year 2023

Ordinal numbers Words that indicate the order of a noun in a series.

el **cuarto** jugador	la **décima** hora
the fourth player	*the tenth hour*

PAST PARTICIPLE A past form of the verb used in compound tenses. The past participle may also be used as an adjective, but it must then agree in number and gender with the word it modifies.

Han **buscado** por todas partes.
They have searched everywhere.

Yo no había **estudiado** para el examen.
I hadn't studied for the exam.

Hay una **ventana abierta** en la sala.
There is an open window in the living room.

PERSON The form of the verb or pronoun that indicates the speaker, the one spoken to, or the one spoken about. In Spanish, as in English, there are three persons: first, second, and third.

Person	Singular	Plural
1st	yo *I*	nosotros/as *we*
2nd	**tú, Ud.** *you*	**vosotros/as, Uds.** *you*
3rd	**él, ella** *he, she*	**ellos, ellas** *they*

PREPOSITION A word or words that describe(s) the relationship, most often in time or space, between two other words.

Anita es **de** California.
Anita is from California.

La chaqueta está **en** el carro.
The jacket is in the car.

Marta se peinó **antes de** salir.
Marta combed her hair before going out.

PRESENT PARTICIPLE In English, a verb form that ends in *-ing*. In Spanish, the present participle ends in **-ndo**, and is often used with **estar** to form a progressive tense.

Mi hermana está **hablando** por teléfono ahora mismo.
My sister is talking on the phone right now.

PRONOUN A word that takes the place of a noun or nouns.

Demonstrative pronoun A pronoun that takes the place of a specific noun.

Quiero **ésta.**
I want this one.

¿Vas a comprar **ése?**
Are you going to buy that one?

Juan prefirió **aquéllos.**
Juan preferred those (over there).

Object pronoun A pronoun that functions as a direct or indirect object of the verb.

Te digo la verdad.
I'm telling you the truth.

Me lo trajo Juan.
Juan brought it to me.

Reflexive pronoun A pronoun that indicates that the action of a verb is performed by the subject on itself. These pronouns are often expressed in English with *-self: myself, yourself*, etc.

Yo **me bañé** antes de salir.
I bathed (myself) before going out.

Elena **se acostó** a las once y media.
Elena went to bed at eleven-thirty.

Relative pronoun A pronoun that connects a subordinate clause to a main clause.

El chico **que** nos escribió viene de visita mañana.
*The boy **who** wrote us is coming to visit tomorrow.*

Ya sé **lo que** tenemos que hacer.
*I already know **what** we have to do.*

Subject pronoun A pronoun that replaces the name or title of a person or thing, and acts as the subject of a verb.

Tú debes estudiar más.
***You** should study more.*

Él llegó primero.
***He** arrived first.*

SUBJECT A noun or pronoun that performs the action of a verb and is often implied by the verb.

María va al supermercado.
***María** goes to the supermarket.*

(Ellos) Trabajan mucho.
***They** work hard.*

Esos **libros** son muy caros.
*Those **books** are very expensive.*

SUPERLATIVE A word or construction used with an adjective or adverb to express the highest or lowest degree of a specific quality among three or more people, places, or things.

De todas mis clases, ésta es la **más interesante**.
*Of all my classes, this is the **most interesting**.*

Raúl es el **menos simpático** de los chicos.
*Raúl is the **least likeable** of the boys.*

TENSE A set of verb forms that indicates the time of an action or state: past, present, or future.

Compound tense A two-word tense made up of an auxiliary verb and a present or past participle. In Spanish, **estar** and **haber** are auxiliary verbs.

En este momento, **estoy estudiando**.
*At this time, **I am studying**.*

El paquete no **ha llegado** todavía.
*The package **has** not **arrived** yet.*

Simple tense A tense expressed by a single verb form.

María **estaba** enferma anoche.
*María **was** sick last night.*

Juana **hablará** con su mamá mañana.
*Juana **will speak** with her mom tomorrow.*

VERB A word that expresses actions or states of being.

Auxiliary verb A verb used with a present or past participle to form a compound tense. **Haber** is the most commonly used auxiliary verb in Spanish.

Los chicos **han** visto los elefantes.
*The children **have** seen the elephants.*

Espero que **hayas** comido.
*I hope you **have** eaten.*

Reflexive verb A verb that describes an action performed by the subject on itself and is always used with a reflexive pronoun.

Me compré un carro nuevo.
*I **bought myself** a new car.*

Pedro y Adela **se levantan** muy temprano.
*Pedro and Adela **get (themselves) up** very early.*

Spelling change verb A verb that undergoes a predictable change in spelling, in order to reflect its actual pronunciation in the various conjugations.

practicar	c→qu	practico	practiqué
dirigir	g→j	dirigí	dirijo
almorzar	z→c	almorzó	almorcé

Stem-changing verb A verb whose stem vowel undergoes one or more predictable changes in the various conjugations.

entender (e:ie)	entiendo
pedir (e:i)	piden
dormir (o:ue, u)	duermo, durmieron

Verb Conjugation Tables

The verb lists

The list of verbs below and the model-verb tables that start on page A-11 show you how to conjugate the verbs taught in **Vistas**. Each verb in the list is followed by a model verb conjugated according to the same pattern. The number in parentheses indicates where in the verb tables you can find the conjugated forms of the model verb. If you want to find out how to conjugate **divertirse**, for example, look up number 33, **sentir**, the model for verbs that follow the e:ie stem-change pattern.

How to use the verb tables

In the tables you will find the infinitive, present and past participles, and all the simple forms of each model verb. The formation of the compound tenses of any verb can be inferred from the table of compound tenses, pages A-11–12, either by combining the past participle of the verb with a conjugated form of **haber** or by combining the present participle with a conjugated form of **estar.**

---

abrazar (z:c) like cruzar (37)

abrir like vivir (3) *except* past participle is **abierto**

aburrir(se) like vivir (3)

acabar like hablar (1)

acampar like hablar (1)

acompañar like hablar (1)

aconsejar like hablar (1)

acordarse (o:ue) like contar (24)

acostarse (o:ue) like contar (24)

adelgazar (z:c) like cruzar (37)

afeitarse like hablar (1)

ahorrar like hablar (1)

alegrarse like hablar (1)

aliviar like hablar (1)

almorzar (o:ue) like contar (24) *except* (z:c)

alquilar like hablar (1)

andar like hablar (1) *except* preterite stem is **anduv-**

anunciar like hablar (1)

apagar (g:gu) like llegar (41)

aplaudir like vivir (3)

apreciar like hablar (1)

aprender like comer (2)

apurarse like hablar (1)

arrancar (c:qu) like tocar (44)

arreglar like hablar (1)

asistir like vivir (3)

aumentar like hablar (1)

ayudar(se) like hablar (1)

bailar like hablar (1)

bajar(se) like hablar (1)

bañarse like hablar (1)

barrer like comer (2)

beber like comer (2)

besar(se) like hablar (1)

borrar like hablar (1)

brindar like hablar (1)

bucear like hablar (1)

buscar (c:qu) like tocar (44)

caber (4)

caer(se) (5)

calentarse (e:ie) like pensar (30)

calzar (z:c) like cruzar (37)

cambiar like hablar (1)

caminar like hablar (1)

cantar like hablar (1)

cargar like llegar (41)

casarse like hablar (1)

cazar (z:c) like cruzar (37)

celebrar like hablar (1)

cenar like hablar (1)

cepillarse like hablar (1)

cerrar (e:ie) like pensar (30)

chatear like hablar (1)

cobrar like hablar (1)

cocinar like hablar (1)

comenzar (e:ie) (z:c) like empezar (26)

comer (2)

compartir like vivir (3)

comprar like hablar (1)

comprender like comer (2)

comprometerse like comer (2)

comunicarse (c:qu) like tocar (44)

conducir (c:zc) (6)

conectar(se) like hablar (1)

confirmar like hablar (1)

conocer (c:zc) (35)

conseguir (e:i) (g:gu) like seguir (32)

conservar like hablar (1)

consumir like vivir (3)

contaminar like hablar (1)

contar (o:ue) (24)

contestar like hablar (1)

contratar like hablar (1)

controlar like hablar (1)

conversar like hablar (1)

correr like comer (2)

costar (o:ue) like contar (24)

creer (y) (36)

cruzar (z:c) (37)

cuidar like hablar (1)

dañar like hablar (1)

dar (7)

deber like comer (2)

decidir like vivir (3)

decir (e:i) (8)

declarar like hablar (1)

dejar like hablar (1)

depositar like hablar (1)

desarrollar like hablar (1)

desayunar like hablar (1)

descansar like hablar (1)

descargar like llegar (41)

describir like vivir (3) *except* past participle is descrito

descubrir like vivir (3) *except* past participle is descubierto

desear like hablar (1)

despedir(se) (e:i) like pedir (29)

despertarse (e:ie) like pensar (30)

destruir (y) (38)

dibujar like hablar (1)

dirigir (g:j) like vivir (3) *except* (g:j)

disfrutar like hablar (1)

divertirse (e:ie) like sentir (33)

divorciarse like hablar (1)

doblar like hablar (1)

doler (o:ue) like volver (34) *except* past participle is regular

dormir(se) (o:ue) (25)

ducharse like hablar (1)

dudar like hablar (1)

durar like hablar (1)

echar like hablar (1)

elegir (e:i) like pedir (29) *except* (g:j)

emitir like vivir (3)

empezar (e:ie) (z:c) (26)

enamorarse like hablar (1)

encantar like hablar (1)

encontrar(se) (o:ue) like contar (24)

enfermarse like hablar (1)

engordar like hablar (1)

enojarse like hablar (1)

enseñar like hablar (1)

ensuciar like hablar (1)

entender (e:ie) (27)

entrenarse like hablar (1)

entrevistar like hablar (1)

enviar (envío) (39)

escalar like hablar (1)

escanear like hablar (1)

escoger (g:j) like proteger (43)

escribir like vivir (3) *except* past participle is **escrito**

escuchar like hablar (1)

esculpir like vivir (3)

esperar like hablar (1)

esquiar (esquío) like enviar (39)

establecer (c:zc) like conocer (35)

estacionar like hablar (1)

estar (9)

estornudar like hablar (1)

estudiar like hablar (1)

evitar like hablar (1)

explicar (c:qu) like tocar (44)

faltar like hablar (1)

fascinar like hablar (1)

firmar like hablar (1)

fumar like hablar (1)

funcionar like hablar (1)

ganar like hablar (1)

gastar like hablar (1)

grabar like hablar (1)

graduarse (gradúo) (40)

guardar like hablar (1)

gustar like hablar (1)

haber (hay) (10)

hablar (1)

hacer (11)

importar like hablar (1)

imprimir like vivir (3)

indicar (c:qu) like tocar (44)

informar like hablar (1)

insistir like vivir (3)

interesar like hablar (1)

invertir (e:ie) like sentir (33)

invitar like hablar (1)

ir(se) (12)

jubilarse like hablar (1)

jugar (u:ue) (g:gu) (28)

lastimarse like hablar (1)

lavar(se) like hablar (1)

leer (y) like creer (36)

levantar(se) like hablar (1)

limpiar like hablar (1)

llamar(se) like hablar (1)

llegar (g:gu) (41)

llenar like hablar (1)

llevar(se) like hablar (1)

llover (o:ue) like volver (34) *except* past participle is regular

luchar like hablar (1)

mandar like hablar (1)

manejar like hablar (1)

mantener(se) (e:ie) like tener (20)

maquillarse like hablar (1)

mejorar like hablar (1)

merendar (e:ie) like pensar (30)

mirar like hablar (1)

molestar like hablar (1)

montar like hablar (1)

morir (o:ue) like dormir (25) *except* past participle is muerto

mostrar (o:ue) like contar (24)

mudarse like hablar (1)

nacer (c:zc) like conocer (35)

nadar like hablar (1)

necesitar like hablar (1)

negar (e:ie) like pensar (30) *except* (g:gu)

nevar (e:ie) like pensar (30)

obedecer (c:zc) like conocer (35)

obtener (e:ie) like tener (20)

ocurrir like vivir (3)

odiar like hablar (1)

ofrecer (c:zc) like conocer (35)

oír (13)

olvidar like hablar (1)

pagar (g:gu) like llegar (41)

parar like hablar (1)

parecer (c:zc) like conocer (35)

pasar like hablar (1)

pasear like hablar (1)

patinar like hablar (1)

pedir (e:i) (29)

peinarse like hablar (1)

pensar (e:ie) (30)

perder (e:ie) like entender (27)

pescar (c:qu) like tocar (44)

pintar like hablar (1)

planchar like hablar (1)

poder (o:ue) (14)

poner(se) (15)

practicar (c:qu) like tocar (44)

preferir (e:ie) like sentir (33)

preguntar like hablar (1)

prender like comer (2)

preocuparse like hablar (1)

preparar like hablar (1)

presentar like hablar (1)

prestar like hablar (1)

probar(se) (o:ue) like contar (24)

prohibir (prohíbo) (42)

proteger (g:j) (43)

publicar (c:qu) like tocar (44)

quedar(se) like hablar (1)

querer (e:ie) (16)

quitar(se) like hablar (1)

recetar like hablar (1)

recibir like vivir (3)

reciclar like hablar (1)

recoger (g:j) like proteger (43)

recomendar (e:ie) like pensar (30)

recordar (o:ue) like contar (24)

reducir (c:zc) like conducir (6)

regalar like hablar (1)

regatear like hablar (1)

regresar like hablar (1)

reír(se) (e:i) (31)

relajarse like hablar (1)

renunciar like hablar (1)

repetir (e:i) like pedir (29)

resolver (o:ue) like volver (34)

respirar like hablar (1)

revisar like hablar (1)

rogar (o:ue) like contar (24) *except* (g:gu)

romper(se) like comer (2) *except* past participle is **roto**

saber (17)

sacar (c:qu) like tocar (44)

sacudir like vivir (3)

salir (18)

saludar(se) like hablar (1)

secar(se) (c:qu) like tocar (44)

seguir (e:i) (32)

sentarse (e:ie) like pensar (30)

sentir(se) (e:ie) (33)

separarse like hablar (1)

ser (19)

servir (e:i) like pedir (29)

solicitar like hablar (1)

sonar (o:ue) like contar (24)

sonreír (e:i) like reír(se) (31)

sorprender like comer (2)

subir like vivir (3)

sudar like hablar (1)

sufrir like vivir (3)

sugerir (e:ie) like sentir (33)

suponer like poner (15)

temer like comer (2)

tener (e:ie) (20)

terminar like hablar (1)

textear like hablar (1)

tocar (c:qu) (44)

tomar like hablar (1)

torcerse (o:ue) like volver (34) *except* (c:z) and past participle is regular; e.g., **yo tuerzo**

toser like comer (2)

trabajar like hablar (1)

traducir (c:zc) like conducir (6)

traer (21)

transmitir like vivir (3)

tratar like hablar (1)

usar like hablar (1)

vender like comer (2)

venir (e:ie) (22)

ver (23)

vestirse (e:i) like pedir (29)

viajar like hablar (1)

visitar like hablar (1)

vivir (3)

volver (o:ue) (34)

votar like hablar (1)

Regular verbs: simple tenses

| Infinitive | INDICATIVE | | | | | SUBJUNCTIVE | | IMPERATIVE |
	Present	Imperfect	Preterite	Future	Conditional	Present	Past	
1 hablar Participles: hablando hablado	hablo hablas habla hablamos habláis hablan	hablaba hablabas hablaba hablábamos hablabais hablaban	hablé hablaste habló hablamos hablasteis hablaron	hablaré hablarás hablará hablaremos hablaréis hablarán	hablaría hablarías hablaría hablaríamos hablaríais hablarían	hable hables hable hablemos habléis hablen	hablara hablaras hablara habláramos hablarais hablaran	 habla tú (no hables) hable Ud. hablemos hablad (no habléis) hablen Uds.
2 comer Participles: comiendo comido	como comes come comemos coméis comen	comía comías comía comíamos comíais comían	comí comiste comió comimos comisteis comieron	comeré comerás comerá comeremos comeréis comerán	comería comerías comería comeríamos comeríais comerían	coma comas coma comamos comáis coman	comiera comieras comiera comiéramos comierais comieran	 come tú (no comas) coma Ud. comamos comed (no comáis) coman Uds.
3 vivir Participles: viviendo vivido	vivo vives vive vivimos vivís viven	vivía vivías vivía vivíamos vivíais vivían	viví viviste vivió vivimos vivisteis vivieron	viviré vivirás vivirá viviremos viviréis vivirán	viviría vivirías viviría viviríamos viviríais vivirían	viva vivas viva vivamos viváis vivan	viviera vivieras viviera viviéramos vivierais vivieran	 vive tú (no vivas) viva Ud. vivamos vivid (no viváis) vivan Uds.

All verbs: compound tenses

PERFECT TENSES

INDICATIVE

Present Perfect		Past Perfect		Future Perfect		Conditional Perfect	
he has ha hemos habéis han	hablado comido vivido	había habías había habíamos habíais habían	hablado comido vivido	habré habrás habrá habremos habréis habrán	hablado comido vivido	habría habrías habría habríamos habríais habrían	hablado comido vivido

SUBJUNCTIVE

Present Perfect		Past Perfect	
haya hayas haya hayamos hayáis hayan	hablado comido vivido	hubiera hubieras hubiera hubiéramos hubierais hubieran	hablado comido vivido

PROGRESSIVE TENSES

INDICATIVE				SUBJUNCTIVE	
Present Progressive	Past Progressive	Future Progressive	Conditional Progressive	Present Progressive	Past Progressive
estoy	estaba	estaré	estaría	esté	estuviera
estás	estabas	estarás	estarías	estés	estuvieras
está	estaba	estará	estaría	esté	estuviera
estamos	estábamos	estaremos	estaríamos	estemos	estuviéramos
estáis	estabais	estaréis	estaríais	estéis	estuvierais
están	estaban	estarán	estarían	estén	estuvieran

(hablando, comiendo, viviendo — for all tenses above)

Irregular verbs

Infinitive	INDICATIVE					SUBJUNCTIVE		IMPERATIVE
	Present	Imperfect	Preterite	Future	Conditional	Present	Past	
4 **caber**	**quepo**	cabía	**cupe**	**cabré**	**cabría**	**quepa**	**cupiera**	
	cabes	cabías	**cupiste**	**cabrás**	**cabrías**	**quepas**	**cupieras**	cabe tú (no **quepas**)
	cabe	cabía	**cupo**	**cabrá**	**cabría**	**quepa**	**cupiera**	**quepa** Ud.
Participles:	cabemos	cabíamos	**cupimos**	**cabremos**	**cabríamos**	**quepamos**	**cupiéramos**	**quepamos**
cabiendo	cabéis	cabíais	**cupisteis**	**cabréis**	**cabríais**	**quepáis**	**cupierais**	cabed (no **quepáis**)
cabido	caben	cabían	**cupieron**	**cabrán**	**cabrían**	**quepan**	**cupieran**	**quepan** Uds.
5 **caer(se)**	**caigo**	caía	caí	caeré	caería	**caiga**	**cayera**	
	caes	caías	**caíste**	caerás	caerías	**caigas**	**cayeras**	cae tú (no **caigas**)
	cae	caía	**cayó**	caerá	caería	**caiga**	**cayera**	**caiga** Ud.
Participles:	caemos	caíamos	**caímos**	caeremos	caeríamos	**caigamos**	**cayéramos**	**caigamos**
cayendo	caéis	caíais	**caísteis**	caeréis	caeríais	**caigáis**	**cayerais**	caed (no **caigáis**)
caído	caen	caían	**cayeron**	caerán	caerían	**caigan**	**cayeran**	**caigan** Uds.
6 **conducir** **(c:zc)**	**conduzco**	conducía	**conduje**	conduciré	conduciría	**conduzca**	**condujera**	
	conduces	conducías	**condujiste**	conducirás	conducirías	**conduzcas**	**condujeras**	conduce tú (no **conduzcas**)
	conduce	conducía	**condujo**	conducirá	conduciría	**conduzca**	**condujera**	**conduzca** Ud.
Participles:	conducimos	conducíamos	**condujimos**	conduciremos	conduciríamos	**conduzcamos**	**condujéramos**	**conduzcamos**
conduciendo	conducís	conducíais	**condujisteis**	conduciréis	conduciríais	**conduzcáis**	**condujerais**	conducid (no **conduzcáis**)
conducido	conducen	conducían	**condujeron**	conducirán	conducirían	**conduzcan**	**condujeran**	**conduzcan** Uds.

7. dar
Participles: dando, dado

	INDICATIVE					SUBJUNCTIVE		IMPERATIVE
	Present	Imperfect	Preterite	Future	Conditional	Present	Past	
	doy	daba	di	daré	daría	dé	diera	
	das	dabas	diste	darás	darías	des	dieras	da tú (no des)
	da	daba	dio	dará	daría	dé	diera	dé Ud.
	damos	dábamos	dimos	daremos	daríamos	demos	diéramos	demos
	dais	dabais	disteis	daréis	daríais	deis	dierais	dad (no deis)
	dan	daban	dieron	darán	darían	den	dieran	den Uds.

8. decir (e:i)
Participles: diciendo, dicho

	INDICATIVE					SUBJUNCTIVE		IMPERATIVE
	Present	Imperfect	Preterite	Future	Conditional	Present	Past	
	digo	decía	dije	diré	diría	diga	dijera	
	dices	decías	dijiste	dirás	dirías	digas	dijeras	di tú (no digas)
	dice	decía	dijo	dirá	diría	diga	dijera	diga Ud.
	decimos	decíamos	dijimos	diremos	diríamos	digamos	dijéramos	digamos
	decís	decíais	dijisteis	diréis	diríais	digáis	dijerais	decid (no digáis)
	dicen	decían	dijeron	dirán	dirían	digan	dijeran	digan Uds.

9. estar
Participles: estando, estado

	INDICATIVE					SUBJUNCTIVE		IMPERATIVE
	Present	Imperfect	Preterite	Future	Conditional	Present	Past	
	estoy	estaba	estuve	estaré	estaría	esté	estuviera	
	estás	estabas	estuviste	estarás	estarías	estés	estuvieras	está tú (no estés)
	está	estaba	estuvo	estará	estaría	esté	estuviera	esté Ud.
	estamos	estábamos	estuvimos	estaremos	estaríamos	estemos	estuviéramos	estemos
	estáis	estabais	estuvisteis	estaréis	estaríais	estéis	estuvierais	estad (no estéis)
	están	estaban	estuvieron	estarán	estarían	estén	estuvieran	estén Uds.

10. haber
Participles: habiendo, habido

	INDICATIVE					SUBJUNCTIVE		IMPERATIVE
	Present	Imperfect	Preterite	Future	Conditional	Present	Past	
	he	había	hube	habré	habría	haya	hubiera	
	has	habías	hubiste	habrás	habrías	hayas	hubieras	
	ha	había	hubo	habrá	habría	haya	hubiera	
	hemos	habíamos	hubimos	habremos	habríamos	hayamos	hubiéramos	
	habéis	habíais	hubisteis	habréis	habríais	hayáis	hubierais	
	han	habían	hubieron	habrán	habrían	hayan	hubieran	

11. hacer
Participles: haciendo, hecho

	INDICATIVE					SUBJUNCTIVE		IMPERATIVE
	Present	Imperfect	Preterite	Future	Conditional	Present	Past	
	hago	hacía	hice	haré	haría	haga	hiciera	
	haces	hacías	hiciste	harás	harías	hagas	hicieras	haz tú (no hagas)
	hace	hacía	hizo	hará	haría	haga	hiciera	haga Ud.
	hacemos	hacíamos	hicimos	haremos	haríamos	hagamos	hiciéramos	hagamos
	hacéis	hacíais	hicisteis	haréis	haríais	hagáis	hicierais	haced (no hagáis)
	hacen	hacían	hicieron	harán	harían	hagan	hicieran	hagan Uds.

12. ir
Participles: yendo, ido

	INDICATIVE					SUBJUNCTIVE		IMPERATIVE
	Present	Imperfect	Preterite	Future	Conditional	Present	Past	
	voy	iba	fui	iré	iría	vaya	fuera	
	vas	ibas	fuiste	irás	irías	vayas	fueras	ve tú (no vayas)
	va	iba	fue	irá	iría	vaya	fuera	vaya Ud.
	vamos	íbamos	fuimos	iremos	iríamos	vayamos	fuéramos	vamos
	vais	ibais	fuisteis	iréis	iríais	vayáis	fuerais	id (no vayáis)
	van	iban	fueron	irán	irían	vayan	fueran	vayan Uds.

13. oír (y)
Participles: oyendo, oído

	INDICATIVE					SUBJUNCTIVE		IMPERATIVE
	Present	Imperfect	Preterite	Future	Conditional	Present	Past	
	oigo	oía	oí	oiré	oiría	oiga	oyera	
	oyes	oías	oíste	oirás	oirías	oigas	oyeras	oye tú (no oigas)
	oye	oía	oyó	oirá	oiría	oiga	oyera	oiga Ud.
	oímos	oíamos	oímos	oiremos	oiríamos	oigamos	oyéramos	oigamos
	oís	oíais	oísteis	oiréis	oiríais	oigáis	oyerais	oíd (no oigáis)
	oyen	oían	oyeron	oirán	oirían	oigan	oyeran	oigan Uds.

Infinitive	INDICATIVE Present	Imperfect	Preterite	Future	Conditional	SUBJUNCTIVE Present	Past	IMPERATIVE
14 poder (o:ue) Participles: **pudiendo** podido	puedo puedes puede podemos podéis pueden	podía podías podía podíamos podíais podían	pude pudiste pudo pudimos pudisteis pudieron	podré podrás podrá podremos podréis podrán	podría podrías podría podríamos podríais podrían	pueda puedas pueda podamos podáis puedan	pudiera pudieras pudiera pudiéramos pudierais pudieran	puede tú (no puedas) pueda Ud. podamos poded (no podáis) puedan Uds.
15 poner Participles: poniendo **puesto**	pongo pones pone ponemos ponéis ponen	ponía ponías ponía poníamos poníais ponían	puse pusiste puso pusimos pusisteis pusieron	pondré pondrás pondrá pondremos pondréis pondrán	pondría pondrías pondría pondríamos pondríais pondrían	ponga pongas ponga pongamos pongáis pongan	pusiera pusieras pusiera pusiéramos pusierais pusieran	pon tú (no pongas) ponga Ud. pongamos poned (no pongáis) pongan Uds.
16 querer (e:ie) Participles: queriendo querido	quiero quieres quiere queremos queréis quieren	quería querías quería queríamos queríais querían	quise quisiste quiso quisimos quisisteis quisieron	querré querrás querrá querremos querréis querrán	querría querrías querría querríamos querríais querrían	quiera quieras quiera queramos queráis quieran	quisiera quisieras quisiera quisiéramos quisierais quisieran	quiere tú (no quieras) quiera Ud. queramos quered (no queráis) quieran Uds.
17 saber Participles: sabiendo sabido	sé sabes sabe sabemos sabéis saben	sabía sabías sabía sabíamos sabíais sabían	supe supiste supo supimos supisteis supieron	sabré sabrás sabrá sabremos sabréis sabrán	sabría sabrías sabría sabríamos sabríais sabrían	sepa sepas sepa sepamos sepáis sepan	supiera supieras supiera supiéramos supierais supieran	sabe tú (no sepas) sepa Ud. sepamos sabed (no sepáis) sepan Uds.
18 salir Participles: saliendo salido	salgo sales sale salimos salís salen	salía salías salía salíamos salíais salían	salí saliste salió salimos salisteis salieron	saldré saldrás saldrá saldremos saldréis saldrán	saldría saldrías saldría saldríamos saldríais saldrían	salga salgas salga salgamos salgáis salgan	saliera salieras saliera saliéramos salierais salieran	sal tú (no salgas) salga Ud. salgamos salid (no salgáis) salgan Uds.
19 ser Participles: siendo sido	soy eres es somos sois son	era eras era éramos erais eran	fui fuiste fue fuimos fuisteis fueron	seré serás será seremos seréis serán	sería serías sería seríamos seríais serían	sea seas sea seamos seáis sean	fuera fueras fuera fuéramos fuerais fueran	sé tú (no seas) sea Ud. seamos sed (no seáis) sean Uds.
20 tener (e:ie) Participles: teniendo tenido	tengo tienes tiene tenemos tenéis tienen	tenía tenías tenía teníamos teníais tenían	tuve tuviste tuvo tuvimos tuvisteis tuvieron	tendré tendrás tendrá tendremos tendréis tendrán	tendría tendrías tendría tendríamos tendríais tendrían	tenga tengas tenga tengamos tengáis tengan	tuviera tuvieras tuviera tuviéramos tuvierais tuvieran	ten tú (no tengas) tenga Ud. tengamos tened (no tengáis) tengan Uds.

	INDICATIVE					SUBJUNCTIVE		IMPERATIVE
Infinitive	Present	Imperfect	Preterite	Future	Conditional	Present	Past	
21 traer	**traigo**	traía	**traje**	traeré	traería	**traiga**	**trajera**	
	traes	traías	**trajiste**	traerás	traerías	**traigas**	**trajeras**	trae tú (no **traigas**)
Participles:	trae	traía	**trajo**	traerá	traería	**traiga**	**trajera**	**traiga** Ud.
trayendo	traemos	traíamos	**trajimos**	traeremos	traeríamos	**traigamos**	**trajéramos**	**traigamos**
traído	traéis	traíais	**trajisteis**	traeréis	traeríais	**traigáis**	**trajerais**	traed (no **traigáis**)
	traen	traían	**trajeron**	traerán	traerían	**traigan**	**trajeran**	**traigan** Uds.
22 venir (e:ie)	**vengo**	venía	**vine**	**vendré**	**vendría**	**venga**	**viniera**	
	vienes	venías	**viniste**	**vendrás**	**vendrías**	**vengas**	**vinieras**	**ven** tú (no **vengas**)
Participles:	**viene**	venía	**vino**	**vendrá**	**vendría**	**venga**	**viniera**	**venga** Ud.
viniendo	venimos	veníamos	**vinimos**	**vendremos**	**vendríamos**	**vengamos**	**viniéramos**	**vengamos**
venido	venís	veníais	**vinisteis**	**vendréis**	**vendríais**	**vengáis**	**vinierais**	venid (no **vengáis**)
	vienen	venían	**vinieron**	**vendrán**	**vendrían**	**vengan**	**vinieran**	**vengan** Uds.
23 ver	**veo**	**veía**	**vi**	veré	vería	**vea**	**viera**	
	ves	**veías**	viste	verás	verías	**veas**	**vieras**	**ve** tú (no **veas**)
Participles:	ve	**veía**	vio	verá	vería	**vea**	**viera**	**vea** Ud.
viendo	vemos	**veíamos**	vimos	veremos	veríamos	**veamos**	**viéramos**	**veamos**
visto	veis	**veíais**	visteis	veréis	veríais	**veáis**	**vierais**	ved (no **veáis**)
	ven	**veían**	vieron	verán	verían	**vean**	**vieran**	**vean** Uds.

Stem-changing verbs

	INDICATIVE					SUBJUNCTIVE		IMPERATIVE
Infinitive	Present	Imperfect	Preterite	Future	Conditional	Present	Past	
24 contar (o:ue)	**cuento**	contaba	conté	contaré	contaría	**cuente**	contara	
	cuentas	contabas	contaste	contarás	contarías	**cuentes**	contaras	**cuenta** tú (no **cuentes**)
Participles:	**cuenta**	contaba	contó	contará	contaría	**cuente**	contara	**cuente** Ud.
contando	contamos	contábamos	contamos	contaremos	contaríamos	contemos	contáramos	contemos
contado	contáis	contabais	contasteis	contaréis	contaríais	contéis	contarais	contad (no **contéis**)
	cuentan	contaban	contaron	contarán	contarían	**cuenten**	contaran	**cuenten** Uds.
25 dormir (o:ue)	**duermo**	dormía	dormí	dormiré	dormiría	**duerma**	**durmiera**	
	duermes	dormías	dormiste	dormirás	dormirías	**duermas**	**durmieras**	**duerme** tú (no **duermas**)
Participles:	**duerme**	dormía	**durmió**	dormirá	dormiría	**duerma**	**durmiera**	**duerma** Ud.
durmiendo	dormimos	dormíamos	dormimos	dormiremos	dormiríamos	**durmamos**	**durmiéramos**	**durmamos**
dormido	dormís	dormíais	dormisteis	dormiréis	dormiríais	**durmáis**	**durmierais**	dormid (no **durmáis**)
	duermen	dormían	**durmieron**	dormirán	dormirían	**duerman**	**durmieran**	**duerman** Uds.
26 empezar (e:ie) (z:c)	**empiezo**	empezaba	**empecé**	empezaré	empezaría	**empiece**	empezara	
	empiezas	empezabas	empezaste	empezarás	empezarías	**empieces**	empezaras	**empieza** tú (no **empieces**)
	empieza	empezaba	empezó	empezará	empezaría	**empiece**	empezara	**empiece** Ud.
Participles:	empezamos	empezábamos	empezamos	empezaremos	empezaríamos	**empecemos**	empezáramos	**empecemos**
empezando	empezáis	empezabais	empezasteis	empezaréis	empezaríais	**empecéis**	empezarais	empezad (no **empecéis**)
empezado	**empiezan**	empezaban	empezaron	empezarán	empezarían	**empiecen**	empezaran	**empiecen** Uds.

Infinitive	INDICATIVE Present	Imperfect	Preterite	Future	Conditional	SUBJUNCTIVE Present	Past	IMPERATIVE
entender (e:ie) Participles: entendiendo entendido	entiendo entiendes entiende entendemos entendéis entienden	entendía entendías entendía entendíamos entendíais entendían	entendí entendiste entendió entendimos entendisteis entendieron	entenderé entenderás entenderá entenderemos entenderéis entenderán	entendería entenderías entendería entenderíamos entenderíais entenderían	entienda entiendas entienda entendamos entendáis entiendan	entendiera entendieras entendiera entendiéramos entendierais entendieran	entiende tú (no entiendas) entienda Ud. entendamos entended (no entendáis) entiendan Uds.
jugar (u:ue) (g:gu) Participles: jugando jugado	juego juegas juega jugamos jugáis juegan	jugaba jugabas jugaba jugábamos jugabais jugaban	jugué jugaste jugó jugamos jugasteis jugaron	jugaré jugarás jugará jugaremos jugaréis jugarán	jugaría jugarías jugaría jugaríamos jugaríais jugarían	juegue juegues juegue juguemos juguéis jueguen	jugara jugaras jugara jugáramos jugarais jugaran	juega tú (no juegues) juegue Ud. juguemos jugad (no juguéis) jueguen Uds.
pedir (e:i) Participles: pidiendo pedido	pido pides pide pedimos pedís piden	pedía pedías pedía pedíamos pedíais pedían	pedí pediste pidió pedimos pedisteis pidieron	pediré pedirás pedirá pediremos pediréis pedirán	pediría pedirías pediría pediríamos pediríais pedirían	pida pidas pida pidamos pidáis pidan	pidiera pidieras pidiera pidiéramos pidierais pidieran	pide tú (no pidas) pida Ud. pidamos pedid (no pidáis) pidan Uds.
pensar (e:ie) Participles: pensando pensado	pienso piensas piensa pensamos pensáis piensan	pensaba pensabas pensaba pensábamos pensabais pensaban	pensé pensaste pensó pensamos pensasteis pensaron	pensaré pensarás pensará pensaremos pensaréis pensarán	pensaría pensarías pensaría pensaríamos pensaríais pensarían	piense pienses piense pensemos penséis piensen	pensara pensaras pensara pensáramos pensarais pensaran	piensa tú (no pienses) piense Ud. pensemos pensad (no penséis) piensen Uds.
reír(se) (e:i) Participles: riendo reído	río ríes ríe reímos reís ríen	reía reías reía reíamos reíais reían	reí reíste rio reímos reísteis rieron	reiré reirás reirá reiremos reiréis reirán	reiría reirías reiría reiríamos reiríais reirían	ría rías ría riamos riáis rían	riera rieras riera riéramos rierais rieran	ríe tú (no rías) ría Ud. riamos reíd (no riáis) rían Uds.
seguir (e:i) (gu:g) Participles: siguiendo seguido	sigo sigues sigue seguimos seguís siguen	seguía seguías seguía seguíamos seguíais seguían	seguí seguiste siguió seguimos seguisteis siguieron	seguiré seguirás seguirá seguiremos seguiréis seguirán	seguiría seguirías seguiría seguiríamos seguiríais seguirían	siga sigas siga sigamos sigáis sigan	siguiera siguieras siguiera siguiéramos siguierais siguieran	sigue tú (no sigas) siga Ud. sigamos seguid (no sigáis) sigan Uds.
sentir (e:ie) Participles: sintiendo sentido	siento sientes siente sentimos sentís sienten	sentía sentías sentía sentíamos sentíais sentían	sentí sentiste sintió sentimos sentisteis sintieron	sentiré sentirás sentirá sentiremos sentiréis sentirán	sentiría sentirías sentiría sentiríamos sentiríais sentirían	sienta sientas sienta sintamos sintáis sientan	sintiera sintieras sintiera sintiéramos sintierais sintieran	siente tú (no sientas) sienta Ud. sintamos sentid (no sintáis) sientan Uds.

27 28 29 30 31 32 33

Infinitive	INDICATIVE					SUBJUNCTIVE		IMPERATIVE
	Present	Imperfect	Preterite	Future	Conditional	Present	Past	
34 volver (o:ue) Participles: volviendo **vuelto**	**vuelvo** **vuelves** **vuelve** volvemos volvéis **vuelven**	volvía volvías volvía volvíamos volvíais volvían	volví volviste volvió volvimos volvisteis volvieron	volveré volverás volverá volveremos volveréis volverán	volvería volverías volvería volveríamos volveríais volverían	**vuelva** **vuelvas** **vuelva** volvamos volváis **vuelvan**	volviera volvieras volviera volviéramos volvierais volvieran	**vuelve** tú (no **vuelvas**) **vuelva** Ud. volvamos volved (no volváis) **vuelvan** Uds.

Verbs with spelling changes only

Infinitive	INDICATIVE					SUBJUNCTIVE		IMPERATIVE
	Present	Imperfect	Preterite	Future	Conditional	Present	Past	
35 conocer (c:zc) Participles: conociendo conocido	**conozco** conoces conoce conocemos conocéis conocen	conocía conocías conocía conocíamos conocíais conocían	conocí conociste conoció conocimos conocisteis conocieron	conoceré conocerás conocerá conoceremos conoceréis conocerán	conocería conocerías conocería conoceríamos conoceríais conocerían	**conozca** **conozcas** **conozca** **conozcamos** **conozcáis** **conozcan**	conociera conocieras conociera conociéramos conocierais conocieran	conoce tú (no **conozcas**) **conozca** Ud. **conozcamos** conoced (no **conozcáis**) **conozcan** Uds.
36 creer (y) Participles: **creyendo** **creído**	creo crees cree creemos creéis creen	creía creías creía creíamos creíais creían	**creí** **creíste** **creyó** **creímos** **creísteis** **creyeron**	creeré creerás creerá creeremos creeréis creerán	creería creerías creería creeríamos creeríais creerían	crea creas crea creamos creáis crean	**creyera** **creyeras** **creyera** **creyéramos** **creyerais** **creyeran**	cree tú (no creas) crea Ud. creamos creed (no creáis) crean Uds.
37 cruzar (z:c) Participles: cruzando cruzado	cruzo cruzas cruza cruzamos cruzáis cruzan	cruzaba cruzabas cruzaba cruzábamos cruzabais cruzaban	**crucé** cruzaste cruzó cruzamos cruzasteis cruzaron	cruzaré cruzarás cruzará cruzaremos cruzaréis cruzarán	cruzaría cruzarías cruzaría cruzaríamos cruzaríais cruzarían	**cruce** **cruces** **cruce** **crucemos** **crucéis** **crucen**	cruzara cruzaras cruzara cruzáramos cruzarais cruzaran	cruza tú (no **cruces**) **cruce** Ud. **crucemos** cruzad (no **crucéis**) **crucen** Uds.
38 destruir (y) Participles: **destruyendo** destruido	**destruyo** **destruyes** **destruye** destruimos destruís **destruyen**	destruía destruías destruía destruíamos destruíais destruían	destruí destruiste **destruyó** destruimos destruisteis **destruyeron**	destruiré destruirás destruirá destruiremos destruiréis destruirán	destruiría destruirías destruiría destruiríamos destruiríais destruirían	**destruya** **destruyas** **destruya** **destruyamos** **destruyáis** **destruyan**	**destruyera** **destruyeras** **destruyera** **destruyéramos** **destruyerais** **destruyeran**	**destruye** tú (no **destruyas**) **destruya** Ud. **destruyamos** destruid (no **destruyáis**) **destruyan** Uds.
39 enviar (envío) Participles: enviando enviado	**envío** **envías** **envía** enviamos enviáis **envían**	enviaba enviabas enviaba enviábamos enviabais enviaban	envié enviaste envió enviamos enviasteis enviaron	enviaré enviarás enviará enviaremos enviaréis enviarán	enviaría enviarías enviaría enviaríamos enviaríais enviarían	**envíe** **envíes** **envíe** enviemos enviéis **envíen**	enviara enviaras enviara enviáramos enviarais enviaran	**envía** tú (no **envíes**) **envíe** Ud. enviemos enviad (no enviéis) **envíen** Uds.

Infinitive	INDICATIVE					SUBJUNCTIVE		IMPERATIVE
	Present	Imperfect	Preterite	Future	Conditional	Present	Past	

40 graduarse (gradúo)
Participles: graduando, graduado

	Present	Imperfect	Preterite	Future	Conditional	Present	Past	IMPERATIVE
	gradúo	graduaba	gradué	graduaré	graduaría	gradúe	graduara	
	gradúas	graduabas	graduaste	graduarás	graduarías	gradúes	graduaras	gradúa tú (no gradúes)
	gradúa	graduaba	graduó	graduará	graduaría	gradúe	graduara	gradúe Ud.
	graduamos	graduábamos	graduamos	graduaremos	graduaríamos	graduemos	graduáramos	graduemos
	graduáis	graduabais	graduasteis	graduaréis	graduaríais	graduéis	graduarais	graduad (no graduéis)
	gradúan	graduaban	graduaron	graduarán	graduarían	gradúen	graduaran	gradúen Uds.

41 llegar (g:gu)
Participles: llegando, llegado

	Present	Imperfect	Preterite	Future	Conditional	Present	Past	IMPERATIVE
	llego	llegaba	llegué	llegaré	llegaría	llegue	llegara	
	llegas	llegabas	llegaste	llegarás	llegarías	llegues	llegaras	llega tú (no llegues)
	llega	llegaba	llegó	llegará	llegaría	llegue	llegara	llegue Ud.
	llegamos	llegábamos	llegamos	llegaremos	llegaríamos	lleguemos	llegáramos	lleguemos
	llegáis	llegabais	llegasteis	llegaréis	llegaríais	lleguéis	llegarais	llegad (no lleguéis)
	llegan	llegaban	llegaron	llegarán	llegarían	lleguen	llegaran	lleguen Uds.

42 prohibir (prohíbo)
Participles: prohibiendo, prohibido

	Present	Imperfect	Preterite	Future	Conditional	Present	Past	IMPERATIVE
	prohíbo	prohibía	prohibí	prohibiré	prohibiría	prohíba	prohibiera	
	prohíbes	prohibías	prohibiste	prohibirás	prohibirías	prohíbas	prohibieras	prohíbe tú (no prohíbas)
	prohíbe	prohibía	prohibió	prohibirá	prohibiría	prohíba	prohibiera	prohíba Ud.
	prohibimos	prohibíamos	prohibimos	prohibiremos	prohibiríamos	prohibamos	prohibiéramos	prohibamos
	prohibís	prohibíais	prohibisteis	prohibiréis	prohibiríais	prohibáis	prohibierais	prohibid (no prohibáis)
	prohíben	prohibían	prohibieron	prohibirán	prohibirían	prohíban	prohibieran	prohíban Uds.

43 proteger (g:j)
Participles: protegiendo, protegido

	Present	Imperfect	Preterite	Future	Conditional	Present	Past	IMPERATIVE
	protejo	protegía	protegí	protegeré	protegería	proteja	protegiera	
	proteges	protegías	protegiste	protegerás	protegerías	protejas	protegieras	protege tú (no protejas)
	protege	protegía	protegió	protegerá	protegería	proteja	protegiera	proteja Ud.
	protegemos	protegíamos	protegimos	protegeremos	protegeríamos	protejamos	protegiéramos	protejamos
	protegéis	protegíais	protegisteis	protegeréis	protegeríais	protejáis	protegierais	proteged (no protejáis)
	protegen	protegían	protegieron	protegerán	protegerían	protejan	protegieran	protejan Uds.

44 tocar (c:qu)
Participles: tocando, tocado

	Present	Imperfect	Preterite	Future	Conditional	Present	Past	IMPERATIVE
	toco	tocaba	toqué	tocaré	tocaría	toque	tocara	
	tocas	tocabas	tocaste	tocarás	tocarías	toques	tocaras	toca tú (no toques)
	toca	tocaba	tocó	tocará	tocaría	toque	tocara	toque Ud.
	tocamos	tocábamos	tocamos	tocaremos	tocaríamos	toquemos	tocáramos	toquemos
	tocáis	tocabais	tocasteis	tocaréis	tocaríais	toquéis	tocarais	tocad (no toquéis)
	tocan	tocaban	tocaron	tocarán	tocarían	toquen	tocaran	toquen Uds.

Guide to Vocabulary

Note on alphabetization

For purposes of alphabetization, **ch** and **ll** are not treated as separate letters, but **ñ** follows **n**. Therefore, in this glossary you will find that **año**, for example, appears after **anuncio**.

Abbreviations used in this glossary

adj.	adjective	*form.*	formal	*pl.*	plural
adv.	adverb	*indef.*	indefinite	*poss.*	possessive
art.	article	*interj.*	interjection	*prep.*	preposition
conj.	conjunction	*i.o.*	indirect object	*pron.*	pronoun
def.	definite	*m.*	masculine	*ref.*	reflexive
d.o.	direct object	*n.*	noun	*sing.*	singular
f.	feminine	*obj.*	object	*sub.*	subject
fam.	familiar	*p.p.*	past participle	*v.*	verb

Spanish-English

A

a *prep.* at; to 1
  ¿A qué hora...? At what time...? 1
  a bordo aboard
  a dieta on a diet 15
  a la derecha de to the right of 2
  a la izquierda de to the left of 2
  a la plancha grilled 8
  a la(s) + *time* at + *time* 1
  a menos que *conj.* unless 13
  a menudo *adv.* often 10
  a nombre de in the name of 5
  a plazos in installments 14
  A sus órdenes. At your service.
  a tiempo *adv.* on time 10
  a veces *adv.* sometimes 10
  a ver let's see
abeja *f.* bee
abierto/a *adj.* open 5, 14
abogado/a *m., f.* lawyer 16
abrazar(se) *v.* to hug; to embrace (each other) 11
abrazo *m.* hug
abrigo *m.* coat 6
abril *m.* April 5
abrir *v.* to open 3
abuelo/a *m., f.* grandfather/ grandmother 3
abuelos *pl.* grandparents 3
aburrido/a *adj.* bored; boring 5
aburrir *v.* to bore 7
aburrirse *v.* to get bored 17
acabar de (+ *inf.*) *v.* to have just done something 6
acampar *v.* to camp 5
accidente *m.* accident 10
acción *f.* action 17
  de acción action (genre) 17

aceite *m.* oil 8
aceptar: ¡Acepto casarme contigo! I'll marry you! 17
acompañar *v.* to accompany 14
aconsejar *v.* to advise 12
acontecimiento *m.* event 18
acordarse (de) (o:ue) *v.* to remember 7
acostarse (o:ue) *v.* to go to bed 7
activo/a *adj.* active 15
actor *m.* actor 16
actriz *f.* actress 16
actualidades *f., pl.* news; current events 18
adelgazar *v.* to lose weight; to slim down 15
además (de) *adv.* furthermore; besides 10
adicional *adj.* additional
adiós *m.* goodbye 1
adjetivo *m.* adjective
administración de empresas *f.* business administration 2
adolescencia *f.* adolescence 9
¿adónde? *adv.* where (to)? (destination) 2
aduana *f.* customs
aeróbico/a *adj.* aerobic 15
aeropuerto *m.* airport 5
afectado/a *adj.* affected 13
afeitarse *v.* to shave 7
aficionado/a *m., f.* fan 4
afirmativo/a *adj.* affirmative
afuera *adv.* outside 5
afueras *f., pl.* suburbs; outskirts 12
agencia de viajes *f.* travel agency
agente de viajes *m., f.* travel agent
agosto *m.* August 5
agradable *adj.* pleasant **agua** *f.* water 8
  agua mineral mineral water 8

aguantar *v.* to endure, to hold up 14
ahora *adv.* now 2
  ahora mismo right now 5
ahorrar *v.* to save (money) 14
ahorros *m., pl.* savings 14
aire *m.* air 13
ajo *m.* garlic 8
al (*contraction of* **a** + **el**) 4
  al aire libre open-air 6
  al contado in cash 14
  (al) este (to the) east 14
  al lado de next to; beside 2
  (al) norte (to the) north 14
  (al) oeste (to the) west 14
  (al) sur (to the) south 14
alcoba *f.* bedroom
alcohol *m.* alcohol 15
alcohólico/a *adj.* alcoholic 15
alegrarse (de) *v.* to be happy 13
alegre *adj.* happy 5
alegría *f.* happiness 9
alemán, alemana *adj.* German 3
alérgico/a *adj.* allergic 10
alfombra *f.* carpet; rug 12
algo *pron.* something; anything 7
algodón *m.* cotton 6
alguien *pron.* someone; somebody; anyone 7
algún, alguno/a(s) *adj.* any; some 7
alimentación *f.* diet
alimento *m.* food
aliviar *v.* to reduce 15
  aliviar el estrés/la tensión to reduce stress/tension 15
allá *adv.* over there 2
allí *adv.* there 2
alma *f.* soul 9
almacén *m.* department store 6
almohada *f.* pillow 12
almorzar (o:ue) *v.* to have lunch 4

almuerzo *m.* lunch 4, 8
aló *interj.* hello (*on the telephone*) 11
alquilar *v.* to rent 12
alquiler *m.* rent (payment) 12
altar *m.* altar 9
altillo *m.* attic 12
alto/a *adj.* tall 3
aluminio *m.* aluminum 13
amo/a de casa *m., f.* homemaker 12
amable *adj.* nice; friendly 5
amarillo/a *adj.* yellow 6
amigo/a *m., f.* friend 3
amistad *f.* friendship 9
amor *m.* love 9
  amor a primera vista love at first sight 9
anaranjado/a *adj.* orange 6
ándale *interj.* come on 14
andar *v.* **en patineta** to skateboard 4
ángel *m.* angel 9
anillo *m.* ring 17
animal *m.* animal 13
aniversario (de bodas) *m.* (wedding) anniversary 9
anoche *adv.* last night 6
anteayer *adv.* the day before yesterday 6
antes *adv.* before 7
  antes de *prep.* before 7
  antes (de) que *conj.* before 13
antibiótico *m.* antibiotic 10
antipático/a *adj.* unpleasant 3
anunciar *v.* to announce; to advertise 18
anuncio *m.* advertisement 16
año *m.* year 5
  año pasado last year 6
apagar *v.* to turn off 11
aparato *m.* appliance
apartamento *m.* apartment 12
apellido *m.* last name 3
apenas *adv.* hardly; scarcely 10
aplaudir *v.* to applaud 17
aplicación *f.* app 11
apreciar *v.* to appreciate 17
aprender (a + *inf.*) *v.* to learn 3
apurarse *v.* to hurry; to rush 15
aquel, aquella *adj.* that (over there) 6
aquél, aquélla *pron.* that (over there) 6
aquello *neuter, pron.* that; that thing; that fact 6
aquellos/as *pl. adj.* those (over there) 6
aquéllos/as *pl. pron.* those (ones) (over there) 6
aquí *adv.* here 1
  Aquí está(n)... Here is/are... 5
árbol *m.* tree 13 **archivo** *m.* file 11
arete *m.* earring 6
argentino/a *adj.* Argentine 3
armario *m.* closet 12
arqueología *f.* archeology 2

arqueólogo/a *m., f.* archeologist 16
arquitecto/a *m., f.* architect 16
arrancar *v.* to start (*a car*) 11
arreglar *v.* to fix; to arrange 11; to straighten up 12
arreglarse *v.* to get ready 7; to fix oneself (*clothes, hair, etc. to go out*) 7
arroba *f.* @ symbol 11
arroz *m.* rice 8
arte *m.* art 2
artes *f., pl.* arts 17
artesanía *f.* craftsmanship; crafts 17
artículo *m.* article 18
artista *m., f.* artist 3
artístico/a *adj.* artistic 17
arveja *f.* pea 8
asado/a *adj.* roast 8
ascenso *m.* promotion 16
ascensor *m.* elevator 5
así *adv.* like this; so (*in such a way*) 10
asistir (a) *v.* to attend 3
aspiradora *f.* vacuum cleaner 12
aspirante *m., f.* candidate; applicant 16
aspirina *f.* aspirin 10
atún *m.* tuna 8
aumentar *v.* to grow; to get bigger 13
aumentar *v.* **de peso** to gain weight 15
aumento *m.* increase
  aumento de sueldo pay raise 16
aunque although
autobús *m.* bus 1
automático/a *adj.* automatic
auto(móvil) *m.* car 5
autopista *f.* highway 11
ave *f.* bird 13
avenida *f.* avenue
aventura *f.* adventure 17
  de aventuras adventure (genre) 17
avergonzado/a *adj.* embarrassed 5
avión *m.* airplane 5
¡Ay! *interj.* Oh!
  ¡Ay, qué dolor! Oh, what pain!
ayer *adv.* yesterday 6
ayudar(se) *v.* to help (each other) 11
azúcar *m.* sugar 8
azul *adj. m., f.* blue 6

B

bailar *v.* to dance 2
bailarín/bailarina *m., f.* dancer 17
baile *m.* dance 17
bajar(se) de *v.* to get off of/out of (a vehicle) 11

bajo/a *adj.* short (*in height*) 3
balcón *m.* balcony 12
balde *m.* bucket 5
ballena *f.* whale 13
baloncesto *m.* basketball 4
banana *f.* banana 8
banco *m.* bank 14
banda *f.* band 17
bandera *f.* flag
bañarse *v.* to take a bath 7
baño *m.* bathroom 7
barato/a *adj.* cheap 6
barco *m.* boat 5
barrer *v.* to sweep 12
  barrer el suelo *v.* to sweep the floor 12
barrio *m.* neighborhood 12
bastante *adv.* enough; rather 10
basura *f.* trash 12
batería *f.* battery 11
baúl *m.* trunk 11
beber *v.* to drink 3
bebida *f.* drink 8
  bebida alcohólica *f.* alcoholic beverage 15
béisbol *m.* baseball 4
bellas artes *f., pl.* fine arts 17
belleza *f.* beauty 14
beneficio *m.* benefit 16
besar(se) *v.* to kiss (each other) 11
beso *m.* kiss 9
biblioteca *f.* library 2
bicicleta *f.* bicycle 4
bien *adv.* well 1
bienestar *m.* well-being 15
bienvenido(s)/a(s) *adj.* welcome 1
billete *m.* paper money; ticket
billón *m.* trillion
biología *f.* biology 2
bisabuelo/a *m., f.* great-grand-father/great-grandmother 3
bistec *m.* steak 8
blanco/a *adj.* white 6
blog *m.* blog 11
(blue)jeans *m., pl.* jeans 6
blusa *f.* blouse 6
boca *f.* mouth 10
boda *f.* wedding 9
boleto *m.* ticket 2, 17
bolsa *f.* purse, bag 6
bombero/a *m., f.* firefighter 16
bonito/a *adj.* pretty 3
borrador *m.* eraser 2
borrar *v.* to erase 11
bosque *m.* forest 13
  bosque tropical tropical forest; rain forest 13
bota *f.* boot 6
botella *f.* bottle 9
  botella de vino bottle of wine 9
botones *m., f. sing.* bellhop 5
brazo *m.* arm 10
brindar *v.* to toast (*drink*) 9
bucear *v.* to scuba dive 4

buen, bueno/a *adj.* good 3, 6
  buena forma good shape (*physical*) 15
  Buenas noches. Good evening; Good night. 1
  Buenas tardes. Good afternoon. 1
  Bueno. Hello. (*on telephone*) 11
  Buenos días. Good morning. 1
bulevar *m.* boulevard
buscador *m.* browser 11
buscar *v.* to look for 2
buzón *m.* mailbox 14

C

caballero *m.* gentleman, sir 8
caballo *m.* horse 5
cabe: no cabe duda de there's no doubt 13
cabeza *f.* head 10
cada *adj. m., f.* each 6
caerse *v.* to fall (down) 10
café *m.* café 4; *adj. m., f.* brown 6; *m.* coffee 8
cafeína *f.* caffeine 15
cafetera *f.* coffee maker 12
cafetería *f.* cafeteria 2
caído/a *p.p.* fallen 14
caja *f.* cash register 6
cajero/a *m., f.* cashier
  cajero automático *m.* ATM 14
calavera de azúcar *f.* skull made out of sugar 9
calcetín (calcetines) *m.* sock(s) 6
calculadora *f.* calculator 2
calentamiento global *m.* global warming 13
calentarse (e:ie) *v.* to warm up 15
calidad *f.* quality 6
calle *f.* street 11
calor *m.* heat
caloría *f.* calorie 15
calzar *v.* to take size... shoes 6
cama *f.* bed 5
cámara digital *f.* digital camera 11
camarero/a *m., f.* waiter/waitress 8
camarón *m.* shrimp 8
cambiar (de) *v.* to change 9
cambio: de cambio in change 2
cambio *m.* **climático** climate change 13
cambio *m.* **de moneda** currency exchange
caminar *v.* to walk 2
camino *m.* road
camión *m.* truck; bus
camisa *f.* shirt 6
camiseta *f.* t-shirt 6
campo *m.* countryside 5
canadiense *adj.* Canadian 3
canal *m.* (TV) channel 11; 17

canción *f.* song 17
candidato/a *m., f.* candidate 18
canela *f.* cinnamon 10
cansado/a *adj.* tired 5
cantante *m., f.* singer 17
cantar *v.* to sing 2
capital *f.* capital city
capó *m.* hood 11
cara *f.* face 7
caramelo *m.* caramel 9
cargador *m.* charger 11
cargar *v.* to charge; to upload 11
carne *f.* meat 8
  carne de res *f.* beef 8
carnicería *f.* butcher shop 14
caro/a *adj.* expensive 6
carpintero/a *m., f.* carpenter 16
carrera *f.* career 16
carretera *f.* highway; (main) road 11
carro *m.* car 11
carta *f.* letter 4; *(playing)* card 5
cartel *m.* poster 12
cartera *f.* wallet 4, 6
cartero *m.* mail carrier 14
casa *f.* house; home 2
casado/a *adj.* married 9
casarse (con) *v.* to get married (to) 9
casi *adv.* almost 10
catorce fourteen 1
cazar *v.* to hunt 13
cebolla *f.* onion 8
celebrar *v.* to celebrate 9
cementerio *m.* cemetery 9
cena *f.* dinner 8
cenar *v.* to have dinner 2
centro *m.* downtown 4
  centro comercial shopping mall 6
cepillarse los dientes/el pelo *v.* to brush one's teeth/one's hair 7
cerámica *f.* pottery 17
cerca de *prep.* near 2
cerdo *m.* pork 8
cereales *m., pl.* cereal; grains 8
cero *m.* zero 1
cerrado/a *adj.* closed 5
cerrar (e:ie) *v.* to close 4
cerveza *f.* beer 8
césped *m.* grass
ceviche *m.* marinated fish dish 8
  ceviche de camarón *m.* lemon-marinated shrimp 8
chaleco *m.* vest
champán *m.* champagne 9
champiñón *m.* mushroom 8
champú *m.* shampoo 7
chaqueta *f.* jacket 6
chatear *v.* to chat 11
chau *fam. interj.* bye 1
cheque *m.* (bank) check 14
chévere *adj., fam.* terrific
chico/a *m., f.* boy/girl 1
chino/a *adj.* Chinese 3
chocar (con) *v.* to run into
chocolate *m.* chocolate 9

choque *m.* collision 18
chuleta *f.* chop (*food*) 8
  chuleta de cerdo *f.* pork chop 8
ciclismo *m.* cycling 4
cielo *m.* sky 13
cien(to) one hundred 2
ciencias *f., pl.* sciences 2
  ciencias ambientales environmental science 2
  de ciencia ficción *f.* science fiction (genre) 17
científico/a *m., f.* scientist 16
cierto/a *adj.* certain 13
  es cierto it's certain 13
  no es cierto it's not certain 13
cima *f.* top, peak 15
cinco five 1
cincuenta fifty 2
cine *m.* movie theater 4
cinta caminadora *f.* treadmill 15
cinturón *m.* belt 6
circulación *f.* traffic 11
cita *f.* date; appointment 9
ciudad *f.* city
ciudadano/a *m., f.* citizen 18
Claro (que sí). *fam.* Of course.
clase *f.* class 2
  clase de ejercicios aeróbicos *f.* aerobics class 15
clásico/a *adj.* classical 17
cliente/a *m., f.* customer 6
clínica *f.* clinic 10
cobrar *v.* to cash (a check) 14
coche *m.* car 11
cocina *f.* kitchen; stove 9, 12
cocinar *v.* to cook 12
cocinero/a *m., f.* cook, chef 16
cofre *m.* hood 14
cola *f.* line 14
colesterol *m.* cholesterol 15
color *m.* color 6
comedia *f.* comedy; play 17
comedor *m.* dining room 12
comenzar (e:ie) *v.* to begin 4
comer *v.* to eat 3
comercial *adj.* commercial; business-related 16
comida *f.* food; meal 4, 8
como like; as 8
¿cómo? what?; how? 1, 2
  ¿Cómo es...? What's... like?
  ¿Cómo está usted? *form.* How are you? 1
  ¿Cómo estás? *fam.* How are you? 1
  ¿Cómo se llama usted? *form.* What's your name? 1
  ¿Cómo te llamas? *fam.* What's your name? 1
cómoda *f.* chest of drawers 12
cómodo/a *adj.* comfortable 5
compañero/a de clase *m., f.* classmate 2
compañero/a de cuarto *m., f.* roommate 2
compañía *f.* company; firm 16

compartir *v.* to share 3
compositor(a) *m., f.* composer 17
comprar *v.* to buy 2
  comprar en línea to buy online 6
compras *f., pl.* purchases
  ir de compras to go shopping 5
comprender *v.* to understand 3
comprobar *v.* to check
comprometerse (con) *v.* to get engaged (to) 9
computación *f.* computer science 2
computadora *f.* computer 1
computadora portátil *f.* portable computer; laptop 11
comunicación *f.* communication 18
comunicarse (con) *v.* to communicate (with) 18
comunidad *f.* community 1
con *prep.* with 2
  Con él/ella habla. Speaking. (*on telephone*) 11
  con frecuencia *adv.* frequently 10
  Con permiso. Pardon me; Excuse me. 1
  con tal (de) que *conj.* provided (that) 13
concierto *m.* concert 17
concordar *v.* to agree
concurso *m.* game show; contest 17
conducir *v.* to drive 6, 11
conductor(a) *m., f.* driver 1
conectarse *v.* **a Internet** to get connected to the Internet 11
conexión *f.* **inalámbrica** wireless connection 11
confirmar *v.* to confirm 5
confirmar *v.* **una reservación** *f.* to confirm a reservation 5
confundido/a *adj.* confused 5
congelador *m.* freezer 12
congestionado/a *adj.* congested 10
conmigo *pron.* with me 4, 9
conocer *v.* to know; to be acquainted with 6
conocido/a *adj.; p.p.* known
conseguir (e:i) *v.* to get; to obtain 4
consejero/a *m., f.* counselor; advisor 16
consejo *m.* advice
conservación *f.* conservation 13
conservar *v.* to conserve 13
construir *v.* to build
consultorio *m.* doctor's office 10
consumir *v.* to consume 15
contabilidad *f.* accounting 2
contador(a) *m., f.* accountant 16
contaminación *f.* pollution 13
  contaminación del aire/del agua air/water pollution 13
contaminado/a *adj.* polluted 13
contaminar *v.* to pollute 13
contar (o:ue) *v.* to count; to tell 4
contento/a *adj.* content 5
contestar *v.* to answer 2
contigo *fam. pron.* with you 5, 9
contraseña *f.* password 11

contratar *v.* to hire 16
control *m.* **remoto** remote control 11
controlar *v.* to control 13
conversación *f.* conversation 1
conversar *v.* to converse, to chat 2
copa *f.* wineglass 12
corazón *m.* heart 10
corbata *f.* tie 6
corredor(a) *m., f.* **de bolsa** stockbroker 16
correo *m.* mail; post office 14
  correo de voz *m.* voice mail 11
  correo electrónico *m.* e-mail 4
correr *v.* to run 3
cortesía *f.* courtesy
cortinas *f., pl.* curtains 12
corto/a *adj.* short (*in length*) 6
cosa *f.* thing 1
costar (o:ue) *v.* to cost 6
costarricense *adj.* Costa Rican 3
cráter *m.* crater 13
creer *v.* to believe 3, 13
  creer (en) *v.* to believe (in) 3
  no creer *v.* not to believe 13
creído/a *adj., p.p.* believed 14
crema de afeitar *f.* shaving cream 5, 7
crimen *m.* crime; murder 18
cruzar *v.* to cross 14
cuaderno *m.* notebook 1
cuadra *f.* (city) block 14
¿cuál(es)? which?; which one(s)? 2
  ¿Cuál es la fecha de hoy? What is today's date? 5
cuadro *m.* picture 12
cuando *conj.* when 7; 13
¿cuándo? when? 2
¿cuánto(s)/a(s)? how much/how many? 1, 2
  ¿Cuánto cuesta...? How much does... cost? 6
  ¿Cuántos años tienes? How old are you?
cuarenta forty 2
cuarto *m.* room 2; 7
  cuarto de baño *m.* bathroom 7
cuarto/a *adj.* fourth 5
  menos cuarto quarter to (time) 1
  y cuarto quarter after (time) 1
cuatro four 1
cuatrocientos/as four hundred 2
cubano/a *adj.* Cuban 3
cubiertos *m., pl.* silverware
cubierto/a *p.p.* covered
cubrir *v.* to cover
cuchara *f.* (table or large) spoon 12
cuchillo *m.* knife 12
cuello *m.* neck 10
cuenta *f.* bill 8; account 14
  cuenta corriente *f.* checking account 14
  cuenta de ahorros *f.* savings account 14
cuento *m.* short story 17
cuerpo *m.* body 10

cuidado *m.* care
cuidar *v.* to take care of 13
cultura *f.* culture 2, 17
cumpleaños *m., sing.* birthday 9
cumplir años *v.* to have a birthday
cuñado/a *m., f.* brother-in-law/ sister-in-law 3
currículum *m.* résumé 16
curso *m.* course 2

D

danza *f.* dance 17
dañar *v.* to damage; to break down 10
dar *v.* to give 6
  dar un consejo *v.* to give advice
  darse con to bump into; to run into (something) 10
  darse prisa *v.* to hurry; to rush 15
de *prep.* of; from 1
  ¿De dónde eres? *fam.* Where are you from? 1
  ¿De dónde es usted? *form.* Where are you from? 1
  ¿De parte de quién? Who is speaking/calling? (*on telephone*) 11
  ¿de quién...? whose...? (*sing.*) 1
  ¿de quiénes...? whose...? (*pl.*) 1
  de algodón (made) of cotton 6
  de aluminio (made) of aluminum 13
  de buen humor in a good mood 5
  de compras shopping 5
  de cuadros plaid 6
  de excursión hiking 4
  de hecho in fact
  de ida y vuelta roundtrip 5
  de la mañana in the morning; A.M. 1
  de la noche in the evening; at night; P.M. 1
  de la tarde in the afternoon; in the early evening; P.M. 1
  de lana (made) of wool 6
  de lunares polka-dotted 6
  de mal humor in a bad mood 5
  de moda in fashion 6
  De nada. You're welcome. 1
  de niño/a as a child 10
  de parte de on behalf of 11
  de plástico (made) of plastic 13
  de rayas striped 6
  de repente suddenly 6
  de seda (made) of silk 6
  de vaqueros western (genre) 17
  de vez en cuando from time to time 10
  de vidrio (made) of glass 13
debajo de *prep.* below; under 2
deber (+ inf.) *v.* should; must; ought to 3

deber *m.* responsibility; obligation 18

debido a due to (the fact that)

débil *adj.* weak 15

decidir (+ *inf.*) *v.* to decide 3

décimo/a *adj.* tenth 5

decir (e:i) *v.* **(que)** to say (that); to tell (that) 4

decir la respuesta to say the answer 4

decir la verdad to tell the truth 4

decir mentiras to tell lies 4

declarar *v.* to declare 18

dedo *m.* finger 10

dedo del pie *m.* toe 10

deforestación *f.* deforestation 13

dejar *v.* to let; to quit; to leave behind 16

dejar de (+ *inf.*) *v.* to stop (*doing something*) 13

dejar una propina *v.* to leave a tip

del (*contraction of* **de** + **el**) of the; from the 1

delante de *prep.* in front of 2

delgado/a *adj.* thin 3

delicioso/a *adj.* delicious 8

demás *adj.* the rest

demasiado *adv.* too much 6

dentista *m., f.* dentist 10

dentro de (diez años) within (ten years) 16; inside

dependiente/a *m., f.* clerk 6

deporte *m.* sport 4

deportista *m.* sports person

deportivo/a *adj.* sports-related 4

depositar *v.* to deposit 14

derecha *f.* right 2

a la derecha de to the right of 2

derecho *adv.* straight (ahead) 14

derechos *m., pl.* rights 18

desarrollar *v.* to develop 13

desastre (natural) *m.* (natural) disaster 18

desayunar *v.* to have breakfast 2

desayuno *m.* breakfast 8

descafeinado/a *adj.* decaffeinated 15

descansar *v.* to rest 2

descargar *v.* to download 11

descompuesto/a *adj.* not working; out of order 11

describir *v.* to describe 3

descrito/a *p.p.* described 14

descubierto/a *p.p.* discovered 14

descubrir *v.* to discover 13

desde *prep.* from 6

desear *v.* to wish; to desire 2

desempleo *m.* unemployment 18

desierto *m.* desert 13

desigualdad *f.* inequality 18

desordenado/a *adj.* disorderly 5

despacio *adv.* slowly 10

despedida *f.* farewell; goodbye

despedir (e:i) *v.* to fire 16

despedirse (de) (e:i) *v.* to say goodbye (to) 18

despejado/a *adj.* clear (*weather*)

despertador *m.* alarm clock 7

despertarse (e:ie) *v.* to wake up 7

después *adv.* afterward; then 7

después de *prep.* after 7

después de que *conj.* after 13

destruir *v.* to destroy 13

detrás de *prep.* behind 2

día *m.* day 1

día de fiesta holiday 9

diario *m.* diary 1; newspaper 18

diario/a *adj.* daily 7

dibujar *v.* to draw 2

dibujo *m.* drawing

dibujos animados *m., pl.* cartoons 17

diccionario *m.* dictionary 1

dicho/a *p.p.* said 14

diciembre *m.* December 5

dictadura *f.* dictatorship 18

diecinueve nineteen 1

dieciocho eighteen 1

dieciséis sixteen 1

diecisiete seventeen 1

diente *m.* tooth 7

dieta *f.* diet 15

comer una dieta equilibrada to eat a balanced diet 15

diez ten 1

difícil *adj.* difficult 3

Diga. Hello. (*on telephone*) 11

diligencia *f.* errand 14

dinero *m.* money 6

dirección *f.* address 14

dirección electrónica *f.* e-mail address 11

director(a) *m., f.* director; (*musical*) conductor 17

dirigir *v.* to direct 17

discriminación *f.* discrimination 18

discurso *m.* speech 18

diseñador(a) *m., f.* designer 16

diseño *m.* design

disfraz *m.* costume 9

disfrutar (de) *v.* to enjoy; to reap the benefits (of) 15

disminuir *v.* to reduce 16

diversión *f.* fun activity; entertainment; recreation 4

divertido/a *adj.* fun

divertirse (e:ie) *v.* to have fun 9

divorciado/a *adj.* divorced 9

divorciarse (de) *v.* to get divorced (from) 9

divorcio *m.* divorce 9

doblar *v.* to turn 14

doble *adj.* double 5

doce twelve 1

doctor(a) *m., f.* doctor 3; 10

documental *m.* documentary 17

documentos de viaje *m., pl.* travel documents

doler (o:ue) *v.* to hurt 10

dolor *m.* ache; pain 10

dolor de cabeza *m.* headache 10

doméstico/a *adj.* domestic 12

domingo *m.* Sunday 2

don *m.* Mr.; sir 1

doña *f.* Mrs.; ma'am 1

donde *adv.* where

¿Dónde está...? Where is...? 2

¿dónde? where? 1, 2

dormir (o:ue) *v.* to sleep 4

dormirse (o:ue) *v.* to go to sleep; to fall asleep 7

dormitorio *m.* bedroom 12

dos two 1

dos veces *f.* twice 6

doscientos/as two hundred 2

drama *m.* drama; play 17

dramático/a *adj.* dramatic 17

dramaturgo/a *m., f.* playwright 17

droga *f.* drug 15

drogadicto/a *m., f.* drug addict 15

ducha *f.* shower 7

ducharse *v.* to take a shower 7

duda *f.* doubt 13

dudar *v.* to doubt 13

no dudar *v.* not to doubt 13

dueño/a *m., f.* owner 8

dulces *m., pl.* sweets; candy 9

durante *prep.* during 7

durar *v.* to last 18

E

e *conj.* (*used instead of* **y** *before words beginning with* **i** *and* **hi**) and

echar *v.* to throw

echar (una carta) al buzón *v.* to put (a letter) in the mailbox; to mail 14

ecología *f.* ecology 13

ecológico/a *adj.* ecological 13

ecologista *m., f.* ecologist 13

economía *f.* economics 2

ecoturismo *m.* ecotourism 13

ecuatoriano/a *adj.* Ecuadorian 3

edad *f.* age 9

edificio *m.* building 12

edificio de apartamentos apartment building 12

(en) efectivo *m.* cash 6

ejercer *v.* to practice/exercise (a degree/profession) 16

ejercicio *m.* exercise 15

ejercicios aeróbicos aerobic exercises 15

ejercicios de estiramiento stretching exercises 15

ejército *m.* army 18

el *m., sing., def. art.* the 1

él *sub. pron.* he 1; *obj. pron.* him

elecciones *f., pl.* election 18

electricista *m., f.* electrician 16

electrodoméstico *m.* electric appliance 12

elegante *adj. m., f.* elegant 6
elegir (e:i) *v.* to elect 18
ella *sub. pron.* she 1; *obj. pron.* her
ellos/as *sub. pron.* they 1; *obj. pron.* them
embarazada *adj.* pregnant 10
emergencia *f.* emergency 10
emitir *v.* to broadcast 18
emocionante *adj. m., f.* exciting
empezar (e:ie) *v.* to begin 4
empleado/a *m., f.* employee 5
empleo *m.* job; employment 16
empresa *f.* company; firm 16
en *prep.* in; on 2
  en casa at home
  en caso (de) que *conj.* in case (that) 13
  en cuanto *conj.* as soon as 13
  en efectivo in cash 14
  en exceso in excess; too much 15
  en línea online 6
  en punto on the dot; exactly; sharp (*time*) 1
  en qué in what; how
  ¿En qué puedo servirles? How can I help you? 5
  en vivo live 7
enamorado/a (de) *adj.* in love (with) 5
enamorarse (de) *v.* to fall in love (with) 9
encantado/a *adj.* delighted; pleased to meet you 1
encantar *v.* to like very much; to love (*inanimate objects*) 7
encima de *prep.* on top of 2
encontrar (o:ue) *v.* to find 4
encontrar(se) (o:ue) *v.* to meet (each other); to run into (each other) 11
  encontrarse con to meet up with 7
encuesta *f.* poll; survey 18
energía *f.* energy 13
  energía nuclear nuclear energy 13
  energía solar solar energy 13
enero *m.* January 5
enfermarse *v.* to get sick 10
enfermedad *f.* illness 10
enfermero/a *m., f.* nurse 10
enfermo/a *adj.* sick 10
enfrente de *adv.* opposite; facing 14
engordar *v.* to gain weight 15
enojado/a *adj.* angry 5
enojarse (con) *v.* to get angry (with) 7
ensalada *f.* salad 8
ensayo *m.* essay 3
enseguida *adv.* right away
enseñar *v.* to teach 2
ensuciar *v.* to get (something) dirty 12
entender (e:ie) *v.* to understand 4
enterarse *v.* to find out 16
entonces *adv.* so, then 5, 7

entrada *f.* entrance 12; ticket
entre *prep.* between; among 2
entregar *v.* to hand in 11
entremeses *m., pl.* appetizers 8
entrenador(a) *m., f.* trainer 15
entrenarse *v.* to train 15
entrevista *f.* interview 16
entrevistador(a) *m., f.* interviewer 16
entrevistar *v.* to interview 16
envase *m.* container 13
enviar *v.* to send; to mail 14
equilibrado/a *adj.* balanced 15
equipaje *m.* luggage 5
equipo *m.* team 4
equivocado/a *adj.* wrong 5
eres *fam.* you are 1
es he/she/it is 1
  Es bueno que... It's good that... 12
  es cierto it's certain 13
  es extraño it's strange 13
  es igual it's the same 5
  Es importante que... It's important that... 12
  es imposible it's impossible 13
  es improbable it's improbable 13
  Es malo que... It's bad that... 12
  Es mejor que... It's better that... 12
  Es necesario que... It's necessary that... 12
  es obvio it's obvious 13
  es posible it's possible 13
  es probable it's probable 13
  es ridículo it's ridiculous 13
  es seguro it's certain 13
  es terrible it's terrible 13
  es triste it's sad 13
  Es urgente que... It's urgent that... 12
  Es la una. It's one o'clock. 1
  es una lástima it's a shame 13
  es verdad it's true 13
esa(s) *f., adj.* that; those 6
ésa(s) *f., pron.* that (one); those (ones) 6
escalar *v.* to climb 4
  escalar montañas to climb mountains 4
escalera *f.* stairs 12
escalón *m.* step 15
escanear *v.* to scan 11
escoger *v.* to choose 8
escribir *v.* to write 3
  escribir un mensaje electrónico to write an e-mail 4
  escribir una carta to write a letter 4
escrito/a *p.p.* written 14
escritor(a) *m., f.* writer 17
escritorio *m.* desk 2
escuchar *v.* to listen (to) 2
  escuchar la radio to listen to

the radio 2
  escuchar música to listen to music 2
escuela *f.* school 1
esculpir *v.* to sculpt 17
escultor(a) *m., f.* sculptor 17
escultura *f.* sculpture 17
ese *m., sing., adj.* that 6
ése *m., sing., pron.* that one 6
eso *neuter, pron.* that; that thing 6
esos *m., pl., adj.* those 6
ésos *m., pl., pron.* those (ones) 6
España *f.* Spain
español *m.* Spanish (*language*) 2
español(a) *adj. m., f.* Spanish 3
espárragos *m., pl.* asparagus 8
especialidad: las especialidades del día today's specials 8
especialización *f.* major 2
espectacular *adj.* spectacular
espectáculo *m.* show 17
espejo *m.* mirror 7
esperar *v.* to hope; to wish 13
  esperar (+ *inf.*) *v.* to wait (for); to hope 2
esposo/a *m., f.* husband/wife; spouse 3
esquí (acuático) *m.* (water) skiing 4
esquiar *v.* to ski 4
esquina *f.* corner 14
está he/she/it is, you are
  Está bien. That's fine.
  Está (muy) despejado. It's (very) clear. (*weather*)
  Está lloviendo. It's raining. 5
  Está nevando. It's snowing. 5
  Está (muy) nublado. It's (very) cloudy. (*weather*) 5
esta(s) *f., adj.* this; these 6
  esta noche tonight
ésta(s) *f., pron.* this (one); these (ones) 6
establecer *v.* to establish 16
estación *f.* station; season 5
  estación de autobuses bus station 5
  estación del metro subway station 5
  estación de tren train station 5
estacionamiento *m.* parking lot 14
estacionar *v.* to park 11
estadio *m.* stadium 2
estado civil *m.* marital status 9
Estados Unidos *m., pl.* (EE.UU.; E.U.) United States
estadounidense *adj. m., f.* from the United States 3
estampilla *f.* stamp 14
estante *m.* bookcase; bookshelves 12
estar *v.* to be 2
  estar a dieta to be on a diet 15

estar aburrido/a to be bored 5   **estar afectado/a (por)** to be affected (by) 13
estar cansado/a to be tired 5
estar contaminado/a to be polluted 13
estar de acuerdo to agree 17
   Estoy de acuerdo. I agree. 17
   No estoy de acuerdo. I don't agree. 17
estar de moda to be in fashion 6
estar de vacaciones *f., pl.* to be on vacation 5
estar en buena forma to be in good shape 15
estar enfermo/a to be sick 10
estar harto/a de... to be sick of... 18
estar listo/a to be ready 5
estar perdido/a to be lost 14
estar roto/a to be broken
estar seguro/a to be sure 5
estar torcido/a to be twisted; to be sprained 10
   No está nada mal. It's not bad at all. 5
estatua *f.* statue 17
este *m.* east 14
este *m., sing., adj.* this 6
éste *m., sing., pron.* this (one) 6
estéreo *m.* stereo
estilo *m.* style
estiramiento *m.* stretching 15
esto *neuter pron.* this; this thing 6
estómago *m.* stomach 10
estornudar *v.* to sneeze 10
estos *m., pl., adj.* these 6
éstos *m., pl., pron.* these (ones) 6
estrella *f.* star 13
   estrella de cine *m., f.* movie star 17
estrés *m.* stress 15
estudiante *m., f.* student 1, 2
estudiantil *adj. m., f.* student 2
estudiar *v.* to study 2
estufa *f.* stove 12
estupendo/a *adj.* stupendous 5
etapa *f.* stage 9
evitar *v.* to avoid 13
examen *m.* test; exam 2
   examen médico physical exam 10
excelente *adj. m., f.* excellent 5
exceso *m.* excess 15
excursión *f.* hike; tour; excursion 4
excursionista *m., f.* hiker
éxito *m.* success
experiencia *f.* experience
explicar *v.* to explain 2
explorar *v.* to explore
expresión *f.* expression
extinción *f.* extinction 13
extranjero/a *adj.* foreign 17

extrañar *v.* to miss 16
extraño/a *adj.* strange 13

F

fábrica *f.* factory 13
fabuloso/a *adj.* fabulous 5
fácil *adj.* easy 3
falda *f.* skirt 6
faltar *v.* to lack; to need 7
familia *f.* family 3
famoso/a *adj.* famous
farmacia *f.* pharmacy 10
fascinar *v.* to fascinate 7
favorito/a *adj.* favorite 4
febrero *m.* February 5
fecha *f.* date 5
¡Felicidades! Congratulations! 9
¡Felicitaciones! Congratulations! 9
feliz *adj.* happy 5
   ¡Feliz cumpleaños! Happy birthday! 9
fenomenal *adj.* great, phenomenal 5
feo/a *adj.* ugly 3
festival *m.* festival 17
fiebre *f.* fever 10
fiesta *f.* party 9
fijo/a *adj.* fixed, set 6
fin *m.* end 4
   fin de semana weekend 4
finalmente *adv.* finally
firmar *v.* to sign (*a document*) 14
física *f.* physics 2
flan (de caramelo) *m.* baked (caramel) custard 9
flexible *adj.* flexible 15
flor *f.* flower 13
folclórico/a *adj.* folk; folkloric 17
folleto *m.* brochure
forma *f.* shape 15
formulario *m.* form 14
foto(grafía) *f.* photograph 1
francés, francesa *adj. m., f.* French 3
frecuentemente *adv.* frequently
frenos *m., pl.* brakes
frente (frío) *m.* (cold) front 5
fresco/a *adj.* cool
frijoles *m., pl.* beans 8
frío/a *adj.* cold
frito/a *adj.* fried 8
fruta *f.* fruit 8
frutería *f.* fruit store 14
fuera *adv.* outside
fuerte *adj. m., f.* strong 15
fumar *v.* to smoke 15
   (no) fumar *v.* (not) to smoke 15
funcionar *v.* to work 11; to function
fútbol *m.* soccer 4
fútbol americano *m.* football 4
futuro/a *adj.* future
   en el futuro in the future

G

gafas (de sol) *f., pl.* (sun)glasses 6
gafas (oscuras) *f., pl.* (sun)glasses
galleta *f.* cookie 9
ganar *v.* to win 4; to earn (money) 16
ganga *f.* bargain 6
garaje *m.* garage; (mechanic's) repair shop 11; garage (*in a house*) 12
garganta *f.* throat 10
gasolina *f.* gasoline 11
gasolinera *f.* gas station 11
gastar *v.* to spend (*money*) 6
gato *m.* cat 13
gemelo/a *m., f.* twin 3
genial *adj.* great 16
gente *f.* people 3
geografía *f.* geography 2
gerente *m., f.* manager 8, 16
gimnasio *m.* gymnasium 4
gobierno *m.* government 13
golf *m.* golf 4
gordo/a *adj.* fat 3
grabar *v.* to record 11
gracias *f., pl.* thank you; thanks 1
   Gracias por invitarme. Thanks for inviting me. 9
graduarse (de/en) *v.* to graduate (from/in) 9
grande *adj.* big; large 3
grasa *f.* fat 15
gratis *adj. m., f.* free of charge 14
grave *adj.* grave; serious 10
gripe *f.* flu 10
gris *adj. m., f.* gray 6
gritar *v.* to scream, to shout
grito *m.* scream 5
guantes *m., pl.* gloves 6
guapo/a *adj.* good-looking 3
guardar *v.* to save (on a computer) 11
guerra *f.* war 18
guía *m., f.* guide
gustar *v.* to be pleasing to; to like 2
   Me gustaría... I would like...
gusto *m.* pleasure 1
   El gusto es mío. The pleasure is mine. 1
   Mucho gusto. Pleased to meet you. 1
   ¡Qué gusto verlo/la! *form.* How nice to see you! 18
   ¡Qué gusto verte! *fam.* How nice to see you! 18

H

haber *(auxiliar)* *v.* to have (done something) 15
habitación *f.* room 5
   habitación doble double room 5
   habitación individual single room 5

hablar *v.* to talk; to speak 2
hacer *v.* to do; to make 4
  Hace buen tiempo. The weather is good. 5
  Hace (mucho) calor. It's (very) hot. (*weather*) 5
  Hace fresco. It's cool. (*weather*) 5
  Hace (mucho) frío. It's (very) cold. (*weather*) 5
  Hace mal tiempo. The weather is bad. 5
  Hace (mucho) sol. It's (very) sunny. (*weather*) 5
  Hace (mucho) viento. It's (very) windy. (*weather*) 5
  hacer cola to stand in line 14
  hacer diligencias to run errands 14
  hacer ejercicio to exercise 15
  hacer ejercicios aeróbicos to do aerobics 15
  hacer ejercicios de estiramiento to do stretching exercises 15
  hacer el papel (de) to play the role (of) 17
  hacer gimnasia to work out 15
  hacer juego (con) to match (with) 6
  hacer la cama to make the bed 12
  hacer las maletas to pack (one's) suitcases 5
  hacer quehaceres domésticos to do household chores 12
  hacer (wind)surf to (wind)surf 5
  hacer turismo to go sightseeing
  hacer un viaje to take a trip 5
  ¿Me harías el honor de casarte conmigo? Would you do me the honor of marrying me? 17
hacia *prep.* toward 14
hambre *f.* hunger
hamburguesa *f.* hamburger 8
hasta *prep.* until 6; toward
  Hasta la vista. See you later. 1
  Hasta luego. See you later. 1
  Hasta mañana. See you tomorrow. 1
  Hasta pronto. See you soon. 1
  hasta que *conj.* until 13
hay there is; there are 1
  Hay (mucha) niebla. It's (very) foggy.
  Hay que It is necessary that
  No hay de qué. You're welcome. 1
  No hay duda de There's no doubt 13
hecho/a *p.p.* done 14
heladería *f.* ice cream shop 14
helado *m.* ice cream 9
helado/a *adj.* iced 8
hermanastro/a *m., f.* stepbrother/stepsister 3

hermano/a *m., f.* brother/sister 3
hermano/a mayor/menor *m., f.* older/younger brother/sister 3
hermanos *m., pl.* siblings (brothers and sisters) 3
hermoso/a *adj.* beautiful 6
hierba *f.* grass 13
hijastro/a *m., f.* stepson/stepdaughter 3
hijo/a *m., f.* son/daughter 3
  hijo/a único/a *m., f.* only child 3
  hijos *m., pl.* children 3
híjole *interj.* wow 6
historia *f.* history 2; story 17
hockey *m.* hockey 4
hola *interj.* hi 1
hombre *m.* man 1
  hombre de negocios *m.* businessman 16
hora *f.* hour 1; the time
horario *m.* schedule 2
horno *m.* oven 12
  horno de microondas *m.* microwave oven 12
horror *m.* horror 17
  de horror horror (genre) 17
hospital *m.* hospital 10
hotel *m.* hotel 5
hoy *adv.* today 2
  hoy día *adv.* nowadays
  Hoy es... Today is... 2
hueco *m.* hole 4
huelga *f.* strike (*labor*) 18
hueso *m.* bone 10
huésped *m., f.* guest 5
huevo *m.* egg 8
humanidades *f., pl.* humanities 2
huracán *m.* hurricane 18

I

ida *f.* one way (*travel*)
idea *f.* idea 18
iglesia *f.* church 4
igualdad *f.* equality 18
igualmente *adv.* likewise 1
impermeable *m.* raincoat 6
importante *adj. m., f.* important 3
importar *v.* to be important to; to matter 7
imposible *adj. m., f.* impossible 13
impresora *f.* printer 11
imprimir *v.* to print 11
improbable *adj. m., f.* improbable 13
impuesto *m.* tax 18
incendio *m.* fire 18
increíble *adj. m., f.* incredible 5
indicar cómo llegar *v.* to give directions 14
individual *adj.* single (*room*) 5
infección *f.* infection 10
informar *v.* to inform 18
informe *m.* report 18

ingeniero/a *m., f.* engineer 3
inglés *m.* English (*language*) 2
inglés, inglesa *adj.* English 3
inodoro *m.* toilet 7
insistir (en) *v.* to insist (on) 12
inspector(a) de aduanas *m., f.* customs inspector 5
inteligente *adj. m., f.* intelligent 3
intento *m.* attempt 11
intercambiar *v.* to exchange
interesante *adj. m., f.* interesting 3
interesar *v.* to be interesting to; to interest 7
internacional *adj. m., f.* international 18
Internet Internet 11
inundación *f.* flood 18
invertir (e:ie) *v.* to invest 16
invierno *m.* winter 5
invitado/a *m., f.* guest 9
invitar *v.* to invite 9
inyección *f.* injection 10
ir *v.* to go 4
  ir a (+ *inf.*) to be going to do something 4
  ir de compras to go shopping 5
  ir de excursión (a las montañas) to go on a hike (in the mountains) 4
  ir de pesca to go fishing
  ir de vacaciones to go on vacation 5
  ir en autobús to go by bus 5
  ir en auto(móvil) to go by car 5
  ir en avión to go by plane 5
  ir en barco to go by boat 5
  ir en metro to go by subway 5
  ir en moto(cicleta) to go by motorcycle 5
  ir en taxi to go by taxi 5
  ir en tren to go by train
irse *v.* to go away; to leave 7
italiano/a *adj.* Italian 3
izquierda *f.* left 2
  a la izquierda de to the left of 2

J

jabón *m.* soap 7
jamás *adv.* never; not ever 7
jamón *m.* ham 8
japonés, japonesa *adj.* Japanese 3
jardín *m.* garden; yard 12
jefe, jefa *m., f.* boss 16
jengibre *m.* ginger 10
joven *adj. m., f., sing.* (**jóvenes** *pl.*) young 3
joven *m., f., sing.* (**jóvenes** *pl.*) young person 1
joyería *f.* jewelry store 14
jubilarse *v.* to retire (*from work*) 9
juego *m.* game
jueves *m., sing.* Thursday 2
jugador(a) *m., f.* player 4

jugar (u:ue) *v.* to play 4
  jugar a las cartas *f., pl.* to play cards 5
jugo *m.* juice 8
  jugo de fruta *m.* fruit juice 8
julio *m.* July 5
jungla *f.* jungle 13
junio *m.* June 5
juntos/as *adj.* together 9
juventud *f.* youth 9

K

kilómetro *m.* kilometer 11

L

la *f., sing., def. art.* the 1; *f., sing., d.o. pron.* her, it, *form.* you 5
laboratorio *m.* laboratory 2
lago *m.* lake 13
lámpara *f.* lamp 12
lana *f.* wool 6
langosta *f.* lobster 8
lápiz *m.* pencil 1
largo/a *adj.* long 6
las *f., pl., def. art.* the 1; *f., pl., d.o. pron.* them; you 5
lástima *f.* shame 13
lastimarse *v.* to injure oneself 10
  lastimarse el pie to injure one's foot 10
lata *f.* (*tin*) can 13
lavabo *m.* sink 7
lavadora *f.* washing machine 12
lavandería *f.* laundromat 14
lavaplatos *m., sing.* dishwasher 12
lavar *v.* to wash 12
  lavar (el suelo, los platos) to wash (the floor, the dishes) 12
lavarse *v.* to wash oneself 7
  lavarse la cara to wash one's face 7
  lavarse las manos to wash one's hands 7
le *sing., i.o. pron.* to/for him, her, *form.* you 6
  Le presento a... *form.* I would like to introduce you to (name). 1
lección *f.* lesson 1
leche *f.* milk 8
lechuga *f.* lettuce 8
leer *v.* to read 3
  leer el correo electrónico to read e-mail 4
  leer un periódico to read a newspaper 4
  leer una revista to read a magazine 4
leído/a *p.p.* read 14
lejos de *prep.* far from 2
lengua *f.* language 2
  lenguas extranjeras *f., pl.* foreign languages 2

lentes de contacto *m., pl.* contact lenses
  lentes (de sol) (sun)glasses
lento/a *adj.* slow 11
les *pl., i.o. pron.* to/for them, you 6
letrero *m.* sign 14
levantar *v.* to lift 15
  levantar pesas to lift weights 15
levantarse *v.* to get up 7
ley *f.* law 13
libertad *f.* liberty; freedom 18
libre *adj. m., f.* free 4
librería *f.* bookstore 2
libro *m.* book 2
licencia de conducir *f.* driver's license 11
limón *m.* lemon 8
limpiar *v.* to clean 12
  limpiar la casa *v.* to clean the house 12
limpio/a *adj.* clean 5
línea *f.* line 4
listo/a *adj.* ready; smart 5
literatura *f.* literature 2
llamar *v.* to call 11
  llamar por teléfono to call on the phone
llamarse *v.* to be called; to be named 7
llanta *f.* tire 11
llave *f.* key 5; wrench 11
llegada *f.* arrival 5
llegar *v.* to arrive 2
llenar *v.* to fill 11, 14
  llenar el tanque to fill the tank 11
  llenar (un formulario) to fill out (a form) 14
lleno/a *adj.* full 11
llevar *v.* to carry 2; to wear; to take 6
  llevar una vida sana to lead a healthy lifestyle 15
  llevarse bien/mal (con) to get along well/badly (with) 9
llorar *v.* to cry 15
llover (o:ue) *v.* to rain 5
  Llueve. It's raining. 5
lluvia *f.* rain
lo *m., sing. d.o. pron.* him, it, *form.* you 5
  ¡Lo he pasado de película! I've had a fantastic time! 18
  lo mejor the best (thing)
  lo que that which; what 12
  Lo siento. I'm sorry. 1
loco/a *adj.* crazy 6
locutor(a) *m., f.* (TV or radio) announcer 18
lodo *m.* mud
los *m., pl., def. art.* the 1; *m. pl., d.o. pron.* them, you 5
luchar (contra/por) *v.* to fight; to struggle (against/for) 18

luego *adv.* then 7; later 1
lugar *m.* place 2, 4
luna *f.* moon 13
lunares *m.* polka dots
lunes *m., sing.* Monday 2
luz *f.* light; electricity 12

M

madrastra *f.* stepmother 3
madre *f.* mother 3
madurez *f.* maturity; middle age 9
maestro/a *m., f.* teacher 16
magnífico/a *adj.* magnificent 5
maíz *m.* corn 8
mal, malo/a *adj.* bad 3
maleta *f.* suitcase 1
mamá *f.* mom
mandar *v.* to order 12; to send; to mail 14
manejar *v.* to drive 11
manera *f.* way
mano *f.* hand 1
manta *f.* blanket 12
mantener *v.* to maintain 15
  mantenerse en forma to stay in shape 15
mantequilla *f.* butter 8
manzana *f.* apple 8
mañana *f.* morning, a.m. 1; tomorrow 1
mapa *m.* map 1, 2
maquillaje *m.* makeup 7
maquillarse *v.* to put on makeup 7
mar *m.* sea 5
maravilloso/a *adj.* marvelous 5
marcador *m.* marker 2
mareado/a *adj.* dizzy; nauseated 10
margarina *f.* margarine 8
mariscos *m., pl.* shellfish 8
marrón *adj. m., f.* brown 6
martes *m., sing.* Tuesday 2
marzo *m.* March 5
más *adv.* more 2
  más de (+ number) more than 8
  más tarde later (on) 7
  más... que more... than 8
masaje *m.* massage 15
matemáticas *f., pl.* mathematics 2
materia *f.* course 2
matrimonio *m.* marriage 9
máximo/a *adj.* maximum 11
mayo *m.* May 5
mayonesa *f.* mayonnaise 8
mayor *adj.* older 3
  el/la mayor *adj.* oldest 8
me *sing., d.o. pron.* me 5; *sing. i.o. pron.* to/for me 6
  Me gusta... I like... 2
  Me gustaría(n)... I would like... 15
  Me llamo... My name is... 1

Me muero por... I'm dying to (for)...
mecánico/a *m., f.* mechanic 11
mediano/a *adj.* medium
medianoche *f.* midnight 1
medias *f., pl.* pantyhose, stockings 6
medicamento *m.* medication 10
medicina *f.* medicine 10
médico/a *m., f.* doctor 3; *adj.* medical 10
medio/a *adj.* half 3
  medio ambiente *m.* environment 13
  medio/a hermano/a *m., f.* half-brother/half-sister 3
  mediodía *m.* noon 1
  medios de comunicación *m., pl.* means of communication; media 18
  y media thirty minutes past the hour (time) 1
mejor *adj.* better 8
  el/la mejor *m., f.* the best 8
mejorar *v.* to improve 13
melocotón *m.* peach 8
menor *adj.* younger 3
  el/la menor *m., f.* youngest 8
menos *adv.* less 10
  menos cuarto..., menos quince... quarter to... (time) 1
  menos de (+ *number*) fewer than 8
  menos... que less... than 8
mensaje *m.* **de texto** text message 11
mensaje electrónico *m.* e-mail message 4
mentira *f.* lie 4
menú *m.* menu 8
mercado *m.* market 6
  mercado al aire libre open-air market 6
merendar (e:ie) *v.* to snack 8; to have an afternoon snack
merienda *f.* afternoon snack 15
mes *m.* month 5
mesa *f.* table 2
mesita *f.* end table 12
  mesita de noche night stand 12
meterse en problemas *v.* to get into trouble 13
metro *m.* subway 5
mexicano/a *adj.* Mexican 3
mí *pron., obj. of prep.* me 9
mi(s) *poss. adj.* my 3
microonda *f.* microwave 12
  horno de microondas *m.* microwave oven 12
miedo *m.* fear
miel *f.* honey 10
mientras *conj.* while 10
miércoles *m., sing.* Wednesday 2
mil *m.* one thousand 2
  mil millones billion
milla *f.* mile
millón *m.* million 2

millones (de) *m.* millions (of)
mineral *m.* mineral 15
minuto *m.* minute
mío(s)/a(s) *poss.* my; (of) mine 11
mirar *v.* to look (at); to watch 2
  mirar (la) televisión to watch television 2
mismo/a *adj.* same 3
mochila *f.* backpack 2
moda *f.* fashion 6
moderno/a *adj.* modern 17
molestar *v.* to bother; to annoy 7
mono *m.* monkey 13
montaña *f.* mountain 4
montar *v.* **a caballo** to ride a horse 5
montón: un montón de a lot of 4
monumento *m.* monument 4
morado/a *adj.* purple 6
moreno/a *adj.* brunet(te) 3
morir (o:ue) *v.* to die 8
mostrar (o:ue) *v.* to show 4
moto(cicleta) *f.* motorcycle 5
motor *m.* motor
muchacho/a *m., f.* boy/girl 3
mucho/a *adj.*, a lot of; much; many 3
  (Muchas) gracias. Thank you (very much); Thanks (a lot). 1
  muchas veces *adv.* a lot; many times 10
  Mucho gusto. Pleased to meet you. 1
mudarse *v.* to move (from one house to another) 12
muebles *m., pl.* furniture 12
muerte *f.* death 9
muerto/a *p.p.* died 14
mujer *f.* woman 1
  mujer de negocios *f.* business woman 16
  mujer policía *f.* female police officer
multa *f.* fine
mundial *adj. m., f.* worldwide
mundo *m.* world 8
muro *m.* wall 15
músculo *m.* muscle 15
museo *m.* museum 4
música *f.* music 2, 17
musical *adj. m., f.* musical 17
músico/a *m., f.* musician 17
muy *adv.* very 1
  (Muy) bien, gracias. (Very) well, thanks. 1

N

nacer *v.* to be born 9
nacimiento *m.* birth 9
nacional *adj. m., f.* national 18
nacionalidad *f.* nationality 1
nada nothing 1; not anything 7
  nada mal not bad at all 5
nadar *v.* to swim 4
nadie *pron.* no one, nobody, not anyone 7

naranja *f.* orange 8
nariz *f.* nose 10
natación *f.* swimming 4
natural *adj. m., f.* natural 13
naturaleza *f.* nature 13
navegador *m.* **GPS** GPS 11
Navidad *f.* Christmas 9
necesario/a *adj.* necessary 12
necesitar (+ *inf.*) *v.* to need 2
negar (e:ie) *v.* to deny 13
  no negar (e:ie) *v.* not to deny 13
negocios *m., pl.* business; commerce 16
negro/a *adj.* black 6
nervioso/a *adj.* nervous 5
nevar (e:ie) *v.* to snow 5
  Nieva. It's snowing. 5
ni...ni neither... nor 7
niebla *f.* fog
nieto/a *m., f.* grandson/granddaughter 3
nieve *f.* snow
ningún, ninguno/a(s) *adj.* no; none; not any 7
niñez *f.* childhood 9
niño/a *m., f.* child 3
no no; not 1
  ¿no? right? 1
  no cabe duda de there is no doubt 13
  no es seguro it's not certain 13
  no es verdad it's not true 13
  No está nada mal. It's not bad at all. 5
  no estar de acuerdo to disagree
  No estoy seguro. I'm not sure.
  no hay there is not; there are not 1
  No hay de qué. You're welcome. 1
  no hay duda de there is no doubt 13
  ¡No me diga(s)! You don't say!
  No me gustan nada. I don't like them at all. 2
  no muy bien not very well 1
  No quiero. I don't want to. 4
  No sé. I don't know.
  No te preocupes. *fam.* Don't worry. 7
  no tener razón to be wrong 3
noche *f.* night 1
nombre *m.* name 1
norte *m.* north 14
norteamericano/a *adj.* (North) American 3
nos *pl., d.o. pron.* us 5; *pl., i.o. pron.* to/for us 6
  Nos vemos. See you. 1
nosotros/as *sub. pron.* we 1; *obj. pron.* us
noticia *f.* news 11
noticias *f., pl.* news 18
noticiero *m.* newscast 18

novecientos/as nine hundred 2
noveno/a *adj.* ninth 5
noventa ninety 2
noviembre *m.* November 5
novio/a *m., f.* boyfriend/ girlfriend 3
nube *f.* cloud 13
nublado/a *adj.* cloudy 5
Está (muy) nublado. It's very cloudy. 5
nuclear *adj. m., f.* nuclear 13
nuera *f.* daughter-in-law 3
nuestro(s)/a(s) *poss. adj.* our 3; our, (of) ours 11
nueve nine 1
nuevo/a *adj.* new 6
número *m.* number 1; (shoe) size 6
nunca *adv.* never; not ever 7
nutrición *f.* nutrition 15
nutricionista *m., f.* nutritionist 15

O

o or 7
o… o; either… or 7
obedecer *v.* to obey 18
obra *f.* work (*of art, literature, music, etc.*) 17
obra maestra *f.* masterpiece 17
obtener *v.* to obtain; to get 16
obvio/a *adj.* obvious 13
océano *m.* ocean
ochenta eighty 2
ocho eight 1
ochocientos/as eight hundred 2
octavo/a *adj.* eighth 5
octubre *m.* October 5
ocupación *f.* occupation 16
ocupado/a *adj.* busy 5
ocurrir *v.* to occur; to happen 18
odiar *v.* to hate 9
oeste *m.* west 14
oferta *f.* offer
oficina *f.* office 12
oficio *m.* trade 16
ofrecer *v.* to offer 6
oído *m.* (sense of) hearing; inner ear 10
oído/a *p.p.* heard 14
oír *v.* to hear 4
ojalá (que) *interj.* I hope (that); I wish (that) 13
ojo *m.* eye 10
olvidar *v.* to forget 10
once eleven 1
ópera *f.* opera 17
operación *f.* operation 10
ordenado/a *adj.* orderly 5
ordinal *adj.* ordinal (*number*)
oreja *f.* (outer) ear 10
organizarse *v.* to organize oneself 12
orquesta *f.* orchestra 17

ortografía *f.* spelling
ortográfico/a *adj.* spelling
os *fam., pl. d.o. pron.* you 5; *fam., pl. i.o. pron.* to/for you 6
otoño *m.* autumn 5
otro/a *adj.* other; another 6
otra vez again

P

paciente *m., f.* patient 10
padrastro *m.* stepfather 3
padre *m.* father 3
padres *m., pl.* parents 3
pagar *v.* to pay 6
pagar a plazos to pay in installments 14
pagar al contado to pay in cash 14
pagar en efectivo to pay in cash 14
pagar la cuenta to pay the bill
página *f.* page 11
página principal *f.* home page 11
país *m.* country 1
paisaje *m.* landscape 5
pájaro *m.* bird 13
palabra *f.* word 1
paleta helada *f.* popsicle 4
pálido/a *adj.* pale 14
pan *m.* bread 8
pan tostado *m.* toasted bread 8
panadería *f.* bakery 14
pantalla *f.* screen 11
pantalla táctil *f.* touch screen
pantalones *m., pl.* pants 6
pantalones cortos *m., pl.* shorts 6
pantuflas *f., pl.* slippers 7
papa *f.* potato 8
papas fritas *f., pl.* fried potatoes; French fries 8
papá *m.* dad
papás *m., pl.* parents
papel *m.* paper 2; role 17
papelera *f.* wastebasket 2
paquete *m.* package 14
par *m.* pair 6
par de zapatos pair of shoes 6
para *prep.* for; in order to; by; used for; considering 11
para que *conj.* so that 13
parabrisas *m., sing.* windshield 11
parar *v.* to stop 11
parecer *v.* to seem 6
pared *f.* wall 12
pareja *f.* (married) couple; partner 9
parientes *m., pl.* relatives 3
parque *m.* park 4
párrafo *m.* paragraph
parte: de parte de on behalf of 11
partido *m.* game; match (*sports*) 4
pasado/a *adj.* last; past 6
pasado *p.p.* passed

pasaje *m.* ticket 5
pasaje de ida y vuelta *m.* roundtrip ticket 5
pasajero/a *m., f.* passenger 1
pasaporte *m.* passport 5
pasar *v.* to go through
pasar la aspiradora to vacuum 12
pasar por la aduana to go through customs
pasar tiempo to spend time
pasarlo bien/mal to have a good/bad time 9
pasatiempo *m.* pastime; hobby 4
pasear *v.* to take a walk; to stroll 4
pasear en bicicleta to ride a bicycle 4
pasear por to walk around
pasillo *m.* hallway 12
pasta *f.* **de dientes** toothpaste 7
pastel *m.* cake; pie 9
pastel de chocolate *m.* chocolate cake 9
pastel de cumpleaños *m.* birthday cake
pastelería *f.* pastry shop 14
pastilla *f.* pill 10
patata *f.* potato 8
patatas fritas *f., pl.* fried potatoes; French fries 8
patinar *v.* to skate 4
patineta *f.* skateboard 4
patio *m.* patio; yard 12
pavo *m.* turkey 8
paz *f.* peace 18
pedir (e:i) *v.* to ask for; to request 4; to order (*food*) 8
pedir prestado *v.* to borrow 14
pedir un préstamo *v.* to apply for a loan 14
peinarse *v.* to comb one's hair 7
película *f.* movie 4
peligro *m.* danger 13
peligroso/a *adj.* dangerous 18
pelirrojo/a *adj.* red-haired 3
pelo *m.* hair 7
pelota *f.* ball 4
peluquería *f.* beauty salon 14
peluquero/a *m., f.* hairdresser 16
penicilina *f.* penicillin
pensar (e:ie) *v.* to think 4
pensar (+ inf.) *v.* to intend to; to plan to (*do something*) 4
pensar en *v.* to think about 4
peor *adj.* worse 8
el/la peor *adj.* the worst 8
pequeño/a *adj.* small 3
pera *f.* pear 8
perder (e:ie) *v.* to lose; to miss 4
perdido/a *adj.* lost 13, 14
Perdón. Pardon me.; Excuse me. 1
perezoso/a *adj.* lazy
perfecto/a *adj.* perfect 5
perfil *m.* profile 11
periódico *m.* newspaper 4
periodismo *m.* journalism 2

periodista *m., f.* journalist 3
permiso *m.* permission
pero *conj.* but 2
perro *m.* dog 13
persona *f.* person 3
personaje *m.* character 17
  personaje principal *m.*
    main character 17
pesas *f. pl.* weights 15
pesca *f.* fishing
pescadería *f.* fish market 14
pescado *m.* fish (*cooked*) 8
pescar *v.* to fish 5
peso *m.* weight 15
pez *m., sing.* (**peces** *pl.*) fish (*live*) 13
pie *m.* foot 10
piedra *f.* stone 13
pierna *f.* leg 10
pimienta *f.* black pepper 8
pintar *v.* to paint 17
pintor(a) *m., f.* painter 16
pintura *f.* painting; picture 12, 17
piña *f.* pineapple
piscina *f.* swimming pool 4
piso *m.* floor (*of a building*) 5
pizarra *f.* whiteboard 2
placer *m.* pleasure
planchar la ropa *v.* to iron the
  clothes 12
planes *m., pl.* plans
planta *f.* plant 13
  planta baja *f.* ground floor 5
plástico *m.* plastic 13
plato *m.* dish (*in a meal*) 8; *m.*
  plate 12
  plato principal *m.* main dish 8
playa *f.* beach 5
plaza *f.* city or town square 4
plazos *m., pl.* periods; time 14
pluma *f.* pen 2
plumero *m.* duster 12
población *f.* population 13
pobre *adj. m., f.* poor 6
pobrecito/a *adj.* poor thing 3
pobreza *f.* poverty
poco *adv.* little 5, 10
poder (o:ue) *v.* to be able to; can 4
  ¿Podría pedirte algo? Could I
    ask you something? 17
  ¿Puedo dejar un recado?
    May I leave a message? 11
poema *m.* poem 17
poesía *f.* poetry 17
poeta *m., f.* poet 17
policía *f.* police (force) 11
política *f.* politics 18
político/a *m., f.* politician 16; *adj.*
  political 18
pollo *m.* chicken 8
  pollo asado *m.* roast chicken 8
poner *v.* to put; to place 4; to turn
  on (*electrical appliances*) 11
  poner la mesa to set the
    table 12
  poner una inyección to give
    an injection 10
  ponerle el nombre to name
    someone/something 9

ponerse (+ *adj.*) *v.* to become
  (+ *adj.*) 7; to put on 7
por *prep.* in exchange for; for;
  by; in; through; around; along;
  during; because of; on account
  of; on behalf of; in search of;
  by way of; by means of 11
  por aquí around here 11
  por ejemplo for example 11
  por eso that's why;
    therefore 11
  por favor please 1
  por fin finally 11
  por la mañana in the
    morning 7
  por la noche at night 7
  por la tarde in the afternoon 7
  por lo menos *adv.* at least 10
  ¿por qué? why? 2
  Por supuesto. Of course.
  por teléfono by phone; on the
    phone
  por último finally 7
porque *conj.* because 2
portátil *adj.* portable 11
portero/a *m., f.* doorman/
  doorwoman 1
porvenir *m.* future 16
  por el porvenir for/to the
    future 16
posesivo/a *adj.* possessive
posible *adj.* possible 13
  es posible it's possible 13
  no es posible it's not
    possible 13
postal *f.* postcard
postre *m.* dessert 9
practicar *v.* to practice 2
  practicar deportes *m., pl.* to
    play sports 4
precio (fijo) *m.* (fixed; set)
  price 6
preferir (e:ie) *v.* to prefer 4
pregunta *f.* question
preguntar *v.* to ask (*a question*) 2
premio *m.* prize; award 17
prender *v.* to turn on 11
prensa *f.* press 18
preocupado/a (por) *adj.* worried
  (about) 5
preocuparse (por) *v.* to worry
  (about) 7
preparar *v.* to prepare 2
preposición *f.* preposition
presentación *f.* introduction
presentar *v.* to introduce; to
  present 17; to put on (*a
  performance*) 17
  Le presento a... I would like
    to introduce you to (name).
    form. 1
  Te presento a... I would like
    to introduce you to (name).
    fam. 1
presiones *f., pl.* pressures 15
prestado/a *adj.* borrowed
préstamo *m.* loan 14

prestar *v.* to lend; to loan 6
primavera *f.* spring 5
primer, primero/a *adj.* first 5
primero *adv.* first 2
primo/a *m., f.* cousin 3
principal *adj. m., f.* main 8
prisa *f.* haste
  darse prisa *v.* to hurry;
    to rush 15
probable *adj. m., f.* probable 13
  es probable it's probable 13
  no es probable it's not
    probable 13
probar (o:ue) *v.* to taste; to try 8
probarse (o:ue) *v.* to try on 7
problema *m.* problem 1
profesión *f.* profession 3; 16
profesor(a) *m., f.* teacher 1, 2
programa *m.* program 1
  programa de computación
    m. software 11
  programa de entrevistas *m.*
    talk show 17
  programa de realidad *m.*
    reality show 17
programador(a) *m., f.* computer
  programmer 3
prohibir *v.* to prohibit 10;
  to forbid
pronombre *m.* pronoun
pronto *adv.* soon 10
propina *f.* tip 8
propio/a *adj.* own
proteger *v.* to protect 13
proteína *f.* protein 15
próximo/a *adj.* next 3, 16
proyecto *m.* project 11
prueba *f.* test; quiz 2
psicología *f.* psychology 2
psicólogo/a *m., f.*
  psychologist 16
publicar *v.* to publish 17
público *m.* audience 17
pueblo *m.* town
puerta *f.* door 2
puertorriqueño/a *adj.* Puerto
  Rican 3
pues *conj.* well
puesto *m.* position; job 16
puesto/a *p.p.* put 14
puro/a *adj.* pure 13

Q

que *pron.* that; which; who 12
  ¿En qué...? In which...?
  ¡Qué...! How...!
  ¡Qué dolor! What pain!
  ¡Qué ropa más bonita!
    What pretty clothes! 6
  ¡Qué sorpresa! What a
    surprise!
  ¿qué? what? 1, 2
  ¿Qué día es hoy? What day is
    it? 2

¿Qué hay de nuevo? What's new? 1

¿Qué hora es? What time is it? 1

¿Qué les parece? What do you (*pl.*) think?

¿Qué onda? What's up? 14

¿Qué pasa? What's happening? What's going on? 1

¿Qué pasó? What happened?

¿Qué precio tiene? What is the price?

¿Qué tal...? How are you?; How is it going? 1

¿Qué talla lleva/usa? What size do you wear? 6

¿Qué tiempo hace? How's the weather? 5

quedar *v.* to be left over; to fit (*clothing*) 7; to be located 14

quedarse *v.* to stay; to remain 7

quehaceres domésticos *m., pl.* household chores 12

querer (e:ie) *v.* to want; to love 4

queso *m.* cheese 8

quien(es) *pron.* who; whom; that 12

¿quién(es)? who?; whom? 1, 2

¿Quién es...? Who is...? 1

¿Quién habla? Who is speaking/calling? (*telephone*) 11

química *f.* chemistry 2

quince fifteen 1

menos quince quarter to (time) 1

y quince quarter after (time) 1

quinceañera *f.* young woman celebrating her fifteenth birthday 9

quinientos/as five hundred 2

quinto/a *adj.* fifth 5

quisiera *v.* I would like

quitar el polvo *v.* to dust 12

quitar la mesa *v.* to clear the table 12

quitarse *v.* to take off 7

quizás *adv.* maybe 5

R

racismo *m.* racism 18

radio *f.* radio (*medium*) 2; *m.* radio (set) 11

radiografía *f.* X-ray 10

rápido *adv.* quickly 10

ratón *m.* mouse 11

ratos libres *m., pl.* spare (free) time 4

raya *f.* stripe

razón *f.* reason

rebaja *f.* sale 6

receta *f.* prescription 10

recetar *v.* to prescribe 10

recibir *v.* to receive 3

reciclaje *m.* recycling 13

reciclar *v.* to recycle 13

recién casado/a *m., f.* newly-wed 9

recoger *v.* to pick up 13

recomendar (e:ie) *v.* to recommend 8, 12

recordar (o:ue) *v.* to remember 4

recorrer *v.* to tour an area

recorrido *m.* tour 13

recuperar *v.* to recover 11

recurso *m.* resource 13

recurso natural *m.* natural resource 13

red *f.* network; Web 11

reducir *v.* to reduce 13

refresco *m.* soft drink 8

refrigerador *m.* refrigerator 12

regalar *v.* to give (a gift) 9

regalo *m.* gift 6

regatear *v.* to bargain 6

región *f.* region; area

regresar *v.* to return 2

regular *adv.* so-so; OK 1

reído *p.p.* laughed 14

reírse (e:i) *v.* to laugh 9

relaciones *f., pl.* relationships

relajarse *v.* to relax 9

reloj *m.* clock; watch 2

renovable *adj.* renewable 13

renunciar (a) *v.* to resign (from) 16

repetir (e:i) *v.* to repeat 4

reportaje *m.* report 18

reportero/a *m., f.* reporter 16

representante *m., f.* representative 18

resfriado *m.* cold (*illness*) 10

residencia estudiantil *f.* dormitory 2

resolver (o:ue) *v.* to resolve; to solve 13

respirar *v.* to breathe 13

responsable *adj.* responsible 8

respuesta *f.* answer

restaurante *m.* restaurant 4

resuelto/a *p.p.* resolved 14

reunión *f.* meeting 16

revisar *v.* to check 11

revisar el aceite *v.* to check the oil 11

revista *f.* magazine 4

rico/a *adj.* rich 6; *adj.* tasty; delicious 8

ridículo/a *adj.* ridiculous 13

río *m.* river 13

rodilla *f.* knee 10

rogar (o:ue) *v.* to beg 12

rojo/a *adj.* red 6

romántico/a *adj.* romantic 17

romper *v.* to break 10

romper (con) *v.* to break up (with) 9

romperse la pierna *v.* to break one's leg 10

ropa *f.* clothing; clothes 6

ropa interior *f.* underwear 6

rosado/a *adj.* pink 6

roto/a *adj.* broken 14

rubio/a *adj.* blond(e) 3

ruso/a *adj.* Russian 3

rutina *f.* routine 7

rutina diaria *f.* daily routine 7

S

sábado *m.* Saturday 2

saber *v.* to know; to know how 6

saber a to taste like 8

sabrosísimo/a *adj.* extremely delicious 8

sabroso/a *adj.* tasty; delicious 8

sacar *v.* to take out

sacar buenas notas to get good grades 2

sacar fotos to take photos 5

sacar la basura to take out the trash 12

sacar(se) un diente to have a tooth removed 10

sacudir *v.* to dust 12

sacudir los muebles to dust the furniture 12

sal *f.* salt 8

sala *f.* living room 12; room

sala de emergencia(s) emergency room 10

salario *m.* salary 16

salchicha *f.* sausage 8

salida *f.* departure; exit 5

salir *v.* to leave 4; to go out

salir con to go out with; to date 4, 9

salir de to leave from 4

salir para to leave for (*a place*) 4

salmón *m.* salmon 8

salón de belleza *m.* beauty salon 14

salud *f.* health 10

saludable *adj.* healthy 10

saludar(se) *v.* to greet (each other) 11

saludo *m.* greeting 1

saludos a... greetings to... 1

sandalia *f.* sandal 6

sandía *f.* watermelon

sándwich *m.* sandwich 8

sano/a *adj.* healthy 10

se *ref. pron.* himself, herself, itself, *form.* yourself, themselves, yourselves 7

se *impersonal* one 10

Se hizo... He/she/it became...

secadora *f.* clothes dryer 12

secarse *v.* to dry (oneself) 7

sección de (no) fumar *f.* (non) smoking section 8

secretario/a *m., f.* secretary 16

secuencia *f.* sequence

sed *f.* thirst

seda *f.* silk 6

sedentario/a *adj.* sedentary 15

seguir (e:i) *v.* to follow; to continue 4

según according to

segundo/a *adj.* second 5

seguro/a *adj.* sure; safe; confident 5

seis six 1

seiscientos/as six hundred 2

sello *m.* stamp 14

selva *f.* jungle 13

semáforo *m.* traffic light 14
semana *f.* week 2
    fin *m.* **de semana** weekend 4
    semana *f.* **pasada** last week 6
semestre *m.* semester 2
sendero *m.* trail; path 13
sentarse (e:ie) *v.* to sit down 7
sentir (e:ie) *v.* to be sorry; to regret 13
sentirse (e:ie) *v.* to feel 7
señor (Sr.); don *m.* Mr.; sir 1
señora (Sra.); doña *f.* Mrs.; ma'am 1
señorita (Srta.) *f.* Miss 1
separado/a *adj.* separated 9
separarse (de) *v.* to separate (from) 9
septiembre *m.* September 5
séptimo/a *adj.* seventh 5
ser *v.* to be 1
    ser aficionado/a (a) to be a fan (of)
    ser alérgico/a (a) to be allergic (to) 10
    ser gratis to be free of charge 14
serio/a *adj.* serious
servicio *m.* service 15
servilleta *f.* napkin 12
servir (e:i) *v.* to serve 8; to help 5
sesenta sixty 2
setecientos/as seven hundred 2
setenta seventy 2
sexismo *m.* sexism 18
sexto/a *adj.* sixth 5
sí *adv.* yes 1
si *conj.* if 4
SIDA *m.* AIDS 18
siempre *adv.* always 7
siete seven 1
silla *f.* seat 2
sillón *m.* armchair 12
similar *adj. m., f.* similar
simpático/a *adj.* nice; likeable 3
sin *prep.* without 13
    sin duda without a doubt
    sin embargo however
    sin que *conj.* without 13
sino but (rather) 7
síntoma *m.* symptom 10
sitio *m.* place 3
sitio *m.* **web** website 11
situado/a *p.p.* located
sobre *m.* envelope 14; *prep.* on; over 2
    sobre todo above all 13
(sobre)población *f.* (over)population 13
sobrino/a *m., f.* nephew/niece 3
sociología *f.* sociology 2
sofá *m.* couch; sofa 12
sol *m.* sun 13
solar *adj. m., f.* solar 13
soldado *m., f.* soldier 18
soleado/a *adj.* sunny
solicitar *v.* to apply (*for a job*) 16
solicitud (de trabajo) *f.* (job) application 16

sólo *adv.* only 6
solo/a *adj.* alone
soltero/a *adj.* single 9
solución *f.* solution 13
sombrero *m.* hat 6
Son las dos. It's two o'clock. 1
sonar (o:ue) *v.* to ring 11
sonreído *p.p.* smiled 14
sonreír (e:i) *v.* to smile 9
sopa *f.* soup 8
sorprender *v.* to surprise 9
sorpresa *f.* surprise 9
sótano *m.* basement 12
soy I am 1
    Soy de... I'm from... 1
su(s) *poss. adj.* his; her; its; *form.* your; their 3
subir(se) a *v.* to get on/into (*a vehicle*) 11
sucio/a *adj.* dirty 5
sudar *v.* to sweat 15
suegro/a *m., f.* father-in-law/ mother-in-law 3
sueldo *m.* salary 16
suelo *m.* floor 12
sueño *m.* sleep
suerte *f.* luck
suéter *m.* sweater 6
sufrir *v.* to suffer 10
    sufrir muchas presiones to be under a lot of pressure 15
    sufrir una enfermedad to suffer an illness 10
sugerir (e:ie) *v.* to suggest 12
supermercado *m.* supermarket 14
suponer *v.* to suppose 4
sur *m.* south 14
sustantivo *m.* noun
suyo(s)/a(s) *poss.* (of) his/her; (of) hers; its; *form.* your, (of) yours, (of) theirs, their 11

T

tabla de (wind)surf *f.* surf board/sailboard 5
tableta *f.* tablet (computer) 11
tal vez *adv.* maybe 5
talentoso/a *adj.* talented 17
talla *f.* size 6
    talla grande *f.* large
taller *m.* **mecánico** garage; mechanic's repair shop 11
también *adv.* also; too 2; 7
tampoco *adv.* neither; not either 7
tan *adv.* so 5
    tan... como as... as 8
    tan pronto como *conj.* as soon as 13
tanque *m.* tank 11
tanto *adv.* so much
    tanto... como as much... as 8
tantos/as... como as many... as 8
tarde *adv.* late 7; *f.* afternoon; evening; P.M. 1
tarea *f.* homework 2

tarjeta *f.* (post) card
tarjeta de crédito *f.* credit card 6
tarjeta de débito *f.* debit card 6
tarjeta postal *f.* postcard
taxi *m.* taxi 5
taza *f.* cup 12
te *sing., fam., d.o. pron.* you 5; *sing., fam., i.o. pron.* to/for you 6
    Te presento a... *fam.* I would like to introduce you to (name). 1
    ¿Te gustaría? Would you like to?
    ¿Te gusta(n)...? Do you like...? 2
té *m.* tea 8
    té helado *m.* iced tea 8
teatro *m.* theater 17
teclado *m.* keyboard 11
técnico/a *m., f.* technician 16
tejido *m.* weaving 17
teleadicto/a *m., f.* couch potato 15
(teléfono) celular *m.* (cell) phone 11
telenovela *f.* soap opera 17
teletrabajo *m.* telecommuting 16
televisión *f.* television 2
televisor *m.* television set 11
temer *v.* to fear; to be afraid 13
temperatura *f.* temperature 10
temporada *f.* period of time 5
temprano *adv.* early 7
tenedor *m.* fork 12
tener *v.* to have 3
    tener... años to be... years old 3
    tener (mucho) calor to be (very) hot 3
    tener (mucho) cuidado to be (very) careful 3
    tener dolor to have pain 10
    tener éxito to be successful 16
    tener fiebre to have a fever 10
    tener (mucho) frío to be (very) cold 3
    tener ganas de (+ *inf.*) to feel like (*doing something*) 3
    tener (mucha) hambre *f.* to be (very) hungry 3
    tener (mucho) miedo (de) to be (very) afraid (of); to be (very) scared (of) 3
    tener miedo (de) que to be afraid that
    tener planes *m., pl.* to have plans
    tener (mucha) prisa to be in a (big) hurry 3
    tener que (+ *inf.*) *v.* to have to (*do something*) 3
    tener razón *f.* to be right 3
    tener (mucha) sed *f.* to be (very) thirsty 3
    tener (mucho) sueño to be (very) sleepy 3
    tener (mucha) suerte to be (very) lucky 3
    tener tiempo to have time 14

tener una cita to have a date; to have an appointment 9
tenis *m.* tennis 4
tensión *f.* tension 15
tercer, tercero/a *adj.* third 5
terco/a *adj.* stubborn 10
terminar *v.* to end; to finish 2
  terminar de (+ inf.) *v.* to finish (*doing something*)
terremoto *m.* earthquake 18
terrible *adj. m., f.* terrible 13
textear *v.* to text 11
ti *obj. of prep., sing., fam.* you 9
tiempo *m.* time 14; weather 5
  tiempo libre free time
tienda *f.* store 6
tierra *f.* land; soil 13
tinto/a *adj.* red (wine) 8
tío/a *m., f.* uncle/aunt 3
tíos *m., pl.* aunts and uncles 3
título *m.* title 16
tiza *f.* chalk
toalla *f.* towel 7
tobillo *m.* ankle 10
tocar *v.* to play (*a musical instrument*) 17; to touch 17
todavía *adv.* yet; still 3, 5
todo *m.* everything 5
todo(s)/a(s) *adj.* all
todos *m., pl.* all of us; *m., pl.* everybody; everyone
todos los días *adv.* every day 10
tomar *v.* to take; to drink 2
  tomar clases *f., pl.* to take classes 2
  tomar el sol to sunbathe 4
  tomar en cuenta to take into account
  tomar fotos *f., pl.* to take photos 5
  tomar la temperatura to take someone's temperature 10
  tomar una decisión to make a decision 15
tomate *m.* tomato 8
tonto/a *adj.* foolish 3
torcerse (o:ue) (el tobillo) *v.* to sprain (one's ankle) 10
tormenta *f.* storm 18
tornado *m.* tornado 18
tortuga (marina) *f.* (sea) turtle 13
tos *f., sing.* cough 10
toser *v.* to cough 10
tostado/a *adj.* toasted 8
tostadora *f.* toaster 12
trabajador(a) *adj.* hard-working 3
trabajar *v.* to work 2
trabajo *m.* job; work 16
traducir *v.* to translate 6
traer *v.* to bring 4
tráfico *m.* traffic 11
tragedia *f.* tragedy 17
traído/a *p.p.* brought 14
traje *m.* suit 6
  traje de baño *m.* bathing suit 6
trajinera *f.* type of barge 3
tranquilo/a *adj.* calm; quiet 15

Tranquilo/a. Relax. 7
Tranquilo/a, cariño. Relax, sweetie. 11
transmitir *v.* to broadcast 18
tratar de (+ inf.) *v.* to try (*to do something*) 15
trece thirteen 1
treinta thirty 1, 2
  y treinta thirty minutes past the hour (time) 1
tren *m.* train 5
tres three 1
trescientos/as three hundred 2
trimestre *m.* trimester; quarter 2
triste *adj.* sad 5
tú *sing., fam. sub. pron.* you 1
tu(s) *fam. poss. adj.* your 3
turismo *m.* tourism
turista *m., f.* tourist 1
turístico/a *adj.* touristic
tuyo(s)/a(s) *fam. poss. pron.* your; (of) yours 11

<hr>

U

Ud. *form. sing.* you 1
Uds. *pl.* you 1
último/a *adj.* last 7
  la última vez the last time 7
un, uno/a *indef. art.* a; one 1
  a la una at one o'clock 1
  una vez once 6
  una vez más one more time
uno one 1
único/a *adj.* only 3; unique 9
universidad *f.* university; college 2
unos/as *m., f., pl. indef. art.* some 1
urgente *adj.* urgent 12
usar *v.* to wear; to use 6
usted (Ud.) *form. sing.* you 1
ustedes (Uds.) *pl.* you 1
útil *adj.* useful
uva *f.* grape 8

<hr>

V

vaca *f.* cow 13
vacaciones *f. pl.* vacation 5
valle *m.* valley 13
vamos let's go 4
vaquero *m.* cowboy 17
  de vaqueros *m., pl.* western (genre) 17
varios/as *adj. m. f., pl.* various; several
vaso *m.* glass 12
veces *f., pl.* times 6
vecino/a *m., f.* neighbor 12
veinte twenty 1
veinticinco twenty-five 1
veinticuatro twenty-four 1
veintidós twenty-two 1
veintinueve twenty-nine 1
veintiocho twenty-eight 1

veintiséis twenty-six 1
veintisiete twenty-seven 1
veintitrés twenty-three 1
veintiún, veintiuno/a *adj.* twenty-one 1
veintiuno twenty-one 1
vejez *f.* old age 9
velocidad *f.* speed 11
  velocidad máxima *f.* speed limit 11
vencer *v.* to expire 14
vendedor(a) *m., f.* salesperson 6
vender *v.* to sell 6
venir *v.* to come 3
ventana *f.* window 2
ver *v.* to see 4
  a ver *v.* let's see
  ver películas *f., pl.* to see movies 4
verano *m.* summer 5
verbo *m.* verb
verdad *f.* truth 4
  (no) es verdad it's (not) true 13
  ¿verdad? right? 1
verde *adj., m. f.* green 6
verduras *pl., f.* vegetables 8
vestido *m.* dress 6
vestirse (e:i) *v.* to get dressed 7
vez *f.* time 6
viajar *v.* to travel 2
viaje *m.* trip 5
viajero/a *m., f.* traveler 5
vida *f.* life 9
video *m.* video 1
videoconferencia *f.* videoconference 16
videojuego *m.* video game 4
vidrio *m.* glass 13
viejo/a *adj.* old 3
viento *m.* wind
viernes *m., sing.* Friday 2
vinagre *m.* vinegar 8
vino *m.* wine 8
  vino blanco *m.* white wine 8
  vino tinto *m.* red wine 8
violencia *f.* violence 18
visitar *v.* to visit 4
  visitar monumentos *m., pl.* to visit monuments 4
visto/a *p.p.* seen 14
vitamina *f.* vitamin 15
viudo/a *adj.* widower/widow 9
vivienda *f.* housing 12
vivir *v.* to live 3
vivo/a *adj.* clever; living
volante *m.* steering wheel 11
volcán *m.* volcano 13
vóleibol *m.* volleyball 4
volver (o:ue) *v.* to return 4
volver a ver(te, lo, la) *v.* to see (you, him, her) again
vos *pron.* you
vosotros/as *fam., pl.* you 1
votar *v.* to vote 18
vuelta *f.* return trip

vuelto/a *p.p.* returned 14
vuestro(s)/a(s) *poss. adj.* your 3;
  your, (of) yours *fam., pl.* 11

Y

y *conj.* and 1
  y cuarto quarter after (time) 1
  y media half-past (time) 1
  y quince quarter after (time) 1
  y treinta thirty (minutes past
    the hour) 1
  ¿Y tú? *fam.* And you? 1
  ¿Y usted? *form.* And you? 1
ya *adv.* already 6
yerno *m.* son-in-law 3
yo *sub. pron.* I 1
yogur *m.* yogurt 8

Z

zanahoria *f.* carrot 8
zapatería *f.* shoe store 14
zapatos de tenis *m., pl.* tennis
  shoes, sneakers 6

English-Spanish

A

a **un/a** *m., f., sing.; indef. art.* 1
@ (*symbol*) **arroba** *f.* 11
a.m. **de la mañana** *f.* 1
able: be able to **poder (o:ue)** *v.* 4
aboard **a bordo**
above all **sobre todo** 13
accident **accidente** *m.* 10
accompany **acompañar** *v.* 14
account **cuenta** *f.* 14
  on account of **por** *prep.* 11
accountant **contador(a)** *m., f.* 16
accounting **contabilidad** *f.* 2
ache **dolor** *m.* 10
acquainted: be acquainted with
  conocer *v.* 6
action (genre) **de acción** *f.* 17
active **activo/a** *adj.* 15
actor **actor** *m.,* **actriz** *f.* 16
addict (*drug*) **drogadicto/a**
  m., f. 15
additional **adicional** *adj.*
address **dirección** *f.* 14
adjective **adjetivo** *m.*
adolescence **adolescencia** *f.* 9
adventure (genre) **de aventuras**
  f. 17
advertise **anunciar** *v.* 18
advertisement **anuncio** *m.* 16
advice **consejo** *m.*
  give advice **dar consejos** 6
advise **aconsejar** *v.* 12
advisor **consejero/a** *m., f.* 16
aerobic **aeróbico/a** *adj.* 15
  aerobics class **clase de**
    ejercicios aeróbicos 15
  to do aerobics **hacer ejercicios**
    aeróbicos 15
affected **afectado/a** *adj.* 13
  be affected (by) **estar** *v.*
    afectado/a (por) 13
affirmative **afirmativo/a** *adj.*
afraid: be (very) afraid (of) **tener**
  (mucho) miedo (de) 3
  be afraid that **tener miedo**
    (de) que
after **después de** *prep.* 7;
  después de que *conj.* 13
afternoon **tarde** *f.* 1
afterward **después** *adv.* 7
again **otra vez**
age **edad** *f.* 9
agree **estar** *v.* **de acuerdo** 17
  I agree. **Estoy de acuerdo.** 17
  I don't agree. **No estoy de**
    acuerdo. 17
agreement **acuerdo** *m.*
AIDS **SIDA** *m.* 18
air **aire** *m.* 13
  air pollution **contaminación**
    del aire 13
airplane **avión** *m.* 5
airport **aeropuerto** *m.* 5
alarm clock **despertador** *m.* 7

alcohol **alcohol** *m.* 15
  to consume alcohol **consumir**
    alcohol 15
alcoholic **alcohólico/a** *adj.* 15
all **todo(s)/a(s)** *adj.*
  all of us **todos**
allergic **alérgico/a** *adj.* 10
  be allergic (to) **ser alérgico/a**
    (a) 10
alleviate **aliviar** *v.*
almost **casi** *adv.* 10
alone **solo/a** *adj.*
along **por** *prep.* 11
already **ya** *adv.* 6
also **también** *adv.* 2; 7
altar **altar** *m.* 9
aluminum **aluminio** *m.* 13
  (made) of aluminum **de**
    aluminio 13
always **siempre** *adv.* 7
American (*North*)
  norteamericano/a *adj.* 3
among **entre** *prep.* 2
amusement **diversión** *f.*
and **y** 1, **e** (*before words beginning*
  with i or hi)
  And you?**¿Y tú?** *fam.* 1;
    ¿Y usted? *form.* 1
angel **ángel** *m.* 9
angry **enojado/a** *adj.* 5
  get angry (with) **enojarse** *v.*
    (con) 7
animal **animal** *m.* 13
ankle **tobillo** *m.* 10
anniversary **aniversario** *m.* 9
  (wedding) anniversary
    aniversario *m.* **(de bodas)** 9
announce **anunciar** *v.* 18
announcer (*TV/radio*) **locutor(a)**
  m., f. 18
annoy **molestar** *v.* 7
another **otro/a** *adj.* 6
answer **contestar** *v.* 2;
  respuesta *f.*
antibiotic **antibiótico** *m.* 10
any **algún, alguno/a(s)** *adj.* 7
anyone **alguien** *pron.* 7
anything **algo** *pron.* 7
apartment **apartamento** *m.* 12
apartment building **edificio de**
  apartamentos 12
app **aplicación** *f.* 11
appear **parecer** *v.*
appetizers **entremeses** *m., pl.* 8
applaud **aplaudir** *v.* 17
apple **manzana** *f.* 8
appliance (electric)
  electrodoméstico *m.* 12
applicant **aspirante** *m., f.* 16
application **solicitud** *f.* 16
  job application **solicitud de**
    trabajo 16
apply (*for a job*) **solicitar** *v.* 16
  apply for a loan **pedir (e:i)** *v.*
    un préstamo 14
appointment **cita** *f.* 9
  have an appointment **tener** *v.*
    una cita 9
appreciate **apreciar** *v.* 17

April **abril** *m.* 5
archeologist **arqueólogo/a**
  m., f. 16
archeology **arqueología** *f.* 2
architect **arquitecto/a** *m., f.* 16
area **región** *f.*
Argentine **argentino/a** *adj.* 3
arm **brazo** *m.* 10
armchair **sillón** *m.* 12
army **ejército** *m.* 18
around **por** *prep.* 11
  around here **por aquí** 11
arrange **arreglar** *v.* 11
arrival **llegada** *f.* 5
arrive **llegar** *v.* 2
art **arte** *m.* 2
  (fine) arts **bellas artes** *f., pl.* 17
article **artículo** *m.* 18
artist **artista** *m., f.* 3
artistic **artístico/a** *adj.* 17
arts **artes** *f., pl.* 17
as **como** 8
  as a child **de niño/a** 10
  as... as **tan... como** 8
  as many... as **tantos/as...**
    como 8
  as much... as **tanto...**
    como 8
  as soon as **en cuanto** *conj.* 13;
    tan pronto como *conj.* 13
ask (*a question*) **preguntar** *v.* 2
  ask for **pedir (e:i)** *v.* 4
asparagus **espárragos** *m., pl.* 8
aspirin **aspirina** *f.* 10
at **a** *prep.* 1; **en** *prep.* 2
  at + *time* **a la(s)** + *time* 1
  at home **en casa**
  at least **por lo menos** 10
  at night **por la noche** 7
  At what time...? **¿A qué**
    hora...? 1
  At your service. **A sus**
    órdenes.
ATM **cajero automático** *m.* 14
attempt **intento** *m.* 11
attend **asistir (a)** *v.* 3
attic **altillo** *m.* 12
audience **público** *m.* 17
August **agosto** *m.* 5
aunt **tía** *f.* 3
  aunts and uncles **tíos** *m., pl.* 3
autumn **otoño** *m.* 5
avenue **avenida** *f.*
avoid **evitar** *v.* 13
award **premio** *m.* 17

B

backpack **mochila** *f.* 2
bad **mal, malo/a** *adj.* 3
  It's bad that... **Es malo**
    que... 12
  It's not bad at all. **No está**
    nada mal. 5
bag **bolsa** *f.* 6
bakery **panadería** *f.* 14

balanced **equilibrado/a** *adj.* 15
  to eat a balanced diet **comer una dieta equilibrada** 15
balcony **balcón** *m.* 12
ball **pelota** *f.* 4
banana **banana** *f.* 8
band **banda** *f.* 17
bank **banco** *m.* 14
bargain **ganga** *f.* 6; **regatear** *v.* 6
baseball (*game*) **béisbol** *m.* 4
basement **sótano** *m.* 12
basketball (*game*) **baloncesto** *m.* 4
bath: take a bath **bañarse** *v.* 7
bathing suit **traje** *m.* **de baño** 6
bathroom **baño** *m.* 7; **cuarto de baño** *m.* 7
battery **batería** *f.* 11
be **ser** *v.* 1; **estar** *v.* 2
  be… years old **tener… años** 3
  be sick of… **estar harto/a de…** 18
beach **playa** *f.* 5
beans **frijoles** *m., pl.* 8
beautiful **hermoso/a** *adj.* 6
beauty **belleza** *f.* 14
  beauty salon **peluquería** *f.* 14; **salón** *m.* **de belleza** 14
because **porque** *conj.* 2
  because of **por** *prep.* 11
become (+ *adj.*) **ponerse (+ adj.)** 7; **convertirse** *v.*
bed **cama** *f.* 5
  go to bed **acostarse (o:ue)** *v.* 7
bedroom **alcoba** *f.*, **recámara** *f.*; **dormitorio** *m.* 12
beef **carne de res** *f.* 8
beer **cerveza** *f.* 8
before **antes** *adv.* 7; **antes de** *prep.* 7; **antes (de) que** *conj.* 13
beg **rogar (o:ue)** *v.* 12
begin **comenzar (e:ie)** *v.* 4; **empezar (e:ie)** *v.* 4
behalf: on behalf of **de parte de** 11
behind **detrás de** *prep.* 2
believe (in) **creer** *v.* **(en)** 3; **creer** *v.* 13
  not to believe **no creer** 13
believed **creído/a** *p.p.* 14
bellhop **botones** *m., f. sing.* 5
below **debajo de** *prep.* 2
belt **cinturón** *m.* 6
benefit **beneficio** *m.* 16
beside **al lado de** *prep.* 2
besides **además (de)** *adv.* 10
best **mejor** *adj.*
  the best **el/la mejor** *m., f.* 8
  lo mejor *neuter*
better **mejor** *adj.* 8
  It's better that… **Es mejor que…** 12
between **entre** *prep.* 2
beverage **bebida** *f.* 8
  alcoholic beverage **bebida alcohólica** *f.* 15
bicycle **bicicleta** *f.* 4

big **grande** *adj.* 3
bill **cuenta** *f.* 8
billion **mil millones**
biology **biología** *f.* 2
bird **ave** *f.* 13; **pájaro** *m.* 13
birth **nacimiento** *m.* 9
birthday **cumpleaños** *m., sing.* 9
  have a birthday **cumplir** *v.* **años**
black **negro/a** *adj.* 6
blanket **manta** *f.* 12
block (city) **cuadra** *f.* 14
blog **blog** *m.* 11
blond(e) **rubio/a** *adj.* 3
blouse **blusa** *f.* 6
blue **azul** *adj. m., f.* 6
boat **barco** *m.* 5
body **cuerpo** *m.* 10
bone **hueso** *m.* 10
book **libro** *m.* 2
bookcase **estante** *m.* 12
bookshelves **estante** *m.* 12
bookstore **librería** *f.* 2
boot **bota** *f.* 6
bore **aburrir** *v.* 7
bored **aburrido/a** *adj.* 5
  be bored **estar** *v.* **aburrido/a** 5
  get bored **aburrirse** *v.* 17
boring **aburrido/a** *adj.* 5
born: be born **nacer** *v.* 9
borrow **pedir (e:i)** *v.* **prestado** 14
borrowed **prestado/a** *adj.*
boss **jefe** *m.*, **jefa** *f.* 16
bother **molestar** *v.* 7
bottle **botella** *f.* 9
  bottle of wine **botella de vino** 9
bottom **fondo** *m.*
boulevard **bulevar** *m.*
boy **chico** *m.* 1; **muchacho** *m.* 3
boyfriend **novio** *m.* 3
brakes **frenos** *m., pl.*
bread **pan** *m.* 8
break **romper** *v.* 10
  break (one's leg) **romperse (la pierna)** 10
  break down **dañar** *v.* 10
  break up (with) **romper** *v.* **(con)** 9
breakfast **desayuno** *m.* 8
  have breakfast **desayunar** *v.* 2
breathe **respirar** *v.* 13
bring **traer** *v.* 4
broadcast **transmitir** *v.* 18; **emitir** *v.* 18
brochure **folleto** *m.*
broken **roto/a** *adj.* 14
  be broken **estar roto/a**
brother **hermano** *m.* 3
brother-in-law **cuñado** *m.* 3
brothers and sisters **hermanos** *m., pl.* 3
brought **traído/a** *p.p.* 14
brown **café** *adj.* 6; **marrón** *adj.* 6
browser **buscador** *m.* 11
brunet(te) **moreno/a** *adj.* 3

brush **cepillar(se)** *v.* 7
  brush one's hair **cepillarse el pelo** 7
  brush one's teeth **cepillarse los dientes** 7
bucket **balde** *m.* 5
build **construir** *v.*
building **edificio** *m.* 12
bump into (*something accidentally*) **darse con** 10; (*someone*) **encontrarse** *v.* 11
bus **autobús** *m.* 1
  bus station **estación** *f.* **de autobuses** 5
business **negocios** *m. pl.* 16
  business administration **administración** *f.* **de empresas** 2
  business-related **comercial** *adj.* 16
businessperson **hombre** *m.* **/ mujer** *f.* **de negocios** 16
busy **ocupado/a** *adj.* 5
but **pero** *conj.* 2; (rather) **sino** *conj.* (*in negative sentences*) 7
butcher shop **carnicería** *f.* 14
butter **mantequilla** *f.* 8
buy **comprar** *v.* 2
  buy online **comprar en línea** 6
by **por** *prep.* 11; **para** *prep.* 11
  by means of **por** *prep.* 11
  by phone **por teléfono**
  by way of **por** *prep.* 11
bye **chau** *interj. fam.* 1

C

café **café** *m.* 4
cafeteria **cafetería** *f.* 2
caffeine **cafeína** *f.* 15
cake **pastel** *m.* 9
  chocolate cake **pastel de chocolate** *m.* 9
calculator **calculadora** *f.* 2
call **llamar** *v.* 11
  be called **llamarse** *v.* 7
  call on the phone **llamar por teléfono**
calm **tranquilo/a** *adj.* 15
calorie **caloría** *f.* 15
camera **cámara** *f.* 11
camp **acampar** *v.* 5
can (*tin*) **lata** *f.* 13
can **poder (o:ue)** *v.* 4
  Could I ask you something? **¿Podría pedirte algo?** 17
Canadian **canadiense** *adj.* 3
candidate **aspirante** *m., f.* 16; **candidato/a** *m., f.* 18
candy **dulces** *m., pl.* 9
capital city **capital** *f.*
car **coche** *m.* 11; **carro** *m.* 11; **auto(móvil)** *m.* 5
caramel **caramelo** *m.* 9
card **tarjeta** *f.*; (*playing*) **carta** *f.* 5

care **cuidado** *m.*
　take care of **cuidar** *v.* 13
career **carrera** *f.* 16
careful: be (very) careful **tener** *v.*
　(mucho) cuidado 3
carpenter **carpintero/a** *m., f.* 16
carpet **alfombra** *f.* 12
carrot **zanahoria** *f.* 8
carry **llevar** *v.* 2
cartoons **dibujos** *m., pl.*
　animados 17
case: in case (that) **en caso (de)**
　que 13
cash (a check) **cobrar** *v.* 14;
　cash **(en) efectivo** 6
　cash register **caja** *f.* 6
　pay in cash **pagar** *v.* **al contado**
　14; **pagar en efectivo** 14
cashier **cajero/a** *m., f.*
cat **gato** *m.* 13
celebrate **celebrar** *v.* 9
celebration **celebración** *f.*
(cell) phone **(teléfono)**
　celular *m.* 11
cemetery **cementerio** *m.* 9
cereal **cereales** *m., pl.* 8
certain **cierto/a** *adj.*; **seguro/a**
　adj. 13
　it's (not) certain **(no) es**
　cierto/seguro 13
chalk **tiza** *f.*
champagne **champán** *m.* 9
change **cambiar** *v.* **(de)** 9
change: in change **de cambio** 2
channel (*TV*) **canal** *m.* 11; 17
character (*fictional*) **personaje**
　m. 17
　(main) character *m.* **personaje**
　(principal) 17
charge **cargar** *v.* 11
charger **cargador** *m.* 11
chat **conversar** *v.* 2; **chatear** *v.* 11
cheap **barato/a** *adj.* 6
check **comprobar (o:ue)** *v.*;
　revisar *v.* 11; (*bank*) **cheque**
　m. 14
　check the oil **revisar el aceite** 11
checking account **cuenta** *f.*
　corriente 14
cheese **queso** *m.* 8
chef **cocinero/a** *m., f.* 16
chemistry **química** *f.* 2
chest of drawers **cómoda** *f.* 12
chicken **pollo** *m.* 8
child **niño/a** *m., f.* 3
childhood **niñez** *f.* 9
children **hijos** *m., pl.* 3
Chinese **chino/a** *adj.* 3
chocolate **chocolate** *m.* 9
　chocolate cake **pastel** *m.* **de**
　chocolate 9
cholesterol **colesterol** *m.* 15
choose **escoger** *v.* 8
chop (*food*) **chuleta** *f.* 8
Christmas **Navidad** *f.* 9
church **iglesia** *f.* 4
cinnamon **canela** *f.* 10
citizen **ciudadano/a** *m., f.* 18
city **ciudad** *f.*

class **clase** *f.* 2
　take classes **tomar clases** 2
classical **clásico/a** *adj.* 17
classmate **compañero/a** *m., f.* **de**
　clase 2
clean **limpio/a** *adj.* 5;
　limpiar *v.* 12
　clean the house *v.* **limpiar la**
　casa 12
clear (*weather*) **despejado/a** *adj.*
　clear the table **quitar la**
　mesa 12
　It's (very) clear. (*weather*)
　Está (muy) despejado.
clerk **dependiente/a** *m., f.* 6
climate change **cambio climático**
　m. 13
climb **escalar** *v.* 4
　climb mountains **escalar**
　montañas 4
clinic **clínica** *f.* 10
clock **reloj** *m.* 2
close **cerrar (e:ie)** *v.* 4
closed **cerrado/a** *adj.* 5
closet **armario** *m.* 12
clothes **ropa** *f.* 6
　clothes dryer **secadora** *f.* 12
clothing **ropa** *f.* 6
cloud **nube** *f.* 13
cloudy **nublado/a** *adj.* 5
　It's (very) cloudy. **Está (muy)**
　nublado. 5
coat **abrigo** *m.* 6
coffee **café** *m.* 8
　coffee maker **cafetera** *f.* 12
cold **frío** *m.* 5;
　(*illness*) **resfriado** *m.* 10
　be (*feel*) (very) cold **tener**
　(mucho) frío 3
　It's (very) cold. (*weather*) **Hace**
　(mucho) frío. 5
college **universidad** *f.* 2
collision **choque** *m.* 18
color **color** *m.* 6
comb one's hair **peinarse** *v.* 7
come **venir** *v.* 3
come on **ándale** *interj.* 14
comedy **comedia** *f.* 17
comfortable **cómodo/a** *adj.* 5
commerce **negocios** *m., pl.* 16
commercial **comercial** *adj.* 16
communicate (with) **comunicarse**
　v. **(con)** 18
communication **comunicación**
　f. 18
　means of communication
　medios *m. pl.* **de**
　comunicación 18
community **comunidad** *f.* 1
company **compañía** *f.* 16;
　empresa *f.* 16
comparison **comparación** *f.*
composer **compositor(a)** *m., f.* 17
computer **computadora** *f.* 1
　computer programmer
　programador(a) *m., f.* 3
　computer science **computación**
　f. 2
concert **concierto** *m.* 17

conductor (*musical*) **director(a)**
　m., f. 17
confident **seguro/a** *adj.* 5
confirm **confirmar** *v.* 5
　confirm a reservation **confirmar**
　una reservación 5
confused **confundido/a** *adj.* 5
congested **congestionado/a**
　adj. 10
Congratulations! **¡Felicidades!**;
　¡Felicitaciones! *f., pl.* 9
conservation **conservación** *f.* 13
conserve **conservar** *v.* 13
considering **para** *prep.* 11
consume **consumir** *v.* 15
container **envase** *m.* 13
contamination **contaminación** *f.*
content **contento/a** *adj.* 5
contest **concurso** *m.* 17
continue **seguir (e:i)** *v.* 4
control **control** *m.*; **controlar** *v.* 13
conversation **conversación** *f.* 1
converse **conversar** *v.* 2
cook **cocinar** *v.* 12; **cocinero/a**
　m., f. 16
cookie **galleta** *f.* 9
cool **fresco/a** *adj.* 5
　It's cool. (*weather*) **Hace**
　fresco. 5
corn **maíz** *m.* 8
corner **esquina** *f.* 14
cost **costar (o:ue)** *v.* 6
Costa Rican **costarricense** *adj.* 3
costume **disfraz** *m.* 9
cotton **algodón** *f.* 6
　(made of) cotton **de algodón** 6
couch **sofá** *m.* 12
couch potato **teleadicto/a**
　m., f. 15
cough **tos** *f.* 10; **toser** *v.* 10
counselor **consejero/a** *m., f.* 16
count **contar (o:ue)** *v.* 4
country (*nation*) **país** *m.* 1
countryside **campo** *m.* 5
(married) couple **pareja** *f.* 9
course **curso** *m.* 2; **materia** *f.* 2
courtesy **cortesía** *f.*
cousin **primo/a** *m., f.* 3
cover **cubrir** *v.*
covered **cubierto/a** *p.p.*
cow **vaca** *f.* 13
crafts **artesanía** *f.* 17
craftsmanship **artesanía** *f.* 17
crater **cráter** *m.* 13
crazy **loco/a** *adj.* 6
create **crear** *v.*
credit **crédito** *m.* 6
　credit card **tarjeta** *f.* **de**
　crédito 6
crime **crimen** *m.* 18
cross **cruzar** *v.* 14
cry **llorar** *v.* 15
Cuban **cubano/a** *adj.* 3
culture **cultura** *f.* 2, 17
cup **taza** *f.* 12
currency exchange **cambio** *m.* **de**
　moneda
current events **actualidades** *f.,*
　pl. 18

curtains **cortinas** *f., pl.* 12
custard (*baked*) **flan** *m.* 9
custom **costumbre** *f.*
customer **cliente/a** *m., f.* 6
customs **aduana** *f.*
   customs inspector **inspector(a)**
     m., f. **de aduanas** 5
cycling **ciclismo** *m.* 4

D

dad **papá** *m.*
daily **diario/a** *adj.* 7
   daily routine **rutina** *f.* **diaria** 7
damage **dañar** *v.* 10
dance **bailar** *v.* 2; **danza** *f.* 17;
   baile *m.* 17
dancer **bailarín/bailarina** *m.,*
   f. 17
danger **peligro** *m.* 13
dangerous **peligroso/a** *adj.* 18
date (*appointment*) **cita** *f.* 9;
   (*calendar*) **fecha** *f.* 5; (*someone*)
   salir *v.* **con (alguien)** 9
   have a date **tener una cita** 9
daughter **hija** *f.* 3
daughter-in-law **nuera** *f.* 3
day **día** *m.* 1
   day before yesterday
     anteayer *adv.* 6
death **muerte** *f.* 9
debit card **tarjeta** *f.* **de débito** 6
decaffeinated **descafeinado/a**
   adj. 15
December **diciembre** *m.* 5
decide **decidir** *v.* (+ *inf.*) 3
declare **declarar** *v.* 18
deforestation **deforestación** *f.* 13
delicious **delicioso/a** *adj.* 8;
   rico/a *adj.* 8; **sabroso/a** *adj.* 8
delighted **encantado/a** *adj.* 1
dentist **dentista** *m., f.* 10
deny **negar (e:ie)** *v.* 13
   not to deny **no negar** 13
department store **almacén** *m.* 6
departure **salida** *f.* 5
deposit **depositar** *v.* 14
describe **describir** *v.* 3
described **descrito/a** *p.p.* 14
desert **desierto** *m.* 13
design **diseño** *m.*
designer **diseñador(a)** *m., f.* 16
desire **desear** *v.* 2
desk **escritorio** *m.* 2
dessert **postre** *m.* 9
destroy **destruir** *v.* 13
develop **desarrollar** *v.* 13
diary **diario** *m.* 1
dictatorship **dictadura** *f.* 18
dictionary **diccionario** *m.* 1
die **morir (o:ue)** *v.* 8
died **muerto/a** *p.p.* 14
diet **dieta** *f.* 15; **alimentación**
   balanced diet **dieta**
     equilibrada 15
   be on a diet **estar a dieta** 15
difficult **difícil** *adj. m., f.* 3

digital camera **cámara** *f.*
   digital 11
dining room **comedor** *m.* 12
dinner **cena** *f.* 8
   have dinner **cenar** *v.* 2
direct **dirigir** *v.* 17
director **director(a)** *m., f.* 17
dirty **ensuciar** *v.*; **sucio/a** *adj.* 5
   get (something) dirty **ensuciar**
     v. 12
disagree **no estar de acuerdo**
disaster **desastre** *m.* 18
discover **descubrir** *v.* 13
discovered **descubierto/a** *p.p.* 14
discrimination **discriminación**
   f. 18
dish **plato** *m.* 8, 12
   main dish *m.* **plato principal** 8
dishwasher **lavaplatos** *m.,*
   sing. 12
disorderly **desordenado/a** *adj.* 5
divorce **divorcio** *m.* 9
divorced **divorciado/a** *adj.* 9
   get divorced (from) **divorciarse**
     v. **(de)** 9
dizzy **mareado/a** *adj.* 10
do **hacer** *v.* 4
   do aerobics **hacer ejercicios**
     aeróbicos 15
   do household chores **hacer**
     quehaceres domésticos 12
   do stretching exercises **hacer**
     ejercicios de estiramiento 15
   (I) don't want to. **No quiero.** 4
doctor **doctor(a)** *m., f.* 3; 10;
   médico/a *m., f.* 3
documentary (*film*) **documental**
   m. 17
dog **perro** *m.* 13
domestic **doméstico/a** *adj.*
   domestic appliance
     electrodoméstico *m.*
done **hecho/a** *p.p.* 14
door **puerta** *f.* 2
doorman/doorwoman **portero/a**
   m., f. 1
dormitory **residencia** *f.*
   estudiantil 2
double **doble** *adj.* 5
   double room **habitación** *f.*
     doble 5
doubt **duda** *f.* 13; **dudar** *v.* 13
   not to doubt **no dudar** 13
   there is no doubt that
     no cabe duda de 13;
     no hay duda de 13
download **descargar** *v.* 11
downtown **centro** *m.* 4
drama **drama** *m.* 17
dramatic **dramático/a** *adj.* 17
draw **dibujar** *v.* 2
drawing **dibujo** *m.*
dress **vestido** *m.* 6
   get dressed **vestirse (e:i)** *v.* 7
drink **beber** *v.* 3; **bebida** *f.* 8;
   tomar *v.* 2
drive **conducir** *v.* 6; **manejar**
   v. 11
driver **conductor(a)** *m., f.* 1

drug **droga** *f.* 15
   drug addict **drogadicto/a**
     m., f. 15
dry (oneself) **secarse** *v.* 7
during **durante** *prep.* 7; **por**
   prep. 11
dust **sacudir** *v.* 12;
   quitar *v.* **el polvo** 12
dust the furniture **sacudir los**
   muebles 12
duster **plumero** *m.* 12

E

each **cada** *adj.* 6
ear (outer) **oreja** *f.* 10
early **temprano** *adv.* 7
earn **ganar** *v.* 16
earring **arete** *m.* 6
earthquake **terremoto** *m.* 18
ease **aliviar** *v.*
east **este** *m.* 14
   to the east **al este** 14
easy **fácil** *adj. m., f.* 3
eat **comer** *v.* 3
ecological **ecológico/a** *adj.* 13
ecologist **ecologista** *m., f.* 13
ecology **ecología** *f.* 13
economics **economía** *f.* 2
ecotourism **ecoturismo** *m.* 13
Ecuadorian **ecuatoriano/a** *adj.* 3
effective **eficaz** *adj. m., f.*
egg **huevo** *m.* 8
eight **ocho** 1
eight hundred **ochocientos/as** 2
eighteen **dieciocho** 1
eighth **octavo/a** 5
eighty **ochenta** 2
either… or **o… o** *conj.* 7
elect **elegir (e:i)** *v.* 18
election **elecciones** *f. pl.* 18
electric appliance
   electrodoméstico *m.* 12
electrician **electricista** *m., f.* 16
electricity **luz** *f.* 12
elegant **elegante** *adj. m., f.* 6
elevator **ascensor** *m.* 5
eleven **once** 1
e-mail **correo** *m.* **electrónico** 4
   e-mail address **dirección** *f.*
     electrónica 11
   e-mail message **mensaje** *m.*
     electrónico 4
   read e-mail **leer** *v.* **el correo**
     electrónico 4
embarrassed **avergonzado/a**
   adj. 5
embrace (each other) **abrazar(se)**
   v. 11
emergency **emergencia** *f.* 10
   emergency room **sala** *f.* **de**
     emergencia(s) 10
employee **empleado/a** *m., f.* 5
employment **empleo** *m.* 16
end **fin** *m.* 4; **terminar** *v.* 2
   end table **mesita** *f.* 12
endure **aguantar** *v.* 14
energy **energía** *f.* 13
engaged: get engaged (to)
   comprometerse *v.* **(con)** 9

engineer **ingeniero/a** *m.*, *f.* 3
English (*language*) **inglés** *m.* 2;
  inglés, inglesa *adj.* 3
enjoy **disfrutar** *v.* **(de)** 15
enough **bastante** *adv.* 10
entertainment **diversión** *f.* 4
entrance **entrada** *f.* 12
envelope **sobre** *m.* 14
environment **medio ambiente**
  m. 13
environmental science **ciencias**
  ambientales 2
equality **igualdad** *f.* 18
erase **borrar** *v.* 11
eraser **borrador** *m.* 2
errand **diligencia** *f.* 14
essay **ensayo** *m.* 3
establish **establecer** *v.* 16
evening **tarde** *f.* 1
event **acontecimiento** *m.* 18
every day **todos los días** 10
everything **todo** *m.* 5
exactly **en punto** 1
exam **examen** *m.* 2
excellent **excelente** *adj.* 5
excess **exceso** *m.* 15
  in excess **en exceso** 15
exchange **intercambiar** *v.*
  in exchange for **por** 11
exciting **emocionante** *adj. m.*, *f.*
excursion **excursión** *f.*
excuse **disculpar** *v.*
Excuse me. (*May I?*) **Con**
  permiso. 1; (*I beg your*
  pardon.) **Perdón.** 1
exercise **ejercicio** *m.* 15;
  hacer *v.* **ejercicio** 15;
  (*a degree/profession*) **ejercer**
  v. 16
exit **salida** *f.* 5
expensive **caro/a** *adj.* 6
experience **experiencia** *f.*
expire **vencer** *v.* 14
explain **explicar** *v.* 2
explore **explorar** *v.*
expression **expresión** *f.*
extinction **extinción** *f.* 13
eye **ojo** *m.* 10

F

fabulous **fabuloso/a** *adj.* 5
face **cara** *f.* 7
facing **enfrente de** *prep.* 14
fact: in fact **de hecho**
factory **fábrica** *f.* 13
fall (down) **caerse** *v.* 10
  fall asleep **dormirse (o:ue)** *v.* 7
  fall in love (with) **enamorarse**
    v. **(de)** 9
fall (season) **otoño** *m.* 5
fallen **caído/a** *p.p.* 14
family **familia** *f.* 3
famous **famoso/a** *adj.*
fan **aficionado/a** *m.*, *f.* 4
  be a fan (of) **ser aficionado/a (a)**
far from **lejos de** *prep.* 2
farewell **despedida** *f.*

fascinate **fascinar** *v.* 7
fashion **moda** *f.* 6
  be in fashion **estar de moda** 6
fast **rápido/a** *adj.*
fat **gordo/a** *adj.* 3; **grasa** *f.* 15
father **padre** *m.* 3
father-in-law **suegro** *m.* 3
favorite **favorito/a** *adj.* 4
fear **miedo** *m.*; **temer** *v.* 13
February **febrero** *m.* 5
feel **sentir(se) (e:ie)** *v.* 7
  feel like (*doing something*) **tener**
    ganas de (+ *inf.*) 3
festival **festival** *m.* 17
fever **fiebre** *f.* 10
  have a fever **tener** *v.* **fiebre** 10
few **pocos/as** *adj. pl.*
  fewer than **menos de**
    (+ *number*) 8
fifteen **quince** 1
  fifteen-year-old girl celebrating her
    birthday **quinceañera** *f.* 9
fifth **quinto/a** 5
fifty **cincuenta** 2
fight (for/against) **luchar** *v.* **(por/**
  contra) 18
figure (*number*) **cifra** *f.*
file **archivo** *m.* 11
fill **llenar** *v.* 11
  fill out (a form) **llenar (un**
    formulario) 14
  fill the tank **llenar el**
    tanque 11
finally **finalmente** *adv.*; **por**
  último 7; **por fin** 11
find **encontrar (o:ue)** *v.* 4
  find (each other) **encontrar(se)**
  find out **enterarse** *v.* 16
fine **multa** *f.*
(fine) arts **bellas artes** *f., pl.* 17
finger **dedo** *m.* 10
finish **terminar** *v.* 2
  finish (*doing something*)
    terminar *v.* **de (+ *inf.*)**
fire **incendio** *m.* 18; **despedir**
  (e:i) *v.* 16
firefighter **bombero/a** *m.*, *f.* 16
firm **compañía** *f.* 16; **empresa**
  f. 16
first **primer, primero/a** 2, 5
fish (*food*) **pescado** *m.* 8;
  pescar *v.* 5; (*live*) **pez** *m., sing.*
  (**peces** *pl.*) 13
  fish market **pescadería** *f.* 14
fishing **pesca** *f.*
fit (*clothing*) **quedar** *v.* 7
five **cinco** 1
five hundred **quinientos/as** 2
fix (*put in working order*) **arreglar**
  v. 11; (*clothes, hair, etc. to*
  go out) **arreglarse** *v.* 7
fixed **fijo/a** *adj.* 6
flag **bandera** *f.*
flexible **flexible** *adj.* 15
flood **inundación** *f.* 18

floor (*of a building*) **piso** *m.* 5;
  suelo *m.* 12
  ground floor **planta baja** *f.* 5
  top floor **planta** *f.* **alta**
flower **flor** *f.* 13
flu **gripe** *f.* 10
fog **niebla** *f.*
folk **folclórico/a** *adj.* 17
follow **seguir (e:i)** *v.* 4
food **comida** *f.* 4, 8
foolish **tonto/a** *adj.* 3
foot **pie** *m.* 10
football **fútbol** *m.* **americano** 4
for **para** *prep.* 11; **por** *prep.* 11
  for example **por ejemplo** 11
  for me **para mí** 8
forbid **prohibir** *v.*
foreign **extranjero/a** *adj.* 17
  foreign languages **lenguas**
    f., pl. **extranjeras** 2
forest **bosque** *m.* 13
forget **olvidar** *v.* 10
fork **tenedor** *m.* 12
form **formulario** *m.* 14
forty **cuarenta** 2
four **cuatro** 1
four hundred **cuatrocientos/as** 2
fourteen **catorce** 1
fourth **cuarto/a** *m.*, *f.* 5
free **libre** *adj. m.*, *f.* 4
  be free (of charge) **ser**
    gratis 14
  free time **tiempo libre**; spare
    (free) time **ratos libres** 4
freedom **libertad** *f.* 18
freezer **congelador** *m.* 12
French **francés, francesa** *adj.* 3
  French fries **papas** *f., pl.*
    fritas 8; **patatas** *f., pl.* **fritas** 8
frequently **frecuentemente** *adv.*;
  con frecuencia *adv.* 10
Friday **viernes** *m., sing.* 2
fried **frito/a** *adj.* 8
  fried potatoes **papas** *f., pl.*
    fritas 8; **patatas** *f., pl.*
    fritas 8
friend **amigo/a** *m.*, *f.* 3
friendly **amable** *adj. m.*, *f.* 5
friendship **amistad** *f.* 9
from **de** *prep.* 1; **desde** *prep.* 6
  from the United States
    estadounidense *m.*, *f.*
    adj. 3
  from time to time **de vez en**
    cuando 10
  I'm from… **Soy de…** 1
front: (cold) front **frente (frío)**
  m. 5
fruit **fruta** *f.* 8
  fruit juice **jugo** *m.* **de fruta** 8
  fruit store **frutería** *f.* 14
full **lleno/a** *adj.* 11
fun **divertido/a** *adj.*
  fun activity **diversión** *f.* 4
  have fun **divertirse (e:ie)** *v.* 9

function **funcionar** *v.*
furniture **muebles** *m., pl.* 12
furthermore **además (de)** *adv.* 10
future **porvenir** *m.* 16
  for/to the future **por el porvenir** 16
  in the future **en el futuro**

G

gain weight **aumentar** *v.* **de peso** 15; **engordar** *v.* 15
game **juego** *m.*; (*match*) **partido** *m.* 4
  game show **concurso** *m.* 17
garage (*in a house*) **garaje** *m.* 12; **garaje** *m.* 11; **taller (mecánico)** 11
garden **jardín** *m.* 12
garlic **ajo** *m.* 8
gas station **gasolinera** *f.* 11
gasoline **gasolina** *f.* 11
gentleman **caballero** *m.* 8
geography **geografía** *f.* 2
German **alemán, alemana** *adj.* 3
get **conseguir (e:i)** *v.* 4; **obtener** *v.* 16
  get along well/badly (with) **llevarse bien/mal (con)** 9
  get bigger **aumentar** *v.* 13
  get bored **aburrirse** *v.* 17
  get connected to the Internet **conectarse** *v.* **a Internet** 11
  get good grades **sacar buenas notas** 2
  get into trouble **meterse en problemas** *v.* 13
  get off of (a vehicle) **bajar(se)** *v.* **de** 11
  get on/into (a vehicle) **subir(se)** *v.* **a** 11
  get out of (a vehicle) **bajar(se)** *v.* **de** 11
  get ready **arreglarse** *v.* 7
  get up **levantarse** *v.* 7
gift **regalo** *m.* 6
ginger **jengibre** *m.* 10
girl **chica** *f.* 1; **muchacha** *f.* 3
girlfriend **novia** *f.* 3
give **dar** *v.* 6; (*as a gift*) **regalar** 9
  give directions **indicar cómo llegar** 14
glass (*drinking*) **vaso** *m.* 12; **vidrio** *m.* 13
  (made) of glass **de vidrio** 13
glasses **gafas** *f., pl.* 6
  sunglasses **gafas** *f., pl.* **de sol** 6
global warming **calentamiento global** *m.* 13
gloves **guantes** *m., pl.* 6
go **ir** *v.* 4
  go away **irse** 7
  go by boat **ir en barco** 5

go by bus **ir en autobús** 5
go by car **ir en auto(móvil)** 5
go by motorcycle **ir en moto(cicleta)** 5
go by plane **ir en avión** 5
go by taxi **ir en taxi** 5
go down **bajar(se)** *v.*
go on a hike **ir de excursión** 4
go out (with) **salir** *v.* **(con)** 9
go up **subir** *v.*
  Let's go. **Vamos.** 4
going to: be going to (*do something*) **ir a (+ *inf.*)** 4
golf **golf** *m.* 4
good **buen, bueno/a** *adj.* 3, 6
  Good afternoon. **Buenas tardes.** 1
  Good evening. **Buenas noches.** 1
  Good morning. **Buenos días.** 1
  Good night. **Buenas noches.** 1
  It's good that… **Es bueno que…** 12
goodbye **adiós** *m.* 1
  say goodbye (to) **despedirse** *v.* **(de) (e:i)** 18
good-looking **guapo/a** *adj.* 3
government **gobierno** *m.* 13
GPS **navegador GPS** *m.* 11
graduate (from/in) **graduarse** *v.* **(de/en)** 9
grains **cereales** *m., pl.* 8
granddaughter **nieta** *f.* 3
grandfather **abuelo** *m.* 3
grandmother **abuela** *f.* 3
grandparents **abuelos** *m., pl.* 3
grandson **nieto** *m.* 3
grape **uva** *f.* 8
grass **hierba** *f.* 13
grave **grave** *adj.* 10
gray **gris** *adj. m., f.* 6
great **fenomenal** *adj. m., f.* 5; **genial** *adj.* 16
great-grandfather **bisabuelo** *m.* 3
great-grandmother **bisabuela** *f.* 3
green **verde** *adj. m., f.* 6
greet (each other) **saludar(se)** *v.* 11
greeting **saludo** *m.* 1
  Greetings to… **Saludos a…** 1
grilled **a la plancha** 8
ground floor **planta baja** *f.* 5
grow **aumentar** *v.* 13
guest (*at a house/hotel*) **huésped** *m., f.* 5 (*invited to a function*) **invitado/a** *m., f.* 9
guide **guía** *m., f.*
gymnasium **gimnasio** *m.* 4

H

hair **pelo** *m.* 7
hairdresser **peluquero/a** *m., f.* 16

half **medio/a** *adj.* 3
  half-brother **medio hermano** *m.* 3
  half-past… (*time*) **…y media** 1
  half-sister **media hermana** *f.* 3
hallway **pasillo** *m.* 12
ham **jamón** *m.* 8
hamburger **hamburguesa** *f.* 8
hand **mano** *f.* 1
hand in **entregar** *v.* 11
handsome **guapo/a** *adj.* 3
happen **ocurrir** *v.* 18
happiness **alegría** *v.* 9
happy **alegre** *adj.* 5; **contento/a** *adj.* 5; **feliz** *adj. m., f.* 5 be happy **alegrarse** *v.* **(de)** 13
  Happy birthday! **¡Feliz cumpleaños!** 9
hard **difícil** *adj. m., f.* 3
hard-working **trabajador(a)** *adj.* 3
hardly **apenas** *adv.* 10
hat **sombrero** *m.* 6
hate **odiar** *v.* 9
have **tener** *v.* 3
  have time **tener tiempo** 14
  have to (*do something*) **tener que (+ *inf.*)** 3
  have a tooth removed **sacar(se) un diente** 10
he **él** 1
head **cabeza** *f.* 10
headache **dolor** *m.* **de cabeza** 10
health **salud** *f.* 10
healthy **saludable** *adj. m., f.* 10; **sano/a** *adj.* 10
  lead a healthy lifestyle **llevar** *v.* **una vida sana** 15
hear **oír** *v.* 4
heard **oído/a** *p.p.* 14
hearing: sense of hearing **oído** *m.* 10
heart **corazón** *m.* 10
heat **calor** *m.*
Hello. (*on the telephone*) **Aló.** 11; **Bueno.** 11; **Diga.** 11
help **ayudar** *v.*; **servir (e:i)** *v.* 5
  help each other **ayudarse** *v.* 11
her **su(s)** *poss. adj.* 3; (of) hers **suyo(s)/a(s)** *poss. pron.* 11
  her **la** *f., sing., d.o. pron.* 5
  to/for her **le** *f., sing., i.o. pron.* 6
here **aquí** *adv.* 1
  Here is/are… **Aquí está(n)…** 5
Hi. **Hola.** 1
highway **autopista** *f.* 11; **carretera** *f.* 11
hike **excursión** *f.* 4
  go on a hike **ir de excursión** 4
hiker **excursionista** *m., f.*
hiking **de excursión** 4
him *m., sing., d.o. pron.* **lo** 5; to/for him **le** *m., sing., i.o. pron.* 6
hire **contratar** *v.* 16

his **su(s)** *poss. adj.* 3; (of) his **suyo(s)/a(s)** *poss. pron.* 11
history **historia** *f.* 2; 17
hobby **pasatiempo** *m.* 4
hockey **hockey** *m.* 4
hold up **aguantar** *v.* 14
hole **hueco** *m.* 4
holiday **día** *m.* **de fiesta** 9
home **casa** *f.* 2
   home page **página** *f.* **principal** 11
homemaker **amo/a** *m., f.* **de casa** 12
homework **tarea** *f.* 2
honey **miel** *f.* 10
hood **capó** *m.* 11; **cofre** *m.* 11
hope **esperar** *v.* (+ *inf.*) 2; **esperar** *v.* 13
   I hope (that) **ojalá (que)** 13
horror (genre) **de horror** *m.* 17
horse **caballo** *m.* 5
hospital **hospital** *m.* 10
hot: be (*feel*) (very) hot **tener (mucho) calor** 3
   It's (very) hot. **Hace (mucho) calor.** 5
hotel **hotel** *m.* 5
hour **hora** *f.* 1
house **casa** *f.* 2
household chores **quehaceres** *m. pl.* **domésticos** 12
housing **vivienda** *f.* 12
How…! **¡Qué…!**
   how **¿cómo?** *adv.* 1, 2
   How are you? **¿Qué tal?** 1
   How are you? **¿Cómo estás?** *fam.* 1
   How are you? **¿Cómo está usted?** *form.* 1
   How can I help you? **¿En qué puedo servirles?** 5
   How is it going? **¿Qué tal?** 1
   How is the weather? **¿Qué tiempo hace?** 5
   How much/many? **¿Cuánto(s)/a(s)?** 1
   How much does… cost? **¿Cuánto cuesta…?** 6
   How old are you? **¿Cuántos años tienes?** *fam.*
however **sin embargo**
hug (each other) **abrazar(se)** *v.* 11
humanities **humanidades** *f., pl.* 2
hundred **cien, ciento** 2
hunger **hambre** *f.*
hungry: be (very) hungry **tener** *v.* **(mucha) hambre** 3
hunt **cazar** *v.* 13
hurricane **huracán** *m.* 18
hurry **apurarse** *v.* 15; **darse prisa** *v.* 15
   be in a (big) hurry **tener** *v.* **(mucha) prisa** 3
hurt **doler (o:ue)** *v.* 10
husband **esposo** *m.* 3

I

I **yo** 1
   I hope (that) **Ojalá (que)** *interj.* 13
   I wish (that) **Ojalá (que)** *interj.* 13
ice cream **helado** *m.* 9
   ice cream shop **heladería** *f.* 14
iced **helado/a** *adj.* 8
   iced tea **té** *m.* **helado** 8
idea **idea** *f.* 18
if **si** *conj.* 4
illness **enfermedad** *f.* 10
important **importante** *adj.* 3
   be important to **importar** *v.* 7
   It's important that… **Es importante que…** 12
impossible **imposible** *adj.* 13
   it's impossible **es imposible** 13
improbable **improbable** *adj.* 13
   it's improbable **es improbable** 13
improve **mejorar** *v.* 13
in **en** *prep.* 2; **por** *prep.* 11
   in the afternoon **de la tarde** 1; **por la tarde** 7
   in a bad mood **de mal humor** 5
   in the direction of **para** *prep.* 11
   in the early evening **de la tarde** 1
   in the evening **de la noche** 1; **por la tarde** 7
   in a good mood **de buen humor** 5
   in the morning **de la mañana** 1; **por la mañana** 7
   in love (with) **enamorado/a (de)** 5
   in search of **por** *prep.* 11
in front of **delante de** *prep.* 2
increase **aumento** *m.*
incredible **increíble** *adj.* 5
inequality **desigualdad** *f.* 18
infection **infección** *f.* 10
inform **informar** *v.* 18
injection **inyección** *f.* 10
   give an injection *v.* **poner una inyección** 10
injure (oneself) **lastimarse** 10
   injure (one's foot) **lastimarse** *v.* **(el pie)** 10
inner ear **oído** *m.* 10
inside **dentro** *adv.*
insist (on) **insistir** *v.* **(en)** 12
installments: pay in installments **pagar** *v.* **a plazos** 14
intelligent **inteligente** *adj.* 3
intend to **pensar** *v.* **(+ *inf.*)** 4
interest **interesar** *v.* 7
interesting **interesante** *adj.* 3
   be interesting to **interesar** *v.* 7
international **internacional** *adj. m., f.* 18

Internet **Internet** 11
   get connected to the Internet **conectarse** *v.* **a Internet** 11
interview **entrevista** *f.* 16; **entrevistar** *v.* 16
interviewer **entrevistador(a)** *m., f.* 16
introduction **presentación** *f.*
   I would like to introduce you to (name). **Le presento a…** *form.* 1; **Te presento a…** *fam.* 1
invest **invertir (e:ie)** *v.* 16
invite **invitar** *v.* 9
iron (clothes) **planchar** *v.* **la ropa** 12
it **lo/la** *sing., d.o., pron.* 5
Italian **italiano/a** *adj.* 3
its **su(s)** *poss. adj.* 3; **suyo(s)/a(s)** *poss. pron.* 11
it's the same **es igual** 5

J

jacket **chaqueta** *f.* 6
January **enero** *m.* 5
Japanese **japonés, japonesa** *adj.* 3
jeans **(blue)jeans** *m., pl.* 6
jewelry store **joyería** *f.* 14
job **empleo** *m.* 16; **puesto** *m.* 16; **trabajo** *m.* 16
   job application **solicitud** *f.* **de trabajo** 16
jog **correr** *v.*
journalism **periodismo** *m.* 2
journalist **periodista** *m., f.* 3
joy **alegría** *f.* 9
juice **jugo** *m.* 8
July **julio** *m.* 5
June **junio** *m.* 5
jungle **selva, jungla** *f.* 13
just **apenas** *adv.*
   have just done something **acabar de (+ *inf.*)** 6

K

key **llave** *f.* 5
keyboard **teclado** *m.* 11
kilometer **kilómetro** *m.* 11
kiss **beso** *m.* 9
   kiss each other **besarse** *v.* 11
kitchen **cocina** *f.* 9, 12
knee **rodilla** *f.* 10
knife **cuchillo** *m.* 12
know **saber** *v.* 6; **conocer** *v.* 6
know how **saber** *v.* 6

L

laboratory **laboratorio** *m.* 2
lack **faltar** *v.* 7
lake **lago** *m.* 13

lamp **lámpara** *f.* 12
land **tierra** *f.* 13
landscape **paisaje** *m.* 5
language **lengua** *f.* 2
laptop (computer) **computadora**
    f. **portátil** 11
large **grande** *adj.* 3
large (*clothing size*) **talla**
    grande
last **durar** *v.* 18; **pasado/a**
    adj. 6; **último/a** *adj.* 7
  last name **apellido** *m.* 3
  last night **anoche** *adv.* 6
  last week **semana** *f.* **pasada** 6
  last year **año** *m.* **pasado** 6
  the last time **la última vez** 7
late **tarde** *adv.* 7
later (on) **más tarde** 7
  See you later. **Hasta la vista.** 1;
    Hasta luego. 1
laugh **reírse (e:i)** *v.* 9
laughed **reído** *p.p.* 14
laundromat **lavandería** *f.* 14
law **ley** *f.* 13
lawyer **abogado/a** *m., f.* 16
lazy **perezoso/a** *adj.*
learn **aprender** *v.* (a + *inf.*) 3
least, at **por lo menos** *adv.* 10
leave **salir** *v.* 4; **irse** *v.* 7
  leave a tip **dejar una**
    propina
  leave behind **dejar** *v.* 16
  leave for (*a place*) **salir para**
  leave from **salir de**
left **izquierda** *f.* 2
  be left over **quedar** *v.* 7
  to the left of **a la izquierda de** 2
leg **pierna** *f.* 10
lemon **limón** *m.* 8
lend **prestar** *v.* 6
less **menos** *adv.* 10
  less… than **menos… que** 8
  less than **menos de** (+ *number*)
lesson **lección** *f.* 1
let **dejar** *v.*
let's see **a ver**
letter **carta** *f.* 4, 14
lettuce **lechuga** *f.* 8
liberty **libertad** *f.* 18
library **biblioteca** *f.* 2
license (*driver's*) **licencia** *f.* **de**
  conducir 11
lie **mentira** *f.* 4
life **vida** *f.* 9
lifestyle: lead a healthy lifestyle
  llevar una vida sana 15
lift **levantar** *v.* 15
  lift weights **levantar pesas** 15
light **luz** *f.* 12
like **como** *prep.* 8; **gustar** *v.* 2
  I like… **Me gusta(n)…** 2
  like this **así** *adv.* 10
  like very much **encantar** *v.*;
    fascinar *v.* 7
  Do you like…? **¿Te**
    gusta(n)…? 2
likeable **simpático/a** *adj.* 3
likewise **igualmente** *adv.* 1

line **línea** *f.* 4; **cola** (*queue*) *f.* 14
listen (to) **escuchar** *v.* 2
  listen to music **escuchar**
    música 2
  listen to the radio **escuchar la**
    radio 2
literature **literatura** *f.* 2
little (*quantity*) **poco** *adv.* 10
live **vivir** *v.* 3; **en vivo** *adj.* 7
living room **sala** *f.* 12
loan **préstamo** *m.* 14; **prestar**
  v. 6, 14
lobster **langosta** *f.* 8
located **situado/a** *adj.*
  be located **quedar** *v.* 14
long **largo/a** *adj.* 6
look (at) **mirar** *v.* 2
look for **buscar** *v.* 2
lose **perder (e:ie)** *v.* 4
  lose weight **adelgazar** *v.* 15
lost **perdido/a** *adj.* 13, 14
  be lost **estar perdido/a** 14
lot, a **muchas veces** *adv.* 10
lot of, a **mucho/a** *adj.* 3; **un**
  montón de 4
love (*another person*) **querer**
  (e:ie) *v.* 4; (*inanimate objects*)
  encantar *v.* 7; **amor** *m.* 9
  in love **enamorado/a** *adj.* 5
  love at first sight **amor a**
    primera vista 9
luck **suerte** *f.*
lucky: be (very) lucky **tener**
  (mucha) suerte 3
luggage **equipaje** *m.* 5
lunch **almuerzo** *m.* 4, 8
  have lunch **almorzar (o:ue)**
    v. 4

M

ma'am **señora (Sra.); doña** *f.* 1
mad **enojado/a** *adj.* 5
magazine **revista** *f.* 4
magnificent **magnífico/a** *adj.* 5
mail **correo** *m.* 14; **enviar** *v.*,
  mandar *v.* 14; **echar (una**
  carta) al buzón 14
  mail carrier **cartero** *m.* 14
mailbox **buzón** *m.* 14
main **principal** *adj. m., f.* 8
maintain **mantener** *v.* 15
major **especialización** *f.* 2
make **hacer** *v.* 4
  make a decision **tomar una**
    decisión 15
  make the bed **hacer la**
    cama 12
makeup **maquillaje** *m.* 7
  put on makeup **maquillarse** *v.* 7
man **hombre** *m.* 1
manager **gerente** *m., f.* 8, 16
many **mucho/a** *adj.* 3
  many times **muchas veces** 10
map **mapa** *m.* 1, 2
March **marzo** *m.* 5
margarine **margarina** *f.* 8

marinated fish **ceviche** *m.* 8
  lemon-marinated shrimp
    ceviche *m.* **de camarón** 8
marital status **estado** *m.* **civil** 9
marker **marcador** *m.* 2
market **mercado** *m.* 6
  open-air market **mercado al**
    aire libre 6
marriage **matrimonio** *m.* 9
married **casado/a** *adj.* 9
  get married (to) **casarse** *v.*
    (con) 9
  I'll marry you! **¡Acepto**
    casarme contigo! 17
marvelous **maravilloso/a** *adj.* 5
massage **masaje** *m.* 15
masterpiece **obra maestra** *f.* 17
match (*sports*) **partido** *m.* 4
match (with) **hacer** *v.*
  juego (con) 6
mathematics **matemáticas**
  f., pl. 2
matter **importar** *v.* 7
maturity **madurez** *f.* 9
maximum **máximo/a** *adj.* 11
May **mayo** *m.* 5
May I leave a message? **¿Puedo**
  dejar un recado? 11
maybe **tal vez** 5; **quizás** 5
mayonnaise **mayonesa** *f.* 8
me **me** *sing., d.o. pron.* 5
  to/for me **me** *sing., i.o. pron.* 6
meal **comida** *f.* 8
means of communication **medios**
  m., pl. **de comunicación** 18
meat **carne** *f.* 8
mechanic **mecánico/a** *m., f.* 11
  mechanic's repair shop **taller**
    mecánico 11
media **medios** *m., pl.* **de**
  comunicación 18
medical **médico/a** *adj.* 10
medication **medicamento** *m.* 10
medicine **medicina** *f.* 10
medium **mediano/a** *adj.*
meet (each other) **encontrar(se)**
  v. 11; **conocer(se)** *v.* 8
  meet up with **encontrarse con** 7
meeting **reunión** *f.* 16
menu **menú** *m.* 8
message **mensaje** *m.*
Mexican **mexicano/a** *adj.* 3
microwave **microonda** *f.* 12
  microwave oven **horno** *m.* **de**
    microondas 12
middle age **madurez** *f.* 9
midnight **medianoche** *f.* 1
mile **milla** *f.*
milk **leche** *f.* 8
million **millón** *m.* 2
  million of **millón de** 2
mine **mío(s)/a(s)** *poss.* 11
mineral **mineral** *m.* 15
  mineral water **agua** *f.*
    mineral 8

minute **minuto** *m.*
mirror **espejo** *m.* 7
Miss **señorita (Srta.)** *f.* 1
miss **perder (e:ie)** *v.* 4; **extrañar** *v.* 16
mistaken **equivocado/a** *adj.*
modern **moderno/a** *adj.* 17
mom **mamá** *f.*
Monday **lunes** *m., sing.* 2
money **dinero** *m.* 6
monkey **mono** *m.* 13
month **mes** *m.* 5
monument **monumento** *m.* 4
moon **luna** *f.* 13
more **más** 2
  more… than **más… que** 8
  more than **más de (+ number)** 8
morning **mañana** *f.* 1
mother **madre** *f.* 3
mother-in-law **suegra** *f.* 3
motor **motor** *m.*
motorcycle **moto(cicleta)** *f.* 5
mountain **montaña** *f.* 4
mouse **ratón** *m.* 11
mouth **boca** *f.* 10
move (*from one house to another*) **mudarse** *v.* 12
movie **película** *f.* 4
  movie star **estrella** *f.* **de cine** 17
  movie theater **cine** *m.* 4
Mr. **señor (Sr.); don** *m.* 1
Mrs. **señora (Sra.); doña** *f.* 1
much **mucho/a** *adj.* 3
mud **lodo** *m.*
murder **crimen** *m.* 18
muscle **músculo** *m.* 15
museum **museo** *m.* 4
mushroom **champiñón** *m.* 8
music **música** *f.* 2, 17
musical **musical** *adj., m., f.* 17
musician **músico/a** *m., f.* 17
must **deber** *v.* (+ *inf.*) 3
my **mi(s)** *poss. adj.* 3; **mío(s)/a(s)** *poss. pron.* 11

N

name **nombre** *m.* 1
  be named **llamarse** *v.* 7
  in the name of **a nombre de** 5
  last name **apellido** *m.* 3
  My name is… **Me llamo…** 1
  name someone/something **ponerle el nombre** 9
napkin **servilleta** *f.* 12
national **nacional** *adj. m., f.* 18
nationality **nacionalidad** *f.* 1
natural **natural** *adj. m., f.* 13
  natural disaster **desastre** *m.* **natural** 18
  natural resource **recurso** *m.* **natural** 13

nature **naturaleza** *f.* 13
nauseated **mareado/a** *adj.* 10
near **cerca de** *prep.* 2
necessary **necesario/a** *adj.* 12
  It is necessary that… **Es necesario que…** 12
neck **cuello** *m.* 10
need **faltar** *v.* 7; **necesitar** *v.* (+ *inf.*) 2
neighbor **vecino/a** *m., f.* 12
neighborhood **barrio** *m.* 12
neither **tampoco** *adv.* 7
neither… nor **ni… ni** *conj.* 7
nephew **sobrino** *m.* 3
nervous **nervioso/a** *adj.* 5
network **red** *f.* 11
never **nunca** *adj.* 7; **jamás** 7
new **nuevo/a** *adj.* 6
newlywed **recién casado/a** *m., f.* 9
news **noticias** *f., pl.* 18; **actualidades** *f., pl.* 18; **noticia** *f.* 11
newscast **noticiero** *m.* 18
newspaper **periódico** 4; **diario** *m.* 18
next **próximo/a** *adj.* 3, 16
  next to **al lado de** *prep.* 2
nice **simpático/a** *adj.* 3; **amable** *adj.* 5
niece **sobrina** *f.* 3
night **noche** *f.* 1
  night stand **mesita** *f.* **de noche** 12
nine **nueve** 1
nine hundred **novecientos/as** 2
nineteen **diecinueve** 1
ninety **noventa** 2
ninth **noveno/a** 5
no **no** 1; **ningún, ninguno/a(s)** *adj.* 7
  no one **nadie** *pron.* 7
nobody **nadie** 7
none **ningún, ninguno/a(s)** *adj.* 7
noon **mediodía** *m.* 1
nor **ni** *conj.* 7
north **norte** *m.* 14
  to the north **al norte** 14
nose **nariz** *f.* 10
not **no** 1
  not any **ningún, ninguno/a(s)** *adj.* 7
  not anyone **nadie** *pron.* 7
  not anything **nada** *pron.* 7
  not bad at all **nada mal** 5
  not either **tampoco** *adv.* 7
  not ever **nunca** *adv.* 7; **jamás** *adv.* 7
  not very well **no muy bien** 1
  not working **descompuesto/a** *adj.* 11
notebook **cuaderno** *m.* 1
nothing **nada** 1; 7
noun **sustantivo** *m.*
November **noviembre** *m.* 5

now **ahora** *adv.* 2
nowadays **hoy día** *adv.*
nuclear **nuclear** *adj. m., f.* 13
  nuclear energy **energía nuclear** 13
number **número** *m.* 1
nurse **enfermero/a** *m., f.* 10
nutrition **nutrición** *f.* 15
nutritionist **nutricionista** *m., f.* 15

O

o'clock: It's… o'clock. **Son las…** 1
  It's one o'clock. **Es la una.** 1
obey **obedecer** *v.* 18
obligation **deber** *m.* 18
obtain **conseguir (e:i)** *v.* 4; **obtener** *v.* 16
obvious **obvio/a** *adj.* 13
  it's obvious **es obvio** 13
occupation **ocupación** *f.* 16
occur **ocurrir** *v.* 18
October **octubre** *m.* 5
of **de** *prep.* 1
  Of course. **Claro que sí.; Por supuesto.**
offer **oferta** *f.*; **ofrecer (c:zc)** *v.* 6
office **oficina** *f.* 12
  doctor's office **consultorio** *m.* 10
often **a menudo** *adv.* 10
Oh! **¡Ay!**
oil **aceite** *m.* 8
OK **regular** *adj.* 1
old **viejo/a** *adj.* 3
old age **vejez** *f.* 9
older **mayor** *adj. m., f.* 3
  older brother, sister **hermano/a mayor** *m., f.* 3
oldest **el/la mayor** 8
on **en** *prep.* 2; **sobre** *prep.* 2
  on behalf of **por** *prep.* 11
  on the dot **en punto** 1
  on time **a tiempo** 10
  on top of **encima de** 2
once **una vez** 6
one **uno** 1
  one hundred **cien(to)** 2
  one million **un millón** *m.* 2
  one more time **una vez más**
  one thousand **mil** 2
onion **cebolla** *f.* 8
online: to buy online **comprar** *v.* **en línea** 6
only **sólo** *adv.* 6; **único/a** *adj.* 3
  only child **hijo/a único/a** *m., f.* 3
open **abierto/a** *adj.* 5, 14; **abrir** *v.* 3
open-air **al aire libre** 6
opera **ópera** *f.* 17
operation **operación** *f.* 10
opposite **enfrente de** *prep.* 14
or **o** *conj.* 7

orange **anaranjado/a** *adj.* 6; **naranja** *f.* 8

orchestra **orquesta** *f.* 17

order **mandar** 12; (*food*) **pedir (e:i)** *v.* 8

in order to **para** *prep.* 11

orderly **ordenado/a** *adj.* 5

ordinal (*numbers*) **ordinal** *adj.*

organize oneself **organizarse** *v.* 12

other **otro/a** *adj.* 6

ought to **deber** *v.* (+ *inf.*) *adj.* 3

our **nuestro(s)/a(s)** *poss. adj.* 3; *poss. pron.* 11

out of order **descompuesto/a** *adj.* 11

outside **afuera** *adv.* 5

outskirts **afueras** *f., pl.* 12

oven **horno** *m.* 12

over **sobre** *prep.* 2

(over)population **(sobre)población** *f.* 13

over there **allá** *adv.* 2

own **propio/a** *adj.*

owner **dueño/a** *m., f.* 8

P

p.m. **de la tarde, de la noche** *f.* 1

pack (one's suitcases) **hacer** *v.* **las maletas** 5

package **paquete** *m.* 14

page **página** *f.* 11

pain **dolor** *m.* 10

have pain **tener** *v.* **dolor** 10

paint **pintar** *v.* 17

painter **pintor(a)** *m., f.* 16

painting **pintura** *f.* 12, 17

pair **par** *m.* 6

pair of shoes **par** *m.* **de zapatos** 6

pale **pálido/a** *adj.* 14

pants **pantalones** *m., pl.* 6

pantyhose **medias** *f., pl.* 6

paper **papel** *m.* 2

Pardon me. (*May I?*) **Con permiso.** 1; (*Excuse me.*) Pardon me. **Perdón.** 1

parents **padres** *m., pl.* 3; **papás** *m., pl.*

park **estacionar** *v.* 11; **parque** *m.* 4

parking lot **estacionamiento** *m.* 14

partner (*one of a married couple*) **pareja** *f.* 9

party **fiesta** *f.* 9

passed **pasado/a** *p.p.*

passenger **pasajero/a** *m., f.* 1

passport **pasaporte** *m.* 5

password **contraseña** *f.* 11

past **pasado/a** *adj.* 6

pastime **pasatiempo** *m.* 4

pastry shop **pastelería** *f.* 14

path **sendero** *m.* 13

patient **paciente** *m., f.* 10

patio **patio** *m.* 12

pay **pagar** *v.* 6

pay in cash **pagar** *v.* **al contado; pagar en efectivo** 14

pay in installments **pagar** *v.* **a plazos** 14

pay the bill **pagar la cuenta**

pea **arveja** *m.* 8

peace **paz** *f.* 18

peach **melocotón** *m.* 8

peak **cima** *f.* 15

pear **pera** *f.* 8

pen **pluma** *f.* 2

pencil **lápiz** *m.* 1

penicillin **penicilina** *f.*

people **gente** *f.* 3

pepper (*black*) **pimienta** *f.* 8

per **por** *prep.* 11

perfect **perfecto/a** *adj.* 5

period of time **temporada** *f.* 5

person **persona** *f.* 3

pharmacy **farmacia** *f.* 10

phenomenal **fenomenal** *adj.* 5

photograph **foto(grafía)** *f.* 1

physical (exam) **examen** *m.* **médico** 10

physician **doctor(a), médico/a** *m., f.* 3

physics **física** *f. sing.* 2

pick up **recoger** *v.* 13

picture **cuadro** *m.* 12; **pintura** *f.* 12

pie **pastel** *m.* 9

pill (tablet) **pastilla** *f.* 10

pillow **almohada** *f.* 12

pineapple **piña** *f.*

pink **rosado/a** *adj.* 6

place **lugar** *m.* 2, 4; **sitio** *m.* 3; **poner** *v.* 4

plaid **de cuadros** 6

plans **planes** *m., pl.*

have plans **tener planes**

plant **planta** *f.* 13

plastic **plástico** *m.* 13

(made) of plastic **de plástico** 13

plate **plato** *m.* 12

play **drama** *m.* 17; **comedia** *f.* 17 **jugar (u:ue)** *v.* 4; (*a musical instrument*) **tocar** *v.* 17; (*a role*) **hacer el papel de** 17; (*cards*) **jugar a (las cartas)** 5; (*sports*) **practicar deportes** 4

player **jugador(a)** *m., f.* 4

playwright **dramaturgo/a** *m., f.* 17

pleasant **agradable** *adj.*

please **por favor** 1

Pleased to meet you. **Mucho gusto.** 1; **Encantado/a.** *adj.* 1

pleasing: be pleasing to **gustar** *v.* 7

pleasure **gusto** *m.* 1; **placer** *m.* The pleasure is mine. **El gusto es mío.** 1

poem **poema** *m.* 17

poet **poeta** *m., f.* 17

poetry **poesía** *f.* 17

police (force) **policía** *f.* 11

political **político/a** *adj.* 18

politician **político/a** *m., f.* 16

politics **política** *f.* 18

polka-dotted **de lunares** 6

poll **encuesta** *f.* 18

pollute **contaminar** *v.* 13

polluted **contaminado/a** *m., f.* 13

be polluted **estar contaminado/a** 13

pollution **contaminación** *f.* 13

pool **piscina** *f.* 4

poor **pobre** *adj., m., f.* 6

poor thing **pobrecito/a** *adj.* 3

popsicle **paleta helada** *f.* 4

population **población** *f.* 13

pork **cerdo** *m.* 8

pork chop **chuleta** *f.* **de cerdo** 8

portable **portátil** *adj.* 11

portable computer **computadora** *f.* **portátil** 11

position **puesto** *m.* 16

possessive **posesivo/a** *adj.*

possible **posible** *adj.* 13

it's (not) possible **(no) es posible** 13

post office **correo** *m.* 14

postcard **postal** *f.*

poster **cartel** *m.* 12

potato **papa** *f.* 8; **patata** *f.* 8

pottery **cerámica** *f.* 17

practice **practicar** *v.* 2; (*a degree/ profession*) **ejercer** *v.* 16

prefer **preferir (e:ie)** *v.* 4

pregnant **embarazada** *adj. f.* 10

prepare **preparar** *v.* 2

preposition **preposición** *f.*

prescribe (*medicine*) **recetar** *v.* 10

prescription **receta** *f.* 10

present **regalo** *m.*; **presentar** *v.* 17

press **prensa** *f.* 18

pressure **presión** *f.*

be under a lot of pressure **sufrir muchas presiones** 15

pretty **bonito/a** *adj.* 3

price **precio** *m.* 6

(fixed, set) price **precio** *m.* **fijo** 6

print **imprimir** *v.* 11

printer **impresora** *f.* 11

prize **premio** *m.* 17

probable **probable** *adj.* 13

it's (not) probable **(no) es probable** 13

problem **problema** *m.* 1

profession **profesión** *f.* 3; 16

professor **profesor(a)** *m., f.*

profile **perfil** *m.* 11

program **programa** *m.* 1

programmer **programador(a)** *m., f.* 3

prohibit **prohibir** *v.* 10

project **proyecto** *m.* 11

promotion (*career*) **ascenso** *m.* 16

pronoun **pronombre** *m.*

protect **proteger** *v.* 13

protein **proteína** *f.* 15

provided (that) **con tal (de) que** *conj.* 13

psychologist **psicólogo/a** *m., f.* 16

psychology **psicología** *f.* 2

publish **publicar** *v.* 17

Puerto Rican **puertorriqueño/a** *adj.* 3

purchases **compras** *f., pl.*

pure **puro/a** *adj.* 13

purple **morado/a** *adj.* 6

purse **bolsa** *f.* 6

put **poner** *v.* 4; **puesto/a** *p.p.* 14
  put (a letter) in the mailbox **echar (una carta) al buzón** 14
  put on (*a performance*) **presentar** *v.* 17
  put on (*clothing*) **ponerse** *v.* 7
  put on makeup **maquillarse** *v.* 7

Q

quality **calidad** *f.* 6

quarter (*academic*) **trimestre** *m.* 2
  quarter after (*time*) **y cuarto** 1; **y quince** 1
  quarter to (*time*) **menos cuarto** 1; **menos quince** 1

question **pregunta** *f.*

quickly **rápido** *adv.* 10

quiet **tranquilo/a** *adj.* 15

quit **dejar** *v.* 16

quiz **prueba** *f.* 2

R

racism **racismo** *m.* 18

radio (*medium*) **radio** *f.* 2
  radio (set) **radio** *m.* 11

rain **llover (o:ue)** *v.* 5; **lluvia** *f.*
  It's raining. **Llueve.** 5; **Está lloviendo.** 5

raincoat **impermeable** *m.* 6

rain forest **bosque** *m.* **tropical** 13

raise (*salary*) **aumento** *m.* **de sueldo** 16

rather **bastante** *adv.* 10

read **leer** *v.* 3; **leído/a** *p.p.* 14
  read e-mail **leer el correo electrónico** 4
  read a magazine **leer una revista** 4
  read a newspaper **leer un periódico** 4

ready **listo/a** *adj.* 5

reality show **programa de realidad** *m.* 17

reap the benefits (of) *v.* **disfrutar** *v.* **(de)** 15

receive **recibir** *v.* 3

recommend **recomendar (e:ie)** *v.* 8; 12

record **grabar** *v.* 11

recover **recuperar** *v.* 11

recreation **diversión** *f.* 4

recycle **reciclar** *v.* 13

recycling **reciclaje** *m.* 13

red **rojo/a** *adj.* 6

red-haired **pelirrojo/a** *adj.* 3

reduce **reducir** *v.* 13; **disminuir** *v.* 16
  reduce stress/tension **aliviar el estrés/la tensión** 15

refrigerator **refrigerador** *m.* 12

region **región** *f.*

regret **sentir (e:ie)** *v.* 13

relatives **parientes** *m., pl.* 3

relax **relajarse** *v.* 9
  Relax. **Tranquilo/a.** 7
  Relax, sweetie. **Tranquilo/a, cariño.** 11

remain **quedarse** *v.* 7

remember **acordarse (o:ue)** *v.* **(de)** 7; **recordar (o:ue)** *v.* 4

remote control **control remoto** *m.* 11

renewable **renovable** *adj.* 13

rent **alquilar** *v.* 12; (payment) **alquiler** *m.* 12

repeat **repetir (e:i)** *v.* 4

report **informe** *m.* 18; **reportaje** *m.* 18

reporter **reportero/a** *m., f.* 16

representative **representante** *m., f.* 18

request **pedir (e:i)** *v.* 4

reservation **reservación** *f.* 5

resign (from) **renunciar (a)** *v.* 16

resolve **resolver (o:ue)** *v.* 13

resolved **resuelto/a** *p.p.* 14

resource **recurso** *m.* 13

responsibility **deber** *m.* 18; **responsabilidad** *f.*

responsible **responsable** *adj.* 8

rest **descansar** *v.* 2

restaurant **restaurante** *m.* 4

résumé **currículum** *m.* 16

retire (from work) **jubilarse** *v.* 9

return **regresar** *v.* 2; **volver (o:ue)** *v.* 4

returned **vuelto/a** *p.p.* 14

rice **arroz** *m.* 8

rich **rico/a** *adj.* 6

ride a bicycle **pasear** *v.* **en bicicleta** 4

ride a horse **montar** *v.* **a caballo** 5

ridiculous **ridículo/a** *adj.* 13
  it's ridiculous **es ridículo** 13

right **derecha** *f.* 2
  be right **tener razón** 3
  right? (*question tag*) **¿no?** 1; **¿verdad?** 1
  right away **enseguida** *adv.*
  right now **ahora mismo** 5
  to the right of **a la derecha de** 2

rights **derechos** *m., pl.* 18

ring **anillo** *m.* 17

ring **sonar (o:ue)** *v.* 11

river **río** *m.* 13

road **carretera** *f.* 11; **camino** *m.*

roast **asado/a** *adj.* 8

roast chicken **pollo** *m.* **asado** 8

romantic **romántico/a** *adj.* 17

room **habitación** *f.* 5; **cuarto** *m.* 2; 7
  living room **sala** *f.* 12

roommate **compañero/a** *m., f.* **de cuarto** 2

roundtrip **de ida y vuelta** 5
  roundtrip ticket **pasaje** *m.* **de ida y vuelta** 5

routine **rutina** *f.* 7

rug **alfombra** *f.* 12

run **correr** *v.* 3
  run errands **hacer diligencias** 14
  run into (*have an accident*) **chocar (con)** *v.*; (*meet accidentally*) **encontrar(se) (o:ue)** *v.* 11; (*run into something*) **darse (con)** 10
  run into (each other) **encontrar(se) (o:ue)** *v.* 11

rush **apurarse, darse prisa** *v.* 15

Russian **ruso/a** *adj.* 3

S

sad **triste** *adj.* 5; 13
  it's sad **es triste** 13

safe **seguro/a** *adj.* 5

said **dicho/a** *p.p.* 14

sailboard **tabla de windsurf** *f.* 5

salad **ensalada** *f.* 8

salary **salario** *m.* 16; **sueldo** *m.* 16

sale **rebaja** *f.* 6

salesperson **vendedor(a)** *m., f.* 6

salmon **salmón** *m.* 8

salt **sal** *f.* 8

same **mismo/a** *adj.* 3

sandal **sandalia** *f.* 6

sandwich **sándwich** *m.* 8

Saturday **sábado** *m.* 2

sausage **salchicha** *f.* 8

save (*on a computer*) **guardar** *v.* 11; save (money) **ahorrar** *v.* 14

savings **ahorros** *m.* 14
  savings account **cuenta** *f.* **de ahorros** 14

say **decir** *v.* 4;
  say (that) **decir (que)** *v.* 4
  say the answer **decir la respuesta** 4

scan **escanear** *v.* 11

scarcely **apenas** *adv.* 10

scared: be (very) scared (of) **tener (mucho) miedo (de)** 3

schedule **horario** *m.* 2

school **escuela** *f.* 1

sciences **ciencias** *f., pl.* 2

science fiction (genre) **de ciencia ficción** *f.* 17

scientist **científico/a** *m., f.* 16
scream **grito** *m.* 5; **gritar** *v.*
screen **pantalla** *f.* 11
scuba dive **bucear** *v.* 4
sculpt **esculpir** *v.* 17
sculptor **escultor(a)** *m., f.* 17
sculpture **escultura** *f.* 17
sea **mar** *m.* 5
  (sea) turtle **tortuga (marina)**
   f. 13
season **estación** *f.* 5
seat **silla** *f.* 2
second **segundo/a** 5
secretary **secretario/a** *m., f.* 16
sedentary **sedentario/a** *adj.* 15
see **ver** *v.* 4
  see (you, him, her) again **volver**
   a ver(te, lo, la)
  see movies **ver películas** 4
  See you. **Nos vemos.** 1
  See you later. **Hasta la vista.** 1;
   Hasta luego. 1
  See you soon. **Hasta pronto.** 1
  See you tomorrow. **Hasta**
   mañana. 1
seem **parecer** *v.* 6
seen **visto/a** *p.p.* 14
sell **vender** *v.* 6
semester **semestre** *m.* 2
send **enviar; mandar** *v.* 14
separate (from) **separarse** *v.*
  (de) 9
separated **separado/a** *adj.* 9
September **septiembre** *m.* 5
sequence **secuencia** *f.*
serious **grave** *adj.* 10
serve **servir (e:i)** *v.* 8
service **servicio** *m.* 15
set (*fixed*) **fijo/a** *adj.* 6
  set the table **poner la mesa** 12
seven **siete** 1
seven hundred **setecientos/as** 2
seventeen **diecisiete** 1
seventh **séptimo/a** 5
seventy **setenta** 2
several **varios/as** *adj. pl.*
sexism **sexismo** *m.* 18
shame **lástima** *f.* 13
  it's a shame **es una lástima** 13
shampoo **champú** *m.* 7
shape **forma** *f.* 15
  be in good shape **estar en**
   buena forma 15
  stay in shape **mantenerse en**
   forma 15
share **compartir** *v.* 3
sharp (*time*) **en punto** 1
shave **afeitarse** *v.* 7
shaving cream **crema** *f.* **de**
  afeitar 5, 7
she **ella** 1
shellfish **mariscos** *m., pl.* 8
ship **barco** *m.*
shirt **camisa** *f.* 6
shoe **zapato** *m.* 6
  shoe size **número** *m.* 6
  shoe store **zapatería** *f.* 14
   tennis shoes **zapatos** *m., pl.*
   de tenis 6

shop **tienda** *f.* 6
shopping, to go **ir de compras** 5
  shopping mall **centro**
   comercial *m.* 6
short (*in height*) **bajo/a** *adj.* 3; (*in*
  length) **corto/a** *adj.* 6
short story **cuento** *m.* 17
shorts **pantalones cortos**
  m., pl. 6
should (*do something*) **deber** *v.*
  (+ *inf.*) 3
shout **gritar** *v.*
show **espectáculo** *m.* 17;
  mostrar (o:ue) *v.* 4
  game show **concurso** *m.* 17
shower **ducha** *f.* 7
shrimp **camarón** *m.* 8
siblings **hermanos/as** *pl.* 3
sick **enfermo/a** *adj.* 10
  be sick **estar enfermo/a** 10
  get sick **enfermarse** *v.* 10
sign **firmar** *v.* 14; **letrero** *m.* 14
silk **seda** *f.* 6
  (made of) silk **de seda** 6
since **desde** *prep.*
sing **cantar** *v.* 2
singer **cantante** *m., f.* 17
single **soltero/a** *adj.* 9
  single room **habitación** *f.*
   individual 5
sink **lavabo** *m.* 7
sir **señor (Sr.), don** *m.* 1;
  caballero *m.* 8
sister **hermana** *f.* 3
sister-in-law **cuñada** *f.* 3
sit down **sentarse (e:ie)** *v.* 7
six **seis** 1
six hundred **seiscientos/as** 2
sixteen **dieciséis** 1
sixth **sexto/a** 5
sixty **sesenta** 2
size **talla** *f.* 6
  shoe size *m.* **número** 6
skate **patinar** 4
skateboard **andar en patineta**
  v. 4
ski **esquiar** *v.* 4
skiing **esquí** *m.* 4
  water-skiing **esquí** *m.*
   acuático 4
skirt **falda** *f.* 6
skull made out of sugar **calavera**
  de azúcar *f.* 9
sky **cielo** *m.* 13
sleep **dormir (o:ue)** *v.* 4; **sueño** *m.*
  go to sleep **dormirse**
   (o:ue) *v.* 7
sleepy: be (very) sleepy **tener**
  (mucho) sueño 3
slender **delgado/a** *adj.* 3
slim down **adelgazar** *v.* 15
slippers **pantuflas** *f., pl.* 7
slow **lento/a** *adj.* 11
slowly **despacio** *adv.* 10
small **pequeño/a** *adj.* 3
smart **listo/a** *adj.* 5
smile **sonreír (e:i)** *v.* 9
smiled **sonreído** *p.p.* 14
smoke **fumar** *v.* 15
  (not) to smoke **(no) fumar** 15

smoking section **sección** *f.* **de**
  fumar 8
  (non) smoking section *f.* **sección**
   de (no) fumar 8
snack **merendar (e:ie)** *v.* 8
  afternoon snack **merienda**
   f. 15
  have a snack **merendar** *v.* 8
sneakers **zapatos** *m., pl.*
  de tenis 6
sneeze **estornudar** *v.* 10
snow **nevar (e:ie)** *v.* 5; **nieve** *f.*
  snowing: It's snowing. **Nieva.** 5;
   Está nevando. 5
so (*in such a way*) **así** *adv.* 10;
  tan *adv.* 5
  so much **tanto** *adv.*
  so-so **regular** 1
  so that **para que** *conj.* 13
soap **jabón** *m.* 7
soap opera **telenovela** *f.* 17
soccer **fútbol** *m.* 4
sociology **sociología** *f.* 2
sock(s) **calcetín (calcetines)** *m.* 6
sofa **sofá** *m.* 12
soft drink **refresco** *m.* 8
software **programa** *m.* **de**
  computación 11
soil **tierra** *f.* 13
solar **solar** *adj., m., f.* 13
  solar energy **energía solar** 13
soldier **soldado** *m., f.* 18
solution **solución** *f.* 13
solve **resolver (o:ue)** *v.* 13
some **algún, alguno/a(s)** *adj.* 7;
  unos/as *indef. art.* 1
somebody **alguien** *pron.* 7
someone **alguien** *pron.* 7
something **algo** *pron.* 7
sometimes **a veces** *adv.* 10
son **hijo** *m.* 3
song **canción** *f.* 17
son-in-law **yerno** *m.* 3
soon **pronto** *adv.* 10
  See you soon. **Hasta pronto.** 1
sorry: be sorry **sentir (e:ie)** *v.* 13
  I'm sorry. **Lo siento.** 1
soul **alma** *f.* 9
soup **sopa** *f.* 8
south **sur** *m.* 14
  to the south **al sur** 14
Spain **España** *f.*
Spanish (*language*) **español** *m.* 2;
  español(a) *adj.* 3
spare (free) time **ratos libres** 4
speak **hablar** *v.* 2
  Speaking. (*on the telephone*)
   Con él/ella habla. 1
special: today's specials **las**
  especialidades del día 8
spectacular **espectacular** *adj.*
  m., f.
speech **discurso** *m.* 18
speed **velocidad** *f.* 11
  speed limit **velocidad** *f.*
   máxima 11
spelling **ortografía** *f.*,
  ortográfico/a *adj.*

spend (*money*) **gastar** *v.* 6
spoon (*table or large*) **cuchara** *f.* 12
sport **deporte** *m.* 4
   sports-related **deportivo/a** *adj.* 4
spouse **esposo/a** *m., f.* 3
sprain (*one's ankle*) **torcerse (o:ue)** *v.* (**el tobillo**) 10
spring **primavera** *f.* 5
(city or town) square **plaza** *f.* 4
stadium **estadio** *m.* 2
stage **etapa** *f.* 9
stairs **escalera** *f.* 12
stamp **estampilla** *f.* 14; **sello** *m.* 14
stand in line **hacer** *v.* **cola** 14
star **estrella** *f.* 13
start (*a vehicle*) **arrancar** *v.* 11
station **estación** *f.* 5
statue **estatua** *f.* 17
status: marital status **estado** *m.* **civil** 9
stay **quedarse** *v.* 7
   stay in shape **mantenerse en forma** 15
steak **bistec** *m.* 8
steering wheel **volante** *m.* 11
step **escalón** *m.* 15
stepbrother **hermanastro** *m.* 3
stepdaughter **hijastra** *f.* 3
stepfather **padrastro** *m.* 3
stepmother **madrastra** *f.* 3
stepsister **hermanastra** *f.* 3
stepson **hijastro** *m.* 3
stereo **estéreo** *m.*
still **todavía** *adv.* 5
stockbroker **corredor(a)** *m., f.* **de bolsa** 16
stockings **medias** *f., pl.* 6
stomach **estómago** *m.* 10
stone **piedra** *f.* 13
stop **parar** *v.* 11
   stop (*doing something*) **dejar de** (**+** *inf.*) 13
store **tienda** *f.* 6
storm **tormenta** *f.* 18
story **cuento** *m.* 17; **historia** *f.* 17
stove **cocina, estufa** *f.* 12
straight **derecho** *adv.* 14
   straight (ahead) **derecho** 14
straighten up **arreglar** *v.* 12
strange **extraño/a** *adj.* 13
   it's strange **es extraño** 13
street **calle** *f.* 11
stress **estrés** *m.* 15
stretching **estiramiento** *m.* 15
   do stretching exercises **hacer ejercicios** *m. pl.* **de estiramiento** 15
strike (*labor*) **huelga** *f.* 18
striped **de rayas** 6
stroll **pasear** *v.* 4
strong **fuerte** *adj. m., f.* 15
struggle (for/against) **luchar** *v.* (**por/contra**) 18

student **estudiante** *m., f.* 1; 2; **estudiantil** *adj.* 2
study **estudiar** *v.* 2
stupendous **estupendo/a** *adj.* 5
style **estilo** *m.*
suburbs **afueras** *f., pl.* 12
subway **metro** *m.* 5
   subway station **estación** *f.* **del metro** 5
success **éxito** *m.*
successful: be successful **tener éxito** 16
such as **tales como**
suddenly **de repente** *adv.* 6
suffer **sufrir** *v.* 10
   suffer an illness **sufrir una enfermedad** 10
sugar **azúcar** *m.* 8
suggest **sugerir (e:ie)** *v.* 12
suit **traje** *m.* 6
suitcase **maleta** *f.* 1
summer **verano** *m.* 5
sun **sol** *m.* 13
sunbathe **tomar** *v.* **el sol** 4
Sunday **domingo** *m.* 2
(sun)glasses **gafas** *f., pl.* (**de sol**) 6
sunny: It's (very) sunny. **Hace (mucho) sol.** 5
supermarket **supermercado** *m.* 14
suppose **suponer** *v.* 4
sure **seguro/a** *adj.* 5
   be sure **estar seguro/a** 5
surf **hacer** *v.* **surf** 5
surfboard **tabla de surf** *f.* 5
surprise **sorprender** *v.* 9; **sorpresa** *f.* 9
survey **encuesta** *f.* 18
sweat **sudar** *v.* 15
sweater **suéter** *m.* 6
sweep the floor **barrer el suelo** 12
sweets **dulces** *m., pl.* 9
swim **nadar** *v.* 4
swimming **natación** *f.* 4
   swimming pool **piscina** *f.* 4
symptom **síntoma** *m.* 10

T

table **mesa** *f.* 2
tablespoon **cuchara** *f.* 12
tablet (computer) **tableta** *f.* 11
take **tomar** *v.* 2; **llevar** *v.* 6
   take care of **cuidar** *v.* 13
   take someone's temperature **tomar** *v.* **la temperatura** 10
   take (*wear*) a shoe size **calzar** *v.* 6
   take a bath **bañarse** *v.* 7
   take a shower **ducharse** *v.* 7
   take off **quitarse** *v.* 7
   take out the trash **sacar** *v.* **la basura** 12
   take photos **tomar** *v.* **fotos** 5; **sacar** *v.* **fotos** 5

talented **talentoso/a** *adj.* 17
talk **hablar** *v.* 2
   talk show **programa** *m.* **de entrevistas** 17
tall **alto/a** *adj.* 3
tank **tanque** *m.* 11
taste **probar (o:ue)** *v.* 8
   taste like **saber a** 8
tasty **rico/a** *adj.* 8; **sabroso/a** *adj.* 8
tax **impuesto** *m.* 18
taxi **taxi** *m.* 5
tea **té** *m.* 8
teach **enseñar** *v.* 2
teacher **profesor(a)** *m., f.* 1, 2; **maestro/a** *m., f.* 16
team **equipo** *m.* 4
technician **técnico/a** *m., f.* 16
telecommuting **teletrabajo** *m.* 16
telephone **teléfono** 11
television **televisión** *f.* 2
   television set **televisor** *m.* 11
tell **contar** *v.* 4; **decir** *v.* 4
   tell (that) **decir** *v.* (**que**) 4
   tell lies **decir mentiras** 4
   tell the truth **decir la verdad** 4
temperature **temperatura** *f.* 10
ten **diez** 1
tennis **tenis** *m.* 4
   tennis shoes **zapatos** *m., pl.* **de tenis** 6
tension **tensión** *f.* 15
tent **tienda** *f.* **de campaña**
tenth **décimo/a** 5
terrible **terrible** *adj. m., f.* 13
   it's terrible **es terrible** 13
terrific **chévere** *adj.*
test **prueba** *f.* 2; **examen** *m.* 2
text **textear** *v.* 11
text message **mensaje** *m.* **de texto** 11
Thank you. **Gracias.** *f., pl.* 1
   Thank you (very much). **(Muchas) gracias.** 1
   Thanks (a lot). **(Muchas) gracias.** 1
   Thanks for inviting me. **Gracias por invitarme.** 9
that **que, quien(es)** *pron.* 12
   that (one) **ése, ésa, eso** *pron.* 6; **ese, esa,** *adj.* 6
   that (over there) **aquél, aquélla, aquello** *pron.* 6; **aquel, aquella** *adj.* 6
   that which **lo que** 12
   that's why **por eso** 11
the **el** *m.,* **la** *f. sing.,* **los** *m.,* **las** *f., pl.* 1
theater **teatro** *m.* 17
their **su(s)** *poss. adj.* 3; **suyo(s)/a(s)** *poss. pron.* 11
them **los/las** *pl., d.o. pron.* 5
   to/for them **les** *pl., i.o. pron.* 6
then (*afterward*) **después** *adv.* 7; (*as a result*) **entonces** *adv.* 5, 7; (*next*) **luego** *adv.* 7
there **allí** *adv.* 2
   There is/are... **Hay...** 1
   There is/are not... **No hay...** 1

therefore **por eso** 11
these **éstos, éstas** *pron.* 6; **estos, estas** *adj.* 6
they **ellos** *m.*, **ellas** *f. pron.* 1
thin **delgado/a** *adj.* 3
thing **cosa** *f.* 1
think **pensar (e:ie)** *v.* 4; (believe) **creer** *v.*
　think about **pensar en** *v.* 4
third **tercero/a** 5
thirst **sed** *f.*
thirsty: be (very) thirsty **tener (mucha) sed** 3
thirteen **trece** 1
thirty **treinta** 1; thirty (*minutes past the hour*) **y treinta; y media** 1
this **este, esta** *adj.*; **éste, ésta, esto** *pron.* 6
those **ésos, ésas** *pron.* 6; **esos, esas** *adj.* 6
those (over there) **aquéllos, aquéllas** *pron.* 6; **aquellos, aquellas** *adj.* 6
thousand **mil** *m.* 2
three **tres** 1
three hundred **trescientos/as** 2
throat **garganta** *f.* 10
through **por** *prep.* 11
Thursday **jueves** *m., sing.* 2
thus (*in such a way*) **así** *adv.*
ticket **boleto** *m.* 2, 17; **pasaje** *m.* 5
tie **corbata** *f.* 6
time **vez** *f.* 6; **tiempo** *m.* 14
　have a good/bad time **pasarlo bien/mal** 9
　I've had a fantastic time. **Lo he pasado de película.** 18
　What time is it? **¿Qué hora es?** 1
　(At) What time...? **¿A qué hora...?** 1
times **veces** *f., pl.* 6
　many times **muchas veces** 10
tip **propina** *f.* 8
tire **llanta** *f.* 11
tired **cansado/a** *adj.* 5
　be tired **estar cansado/a** 5
title **título** *m.* 16
to **a** *prep.* 1
toast (*drink*) **brindar** *v.* 9
　toast **pan** *m.* **tostado** 8
toasted **tostado/a** *adj.* 8
　toasted bread **pan tostado** *m.* 8
toaster **tostadora** *f.* 12
today **hoy** *adv.* 2
　Today is... **Hoy es...** 2
toe **dedo** *m.* **del pie** 10
together **juntos/as** *adj.* 9
toilet **inodoro** *m.* 7
tomato **tomate** *m.* 8
tomorrow **mañana** *f.* 1
　See you tomorrow. **Hasta mañana.** 1
tonight **esta noche** *adv.*
too **también** *adv.* 2; 7
　too much **demasiado** *adv.* 6; **en exceso** 15

tooth **diente** *m.* 7
toothpaste **pasta** *f.* **de dientes** 7
top **cima** *f.* 15
tornado **tornado** *m.* 18
touch **tocar** *v.* 17
touch screen **pantalla táctil** *f.*
tour **excursión** *f.* 4; **recorrido** *m.* 13
tour an area **recorrer** *v.*
tourism **turismo** *m.*
tourist **turista** *m., f.* 1; **turístico/a** *adj.*
toward **hacia** *prep.* 14; **para** *prep.* 11
towel **toalla** *f.* 7
town **pueblo** *m.*
trade **oficio** *m.* 16
traffic **circulación** *f.* 11; **tráfico** *m.* 11
　traffic light **semáforo** *m.* 14
tragedy **tragedia** *f.* 17
trail **sendero** *m.* 13
train **entrenarse** *v.* 15; **tren** *m.* 5
　train station **estación** *f.* **de tren** 5
trainer **entrenador(a)** *m., f.* 15
translate **traducir** *v.* 6
trash **basura** *f.* 12
travel **viajar** *v.* 2
　travel agency **agencia** *f.* **de viajes**
　travel agent **agente** *m., f.* **de viajes**
traveler **viajero/a** *m., f.* 5
treadmill **cinta caminadora** *f.* 15
tree **árbol** *m.* 13
trillion **billón** *m.*
trimester **trimestre** *m.* 2
trip **viaje** *m.* 5
　take a trip **hacer un viaje** 5
tropical forest **bosque** *m.* **tropical** 13
true: it's (not) true **(no) es verdad** 13
trunk **baúl** *m.* 11
truth **verdad** *f.* 4
try **intentar** *v.*; **probar (o:ue)** *v.* 8
　try (*to do something*) **tratar de (+ inf.)** 15
　try on **probarse (o:ue)** *v.* 7
t-shirt **camiseta** *f.* 6
Tuesday **martes** *m., sing.* 2
tuna **atún** *m.* 8
turkey **pavo** *m.* 8
turn **doblar** *v.* 14
　turn off (*electricity/appliance*) **apagar** *v.* 11
　turn on (*electricity/appliance*) **poner** *v.* 11; **prender** *v.* 11
twelve **doce** 1
twenty **veinte** 1
twenty-eight **veintiocho** 1
twenty-five **veinticinco** 1
twenty-four **veinticuatro** 1
twenty-nine **veintinueve** 1
twenty-one **veintiuno** 1; **veintiún, veintiuno/a** *adj.* 1

twenty-seven **veintisiete** 1
twenty-six **veintiséis** 1
twenty-three **veintitrés** 1
twenty-two **veintidós** 1
twice **dos veces** 6
twin **gemelo/a** *m., f.* 3
two **dos** 1
　two hundred **doscientos/as** 2

U

ugly **feo/a** *adj.* 3
uncle **tío** *m.* 3
under **debajo de** *prep.* 2
understand **comprender** *v.* 3; **entender (e:ie)** *v.* 4
underwear **ropa interior** 6
unemployment **desempleo** *m.* 18
unique **único/a** *adj.* 9
United States **Estados Unidos (EE.UU.)** *m. pl.*
university **universidad** *f.* 2
unless **a menos que** *conj.* 13
unmarried **soltero/a** *adj.* 9
unpleasant **antipático/a** *adj.* 3
until **hasta** *prep.* 6; **hasta que** *conj.* 13
upload **cargar** *v.* 11
urgent **urgente** *adj.* 12
　It's urgent that... **Es urgente que...** 12
us **nos** *pl., d.o. pron.* 5
　to/for us **nos** *pl., i.o. pron.* 6
use **usar** *v.* 6
used for **para** *prep.* 11
useful **útil** *adj. m., f.*

V

vacation **vacaciones** *f., pl.* 5
　be on vacation **estar de vacaciones** 5
　go on vacation **ir de vacaciones** 5
vacuum **pasar** *v.* **la aspiradora** 12
　vacuum cleaner **aspiradora** *f.* 12
valley **valle** *m.* 13
various **varios/as** *adj. m., f. pl.*
vegetables **verduras** *pl., f.* 8
verb **verbo** *m.*
very **muy** *adv.* 1
　(Very) well, thank you. **(Muy) bien, gracias.** 1
video **video** *m.* 1
　video game **videojuego** *m.* 4
videoconference **videoconferencia** *f.* 16
vinegar **vinagre** *m.* 8
violence **violencia** *f.* 18
visit **visitar** *v.* 4
　visit monuments **visitar monumentos** 4

vitamin **vitamina** *f.* 15
voice mail **correo de voz** *m.* 11
volcano **volcán** *m.* 13
volleyball **vóleibol** *m.* 4
vote **votar** *v.* 18

W

wait (for) **esperar** *v.* **(+ *inf.*)** 2
waiter/waitress **camarero/a** *m., f.* 8
wake up **despertarse (e:ie)** *v.* 7
walk **caminar** *v.* 2
  take a walk **pasear** *v.* 4
  walk around **pasear por** 4
wall **pared** *f.* 12; **muro** *m.* 15
wallet **cartera** *f.* 4, 6
want **querer (e:ie)** *v.* 4
war **guerra** *f.* 18
warm up **calentarse (e:ie)** *v.* 15
wash **lavar** *v.* 12
  wash one's face/hands **lavarse la cara/las manos** 7
  wash (the floor, the dishes) **lavar (el suelo, los platos)** 12
  wash oneself **lavarse** *v.* 7
washing machine **lavadora** *f.* 12
wastebasket **papelera** *f.* 2
watch **mirar** *v.* 2; **reloj** *m.* 2
  watch television **mirar (la) televisión** 2
water **agua** *f.* 8
  water pollution **contaminación del agua** 13
  water-skiing **esquí** *m.* **acuático** 4
way **manera** *f.*
we **nosotros(as)** *m., f.* 1
weak **débil** *adj. m., f.* 15
wear **llevar** *v.* 6; **usar** *v.* 6
weather **tiempo** *m.*
  The weather is bad. **Hace mal tiempo.** 5
  The weather is good. **Hace buen tiempo.** 5
weaving **tejido** *m.* 17
Web **red** *f.* 11
website **sitio** *m.* **web** 11
wedding **boda** *f.* 9
Wednesday **miércoles** *m., sing.* 2
week **semana** *f.* 2
weekend **fin** *m.* **de semana** 4
weight **peso** *m.* 15
  lift weights **levantar** *v.* **pesas** *f., pl.* 15
welcome **bienvenido(s)/a(s)** *adj.* 1
well: (Very) well, thanks. **(Muy) bien, gracias.** 1
well-being **bienestar** *m.* 15
well organized **ordenado/a** *adj.* 5

west **oeste** *m.* 14
  to the west **al oeste** 14 western (*genre*) **de vaqueros** 17
whale **ballena** *f.* 13
what **lo que** *pron.* 12
what? **¿qué?** 1
  At what time...? **¿A qué hora...?** 1
  What a pleasure to...! **¡Qué gusto (+ *inf.*)...!** 18
  What day is it? **¿Qué día es hoy?** 2
  What do you guys think? **¿Qué les parece?**
  What happened? **¿Qué pasó?**
  What is today's date? **¿Cuál es la fecha de hoy?** 5
  What nice clothes! **¡Qué ropa más bonita!** 6
  What size do you wear? **¿Qué talla lleva (usa)?** 6
  What time is it? **¿Qué hora es?** 1
  What's going on? **¿Qué pasa?** 1
  What's happening? **¿Qué pasa?** 1
  What's... like? **¿Cómo es...?**
  What's new? **¿Qué hay de nuevo?** 1
  What's the weather like? **¿Qué tiempo hace?** 5
  What's up? **¿Qué onda?** 14
  What's wrong? **¿Qué pasó?**
  What's your name? **¿Cómo se llama usted?** *form.* 1; **¿Cómo te llamas (tú)?** *fam.* 1
when **cuando** *conj.* 7; 13
When? **¿Cuándo?** 2
where **donde**
where (to)? (*destination*) **¿adónde?** 2; (*location*) **¿dónde?** 1, 2
  Where are you from? **¿De dónde eres (tú)?** *fam.* 1; **¿De dónde es (usted)?** *form.* 1
  Where is...? **¿Dónde está...?** 2
which **que** *pron.,* **lo que** *pron.* 12
which? **¿cuál?** 2; **¿qué?** 2
  In which...? **¿En qué...?**
  which one(s)? **¿cuál(es)?** 2
while **mientras** *conj.* 10
white **blanco/a** *adj.* 6
  white wine **vino blanco** 8
whiteboard **pizarra** *f.* 2
who **que** *pron.* 12; **quien(es)** *pron.* 12
who? **¿quién(es)?** 1, 2
  Who is...? **¿Quién es...?** 1
  Who is speaking? (*on telephone*) **¿Quién habla?** 11
  Who is speaking/calling? (*on telephone*) **¿De parte de quién?** 11

whole **todo/a** *adj.*
whom **quien(es)** *pron.* 12
whose? **¿de quién(es)?** 1
why? **¿por qué?** 2 widower/widow **viudo/a** *adj.* 9
wife **esposa** *f.* 3
win **ganar** *v.* 4
wind **viento** *m.*
window **ventana** *f.* 2
windshield **parabrisas** *m., sing.* 11
windsurf **hacer** *v.* **windsurf** 5
windy: It's (very) windy. **Hace (mucho) viento.** 5
wine **vino** *m.* 8
  red wine **vino tinto** 8
  white wine **vino blanco** 8
wineglass **copa** *f.* 12
winter **invierno** *m.* 5
wireless connection **conexión inalámbrica** *f.* 11
wish **desear** *v.* 2; **esperar** *v.* 13
  I wish (that) **ojalá (que)** 13
with **con** *prep.* 2
  with me **conmigo** 4; 9
  with you **contigo** *fam.* 5, 9
within (ten years) **dentro de (diez años)** *prep.* 16
without **sin** *prep.* 2; **sin que** *conj.* 13
woman **mujer** *f.* 1
wool **lana** *f.* 6
  (made of) wool **de lana** 6
word **palabra** *f.* 1
work **trabajar** *v.* 2; **funcionar** *v.* 11; **trabajo** *m.* 16
  work (*of art, literature, music, etc.*) **obra** *f.* 17
  work out **hacer gimnasia** 15
world **mundo** *m.* 8
worldwide **mundial** *adj. m., f.*
worried (about) **preocupado/a (por)** *adj.* 5
worry (about) **preocuparse** *v.* **(por)** 7
  Don't worry. **No te preocupes.** *fam.* 7
worse **peor** *adj. m., f.* 8
worst **el/la peor** 8
Would you like to...? **¿Te gustaría...?** *fam.*
Would you do me the honor of marrying me? **¿Me harías el honor de casarte conmigo?** 17
wow **híjole** *interj.* 6
wrench **llave** *f.* 11
write **escribir** *v.* 3
  write a letter/an e-mail **escribir una carta/un mensaje electrónico** 4
writer **escritor(a)** *m., f* 17
written **escrito/a** *p.p.* 14
wrong **equivocado/a** *adj.* 5
  be wrong **no tener razón** 3

X

X-ray **radiografía** *f.* 10

Y

yard **jardín** *m.* 12; **patio** *m.* 12
year **año** *m.* 5
    be... years old **tener...
        años** 3
yellow **amarillo/a** *adj.* 6
yes **sí** *interj.* 1
yesterday **ayer** *adv.* 6
yet **todavía** *adv.* 5
yogurt **yogur** *m.* 8
you **tú** *fam.* **usted (Ud.)** *form.*
    sing. **vosotros/as** *m., f. fam. pl.*
    ustedes (Uds.) *pl.* 1; (to, for)
    you *fam. sing.* **te** *pl.* **os** 6; *form.*
    sing. **le** *pl.* **les** 6
    you **te** *fam., sing.,* **lo/la** *form.,*
        sing., **os** *fam., pl.,* **los/las**
        pl., d.o. pron. 5
You don't say! **¡No me digas!**
    fam.; **¡No me diga!** *form.*
You're welcome. **De nada.** 1; **No
    hay de qué.** 1

young **joven** *adj., sing.* (**jóvenes**
    pl.) 3
    young person **joven** *m., f., sing.*
    (**jóvenes** *pl.*) 1
    young woman **señorita
        (Srta.)** *f.*
younger **menor** *adj. m., f.* 3
younger: younger brother, sister *m.,*
    f. **hermano/a menor** 3
youngest **el/la menor** *m., f.* 8
your **su(s)** *poss. adj. form.* 3;
    tu(s) *poss. adj. fam. sing.* 3;
    vuestro/a(s) *poss. adj. fam.*
    pl. 3
your(s) *form.* **suyo(s)/a(s)** *poss.*
    pron. form. 11; **tuyo(s)/a(s)**
    poss. fam. sing. 11; **vuestro(s)**
    /a(s) *poss. fam.* 11
youth *f.* **juventud** 9

Z

zero **cero** *m.* 1

Comics

31 © Joaquin Salvador Lavado (QUINO) Toda Mafalda - Ediciones de La Flor, 1993.

394-395 TUTE.

Literature

499 © Fundación mario Benedetti c/o Schavelzon Graham Agencia Literaria www.schavelzongraham.com

531 Cecilia de Menéndez Leal

565 de Burgos, Julia. "Julia de Burgos: yo misma fui mi ruta" from Song of the Simple Truth: The Complete Poems of Julia de Burgos. Willimantic: Curbstone Press, 1995.

601 Courtesy of Luisa Valenzuela.

Short Films

146 Courtesy of FeelSales/ContentLine.

534-535 Courtesy of Instituto Mexicano de Cinematografía (IMCINE).

568-569 Courtesy of Elemental Films.

604 By Jorge Naranjo and Nana Films (http://vimeo.com/35170814).

TV Clips

34 Courtesy of Edgardo Tettamanti.

72 © Cencosud Supermercados

110 Courtesy of Banco Galicia.

184 Courtesy of Visit Panama.

220 Courtesy of Juguettos.

256 Courtesy of Asepxia, Genommalab and Kepel & Mata.

294 Courtesy of Andres Felipe Roa.

326 Courtesy of Javier Ugarte (director).

362 Courtesy of Getting Better Creative Studio.

398 Courtesy of Popularlibros.com

436 Courtesy of Conforama España

470 Courtesy of Entropic Films.

502 Courtesy of Ogilvy & Mathers Honduras.

636 By permission of Subdirector de la Secretaria de Comunicaciones, Gobierno de Chile.

Photography Credits

Cover: Anna Gorin/Getty Images; (sky) Eric Lowenbach/Getty Images.

Front Matter (SE): iii: Andres Rodriguez/Shutterstock.

Front Matter (IAE): IAE-36: Rido/123RF.

Lesson 1: 1: Lumi Images/Alamy; **2:** John Henley/Getty Images; **3:** Martín Bernetti; **10:** (l) Rachel Distler; (r) Ali Burafi; **11:** (t) Hans Georg Roth/Getty Images; (ml) Elisabetta A. Villa/Getty Images; (mr) Paola Rios; (b) Chelsea Lauren/Variety/REX/Shutterstock; **12:** (l) Janet Dracksdorf; (r) Tom Grill/Corbis, **16:** (l) José Girarte/iStockphoto; (r) Blend Images/Alamy; **19:** (l) Goodluz/Shutterstock; (m) Anne Loubet; (r) Digi4tal Vision/Getty Images; **28:** (all) Martín Bernetti; **31:** (tl) Ana Cabezas Martín; (tml) Martín Bernetti; (tmr) Shvadchak Vasyl/123RF; (tr) Vanessa Bertozzi; (bl) Jan Pietruszka/Deposit Photos; (bm) Sanek70974/Fotolia; (br) Ramiro Isaza/Fotocolombia; **32:** Carolina Zapata; **33:** Paula Díez; **36:** (t) Robert Huberman/Alamy; (b) Photogal/Shutterstock; **37:** (tl) Timolina/Deposit Photos; (tr) Sean Drakes/Alamy; (ml) Stocksnapper/123RF; (mr) Toronto-Images.Com/Shutterstock; (b) Andres R/Shutterstock.

Lesson 2: 39: Radius Images/MaXx Images; **48:** (l) Martin Bernetti; (r) Pablo Corral/Getty Images; **49:** (t) Murle/Alamy; (m) Paul Almasy/Getty Images; (b) S Bukley/Shutterstock; **57:** Stephen Coburn/Shutterstock; **59:** (l) Paola Rios-Schaaf; (r) Image Source/Corbis; **68:** Jose Blanco; **69:** PNC/Media Bakery; **70:** (t) Martín Bernetti; (b) Aspen Photo/Shutterstock; **71:** Nora y Susana/Fotocolombia; **74:** (tl) Jose Blanco; (tr) Jose Blanco; (bl) Jose Tandem/Deposit Photos; (br) Iconotec/Fotosearch; **75:** (tl) Jacquelyn Martin/AP/REX/Shutterstock; (tr) Jose Blanco; (ml) Jose Blanco; (mr) Pete Goding/SIME/eStockphoto; (b) David Ramos/Getty Images.

Lesson 3: 77: Paul Bradbury/AGE Fotostock; **80:** (tl) Anne Loubet; (tr) Elena Kouptsova-Vasic/Shutterstock; (ml) Ana Cabezas Martin; (mr) Blend Images/Alamy; (bl) Martín Bernetti; (br) Bikerider London/Shutterstock; **86:** (tl) David Cantor/AP Images; (tr) Rafael Perez/Reuters; (b) Jeff Vespa/WireImage/Getty Images; **87:** (t) Chelsea Lauren/REX/Shutterstock; (ml) Marc Piasecki/Getty Images; (m) Eamonn McCormack/WireImage/Getty Images; (mr) Carlos Alvarez/Getty Images; (b) PG/Splash News/Newscom; **90:** (l) VaLiza/Shutterstock; (r) Fotoluminate/123RF; **92:** Andres Rodriguez/Alamy; **97:** (l) Tyler Olsen/Fotolia; (r) Blend Images/Alamy; **98:** Aldo Murillo/iStockphoto; **102:** (tl) Shakzu/Fotolia; (tm) Mihailomilovanovic/iStockphoto; (tr) Rosa Images/Media Bakery; (bl) Onoky/Fotolia; (bm) Jamie Grill/Getty Images; (br) Paula Diez; **106:** (t) Glow Images/AGE Fotostock; (m) Hill Street Studios/Media Bakery; (b) GM Visuals/AGE Fotostock; **107:** (t) Nora y Susana/Fotocolombia; (m) Chuck Savage/Getty Images; (b) Antonio Diaz/Shutterstock; **108:** Janet Dracksdorf; **109:** ASIFE/Alamy; **112:** (t) Wildlife GmbH/Alamy; (ml) John Beatty/Getty Images; (mr) Ecuadorpostales/Shutterstock; (bl) Onairda/Getty Images; (br) Lauren Krolick; **113:** (tl) Michael S. Nolan/AGE Fotostock; (tr) Pablo Corral/Getty Images; (ml) Marin Stefani; (mr) Fotos593/Shutterstock; (b) Patricio Hidalgo/Alamy.

Lesson 4: 115: Manu Prats/Offset; **117:** George Shelley/Getty Images; **119:** Nora y Susana/Fotocolombia; **124:** (l) Javier Soriano/AFP/Getty Images; (r) Fernando Bustamante/AP Images; **125:** (t) Photoworks/Shutterstock; (m) Zuma Press/Alamy; (b) RB/Bauer-Griffin/Getty Images; **127:** (t) Radu Bercan/Shutterstock; (ml) Fotomicar/Shutterstock; (mm) David R. Frazier Photolibrary/Alamy; (mr) Iakov Filimonov/123RF; (bl) Henn Photography/Getty Images; (bm) Sigrid Olsson/AGE Fotostock; (br) Janet Dracksdorf; **135:** Warner Bros Pictures/Everett Collection; **139:** Anne Loubet; **141:** Agan/Shutterstock; **142:** Jolopes/Fotolia; **143:** Fernando Llano/AP Images; **144:** Paula Diez; **145:** Rick Gomez/Getty Images; **148:** (tl) Randy Miramontez/Shutterstock; (tr) Self-Portrait with Thorn Necklace and Hummingbird, 1940 (oil on canvas), Kahlo, Frida (1907-54)/ Harry Ransom Center, University of Texas at Austin, Austin, USA / Leemage / Bridgeman Images; (bl) Ruben Varela; (br) Carolina Zapata; **149:** (tl) Radius Images/Alamy; (tr) Bettmann/Getty Images; (mt) Corel/Corbis; (mb) David R. Frazier Photolibrary/Alamy; (b) Diego Grandi/Alamy.

Lesson 5: 151: Gemma Ferrando/Offset; **162:** (l) Emporarcosar/Shutterstock; (r) Efrain Padro/Alamy; **163:** (t) AFP/Getty Images; (m) Pierre-Yves Babelon/123RF; (b) Neilson Barnard/Getty Images; **165:** (tl) Nenetus/Fotolia; (tr) Hart Creations/iStockphoto; (bl) Fotografixx/iStockphoto; (br) Mediaphotos/iStockphoto; **167:** Ronnie Kaufman/Getty Images; **180:** Janet Dracksdorf; **181:** (tl) Corel/Corbis; (tr) Dudarev Mikhail/Shutterstock; (m) Epicstockmedia/123RF; (b) Volodymyr Goinyk/Shutterstock; **182:** Carolina Zapata; **186:** (tl) Eddie Toro/123RF; (tr) Jose Blanco; (bl) Israel Pabon/Shutterstock; (br) Capricornis Photographic/Shutterstock; **187:** (tl) Jose Blanco; (tr) Lawrence Manning/Getty Images; (ml) Michele Falzone/Getty Images; (mr) Daniel Alvarez/123RF; (b) Ricardo Arduengo/Getty Images.

Lesson 6: 189: Antonio Diaz/Shutterstock; **198:** (l) Jose Caballero Digital Press Photos/Newscom; (r) Janet Dracksdorf; **199:** (t) Carlos Alvarez/Getty Images; (ml) Guiseppe Carace/Getty Images; (mr) Mark Mainz/Getty Images; (b) John Parra/Getty Images; **201:** Jack Hollingsworth/Corbis; **204:** (all) Pascal Pernix; **209:** (tl) Mauro Grigollo/AGE Fotostock; (tr) Syda Productions/AGE Fotostock; (bl) James Carman/AGE Fotostock; (br) Ben Welsh/AGE Fotostock; **210:** (all) Paula Díez; **211:** Paula Díez; **216-217:** (collage) Paula Díez; Karkas/Shutterstock; Elnur/Shutterstock; Paul Buturlimov/Shutterstock; Sergey Peterman/Shutterstock; Andrey Armyagov/Shutterstock; Polryaz/Shutterstock; Paula Díez; Vladyslav Starozhylov/Shutterstock; Fadedink.net/Shutterstock; V.S. Anandhakrishna/Shutterstock; Sagir/Shutterstock; **218:** Noam/Fotolia; **219:** Martín Bernetti; **222:** (all) Pascal Pernix; **223:** (tl) Don Emmert/AFP/Getty Images; (tr) Pascal Pernix; (ml) Pascal Pernix; (mr) Road Movie Prods/Kobal/REX/Shutterstock; (b) James Bloor Griffiths/Shutterstock.

Lesson 7: 225: Media Bakery; 228: (tl) PhotoAlto/Alamy; (tr) Radnatt/Fotolia; (tml) Bernd Vogel/Getty Images; (tmr) Blend Images/Media Bakery; (bml) Kemler/iStockphoto; (bmr) Paula Diez; (bl) Zeljkosantrac/iStockphoto; (br) Paula Diez; 234: Stewart Cohen/Blend Images/Corbis; 235: (t) Ali Burafi (m) Janet Dracksdorf; (b) Tommy Lindholm/Alamy; 237: (l) Paula Diez; (r) PeopleImages/Getty Images; 239: (l) Paula Diez; (r) Igor Mojzes/123RF; 242: Jose Blanco; 243: Anya Berkut/Fotolia; 252-253: Didem Hizar/Fotolia; 254: I Love Images/Alamy; 255: Hill Street Studios/Getty Images; 258: (t) Christian Vinces/Shutterstock; (ml) Reiner Elsen/Alamy; (mr) Ian Wood/Alamy; (bl) Juan Manuel Serrano Arce/Getty Images; (br) Oscar Espinosa/123RF; 259: (tl) Martín Bernetti; (tr) Nicolamargaret/Getty Images; (ml) Manual Romaris/Getty Images; (mr) Marshall Bruce/iStockphoto; (b) Jarno Gonzalez Zarraonandia/Shutterstock.

Lesson 8: 261: Terry Vine/Media Bakery; 265: Lauren Krolick; 267: (l) Monkey Business/Shutterstock; (r) Anne Loubet; 272: (t) Rachel Distler; (b) Greg Elms/Lonely Planet Images/Getty Images; 273: (t) Pablo Cuadra/Getty Images; (ml) Rafael Rios; (mr) Studio Bonisolli/Stockfood; (b) Gerardo Mora/ Getty Images; 275: (t) Vanessa Bertozzi; (ml) Annie Pickert Fuller; (mm) Martin Bernetti; (mr) Margouillat Photo/Shutterstock; (bl) Susan Schmitz/ Shutterstock; (bm) Nitr/Shutterstock; (br) Adlife Marketing/iStockphoto; 276: Paula Diez; 278: (l) Pixtal/AGE Fotostock; (r) Jose Blanco; 282: (l) Andresr/Shutterstock; (r) Jose Blanco; 283: (l) Jose Blanco; (r) Monkey Business/Shutterstock; 292: Vanessa Bertozzi; 293: Jack Hollingsworth/Getty Images; 296: (t) Henryk Sadura/Shutterstock; (m) Martin Engelmann/Media Bakery; (b) Henryk Sadura/Shutterstock; 297: (tl) Jenkedco/Shutterstock; (tr) Robert Matton AB/Alamy; (ml) Vladimir Korostyshevskiy/Shutterstock; (mr) Tom Salyer/Alamy; (b) Phil Clarke Hill/In Pictures/Getty Images.

Lesson 9: 299: Jupiter Images/Getty Images; 303: Cathy Yeulet/123RF; 308: (l) Javier Larrea/AGE Fotostock; (r) PictureNet/Getty Images; 309: (t) GDA/ El Mercurio/Chile/El Mercurio de Chile/Newscom; (m) GDA/El Mercurio/Chile/El Mercurio de Chile/Newscom; (b) Tim Mosenfelder/Getty Images; 322: (t) Katrina Brown/123RF; (b) Digital Vision/Media Bakery; 323: Carlos Hernandez/Media Bakery; 324: Blend Images/Alamy; 328: (tl) Lauren Krolick; (tr) Lauren Krolick; (ml) Kathryn Alena-Korf; (mr) Lauren Krolick; (bl) Bettmann/Getty Images; (br) Martin Bernetti/AFP/Getty Images; 329: (tl) Lars Rosen Gunnilstam; (tr) Lauren Krolick; (ml) Nikolay Starchenko/Shutterstock; (mr) Lauren Krolick; (b) Bruce R. Korf.

Lesson 10: 331: Custom Medical Stock Photo/Alamy; 340: (t) Ali Burafi; (b) Andresr/Shutterstock; 341: (t) Courtesy of Arizona State University Hispanic Research Center; (ml) Phootlicensors International AG/Alamy; (mr) AFP/Getty Images; (b) Jealex Photo/Getty Images; 345: ISO K Photography/ Fotolia; 349: Oscar Artavia Solano; 355: Martin Bernetti; 358: Dream Pictures/Getty Images; 359: Danita Delimont/Newscom; 360: Anthony Redpath/ Masterfile; 361: Paula Diez; 364: (tl) Oscar Artavia Solano; (tr) Oscar Artavia Solano; (ml) Timothy A. Clary/AFP/Getty Images; (mm) Oscar Artavia Solano; (mr) Oscar Artavia Solano; 365: (tl) Nik Wheeler/Alamy; (tr) Atlantide Phototravel/Getty Images; (tml) Jacques M. Chenet/Corbis; (tmr) Megapress/Alamy; (m) Oscar Artavia Solano; (b) E. Rojas/Shutterstock.

Lesson 11: 367: Stefan Dahl Langstrup/Alamy; 376: (l) GM Visuals/AGE Fotostock; (r) Quka/Shutterstock; 377: (t) Zsolt Nyulaszi/Shutterstock; (bl) M. Timothy O'Keefe/Alamy; (br) Difusion/El Comercio de Peru/Newscom; 381: LdF/iStockphoto; 385: Katie Wade; 386: (all) Paula Diez; 387: (tl) AGE Fotostock; (tr) Ali Burafi; (bl) JGI/Jamie Grill/Getty Images; (br) Paula Diez; 390: (t) Gmnicholas/iStockphoto; (ml) Elen 418/Shutterstock; (mm) Aleksandr Kurganov/Shutterstock; (mr) Liliana Bobadilla; (bl) LdF/iStockphoto; (bm) Auris/iStockphoto; (br) Scanrail1/Shutterstock; 396: Chad Johnson/Masterfile; 397: Morchella/Fotolia;400: (t) Ali Burafi; (ml) María Eugenia Corbo; (mr) Ali Burafi; (bl) F. Neukirchen/AGE Fotostock; (br) Lauren Krolick; 401: (tl) María Eugenia Corbo; (tr) Ali Burafi; (ml) Ali Burafi; (mr) Rocharibeiro/Shutterstock; (b) Ali Burafi.

Lesson 12: 403: Gravity Images/Getty Images; 407: (t) Terry J/iStockphoto; (b) Harry Neave/Fotolia; 412: (l) Dusko Despotovic; (r) Martín Bernetti; 413: (tl) Fran Fernandez; (tr) Rafal Cichaway/123RF; (b) AB1/Adriana M. Barraza/WENN/Newscom; 415: (l) JGI/Tom Grill/Media Bakery; (r) Anne Loubet; 416: Blend Images/Alamy; 432: Wilmar Photography/Alamy; 434: Dragon Images/Shutterstock; 435: Jolanda Van Den Oudenalder/123RF; 438: (tl) Sergi Reboredo/Alamy; (tr) Melba/AGE Fotostock; (m) Claudio Lovo/Shutterstock; (b) Hernan H. Hernandez/Shutterstock; 439: (tl) Galina vina/Shutterstock; (tr) Danny Lehman/Corbis; (bl) Courtesy of www.Tahiti-Tourisme.com; (br) Jupiter Images/Getty Images.

Lesson 13: 441: Blend Images/Alamy; 443: (tl) Gaccworship/Big Stock; (tr) Goodshoot/Alamy; (bl) National Geographic Singles 65/Inmagine; (br) Les Cunliffe/123RF; 450: (t) Lauren Krolick; (b) Digital Vision/Fotosearch; 451: (t) Oscar Garces/AGE Fotostock; (m) David South/Alamy; (bl) David Liittschwager/Getty Images; (br) Agencia el Universal GDA Photo Service/Newscom; 454: Andy Shchekalev/123RF; 459: (all) Courtesy of Mary Axtmann; 466: (l) Apisit Sorin/EyeEm/Getty Images; 466-467: (t) Borja Andreu/Shutterstock; (b) Yeryomina Anastassiya/Shutterstock; 467: (r) Kitzzeh/ Shutterstock; 468: Frederic Prochassen/123RF; 472: (tl) Andrey Gontarev/Shutterstock; (tr) Foto593/Shutterstock; (m) Jose Blanco; (b) Santiago Saldarriaga GDA Photo Service/Newscom; 473: (tl) Ulf Andersen/Getty Images; (tr) Monica Maria Gonzalez; (ml) Jeremy Horner/Getty Images; (mr) Jess Kraft/Shutterstock; (b) Ardea.com/Mary Evans/Renato Granieri/AGE Fotostock.

Lesson 14: 475: Hilary Jane Morgan/AGE Fotostock; 484: (l) Stuwdamdorp/Alamy; (r) David Wall/Alamy; 485: (t) John Mitchell/Alamy; (m) Courtesy of the Barragan Foundation; (b) GV Cruz/WireImage/Alamy; 491: Paula Diez; 498-499: Filo/Getty Images; 500: Masterfile RF; 501: Paula Diez; 504: (t) Janne Hamalainen/Shutterstock; (m) Alexander Chaikin/Shutterstock; (b) F. Neukirchen/AGE Fotostock; 505: (tl) Julio Etchart/Alamy; (tr) Daniel Romero/VW Pics/Getty Images; (ml) Ken Welsh/Alamy; (mr) Nehophoto/Shutterstock; (b) Vladimir Melnik/Shutterstock.

Lesson 15: 507: Henglein and Steets/AGE Fotostock; 511: Javier Larrea/AGE Fotostock; 516: (l) Posztos/Shutterstock; (r) Oscar Artavia Solano; 517: (t) David Mercado/Reuters/Newscom; (m) Stockcreations/Shutterstock; (b) Courtesy of Chila Jatun; 524: Diego Cervo/iStockphoto; 530-531: Michael Klippfeld/Getty Images; 532: Martin Bernetti; 533: Javier Larrea/AGE Fotostock; 538: (tl) Elzbieta Sekowska/Shutterstock; (tr) Massimo Borchi/ SIME/eStock Photo; (b) Peter Langer/AGE Fotostock; 539: (tl) Daniel Wiedmann/Shutterstock; (tr) Anders Ryman/Alamy; (ml) VHL; (mr) Ben Pipe/ SIME/eStockphoto; (b) Jess Kraft/Shutterstock.

Lesson 16: 541: Caiaimage/Lukasz Olek/Getty Images; 545: (t) Orange Line Media/Shutterstock; (b)Paula Diez; 550: PhotoAlto sas/Alamy; 551: (t) VHL; (m) Galen Rowell/Getty Images; (b) Courtesy of Eterno Fotoarte; 560: Pezography/Bigstock; 561: RJ Lerich/Bigstock; 564: (t) Courtesy of María Consuelo Sáez de Burgos; (b) Frida Khalo. Las dos Fridas. 1939. 2014 Banco de Mexico Diego Rivera Frida Kahlo Museums Trust, Mexico, D.F./Artists Rights Society (ARS), New York. Photo credit: Schalkwijk/Art Resource, NY; 566: Martin Bernetti; 567: Paula Diez; 572: (tl) Endless Traveller/Shutterstock; (tr) RJ Lerich/Shutterstock; (m) Tobe_dw/Shutterstock; (b) Johnny Louis/FilmMagic/Getty Images; 573: (tl) Grigory Kubatyan/Shutterstock; (tr) Dennis Drenner/Washington Post/Getty Images; (ml) Holdeneye/Shutterstock; (mr) Thornton Cohen/Alamy; (b) Scott B. Rosen/Alamy; 574: (tl) Salim October/ Shutterstock; (tr) Daniel Indiana/Shutterstock; (b) Werner Otto/Alamy; 575: (tl) Alvaro Leiva/Alamy; (tr) Aspen Photo/Shutterstock; (ml) Lucas Vallecillos/ AGE Fotostock; (mr) Evannovostro/Shutterstock; (b) AKG-Images/The Image Works.

Lesson 17: 577: Dragon Images/Shutterstock; 581: Andres Rodriguez/Fotolia; 586: (l) Exposicion Cuerpo Plural, Museo de Arte Contemporaneo Caracas, Venezuela, Octubre 2005 (Sala1). Fotografia Morella Munox-Tebar. Archivo Mac; (r) Art Resource, NY; 587: (t) Eric Roberts/VIP Productions/ Getty Images; (m) Museo de Antioquia; (b) Courtesy of Ángel Lopez; 590: GM Visuals/Media Bakery; 591: DC Comics/DC Entertainment/Album/ Newscom; 600-601: (background) Bro Studio/Shutterstock; (foreground) Juanmonino/Getty Images; 602: Lichtmaster/Shutterstock; 606: (tl) John Coletti/Getty Images; (tr) L. Kragt Bakker/Shutterstock; (bl) Leif Skogfors/Getty Images; (br) Andre Nantel/Shutterstock; 607: (tl) Edfuentesg/iStock- photo; (tr) Ondrej Prosicky/Shutterstock; (ml) Jose Cabezas/Reuters/Newscom; (mr) Sheridan Stancliff/Exactostock-1491/Superstock; (b) Corbis; 608: (tl) B & T Media Group Inc/Shutterstock; (tr) Philippe Turpin/AGE Fotostock; (bl) Sandra A. Dunlap/Shutterstock; (br) Christian Kober/ Alamy; 609: (tl) Vik Vojtech/AGE Fotostock; (tr) Elmer Martinez/Stringer/Getty Images; (ml) Jose Antonio Velasquez. San Antonio de Oriente. 1957. Collection OAS AMA/Art Museum of Americas; (mr) B Trapp/AGE Fotostock; (b) Martin Bernetti.

Lesson 18: 611: Nano Calvo/AGE Fotostock; 615: (t) Robert Paul Van Beets/Shutterstock; (b) VHL; 620: (l) Jose Blanco; (r) TravelStockCollection - Homer Sykes/Alamy; 621: (t) Haakon Mosvold LarsenAFP/Getty Images; (b) Juan Aguado/Redferns/Getty Images; 624: Anne Loubet; 629: (l) John ambik/Alamy; (r) Globe Guide Media/Shutterstock; 634: Joel Nito/Stringer/Getty Images; 635: Dream Pictures/Getty Images; 638: (t) Julian Peters otography/Getty Images; (bl) Ian Trower/Getty Images; (br) VHL; 639: (tl) De Agostini/G. Kiner/Getty Images; (tr) Christian Rizzi/AFP/Getty mages; (ml) Hugh Percival/Fotolia; (mr) Thomas Vinke/Getty Images; (b) Jorge Saenz/AP Images; 640: (tl) Peter Groenendijk/Robert Harding/ Media Bakery; (tr) Hans Neleman/Getty Images; (b) Maria Eugenia Corbo; 641: (tl) Janet Dracksdorf; (tr) Jonathon Larsen/Diadem Images/Alamy; (ml) Richard I'Anson/Getty Images; (mr) JMN/Cover/Getty Images; (b) Maria Eugenia Corbo.

Back Cover: Demaerre/iStockphoto.

About the Authors

José A. Blanco founded Vista Higher Learning in 1998. A native of Barranquilla, Colombia, Mr. Blanco holds a B.A. in Literature from the University of California, Santa Cruz, and a M.A. in Hispanic Studies from Brown University. He has worked as a writer, editor, and translator for Houghton Mifflin and D.C. Heath and Company and has taught Spanish at the secondary and university levels. Mr. Blanco is also the co-author of several other Vista Higher Learning programs: **Panorama, Aventuras,** and **¡Viva!** at the introductory level; **Enlaces, Facetas, Enfoques, Imagina,** and **Sueña** at the intermediate level; and **Revista** at the advanced conversation level.

Philip Redwine Donley received his M.A. in Hispanic Literature from the University of Texas at Austin in 1986 and his Ph.D. in Foreign Language Education from the University of Texas at Austin in 1997. Dr. Donley taught Spanish at Austin Community College, Southwestern University, and the University of Texas at Austin. He published articles and conducted workshops about language anxiety management, and the development of critical thinking skills, and was involved in research about teaching languages to the visually impaired. Dr. Donley was also the co-author of **Aventuras** and **Panorama,** two other introductory college Spanish textbook programs published by Vista Higher Learning.

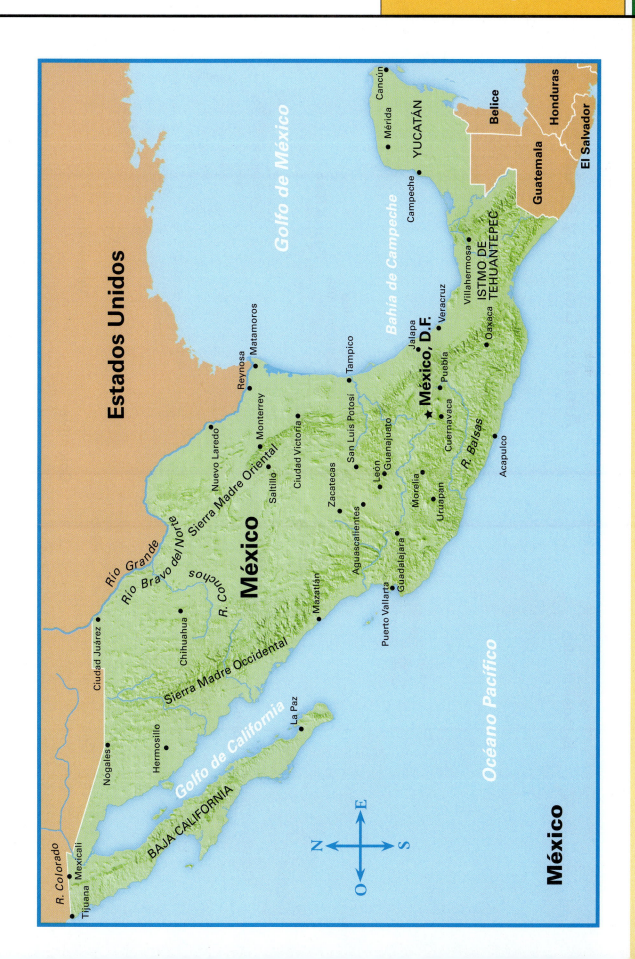

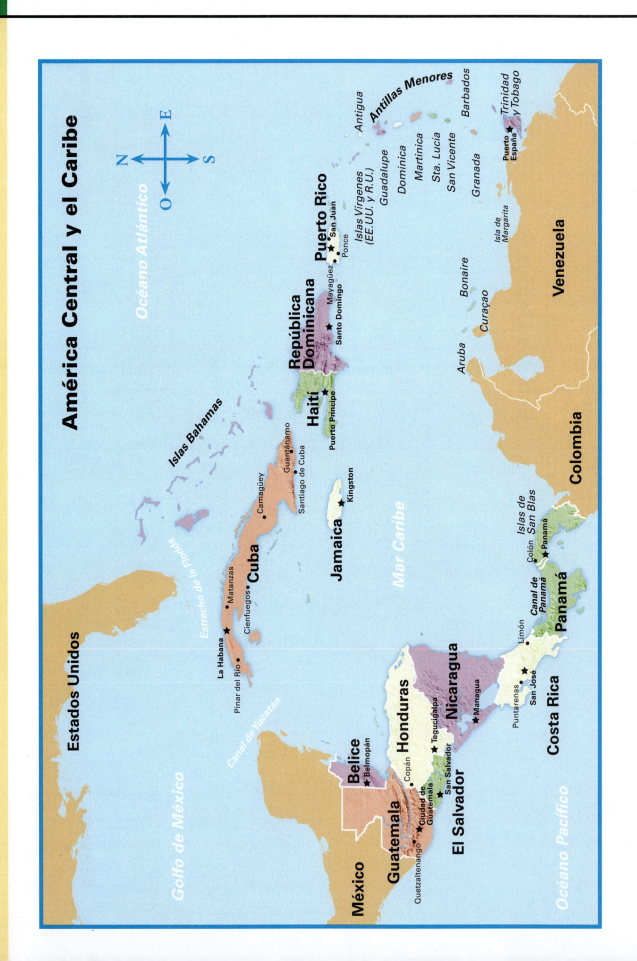

América Central y el Caribe

N · E · S · O

Océano Atlántico

Golfo de México

Estados Unidos

México

Islas Bahamas

Estrecho de la Florida

La Habana
Pinar del Río
Matanzas
Cienfuegos
Camagüey
Cuba
Guantánamo
Santiago de Cuba

Jamaica
Kingston

Canal de Yucatán

Guatemala
Quetzaltenango
Ciudad de Guatemala
Copán
Belice
Belmopán
Honduras
Tegucigalpa
El Salvador
San Salvador
Nicaragua
Managua

Costa Rica
San José
Puntarenas
Limón
Panamá
Canal de Panamá
Colón
Panamá
Islas de San Blas

Mar Caribe

Haití
Puerto Príncipe
República Dominicana
Santo Domingo
Mayagüez
Ponce
Puerto Rico
San Juan

Islas Vírgenes
(EE.UU. y R.U.)

Antigua
Guadalupe
Dominica
Martinica
Sta. Lucía
San Vicente
Granada
Barbados

Antillas Menores

Aruba
Curaçao
Bonaire
Isla de Margarita

Trinidad y Tobago
Puerto España

Venezuela

Colombia

Océano Pacífico

Mar Caribe

Barranquilla • Maracaibo

Caracas

Venezuela

★ Puerto España
Trinidad y Tobago

• Medellín

Colombia ★ Bogotá

R. Orinoco

• Georgetown

Guyana • Paramaribo

★ Cayena

Surinam

Guayana Francesa

• Cali

Pasto •

★ Quito

Ecuador
• Guayaquil

• Iquitos

Perú

R. Negro

R. Amazonas

Manaus •

• Belém

R. Madeira

Cordillera de los Andes

Lima ★

• Cuzco

Lago Titicaca

Arequipa •

• Arica

★ La Paz

Bolivia

Sucre ★

Brasil

★ Brasilia

• Recife

• Salvador

R. Paraguay

Océano Pacífico

• Iquique

• Antofagasta

• Belo Horizonte

R. Paraná

Paraguay

São Paulo • • Río de Janeiro
• Santos

• Salta

Asunción ★

Chile

R. Paraná

R. Uruguay

• Córdoba

• Porto Alegre

• Valparaíso
• Mendoza

★ Santiago

• Rosario

Buenos Aires ★

Uruguay
• Montevideo

Argentina

• Concepción

Cordillera de los Andes

Océano Atlántico

• Bahía Blanca

Puerto Montt •

N

O — E

S

Estrecho de Magallanes

Islas Malvinas

• Punta Arenas

Tierra del Fuego

América del Sur

Islas Galápagos

Océano Pacífico

Isla Pinta •

Isla Marchena

Isla Genovesa

Isla Isabela

Línea Ecuatorial

ECUADOR

Volcán Darwin •

Isla Santiago
(San Salvador)

Isla Fernandina

Puerto Ayora •

Isla Santa Cruz

Isla San Cristóbal

Santo Tomás •

Puerto Barquerizo Moreno

Isla Santa María •

Isla Española